5 language
VISUAL
dictionary

5 language VISUAL dictionary

A DORLING KINDERSLEY BOOK

DK

London, New York, Melbourne, Munich, Delhi

Senior Editor Angeles Gavira
Senior Art Editor Ina Stradins
DTP Designer Rajen Shah
Production Controller Melanie Dowland
Picture Researcher Anna Grapes
Managing Editor Liz Wheeler
Managing Art Editor Phil Ormerod
Category Publisher Jonathan Metcalf

Designed for Dorling Kindersley by WaltonCreative.com
Art Editor Colin Walton, assisted by Tracy Musson
Designers Peter Radcliffe, Earl Neish, Ann Cannings
Picture Research Marissa Keating

Language content for Dorling Kindersley by
g-and-w PUBLISHING
Managed by Jane Wightwick, assisted by Ana Bremón
Translation and editing by Ana Bremón, Renate Betson,
Marc Vitale, Christine Arthur
Additional input by Dr. Arturo Pretel, Martin Prill,
Frédéric Monteil, Meinrad Prill, Mari Bremón,
Oscar Bremón, Anunchi Bremón, Leila Gaafar

First published in Great Britain in 2003
by Dorling Kindersley Limited,
80 Strand, London WC2R 0RL
Copyright © 2003 Dorling Kindersley Limited
A Penguin Company

8 9 10
ISBN 978-0-7513-3681-8
024-AF008-Jan/03

Colour reproduction by Colourscan, Singapore
Printed and bound in Slovakia by Neografia

See our complete catalogue at
www.dk.com

contents
table des matières
Inhalt
contenido
sommario

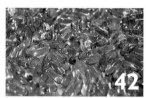

42

health
la santé
die Gesundheit
la salud
la salute

146

eating out
sortir manger
auswärts essen
comer fuera
mangiare fuori

252

leisure
le temps libre
die Freizeit
el ocio
il tempo libero

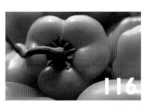

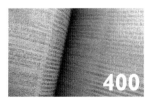

about the dictionary

The use of pictures is proven to aid understanding and the retention of information. Working on this principle, this highly-illustrated multilingual dictionary presents a large range of useful current vocabulary in five European languages.

The dictionary is divided thematically and covers most aspects of the everyday world in detail, from the restaurant to the gym, the home to the workplace, outer space to the animal kingdom. You will also find additional words and phrases for conversational use and for extending your vocabulary.

This is an essential reference tool for anyone interested in languages – practical, stimulating, and easy-to-use.

A few things to note
The five languages are always presented in the same order – English, French, German, Spanish, and Italian.

Other than in English, nouns are given with their definite articles reflecting the gender (masculine, feminine, or neuter) and number (singular or plural), for example:

seed	almonds
la graine	les amandes
der Samen	die Mandeln
la semilla	las almendras
il seme	le mandorle

Verbs are indicated by a (v) after the English, for example:

harvest (v) • récolter • ernten • recolectar • raccogliere

Each language also has its own index at the back of the book. Here you can look up a word in any of the five languages and be referred to the page number(s) where it appears. The gender is shown using the following abbreviations:

m = masculine
f = feminine
n = neuter

à propos du dictionnaire

Il est bien connu que les illustrations nous aident à comprendre et retenir l'information. Fondé sur ce principe, ce dictionnaire multilingue richement illustré présente un large éventail de vocabulaire courant et utile dans cinq langues européennes.

Le dictionnaire est divisé de façon thématique et couvre en détail la plupart des aspects du monde quotidien, du restaurant au gymnase, de la maison au lieu de travail, de l'espace au monde animal. Vous y trouverez également des mots et expressions supplémentaires pour la conversation et pour enrichir votre vocabulaire.

Il s'agit d'un outil de référence essentiel pour tous ceux qui s'intéressent aux langues – pratique, stimulant et d'emploi facile.

Quelques points à noter
Les cinq langues sont toujours présentées dans le même ordre – anglais, français, allemand, espagnol et italien.

Sauf en anglais, les noms sont donnés avec leurs articles définis qui indiquent leur genre (masculin, féminin ou neutre) et leur nombre (singulier ou pluriel):

seed	almonds
la graine	les amandes
der Samen	die Mandeln
la semilla	las almendras
il seme	le mandorle

Les verbes sont indiqués par un (v) après l'anglais, par exemple:

harvest (v) • récolter • ernten • recolectar • raccogliere

Chaque langue a également son propre index à la fin du livre. Vous pourrez y vérifier un mot dans n'importe laquelle des cinq langues et vous serez renvoyé au(x) numéro(s) de(s) page(s) où il figure. Le genre est indiqué par les abréviations suivantes:

m = masculin
f = féminin
n = neutre

über das Wörterbuch

Bilder helfen erwiesenermaßen, Informationen zu verstehen und zu behalten. Dieses mehrsprachige Wörterbuch enthält eine Fülle von Illustrationen und präsentiert gleichzeitig ein umfangreiches aktuelles Vokabular in fünf europäischen Sprachen.

Das Wörterbuch ist thematisch gegliedert und behandelt eingehend die meisten Bereiche des heutigen Alltags, vom Restaurant und Fitnesscenter, Heim und Arbeitsplatz bis zum Tierreich und Weltraum. Es enthält außerdem Wörter und Redewendungen, die für die Unterhaltung nützlich sind und das Vokabular erweitern.

Dies ist ein wichtiges Nachschlagewerk für jeden, der sich für Sprachen interessiert – es ist praktisch, anregend und leicht zu benutzen.

Einige Anmerkungen
Die fünf Sprachen werden immer in der gleichen Reihenfolge aufgeführt – Englisch, Französisch, Deutsch, Spanisch und Italienisch.

Außer für Englisch werden Substantive mit den bestimmten Artikeln, die das Geschlecht (Maskulinum, Femininum oder Neutrum) und den Numerus (Singular oder Plural) ausdrücken, angegeben, zum Beispiel:

seed	almonds
la graine	les amandes
der Samen	die Mandeln
la semilla	las almendras
il seme	le mandorle

Die Verben sind durch ein (v) nach dem englischen Wort gekennzeichnet:

harvest (v) • récolter • ernten • recolectar • raccogliere

Am Ende des Buchs befinden sich Register für jede Sprache. Sie können dort ein Wort in einer der fünf Sprachen und die jeweilige Seitenzahl nachsehen. Die Geschlechtsangabe erfolgt mit folgenden Abkürzungen:

m = Maskulinum
f = Femininum
n = Neutrum

sobre el diccionario

Está comprobado que el empleo de fotografías ayuda a la comprensión y a la retención de información. Partiendo de este principio, este diccionario plurilíngüe y altamente ilustrado ofrece un amplio vocabulario útil y actual en cinco idiomas europeos.

El diccionario está estructurado temáticamente y cubre con detalle la mayoría de los aspectos del mundo cotidiano, desde el restaurante al gimnasio, la casa al lugar de trabajo, el espacio al reino animal. Encontrará también palabras y frases adicionales para su uso en conversación y para ampliar su vocabulario.

Se trata de una herramienta de referencia esencial para cualquiera que esté interesado en los idiomas – práctica, estimulante y fácil de usar.

Algunos puntos que tener en cuenta
Los cinco idiomas se presentan siempre en el mismo orden: inglés, francés, alemán, español e italiano.

Salvo en inglés, los sustantivos van precedidos del artículo definido correspondiente, que refleja el género (masculino, femenino o neutro) y el número (singular/plural), por ejemplo:

seed   almonds
la graine   les amandes
der Samen   **die Mandeln**
la semilla   las almendras
il seme   le mandorle

Los verbos se señalan mediante (v) después del inglés, por ejemplo:

harvest (*v*) • récolter • ernten • cosechar • raccogliere

Cada idioma dispone de su propio índice. Aquí podrá consultar cualquier palabra de las cinco lenguas y se verá remitido a la página en la que figura. El género se indica utilizando las siguientes abreviaturas:

m = masculino
f = femenino
n = neutro

informazioni sul dizionario

È dimostrato che l'uso di immagini aiuti a capire e memorizzare le informazioni. Applicando tale principio, abbiamo realizzato questo dizionario multilingue, corredato da numerosissime illustrazioni, che presenta un ampio ventaglio di vocaboli utili in cinque lingue europee.

Il dizionario è diviso in vari argomenti ed esamina dettagliatamente molti aspetti del mondo moderno, dal ristorante alla palestra, dalla casa all'ufficio, dallo spazio al regno animale. L'opera contiene inoltre frasi e vocaboli utili per conversare e per estendere il proprio vocabolario.

È un'opera di consultazione essenziale per tutti gli appassionati delle lingue – pratica, stimolante e facile da usare.

Indicazioni
Le cinque lingue vengono presentate sempre nello stesso ordine: inglese, francese, tedesco, spagnolo e italiano.

In tutte le lingue, tranne l'inglese, i sostantivi vengono riportati con il relativo articolo determinativo, che indica il genere (maschile, femminile o neutro) e il numero (singolare o plurale), come ad esempio:

seed   almonds
la graine   les amandes
der Samen   **die Mandeln**
la semilla   las almendras
il seme   le mandorle

I verbi sono contraddistinti da una (v) dopo il vocabolo inglese, come ad esempio:

harvest (*v*) • récolter • ernten • recolectar • raccogliere

Alla fine del libro ogni lingua ha inoltre il proprio indice, che consente di cercare un vocabolo in una qualsiasi delle cinque lingue e di trovare il rimando alla pagina che gli corrisponde. Il genere è indicato dalle seguenti abbreviazioni:

m = maschile
f = femminile
n = neutro

how to use this book

Whether you are learning a new language for business, pleasure, or in preparation for a holiday abroad, or are hoping to extend your vocabulary in an already familiar language, this dictionary is a valuable learning tool which you can use in a number of different ways.

When learning a new language, look out for cognates (words that are alike in different languages) and false friends (words that *look* alike but carry significantly different meanings). You can also see where the languages have influenced each other. For example, English has imported many terms for food from other European languages but, in turn, exported terms used in technology and popular culture.

You can compare two or three languages or all five, depending on how wide your interests are.

Practical learning activities
• As you move about your home, workplace, or college, try looking at the pages which cover that setting. You could then close the book, look around you and see how many of the objects and features you can name.

• Challenge yourself to write a story, letter, or dialogue using as many of the terms on a particular page as possible. This will help you retain the vocabulary and remember the spelling. If you want to build up to writing a longer text, start with sentences incorporating 2–3 words.

• If you have a very visual memory, try drawing or tracing items from the book onto a piece of paper, then close the book and fill in the words below the picture.

• Once you are more confident, pick out words in a foreign-language index and see if you know what they mean before turning to the relevant page to check if you were right.

comment utiliser ce livre

Que vous appreniez une nouvelle langue pour les affaires, le plaisir ou pour préparer vos vacances, ou encore si vous espérez élargir votre vocabulaire dans une langue qui vous est déjà familière, ce dictionnaire sera pour vous un outil d'apprentissage précieux que vous pourrez utiliser de plusieurs manières.

Lorsque vous apprenez une nouvelle langue, recherchez les mots apparentés (mots qui se ressemblent dans différentes langues) et les faux amis (mots qui se ressemblent mais ont des significations nettement différentes). Vous pouvez aussi voir comment les langues se sont influencées. Par exemple, l'anglais a importé des autres langues européennes de nombreux termes désignant la nourriture mais, en retour, exporté des termes employés dans le domaine de la technologie et de la culture populaire.

Vous pouvez comparer deux ou trois langues ou bien toutes les cinq, selon votre intérêt.

Activités pratiques d'apprentissage
• Lorsque vous vous déplacez dans votre maison, au travail ou à l'université, essayez de regarder les pages qui correspondent à ce contexte. Vous pouvez ensuite fermer le livre, regarder autour de vous et voir combien d'objets vous pouvez nommer.

• Forcez-vous à écrire une histoire, une lettre ou un dialogue en employant le plus de termes possibles choisis dans une page. Ceci vous aidera à retenir le vocabulaire et son orthographe. Si vous souhaitez pouvoir écrire un texte plus long, commencez par des phrases qui incorporent 2 à 3 mots.

• Si vous avez une mémoire très visuelle, essayez de dessiner ou de décalquer des objets du livre sur une feuille de papier, puis fermez le livre et inscrivez les mots sous l'image.

• Une fois que vous serez plus sûr de vous, choisissez des mots dans l'index de la langue étrangère et essayez de voir si vous en connaissez le sens avant de vous reporter à la page correspondante pour vérifier.

die Benutzung des Buchs

Ganz gleich, ob Sie eine Sprache aus Geschäftsgründen, zum Vergnügen oder als Vorbereitung für einen Auslandsurlaub lernen, oder Ihr Vokabular in einer Ihnen bereits vertrauten Sprache erweitern möchten, dieses Wörterbuch ist ein wertvolles Lernmittel, das Sie auf vielfältige Art und Weise benutzen können.

Wenn Sie eine neue Sprache lernen, achten Sie auf Wörter, die in verschiedenen Sprachen ähnlich sind sowie auf falsche Freunde (Wörter, die ähnlich aussehen aber wesentlich andere Bedeutungen haben). Sie können ebenfalls feststellen, wie die Sprachen einander beeinflusst haben. Englisch hat zum Beispiel viele Ausdrücke für Nahrungsmittel aus anderen europäischen Sprachen übernommen und andererseits viele Begriffe aus der Technik und Popkultur ausgeführt.

Sie können je nach Ihrem Interesse zwei oder drei, oder auch alle fünf Sprachen miteinander vergleichen.

Praktische Übungen
• Versuchen Sie sich zu Hause, am Arbeits- oder Studienplatz den Inhalt der Seiten einzuprägen, die Ihre Umgebung behandeln. Schließen Sie dann das Buch und prüfen Sie, wie viele Gegenstände Sie in den anderen Sprachen sagen können.

• Schreiben Sie eine Geschichte, einen Brief oder Dialog und benutzen Sie dabei möglichst viele Ausdrücke von einer bestimmten Seite des Wörterbuchs. Dies ist eine gute Methode, sich das Vokabular und die Schreibweise einzuprägen. Sie können mit kurzen Sätzen von zwei bis drei Worten anfangen und dann nach und nach längere Texte schreiben.

• Wenn Sie ein visuelles Gedächtnis haben, können Sie Gegenstände aus dem Buch abzeichnen oder abpausen. Schließen Sie dann das Buch und schreiben Sie die passenden Wörter unter die Bilder.

• Wenn Sie mehr Sicherheit haben, können Sie Wörter aus einem der Fremdsprachenregister aussuchen und deren Bedeutung aufschreiben, bevor Sie auf der entsprechenden Seite nachsehen.

cómo utilizar este libro

Ya se encuentre aprendiendo un idioma nuevo por motivos de trabajo, placer, o para preparar sus vacaciones al extranjero, o ya quiera ampliar su vocabulario en un idioma que ya conoce, este diccionario es un instrumento muy valioso que podrá utilizar de distintas maneras.

Cuando esté aprendiendo un idioma nuevo, busque palabras similares en distintos idiomas y palabras que parecen similares pero que poseen significados totalmente distintos. También podrá observar cómo los idiomas se influyen unos a otros. Por ejemplo, la lengua inglesa ha importado muchos términos de comida de otras lenguas pero, a cambio, ha exportado términos empleados en tecnología y cultura popular.

Podrá comparar dos o tres idiomas o los cinco, dependiendo de lo ámplio que sean sus interéses.

Actividades prácticas de aprendizaje
• Mientras se desplaza por su casa, lugar de trabajo o colegio, intente mirar las páginas que se refieren a ese lugar. Podrá entonces cerrar el libro, mirar a su alrededor y ver cuántos objetos o características puede nombrar.

• Desafíese a usted mismo a escribir una historia, carta o diálogo empleando tantos términos de una página concreta como le sea posible. Esto le ayudará a retener vocabulario y recordar la ortografía. Si quiere ir progresando para poder escribir un texto más largo, comience con frases que incorporen dos ó tres palabras.

• Si tiene buena memoria visual, intente dibujar o calcar objetos del libro; luego cierre el libro y escriba las palabras correspondientes debajo del dibujo.

• Cuando se sienta más seguro, escoja al azar palabras del índice de uno de los idiomas y vea si sabe lo que significan antes de consultar la página correspondiente para comprobarlo.

come usare questo libro

Che stiate imparando una lingua nuova a scopo di lavoro, per diletto o in preparazione per una vacanza all'estero, o desideriate estendere il vostro vocabolario in una lingua che vi è già familiare, questo dizionario è uno strumento di apprendimento prezioso che potete usare in vari modi diversi.

Quando imparate una lingua nuova, cercate le parole affini per origine (che sono quindi simili nelle varie lingue) ma occhio alle false analogie (vocaboli che sembrano uguali ma hanno significati molto diversi). Questo dizionario mostra inoltre come le lingue hanno influito l'una sull'altra (l'inglese, per esempio, ha importato dalle altre lingue europee molti vocaboli relativi agli alimenti ma ne ha esportati molti altri relativi alla tecnologia e alla cultura popolare) e vi consente di confrontare due, tre o anche tutte e cinque le lingue, a seconda di quelle che vi interessano.

Attività pratiche di apprendimento
• Girando per casa, in ufficio, a scuola, guardate le pagine relative all'ambiente in cui vi trovate, poi chiudete il libro, guardatevi attorno e cercate di ricordare il nome del maggior numero possibile di oggetti e strutture.

• Provate a scrivere un racconto, una lettera o un dialogo usando il maggior numero possibile dei vocaboli riportati su di una pagina in particolare. Vi aiuterà a memorizzare i vocaboli e a ricordare come si scrivono. Se volete scrivere testi più lunghi, cominciate con delle frasi che comprendano 2 o 3 delle parole.

• Se avete una memoria molto visiva, prendete un foglio di carta e disegnatevi o ricopiatevi le immagini che appaiono nel libro, quindi chiudete il libro e scrivete le parole sotto alle immagini.

• Quando vi sentite più sicuri, scegliete dei vocaboli dall'indice di una lingua straniera e cercate di ricordarne i significati, trovando poi le pagine corrispondenti per verificare che siano giusti.

people
les gens
die Menschen
la gente
la gente

body • le corps • der Körper • el cuerpo • il corpo

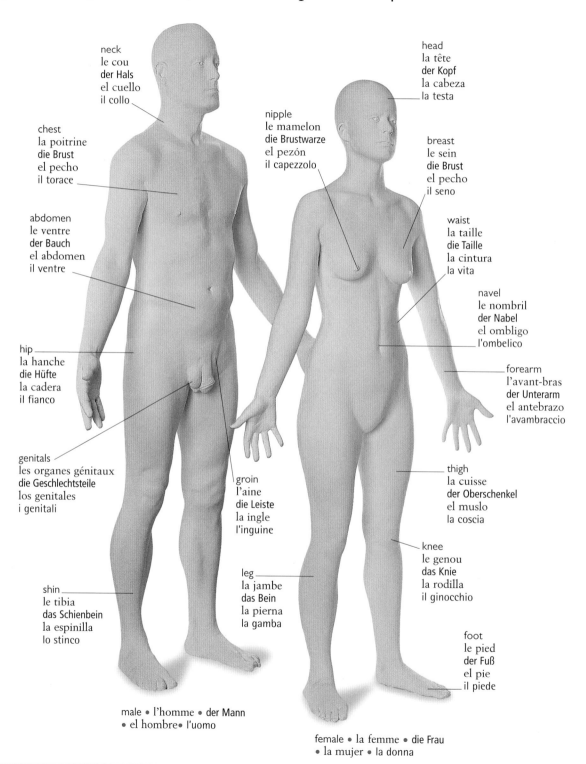

neck
le cou
der Hals
el cuello
il collo

head
la tête
der Kopf
la cabeza
la testa

nipple
le mamelon
die Brustwarze
el pezón
il capezzolo

breast
le sein
die Brust
el pecho
il seno

chest
la poitrine
die Brust
el pecho
il torace

waist
la taille
die Taille
la cintura
la vita

abdomen
le ventre
der Bauch
el abdomen
il ventre

navel
le nombril
der Nabel
el ombligo
l'ombelico

hip
la hanche
die Hüfte
la cadera
il fianco

forearm
l'avant-bras
der Unterarm
el antebrazo
l'avambraccio

genitals
les organes génitaux
die Geschlechtsteile
los genitales
i genitali

groin
l'aine
die Leiste
la ingle
l'inguine

thigh
la cuisse
der Oberschenkel
el muslo
la coscia

knee
le genou
das Knie
la rodilla
il ginocchio

shin
le tibia
das Schienbein
la espinilla
lo stinco

leg
la jambe
das Bein
la pierna
la gamba

foot
le pied
der Fuß
el pie
il piede

male • l'homme • der Mann
• el hombre• l'uomo

female • la femme • die Frau
• la mujer • la donna

english • français • deutsch • español • italiano

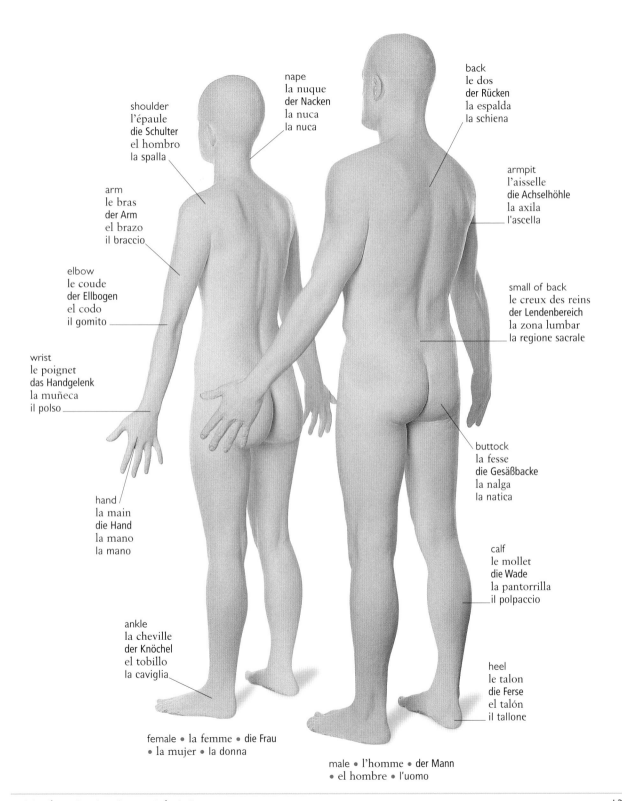

shoulder
l'épaule
die Schulter
el hombro
la spalla

nape
la nuque
der Nacken
la nuca
la nuca

back
le dos
der Rücken
la espalda
la schiena

arm
le bras
der Arm
el brazo
il braccio

armpit
l'aisselle
die Achselhöhle
la axila
l'ascella

elbow
le coude
der Ellbogen
el codo
il gomito

small of back
le creux des reins
der Lendenbereich
la zona lumbar
la regione sacrale

wrist
le poignet
das Handgelenk
la muñeca
il polso

buttock
la fesse
die Gesäßbacke
la nalga
la natica

hand
la main
die Hand
la mano
la mano

calf
le mollet
die Wade
la pantorrilla
il polpaccio

ankle
la cheville
der Knöchel
el tobillo
la caviglia

heel
le talon
die Ferse
el talón
il tallone

female • la femme • die Frau
• la mujer • la donna

male • l'homme • der Mann
• el hombre • l'uomo

face • le visage • das Gesicht • la cara • la faccia

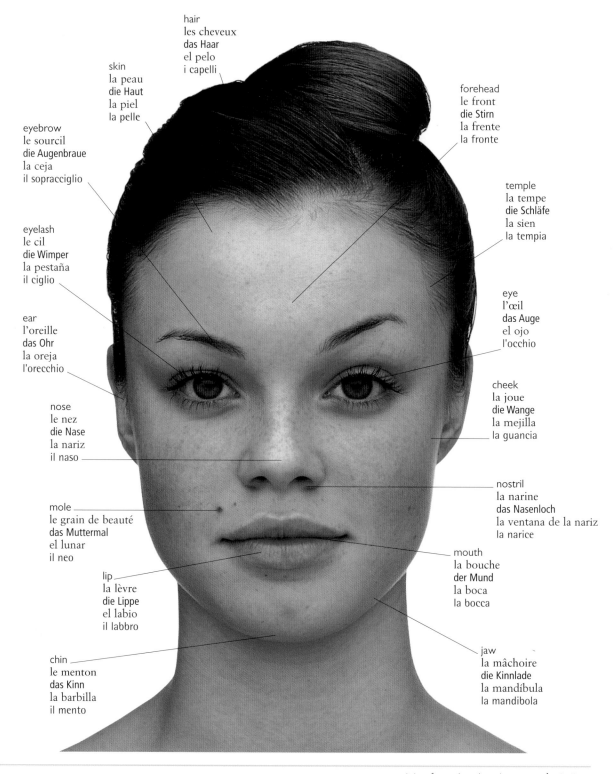

hair
les cheveux
das Haar
el pelo
i capelli

skin
la peau
die Haut
la piel
la pelle

forehead
le front
die Stirn
la frente
la fronte

eyebrow
le sourcil
die Augenbraue
la ceja
il sopracciglio

temple
la tempe
die Schläfe
la sien
la tempia

eyelash
le cil
die Wimper
la pestaña
il ciglio

eye
l'œil
das Auge
el ojo
l'occhio

ear
l'oreille
das Ohr
la oreja
l'orecchio

cheek
la joue
die Wange
la mejilla
la guancia

nose
le nez
die Nase
la nariz
il naso

nostril
la narine
das Nasenloch
la ventana de la nariz
la narice

mole
le grain de beauté
das Muttermal
el lunar
il neo

mouth
la bouche
der Mund
la boca
la bocca

lip
la lèvre
die Lippe
el labio
il labbro

chin
le menton
das Kinn
la barbilla
il mento

jaw
la mâchoire
die Kinnlade
la mandíbula
la mandibola

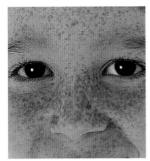

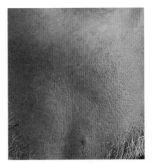

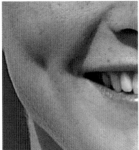

wrinkle • la ride • die Falte
• la arruga • la ruga

freckle • la tache de rousseur
• die Sommersprosse •
la peca • la lentiggine

pore • le pore • die Pore
• el poro • il poro

dimple • la fossette
• das Grübchen • el hoyuelo
• la fossetta

hand • la main • **die Hand** • la mano • la mano

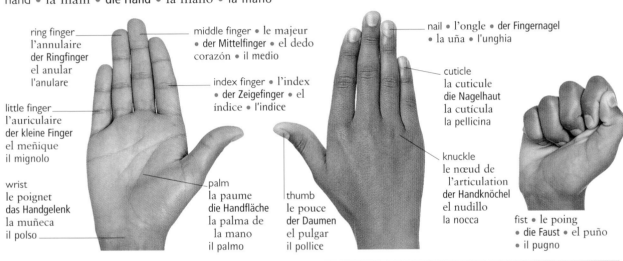

ring finger
l'annulaire
der Ringfinger
el anular
l'anulare

middle finger • le majeur
• der Mittelfinger • el dedo
corazón • il medio

nail • l'ongle • der Fingernagel
• la uña • l'unghia

index finger • l'index
• der Zeigefinger • el
índice • l'indice

cuticle
la cuticule
die Nagelhaut
la cutícula
la pellicina

little finger
l'auriculaire
der kleine Finger
el meñique
il mignolo

knuckle
le nœud de
l'articulation
der Handknöchel
el nudillo
la nocca

wrist
le poignet
das Handgelenk
la muñeca
il polso

palm
la paume
die Handfläche
la palma de
la mano
il palmo

thumb
le pouce
der Daumen
el pulgar
il pollice

fist • le poing
• die Faust • el puño
• il pugno

foot • le pied • **der Fuß** • el pie • il piede

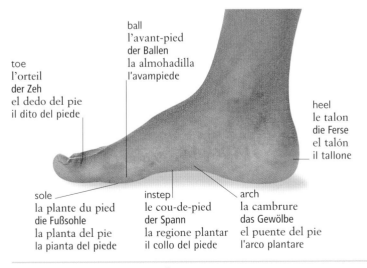

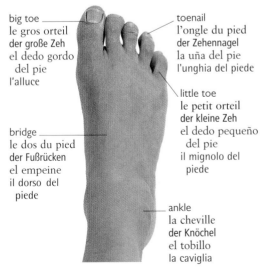

ball
l'avant-pied
der Ballen
la almohadilla
l'avampiede

big toe
le gros orteil
der große Zeh
el dedo gordo
del pie
l'alluce

toenail
l'ongle du pied
der Zehennagel
la uña del pie
l'unghia del piede

toe
l'orteil
der Zeh
el dedo del pie
il dito del piede

heel
le talon
die Ferse
el talón
il tallone

bridge
le dos du pied
der Fußrücken
el empeine
il dorso del
piede

little toe
le petit orteil
der kleine Zeh
el dedo pequeño
del pie
il mignolo del
piede

sole
la plante du pied
die Fußsohle
la planta del pie
la pianta del piede

instep
le cou-de-pied
der Spann
la regione plantar
il collo del piede

arch
la cambrure
das Gewölbe
el puente del pie
l'arco plantare

ankle
la cheville
der Knöchel
el tobillo
la caviglia

muscles • les muscles • die Muskeln • los músculos • i muscoli

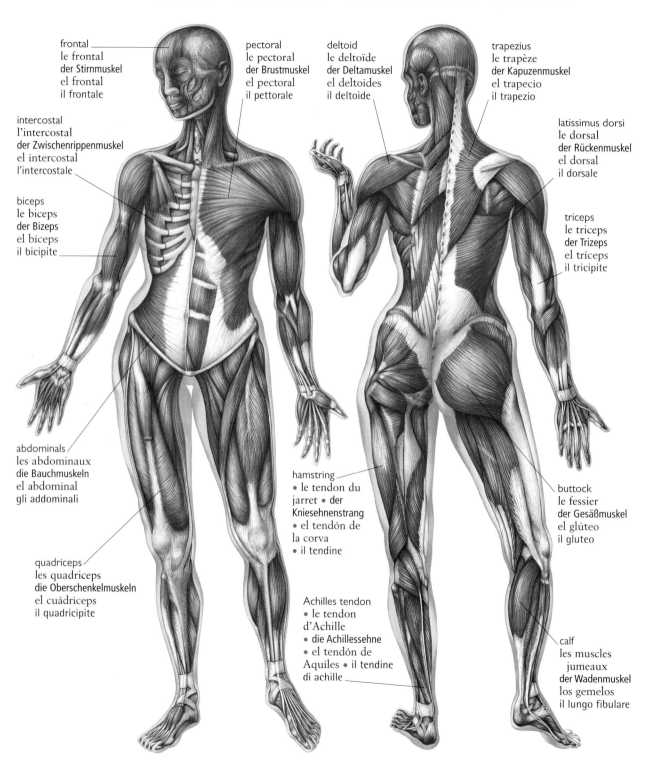

frontal
le frontal
der Stirnmuskel
el frontal
il frontale

pectoral
le pectoral
der Brustmuskel
el pectoral
il pettorale

deltoid
le deltoïde
der Deltamuskel
el deltoides
il deltoide

trapezius
le trapèze
der Kapuzenmuskel
el trapecio
il trapezio

intercostal
l'intercostal
der Zwischenrippenmuskel
el intercostal
l'intercostale

latissimus dorsi
le dorsal
der Rückenmuskel
el dorsal
il dorsale

biceps
le biceps
der Bizeps
el bíceps
il bicipite

triceps
le triceps
der Trizeps
el tríceps
il tricipite

abdominals
les abdominaux
die Bauchmuskeln
el abdominal
gli addominali

hamstring
• le tendon du
jarret • **der
Kniesehnenstrang**
• el tendón de
la corva
• il tendine

buttock
le fessier
der Gesäßmuskel
el glúteo
il gluteo

quadriceps
les quadriceps
die Oberschenkelmuskeln
el cuádriceps
il quadricipite

Achilles tendon
• le tendon
d'Achille
• **die Achillessehne**
• el tendón de
Aquiles • il tendine
di achille

calf
les muscles
jumeaux
der Wadenmuskel
los gemelos
il lungo fibulare

skeleton • le squelette • das Skelett • el esqueleto • lo scheletro

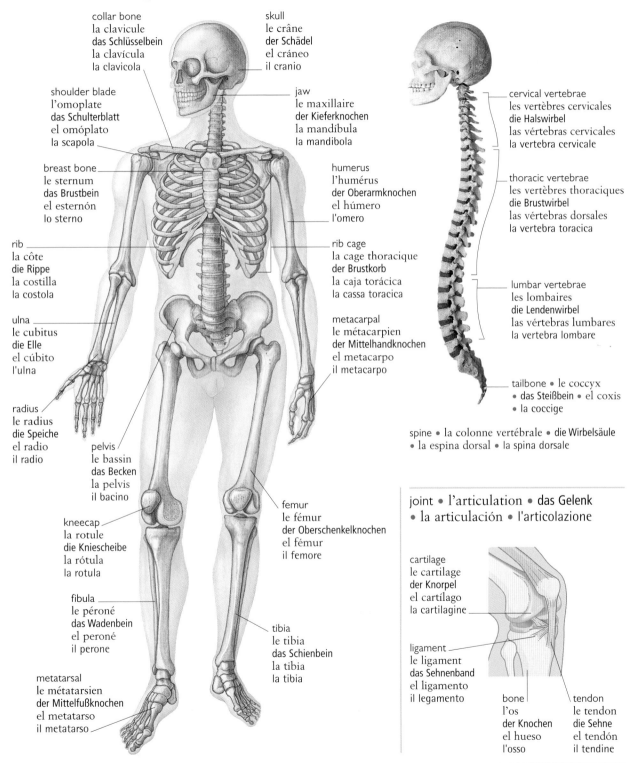

collar bone
la clavicule
das Schlüsselbein
la clavícula
la clavicola

shoulder blade
l'omoplate
das Schulterblatt
el omóplato
la scapola

breast bone
le sternum
das Brustbein
el esternón
lo sterno

rib
la côte
die Rippe
la costilla
la costola

ulna
le cubitus
die Elle
el cúbito
l'ulna

radius
le radius
die Speiche
el radio
il radio

pelvis
le bassin
das Becken
la pelvis
il bacino

kneecap
la rotule
die Kniescheibe
la rótula
la rotula

fibula
le péroné
das Wadenbein
el peroné
il perone

metatarsal
le métatarsien
der Mittelfußknochen
el metatarso
il metatarso

skull
le crâne
der Schädel
el cráneo
il cranio

jaw
le maxillaire
der Kieferknochen
la mandíbula
la mandibola

humerus
l'humérus
der Oberarmknochen
el húmero
l'omero

rib cage
la cage thoracique
der Brustkorb
la caja torácica
la cassa toracica

metacarpal
le métacarpien
der Mittelhandknochen
el metacarpo
il metacarpo

femur
le fémur
der Oberschenkelknochen
el fémur
il femore

tibia
le tibia
das Schienbein
la tibia
la tibia

cervical vertebrae
les vertèbres cervicales
die Halswirbel
las vértebras cervicales
la vertebra cervicale

thoracic vertebrae
les vertèbres thoraciques
die Brustwirbel
las vértebras dorsales
la vertebra toracica

lumbar vertebrae
les lombaires
die Lendenwirbel
las vértebras lumbares
la vertebra lombare

tailbone • le coccyx
• das Steißbein • el coxis
• la coccige

spine • la colonne vertébrale • die Wirbelsäule
• la espina dorsal • la spina dorsale

joint • l'articulation • das Gelenk
• la articulación • l'articolazione

cartilage
le cartilage
der Knorpel
el cartílago
la cartilagine

ligament
le ligament
das Sehnenband
el ligamento
il legamento

bone
l'os
der Knochen
el hueso
l'osso

tendon
le tendon
die Sehne
el tendón
il tendine

internal organs • les organes internes • die inneren Organe • los órganos internos • gli organi interni

thyroid gland
la thyroïde
die Schilddrüse
el tiroides
la tiroide

liver
le foie
die Leber
el hígado
il fegato

windpipe
la trachée
die Luftröhre
la tráquea
la trachea

duodenum
le duodénum
der Zwölffingerdarm
el duodeno
il duodeno

lung
le poumon
die Lunge
el pulmón
il polmone

kidney
le rein
die Niere
el riñón
il rene

heart
le cœur
das Herz
el corazón
il cuore

stomach
l'estomac
der Magen
el estómago
lo stomaco

pancreas
le pancréas
**die Bauchspeichel-
drüse**
el páncreas
il pancreas

spleen
la rate
die Milz
el bazo
la milza

small intestine
l'intestin grêle
der Dünndarm
el intestino
delgado
l'intestino tenue

large intestine
le gros intestin
der Dickdarm
el intestino
grueso
l'intestino crasso

appendix
l'appendice
der Blinddarm
el apéndice
l'appendice

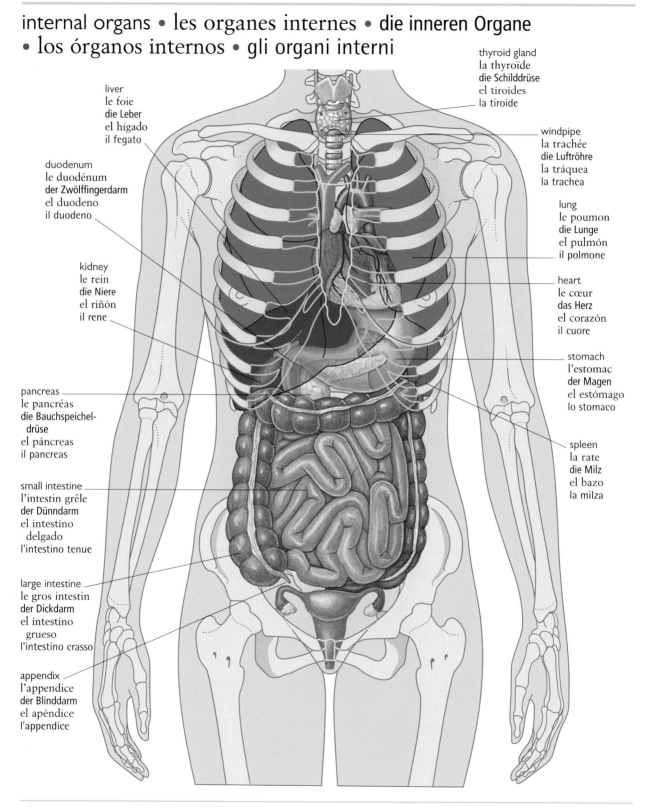

head • la tête • der Kopf • la cabeza • la testa

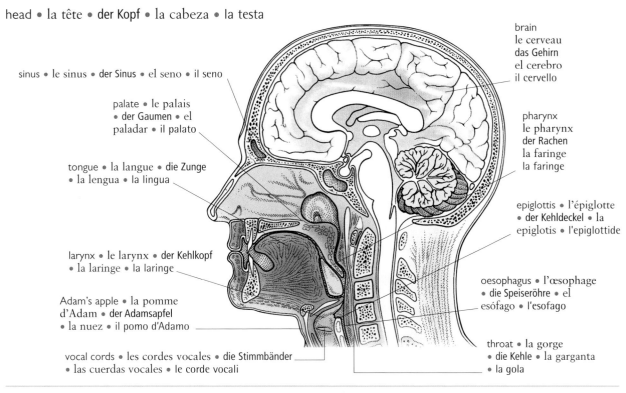

brain
le cerveau
das Gehirn
el cerebro
il cervello

sinus • le sinus • der Sinus • el seno • il seno

palate • le palais • der Gaumen • el paladar • il palato

tongue • la langue • die Zunge • la lengua • la lingua

pharynx
le pharynx
der Rachen
la faringe
la faringe

epiglottis • l'épiglotte • der Kehldeckel • la epiglotis • l'epiglottide

larynx • le larynx • der Kehlkopf • la laringe • la laringe

Adam's apple • la pomme d'Adam • der Adamsapfel • la nuez • il pomo d'Adamo

oesophagus • l'œsophage • die Speiseröhre • el esófago • l'esofago

vocal cords • les cordes vocales • die Stimmbänder • las cuerdas vocales • le corde vocali

throat • la gorge • die Kehle • la garganta • la gola

body systems • les systèmes du corps • die Körpersysteme • los sistemas • i sistemi corporali

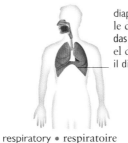

diaphragm
le diaphragme
das Zwerchfell
el diafragma
il diaframma

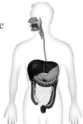

respiratory • respiratoire • das Atmungssystem • respiratorio • respiratorio

digestive • digestif • das Verdauungssystem • digestivo • digestivo

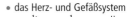

vein
la veine
die Vene
la vena
la vena

artery
l'artère
die Arterie
la arteria
l'arteria

cardiovascular • cardio-vasculaire • das Herz- und Gefäßsystem • cardiovascular • cardiovascolare

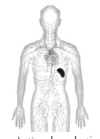

lymphatic • lymphatique • das lymphatische System • linfático • linfatico

urinary • urinaire • das Harnsystem • urinario • urinario

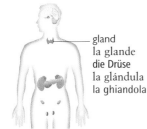

gland
la glande
die Drüse
la glándula
la ghiandola

endocrine • endocrine • das endokrine System • endocrino • endocrino

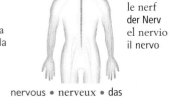

nerve
le nerf
der Nerv
el nervio
il nervo

nervous • nerveux • das Nervensystem • nervioso • nervoso

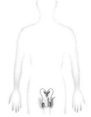

reproductive • reproducteur • das Fortpflanzungssystem • reproductor • riproduttivo

reproductive organs • les organes de reproduction • die Fortpflanzungsorgane • los órganos reproductores • gli organi riproduttivi

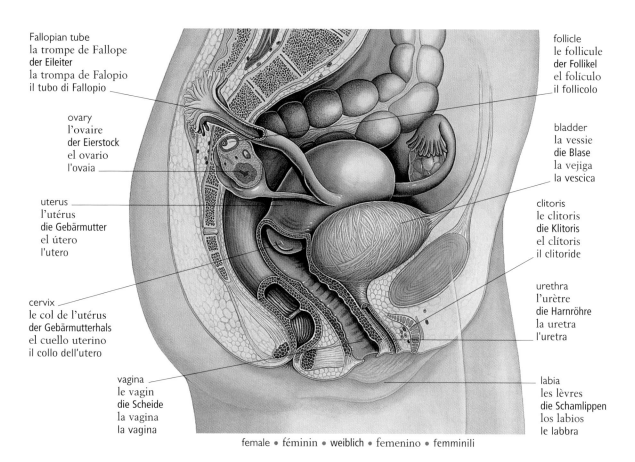

Fallopian tube
la trompe de Fallope
der Eileiter
la trompa de Falopio
il tubo di Fallopio

ovary
l'ovaire
der Eierstock
el ovario
l'ovaia

uterus
l'utérus
die Gebärmutter
el útero
l'utero

cervix
le col de l'utérus
der Gebärmutterhals
el cuello uterino
il collo dell'utero

vagina
le vagin
die Scheide
la vagina
la vagina

follicle
le follicule
der Follikel
el folículo
il follicolo

bladder
la vessie
die Blase
la vejiga
la vescica

clitoris
le clitoris
die Klitoris
el clítoris
il clitoride

urethra
l'urètre
die Harnröhre
la uretra
l'uretra

labia
les lèvres
die Schamlippen
los labios
le labbra

female • féminin • weiblich • femenino • femminili

reproduction • la reproduction • die Fortpflanzung • la reproducción • la riproduzione

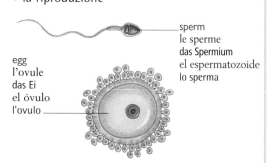

sperm
le sperme
das Spermium
el espermatozoide
lo sperma

egg
l'ovule
das Ei
el óvulo
l'ovulo

fertilization • la fertilisation • die Befruchtung • la fecundación • la fertilizzazione

hormone	impotent	menstruation
l'hormone	impuissant	les règles
das Hormon	impotent	die Menstruation
la hormona	impotente	la menstruación
l'ormone	impotente	la mestruazione
ovulation	fertile	intercourse
l'ovulation	fécond	les rapports sexuels
der Eisprung	fruchtbar	der Geschlechtsverkehr
la ovulación	fértil	las relaciones sexuales
l'ovulazione	fecondo	il coito
infertile	conceive	sexually transmitted disease
stérile	concevoir	la maladie sexuellement transmissible
steril	empfangen	die Geschlechtskrankheit
estéril	concebir	la enfermedad de transmisión sexual
sterile	concepire	la malattia trasmissibile per via sessuale

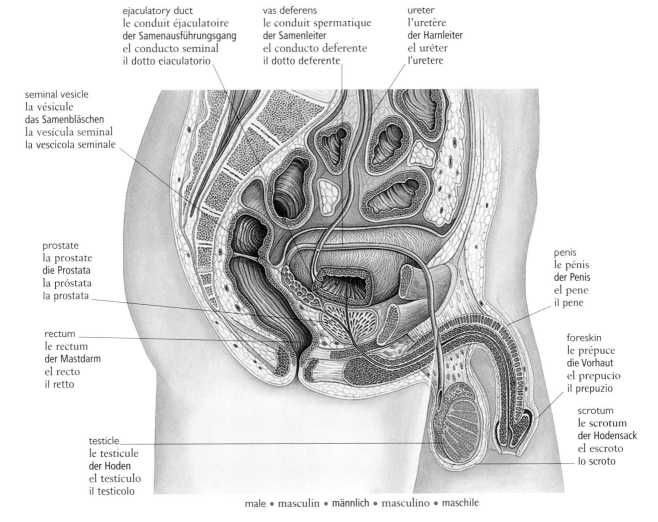

ejaculatory duct
le conduit éjaculatoire
der Samenausführungsgang
el conducto seminal
il dotto eiaculatorio

vas deferens
le conduit spermatique
der Samenleiter
el conducto deferente
il dotto deferente

ureter
l'uretère
der Harnleiter
el uréter
l'uretere

seminal vesicle
la vésicule
das Samenbläschen
la vesícula seminal
la vescicola seminale

prostate
la prostate
die Prostata
la próstata
la prostata

penis
le pénis
der Penis
el pene
il pene

rectum
le rectum
der Mastdarm
el recto
il retto

foreskin
le prépuce
die Vorhaut
el prepucio
il prepuzio

scrotum
le scrotum
der Hodensack
el escroto
lo scroto

testicle
le testicule
der Hoden
el testículo
il testicolo

male • masculin • männlich • masculino • maschile

contraception • la contraception • die Empfängnisverhütung • la anticoncepción • la contraccezione

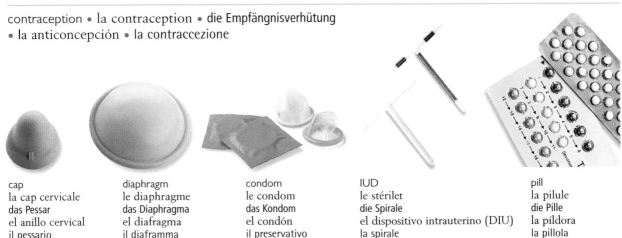

cap
la cap cervicale
das Pessar
el anillo cervical
il pessario

diaphragm
le diaphragme
das Diaphragma
el diafragma
il diaframma

condom
le condom
das Kondom
el condón
il preservativo

IUD
le stérilet
die Spirale
el dispositivo intrauterino (DIU)
la spirale

pill
la pilule
die Pille
la píldora
la pillola

family • la famille • die Familie • la familia • la famiglia

grandmother • la grand-mère • die Großmutter • la abuela • la nonna

grandfather • le grand-père • der Großvater • el abuelo • il nonno

uncle • l'oncle • der Onkel • el tío • lo zio

aunt • la tante • die Tante • la tía • la zia

father • le père • der Vater • el padre • il padre

mother • la mère • die Mutter • la madre • la madre

cousin • le cousin • der Cousin • el primo • il cugino

brother • le frère • der Bruder • el hermano • il fratello

sister • la sœur • die Schwester • la hermana • la sorella

wife • la femme • die Ehefrau • la mujer • la moglie

daughter-in-law • la belle-fille • die Schwiegertochter • la nuera • la nuora

son • le fils • der Sohn • el hijo • il figlio

daughter • la fille • die Tochter • la hija • la figlia

son-in-law • le gendre • der Schwiegersohn • el yerno • il genero

grandson • le petit-fils • der Enkel • el nieto • il nipote

granddaughter • la petite-fille • die Enkelin • la nieta • la nipote

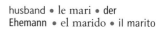

husband • le mari • der Ehemann • el marido • il marito

relatives	parents	grandchildren	stepmother	stepson	generation
les parents	les parents	les petits-enfants	la belle-mère	le beau-fils	la génération
die Verwandten	die Eltern	die Enkelkinder	die Stiefmutter	der Stiefsohn	die Generation
los parientes	los padres	los nietos	la madrastra	el hijastro	la generación
i parenti	i genitori	i nipoti	la matrigna	il figliastro	la generazione

grandparents	children	stepfather	stepdaughter	partner	twins
les grands-parents	les enfants	le beau-père	la belle-fille	le/la partenaire	les jumeaux
die Großeltern	die Kinder	der Stiefvater	die Stieftochter	der Partner/die Partnerin	die Zwillinge
los abuelos	los niños	el padrastro	la hijastra	el/la compañero/-a	los gemelos
i nonni	i bambini	il patrigno	la figliastra	il/la compagno/-a	i gemelli

stages • les stades • die Stadien • las etapas • le fasi

mother-in-law
• la belle-mère
• die Schwiegermutter
• la suegra • la suocera

father-in-law
• le beau-père
• der Schwiegervater
• el suegro • il suocero

baby • le bébé
• das Baby • el bebé
• il bebè

child • l'enfant
• das Kind • el niño
• il bambino

brother-in-law
• le beau-frère
• der Schwager • el
cuñado • il cognato

sister-in-law • la belle-
sœur • die Schwägerin
• la cuñada
• la cognata

boy • le garçon
• der Junge • el chico
• il ragazzo

girl • la fille
• das Mädchen
• la chica • la ragazza

niece • la nièce
• die Nichte • la
sobrina • la nipote

nephew • le neveu
• der Neffe • el
sobrino • il nipote

Mrs
Madame
Frau
Señora
Signora

teenager • l'adolescente
• die Jugendliche
• la adolescente
• l'adolescente

adult • l'adulte • der
Erwachsene • el adulto
• l'adulto

titles • les titres • die Anreden • los tratamientos • gli appellativi

Miss	Mr
Mademoiselle	Monsieur
Fräulein	Herr
Señorita	Señor
Signorina	Signore

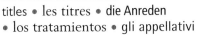

man • l'homme
• der Mann
• el hombre • l'uomo

woman • la femme
• die Frau • la mujer
• la donna

relationships • les relations • die Beziehungen • las relaciones • i rapporti

manager
le chef
der Chef
el jefe
il capo

assistant
l'assistante
die Assistentin
la ayudante
l'assistente

business partner
l'associée
die Geschäftspartnerin
la socia
la socia

employer
l'employeuse
die Arbeitgeberin
la empresaria
il datore di lavoro

employee
l'employé
der Mitarbeiter
el empleado
l'impiegato

colleague
le collègue
der Kollege
el compañero
il collega

office • le bureau • das Büro • la oficina • l'ufficio

neighbour • le voisin • der Nachbar • el vecino • il vicino

friend • l'ami • der Freund • el amigo • l'amico

acquaintance • la connaissance • der Bekannte • el conocido • il conoscente

penfriend • le correspondant • der Brieffreund • el amigo por correspondencia • l'amico di penna

boyfriend
le petit ami
der Freund
el novio
il ragazzo

girlfriend
la petite amie
die Freundin
la novia
la ragazza

fiancé
le fiancé
der Verlobte
el prometido
il fidanzato

fiancée
la fiancée
die Verlobte
la prometida
la fidanzata

couple • le couple • das Paar • la pareja • la coppia

engaged couple • les fiancés • die Verlobten • la pareja de prometidos • i fidanzati

emotions • les émotions • die Gefühle • las emociones • le emozioni

smile
le sourire
das Lächeln
la sonrisa
il sorriso

happy • heureux • glücklich
• contento • felice

sad • triste • traurig • triste
• triste

excited • excité • aufgeregt
• alboratado • eccitato

bored • ennuyé • gelangweilt
• aburrido • annoiato

surprised • surpris
• überrascht • sorprendido
• sorpreso

scared • effrayé • erschrocken
• asustado • spaventato

frown • le froncement
de sourcils • das
Stirnrunzeln • el ceño
fruncido • aggrottare
la fronte

angry • fâché • verärgert
• enfadado • arrabbiato

confused • confus • verwirrt
• confuso • confuso

worried • inquiet • besorgt
• preocupado • preoccupato

nervous • nerveux • nervös
• nervioso • nervoso

proud • fier • stolz
• orgulloso • fiero

confident • sûr de soi
• selbstsicher • seguro de sí
mismo • sicuro di sé

embarrassed • gêné
• verlegen • avergonzado
• imbarazzato

shy • timide • schüchtern
• tímido • timido

upset	laugh (v)	sigh (v)	shout (v)
consterné	rire	soupirer	crier
bestürzt	lachen	seufzen	schreien
consternado	reír	suspirar	gritar
turbato	ridere	sospirare	gridare
shocked	cry (v)	faint (v)	yawn (v)
choqué	pleurer	s'évanouir	bâiller
schockiert	weinen	in Ohnmacht fallen	gähnen
horrorizado	llorar	desmayarse	bostezar
scandalizzato	piangere	svenire	sbadigliare

life events • les événements de la vie • die Ereignisse des Lebens • los acontecimientos de una vida • gli avvenimenti della vita

be born (v) • naître • **geboren werden** • nacer • nascere

start school (v) • commencer à l'école • **zur Schule kommen** • empezar el colegio • iniziare la scuola

make friends (v) • se faire des amis • **sich befreunden** • hacer amigos • fare amicizia

graduate (v) • obtenir sa licence • **graduieren** • licenciarse • laurearsi

get a job (v) • trouver un emploi • **eine Stelle bekommen** • conseguir un trabajo • trovare un lavoro

fall in love (v) • tomber amoureux • **sich verlieben** • enamorarse • innamorarsi

get married (v) • se marier • **heiraten** • casarse • sposarsi

have a baby (v) • avoir un bébé • **ein Baby bekommen** • tener un hijo • avere un bambino

wedding • le mariage • **die Hochzeit** • la boda • il matrimonio

divorce • le divorce • **die Scheidung** • el divorcio • il divorzio

funeral • l'enterrement • **das Begräbnis** • el funeral • il funerale

christening	die (v)
le baptême	mourir
die Taufe	sterben
el bautizo	morir
il battesimo	morire
bar mitzvah	make a will (v)
la bar-mitsvah	faire son testament
die Bar Mizwa	sein Testament machen
el bar mitzvah	hacer testamento
il bar mitzvah	fare testamento
anniversary	birth certificate
l'anniversaire	l'acte de naissance
der Hochzeitstag	die Geburtsurkunde
el aniversario	la partida de nacimiento
l'anniversario	il certificato di nascita
emigrate (v)	wedding reception
émigrer	le repas de noces
emigrieren	die Hochzeitsfeier
emigrar	la boda
emigrare	il ricevimento nuziale
retire (v)	honeymoon
prendre sa retraite	le voyage de noces
in den Ruhestand treten	die Hochzeitsreise
jubilarse	la luna de miel
andare in pensione	il viaggio di nozze

english • français • deutsch • español • italiano

celebrations • les fêtes • die Feste • las celebraciones • le celebrazioni

birthday party
la fête
die Geburtstagsfeier
la fiesta de cumpleaños
la festa di compleanno

card
la carte
die Karte
la tarjeta
la cartolina

birthday • l'anniversaire • der Geburtstag • el cumpleaños • il compleanno

present
le cadeau
das Geschenk
el regalo
il regalo

Christmas • le Noël • Weihnachten • la Navidad • il Natale

festivals • les fêtes • die Feste • las fiestas • le feste

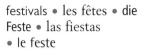

Passover • la Pâque • das Passah • la Pascua judía • la Pasqua ebraica

New Year • le Nouvel An • das Neujahr • el Año Nuevo • il Capodanno

carnival • le carnaval • der Karneval • el carnaval • il carnevale

procession
le défilé
der Umzug
el desfile
la processione

Ramadan • le Ramadan • der Ramadan • el Ramadán • il Ramadan

ribbon
le ruban
das Band
la cinta
il nastro

Thanksgiving • la fête de Thanksgiving • der Thanksgiving Day • el día de Acción de Gracias • il giorno del ringraziamento

Easter • Pâques • das Ostern • la Pascua • la Pasqua

Halloween • la veille de la Toussaint • das Halloween • la víspera de Todos los Santos • la vigilia d'Ognissanti

Diwali • la Diwali • das Diwali • el Diwali • il Diwali

appearance
l'apparence
die äußere Erscheinung
el aspecto
l'aspetto

children's clothing • les vêtements d'enfants • die Kinderkleidung • la ropa de niño • l'abbigliamento da bambino

baby • le bébé • das Baby • el bebé • il bebé

snowsuit • la combinaison de neige • der Schneeanzug • el buzo • la tutina da neve

vest • le tricot de corps • das Hemdchen • el body • la camicetta

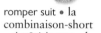

popper
le bouton-pression
der Druckknopf
el corchete
il bottone automatico

babygro • la grenouillère • der Strampelanzug • el pelele • la tutina

sleepsuit • le pyjama • der Schlafanzug • el pijama • il pigiamino

romper suit • la combinaison-short • der Spielanzug • la ranita • il pagliaccetto

bib • le bavoir • das Lätzchen • el babero • il bavaglino

mittens • les moufles • die Babyhandschuhe • las manoplas • i guanti

booties • les chaussons • die Babyschuhe • los patucos • le scarpette

terry nappy • la couche éponge • die Stoffwindel • el pañal de felpa • il pannolino di spugna

disposable nappy • la couche jetable • die Wegwerfwindel • el pañal desechable • il pannolino usa e getta

plastic pants • la culotte en plastique • das Gummihöschen • las braguitas de plástico • le mutande di plastica

---

toddler • le petit enfant • das Kleinkind • el niño pequeño • il bambino piccolo

t-shirt
le t-shirt
das T-Shirt
la camiseta
la maglietta

dungarees
la salopette
die Latzhose
los pantalones con peto
la salopette

sunhat • le chapeau de soleil • der Sonnenhut • el gorro para el sol • il cappello per il sole

skirt
la jupe
der Rock
la falda
la gonna

apron • le tablier • die Schürze • el delantal • il grembiulino

shorts
le bermuda
die Shorts
los pantalones cortos
i pantaloncini

child • l'enfant • das Kind • el niño • il bambino

dress • la robe
• das Kleid • el
vestido • il vestito

hood
la capuche
die Kapuze
la capucha
il cappuccio

jeans
le jean
die Jeans
los pantalones
vaqueros
i jeans

sandals
les sandales
die Sandalen
las sandalias
i sandali

summer • l'été • der
Sommer • el verano
• l'estate

raincoat • l'imperméable
• der Regenmantel
• el impermeable
• l'impermeabile

backpack
le sac à dos
der Rucksack
la mochila
lo zaino

autumn • l'automne
• der Herbst • el otoño
• l'autunno

toggle
le bouton
der Knebelknopf
la muletilla
l'olivetta

duffel coat • le duffel-
coat • der Dufflecoat • la
trenca • il montgomery

scarf
l'écharpe
der Schal
la bufanda
la sciarpa

anorak
l'anorak
der Anorak
el anorak
il piumino

wellington boots
• les bottes de
caoutchouc
• die Gummistiefel
• las botas de
agua • le galosce

winter • l'hiver • der
Winter • el invierno
• l'inverno

dressing gown
la robe de chambre
der Morgenrock
la bata
la vestaglia

logo
le logo
das Logo
el logotipo
il logo

trainers
les baskets
die Sportschuhe
las zapatillas de deporte
le scarpe da ginnastica

football strip • la tenue de
foot • das Fußballtrikot
• la equipación • la
tenuta da calcio

tracksuit • le
survêtement • der
Trainingsanzug • el
chándal • la tuta

leggings • les leggings
• die Leggings • las
mallas • il pantacollant

nightie
la chemise de nuit
das Nachthemd
el camisón
la camicia da notte

slippers
les pantoufles
die Hausschuhe
las zapatillas
le pantofole

nightwear • les vêtements de nuit • die Nachtwäsche
• la ropa para dormir • gli indumenti per la notte

natural fibre	Is it machine washable?
la fibre naturelle	C'est lavable en machine?
die Naturfaser	Ist es waschmaschinenfest?
la fibra natural	¿Se puede lavar a máquina?
la fibra naturale	È lavabile in lavatrice?
synthetic	Will this fit a two-year-old?
synthétique	C'est la bonne taille pour deux ans?
synthetisch	Passt das einem Zweijährigen?
sintético	¿Le valdrá esto a un niño de dos años?
sintetico	È la taglia giusta per un bambino di due anni?

men's clothing • les vêtements pour hommes • die Herrenkleidung • la ropa de caballero • l'abbigliamento da uomo

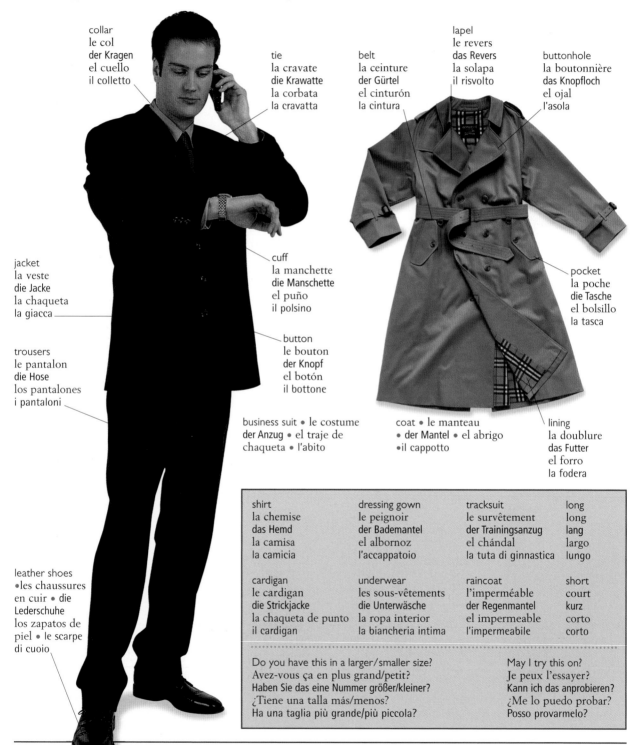

collar
le col
der Kragen
el cuello
il colletto

tie
la cravate
die Krawatte
la corbata
la cravatta

belt
la ceinture
der Gürtel
el cinturón
la cintura

lapel
le revers
das Revers
la solapa
il risvolto

buttonhole
la boutonnière
das Knopfloch
el ojal
l'asola

jacket
la veste
die Jacke
la chaqueta
la giacca

cuff
la manchette
die Manschette
el puño
il polsino

pocket
la poche
die Tasche
el bolsillo
la tasca

trousers
le pantalon
die Hose
los pantalones
i pantaloni

button
le bouton
der Knopf
el botón
il bottone

business suit • le costume
der Anzug • el traje de
chaqueta • l'abito

coat • le manteau
• der Mantel • el abrigo
•il cappotto

lining
la doublure
das Futter
el forro
la fodera

leather shoes
•les chaussures
en cuir • die
Lederschuhe
los zapatos de
piel • le scarpe
di cuoio

shirt	dressing gown	tracksuit	long
la chemise	le peignoir	le survêtement	long
das Hemd	der Bademantel	der Trainingsanzug	lang
la camisa	el albornoz	el chándal	largo
la camicia	l'accappatoio	la tuta di ginnastica	lungo
cardigan	underwear	raincoat	short
le cardigan	les sous-vêtements	l'imperméable	court
die Strickjacke	die Unterwäsche	der Regenmantel	kurz
la chaqueta de punto	la ropa interior	el impermeable	corto
il cardigan	la biancheria intima	l'impermeabile	corto

Do you have this in a larger/smaller size?
Avez-vous ça en plus grand/petit?
Haben Sie das eine Nummer größer/kleiner?
¿Tiene una talla más/menos?
Ha una taglia più grande/più piccola?

May I try this on?
Je peux l'essayer?
Kann ich das anprobieren?
¿Me lo puedo probar?
Posso provarmelo?

blazer • le blazer • der Blazer
• el blazer • il blazer

sports jacket • la veste de
sport • das Sportjackett • la
americana sport • la giacca
sportiva

waistcoat • le gilet
• die Weste • el
chaleco • il gilet

v-neck
l'encolure en V
der V-Ausschnitt
el cuello de pico
il collo a V

round neck
le col rond
der runde Ausschnitt
el cuello redondo
il girocollo

t-shirt
le t-shirt
das T-Shirt
la camiseta
la maglietta

anorak • l'anorak • der
Anorak • el chaquetón
• il giaccone

sweatshirt • le sweat-shirt
• das Sweatshirt • la sudadera
• la felpa

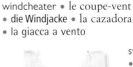

windcheater • le coupe-vent
• die Windjacke • la cazadora
• la giacca a vento

sweatpants
• le pantalon
de jogging
• die Trainingshose
• los pantalones
de chándal
• i pantaloni
della tuta

sweater • le pullover
• der Pullover • el jersey
• il maglione

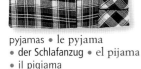

pyjamas • le pyjama
• der Schlafanzug • el pijama
• il pigiama

vest • le tricot de corps
• das Unterhemd • la camiseta
de tirantes • la canottiera

casual wear • les vêtements
sport • die Freizeitkleidung
• la ropa sport • il casual

shorts • le short • die Shorts
• los pantalones cortos
• i calzoncini

briefs • le slip • der Slip
• los calzoncillos • lo slip

boxer shorts • le caleçon
• die Boxershorts • los bóxer •
i boxer

socks • les chaussettes
• die Strümpfe • los calcetines
• i calzini

women's clothing • les vêtements pour femmes • die Damenkleidung • la ropa de señora • l'abbigliamento da donna

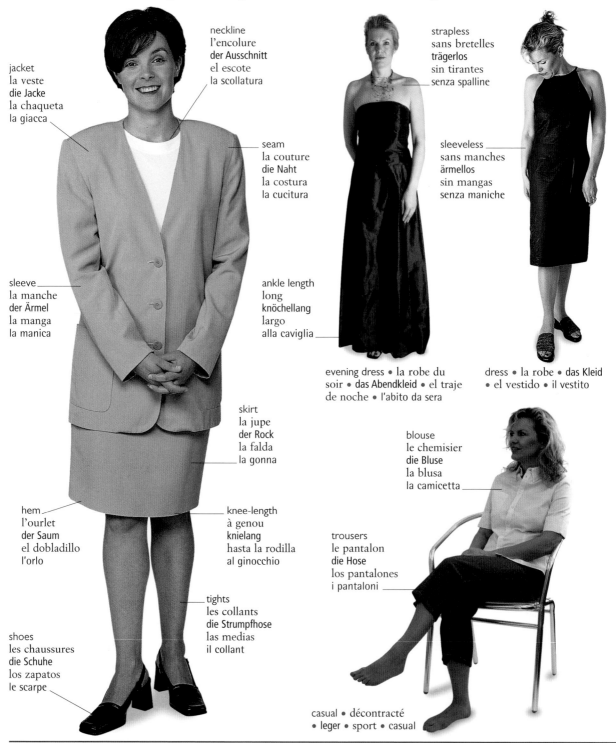

neckline
l'encolure
der Ausschnitt
el escote
la scollatura

jacket
la veste
die Jacke
la chaqueta
la giacca

seam
la couture
die Naht
la costura
la cucitura

strapless
sans bretelles
trägerlos
sin tirantes
senza spalline

sleeveless
sans manches
ärmellos
sin mangas
senza maniche

sleeve
la manche
der Ärmel
la manga
la manica

ankle length
long
knöchellang
largo
alla caviglia

evening dress • la robe du soir • das Abendkleid • el traje de noche • l'abito da sera

dress • la robe • das Kleid • el vestido • il vestito

skirt
la jupe
der Rock
la falda
la gonna

blouse
le chemisier
die Bluse
la blusa
la camicetta

hem
l'ourlet
der Saum
el dobladillo
l'orlo

knee-length
à genou
knielang
hasta la rodilla
al ginocchio

trousers
le pantalon
die Hose
los pantalones
i pantaloni

tights
les collants
die Strumpfhose
las medias
il collant

shoes
les chaussures
die Schuhe
los zapatos
le scarpe

casual • décontracté • leger • sport • casual

lingerie • la lingerie • die Unterwäsche • la lencería • la biancheria intima

negligée • le négligé • das Negligé • el salto de cama • il négligé

slip • le caraco • der Unterrock • la combinación • la sottoveste

strap
la bretelle
der Träger
el tirante
la spallina

camisole • la camisole • das Mieder • la camisola • il corsetto

suspenders
la jarretelle
der Strumpfhalter
el liguero
il reggicalze

basque • la guêpière • das Bustier • el corsé • il bustino

stockings • les bas • die Strümpfe • las medias • le calze

tights • le collant • die Strumpfhose • las medias • il collant

vest
la chemise
das Unterhemd
la camiseta de tirantes
la canottiera

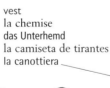

bra • le soutien-gorge • der Büstenhalter • el sujetador • il reggiseno

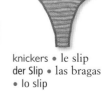

knickers • le slip der Slip • las bragas • lo slip

nightdress • la chemise de nuit • das Nachthemd • el camisón • la camicia da notte

wedding • le mariage • die Hochzeit • la boda • il matrimonio

lace
la dentelle
die Spitze
el encaje
il pizzo

veil
le voile
der Schleier
el velo
il velo

bouquet
le bouquet
das Bukett
el ramo de flores
il bouquet

train
la traîne
die Schleppe
la cola
lo strascico

wedding dress • la robe de mariée • das Hochzeitskleid • el vestido de novia • l'abito da sposa

corset	tailored
le corset	ajusté
das Korsett	maßgeschneidert
el corsé	de sastre
il busto	attillato
garter	halter neck
la jarretière	dos-nu
das Strumpfband	rückenfrei
la liga	con los hombros al aire
la giarrettiera	allacciato dietro il collo
shoulder pad	sports bra
l'épaulette	le soutient-gorge sport
das Schulterpolster	der Sport-BH
la hombrera	el sujetador deportivo
la spallina	il reggiseno sportivo
waistband	underwired
la ceinture	à armature
der Rockbund	mit Formbügeln
la cinturilla	con aros
il girovita	con armatura

accessories • les accessoires • die Accessoires • los complementos • gli accessori

cap • la casquette • die Mütze • la gorra • il berretto

hat • le chapeau • der Hut • el sombrero • il cappello

scarf • le foulard • das Halstuch • el pañuelo • il foulard

buckle
la boucle
die Gürtelschnalle
la hebilla
la fibbia

belt • la ceinture • der Gürtel • el cinturón • la cinta

handle
le manche
der Griff
el asa
il manico

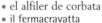

handkerchief • le mouchoir • das Taschentuch • el pañuelo • il fazzoletto

bow tie • le nœud papillon • die Fliege • la pajarita • la farfalla

tie-pin • l'épingle de cravate • die Krawattennadel • el alfiler de corbata • il fermacravatta

gloves • les gants • die Handschuhe • los guantes • i guanti

tip
la pointe
die Spitze
la punta
la punta

umbrella • le parapluie • der Regenschirm • el paraguas • l'ombrello

---

jewellery • les bijoux • der Schmuck • las joyas • i gioielli

pendant • le pendentif • der Anhänger • el colgante • il ciondolo

brooch • la broche • die Brosche • el broche • la spilla

cufflink • le bouton de manchette • der Manschettenknopf • el gemelo • il gemello

string of pearls
le rang de perles
die Perlenkette
el collar de perlas
il filo di perle

earring • la boucle d'oreille • der Ohrring • el pendiente • l'orecchino

link
le maillon
das Glied
el eslabón
la maglia

clasp
le fermoir
der Verschluss
el cierre
il fermaglio

ring
la bague
der Ring
el anillo
l'anello

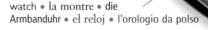

stone
la pierre
der Edelstein
la piedra
la pietra

necklace
le collier
die Halskette
el collar
la collana

watch • la montre • die Armbanduhr • el reloj • l'orologio da polso

bracelet • le bracelet • das Armband • la pulsera • il bracciale

chain • la chaîne • die Kette • la cadena • la catena

jewellery box • la boîte à bijoux • der Schmuckkasten • el joyero • il portagioielli

bags • les sacs • die Taschen • los bolsos • le borse

fastening
le fermoir
der Verschluss
el cierre
la cinghia

shoulder strap
la bretelle
der Schulterriemen
la correa
la tracolla

handles
les poignées
die Griffe
las asas
i manici

wallet • le portefeuille • die Brieftasche • la cartera • il portafoglio

purse • le porte-monnaie • das Portmonee • el monedero • il portamonete

shoulder bag • le sac à bandoulière • die Umhängetasche • el bolso de bandolera • la borsa a tracolla

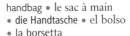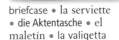

holdall • le fourre-tout • die Reisetasche • la bolsa de viaje • la borsa da viaggio

briefcase • la serviette • die Aktentasche • el maletín • la valigetta

handbag • le sac à main • die Handtasche • el bolso • la borsetta

backpack • le sac à dos • der Rucksack • la mochila • lo zainetto

---

shoes • les chaussures • die Schuhe • los zapatos • le scarpe

eyelet
l'œillet
die Öse
el ojal
l'occhiello

lace
le lacet
der Schnürsenkel
el cordón
il laccio

tongue • la languette • die Zunge • la lengüeta • la lingua

heel
le talon
der Absatz
el tacón
il tacco

sole
la semelle
die Sohle
la suela
la suola

walking boot • le pataugas • der Wanderschuh • la bota de montaña • la scarpa da trekking

trainer • la basket • der Sportschuh • la zapatilla deportiva • la scarpa da ginnastica

lace-up • la chaussure lacée • der Schnürschuh • el zapato con cordones • la scarpa con i lacci

leather shoe • la chaussure de cuir • der Lederschuh • el zapato de piel • la scarpa di cuoio

flip-flop • la tong • die Strandsandale • la chancla • la ciabatta

high heel shoe • la chaussure à talon • der Schuh mit hohem Absatz • el zapato de tacón • la scarpa con il tacco alto

platform shoe • la chaussure à semelle compensée • der Plateauschuh • el zapato de plataforma • lo zatterone

sandal • la sandale • die Sandale • la sandalia • il sandalo

slip-on • le mocassin • der Slipper • el mocasín • il mocassino

brogue • le richelieu • der Herrenhalbschuh • el zapato de caballero • la scarpa da uomo

hair • les cheveux • das Haar • el pelo • i capelli

comb
le peigne
der Kamm
el peine
il pettine

comb (v) • peigner • kämmen
• peinar • pettinare

brush
la brosse
die Haarbürste
el cepillo
la spazzola

brush (v) • brosser • bürsten
• cepillar • spazzolare

rinse (v) • rincer • ausspülen
• enjuagar • sciacquare

hairdresser
la coiffeuse
die Friseurin
la peluquera
la parrucchiera

sink
le lavabo
das Waschbecken
el lavabo
il lavandino

client
la cliente
die Kundin
la cliente
la cliente

wash (v) • laver • waschen • lavar • lavare

robe
le peignoir
der Frisierumhang
la bata
il grembiule

cut (v) • couper • schneiden
• cortar • tagliare

blow dry (v) • sécher • föhnen
• secar con el secador
• asciugare con il fon

set (v) • faire une mise en
plis • legen • marcar
• mettere in piega

---

accessories • les accessoires • die Frisierartikel • los accesorios • gli accesori

hairdryer • le
sèche-cheveux
• der Föhn
• el secador
• l'asciugacapelli

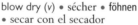

shampoo • le shampoing
• das Shampoo • el
champú • lo shampoo

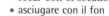

conditioner • l'après-
shampooing • die Haarspülung
• el suavizante • il balsamo

gel • le gel • das
Haargel • el gel
• il gel

hairspray • la laque
• das Haarspray • la laca
• la lacca

curling tongs
• le fer à friser
• der Lockenstab
• las tenacillas
• l'arricciacapelli

scissors • les ciseaux
• die Schere • las
tijeras • le forbici

hairband • le serre-tête
• der Haarreif • la diadema
• il cerchietto

curler • le bigoudi
• der Lockenwickler
• el rulo • i bigodini

hairpin • la pince à cheveux
• die Haarklammer • la
horquilla • la molletta

english • français • deutsch • español • italiano

styles • les coiffures • **die Frisuren** • los estilos • le acconciature

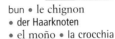

ponytail • la queue de cheval • **der Pferdeschwanz** • la cola de caballo • la coda di cavallo

plait • la natte • **der Zopf** • la trenza • la treccia

french pleat • le rouleau • **die Hochfrisur** • el moño francés • la piega alla francese

bun • le chignon • **der Haarknoten** • el moño • la crocchia

pigtails • les couettes • **die Rattenschwänze** • las coletas • i codini

ribbon
le ruban
das Band
la cinta
il nastro

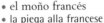

bob • au carré • **der Pagenschnitt** • la melena • il caschetto

crop • la coupe courte • **der Kurzhaarschnitt** • el pelo corto • l'acconciatura corta

curly • frisé • **kraus** • rizado • ricci

perm • la permanente • **die Dauerwelle** • la permanente • la permanente

straight • raide • **glatt** • liso • lisci

roots
les racines
die Wurzeln
las raíces
le radici

highlights • les reflets • **die Strähnchen** • los reflejos • la ciocca

bald • chauve • **kahl** • calvo • calvo

wig • la perruque • **die Perücke** • la peluca • la parrucca

hairtie	greasy
l'élastique pour cheveux	gras
das Haarband	fettig
la goma del pelo	graso
l'elastico	grassi
trim (v)	dry
rafraîchir	sec
nachschneiden	trocken
cortar las puntas	seco
spuntare	secchi
barber	normal
le coiffeur	normal
der Friseur	normal
el peluquero	normal
il barbiere	normali
dandruff	scalp
les pellicules	le cuir chevelu
die Schuppen	die Kopfhaut
la caspa	el cuero cabelludo
la forfora	il cuoio capelluto
split ends	straighten (v)
les fourches	décrêper
die gespaltenen Haarspitzen	glätten
las puntas abiertas	alisar
le doppie punte	lisciare

colours • les couleurs • **die Haarfarben** • los colores • i colori

blonde • blond • blond • rubio • biondo

brunette • châtain • **brünett** • castaño • bruno

auburn • auburn • **rotbraun** • rojizo • castano

ginger • roux • **rot** • pelirrojo • rosso

black • noir • **schwarz** • negro • nero

grey • gris • **grau** • canoso • grigio

white • blanc • **weiß** • blanco • bianco

dyed • teint • **gefärbt** • teñido • tinto

beauty • la beauté • die Schönheit • la belleza • la bellezza

hair dye
la teinture de cheveux
das Haarfärbemittel
el tinte para el pelo
la tintura per capelli

eye shadow
le fard à paupières
der Lidschatten
la sombra de ojos
l'ombretto

mascara
le mascara
die Wimperntusche
el rímel
il mascara

eyeliner
l'eye-liner
der Eyeliner
el lápiz de ojos
la matita per gli occhi

blusher
le fard à joues
das Puderrouge
el colorete
il fard

foundation
le fond de teint
die Grundierung
el fondo de maquillaje
il fondotinta

lipstick
le rouge à lèvres
der Lippenstift
el pintalabios
il rossetto

make-up • le maquillage • das Make-up • el maquillaje • il trucco

eyebrow pencil • le crayon à sourcils • der Augenbrauenstift • el lápiz de cejas • la matita per le sopracciglia

eyebrow brush • la brosse à sourcils • das Brauenbürstchen • el cepillo para las cejas • la spazzolina per le sopracciglia

tweezers • la pince à épiler • die Pinzette • las pinzas • le pinzette

lip gloss • le brillant à lèvres • das Lipgloss • el brillo de labios • lo smalto per le labbra

lip brush • le pinceau à lèvres • der Lippenpinsel • el pincel de labios • il pennello per le labbra

lip liner • le crayon à lèvres • der Lippenkonturenstift • el perfilador • il marcatore per le labbra

brush • le pinceau • der Puderpinsel • la brocha • il pennello

concealer • le correcteur • der Korrekturstift • el lápiz corrector • il correttore

mirror
le miroir
der Spiegel
el espejo
lo specchio

face powder
la poudre
der Gesichtspuder
los polvos compactos
la cipria

powder puff
la houppette
die Puderquaste
la borla
il piumino

compact • le poudrier • die Puderdose • la polvera • il porta cipria

beauty treatments • les soins de beauté • die Schönheitsbehandlungen • los tratamientos de belleza • i trattamenti di bellezza

face pack • le masque de beauté • die Gesichtsmaske • la mascarilla • la maschera di bellezza

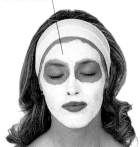

facial • le soin du visage • die Gesichtsbehandlung • la limpieza de cutis • il trattamento per il viso

sunbed • le lit U.V. • die Sonnenbank • la cama de rayos ultravioletas • il lettino solare

exfoliate • exfolier • das Peeling • exfoliar • esfoliare

wax • l'épilation • die Enthaarung • la depilación a la cera • la ceretta

pedicure • la pédicurie • die Pediküre • la pedicura • la pedicure

manicure • la manucure • die Maniküre • la manicura • la manicure

nail file • la lime à ongles • die Nagelfeile • la lima de uñas • la limetta

nail varnish remover le dissolvant der Nagellackentferner el quitaesmalte l'acetone

nail varnish • le vernis à ongles • der Nagellack • el esmalte de uñas • lo smalto per le unghie

nail scissors les ciseaux à ongles die Nagelschere las tijeras de uñas le forbicine per le unghie

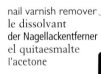

nail clippers le coupe-ongles der Nagelknipser el cortaúñas il tagliaunghie

toiletries • les accessoires de toilette • die Toilettenartikel • los artículos de tocador • gli articoli da toeletta

cleanser • le démaquillant • der Reiniger • la leche limpiadora • il latte detergente

toner • le tonique • das Gesichtswasser • el tónico facial • la lozione tonificante

moisturizer • la crème hydratante • die Feuchtigkeitscreme • la crema hidratante • la crema idratante

self-tanning cream • l'autobronzant • die Selbstbräunungscreme • la crema autobronceadora • la crema autoabbronzante

perfume • le parfum • das Parfum • el perfume • il profumo

eau de toilette • l'eau de toilette • das Eau de Toilette • el agua de colonia • l'acqua di colonia

complexion	oily	tan
le teint	gras	le bronzage
der Teint	fettig	die Sonnenbräune
el cutis	graso	el bronceado
la carnagione	grasso	l'abbronzatura
fair	sensitive	tattoo
clair	sensible	le tatouage
hell	empfindlich	die Tätowierung
claro	sensible	el tatuaje
chiaro	sensibile	il tatuaggio
dark	hypoallergenic	cotton balls
foncé	hypoallergénique	les boules de coton
dunkel	hypoallergen	die Wattebällchen
moreno	hipoalergénico	las bolas de algodón
scuro	ipoallergenico	i batuffoli di ovatta
dry	shade	anti-wrinkle
sec	le ton	antirides
trocken	der Farbton	Antifalten-
seco	el tono	antiarrugas
secco	la tonalità	antirughe

health
la santé
die Gesundheit
la salud
la salute

illness • la maladie • die Krankheit • la enfermedad • la malattia

fever • la fièvre • das Fieber • la fiebre • la febbre

headache • le mal de tête • die Kopfschmerzen • el dolor de cabeza • il mal di testa

nosebleed • le saignement de nez • das Nasenbluten • la hemorragia nasal • l'emorragia nasale

cough • la toux • der Husten • la tos • la tosse

sneeze • l'éternuement • das Niesen • el estornudo • lo starnuto

cold • le rhume • die Erkältung • el resfriado • il raffreddore

flu • la grippe • die Grippe • la gripe • l'influenza

inhaler
l'inhalateur
der Inhalationsapparat
el inhalador
l'inalatore

asthma • l'asthme • das Asthma • el asma • l'asma

cramps • les crampes • die Krämpfe • los retortijones • i crampi

nausea • la nausée • die Übelkeit • las náuseas • la nausea

chickenpox • la varicelle • die Windpocken • la varicela • la varicella

rash • l'éruption • der Hautausschlag • el sarpullido • lo sfogo

heart attack	diabetes	eczema	chill	vomit (v)	diarrhoea
la crise cardiaque	le diabète	l'eczéma	le refroidissement	vomir	la diarrhée
der Herzinfarkt	die Zuckerkrankheit	das Ekzem	die Verkühlung	sich übergeben	der Durchfall
el infarto	la diabetes	el eccema	el resfriado	vomitar	la diarrea
l'infarto	il diabete	l'eczema	l'infreddatura	vomitare	la diarrea
stroke	hayfever	infection	stomach ache	epilepsy	measles
l'attaque	le rhume des foins	l'infection	le mal d'estomac	l'épilepsie	la rougeole
der Schlaganfall	der Heuschnupfen	die Infektion	die Magenschmerzen	die Epilepsie	die Masern
el derrame cerebral	la fiebre del heno	la infección	el dolor de estómago	la epilepsia	el sarampión
l'ictus	la febbre da fieno	l'infezione	il mal di stomaco	l'epilessia	il morbillo
blood pressure	allergy	virus	faint (v)	migraine	mumps
la tension	l'allergie	le virus	s'évanouir	la migraine	les oreillons
der Blutdruck	die Allergie	der Virus	in Ohnmacht fallen	die Migräne	der Mumps
la tensión arterial	la alergia	el virus	desmayarse	la jaqueca	las paperas
la pressione del sangue	l'allergia	il virus	svenire	l'emicrania	gli orecchioni

doctor • le médecin • der Arzt • el médico • il medico

consultation • la consultation • die Arztbesuch • la visita • la visita

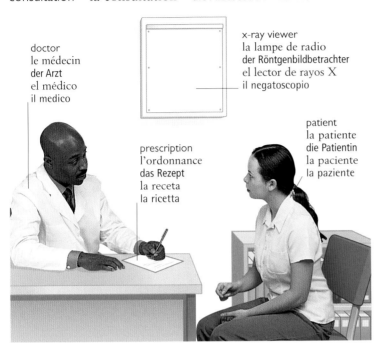

doctor
le médecin
der Arzt
el médico
il medico

x-ray viewer
la lampe de radio
der Röntgenbildbetrachter
el lector de rayos X
il negatoscopio

prescription
l'ordonnance
das Rezept
la receta
la ricetta

patient
la patiente
die Patientin
la paciente
la paziente

height bar
la toise
der Messleiste
el medidor de altura
il misuratore di altezza

nurse
l'infirmière
die Krankenschwester
la enfermera
l'infermiera

scales
la balance
die Personenwaage
la báscula
la bilancia

blood pressure gauge • le tensiomètre
• das Blutdruckmessgerät • el indicador para medir
la tensión • il misuratore di pressione

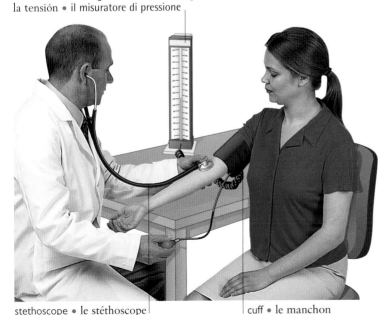

stethoscope • le stéthoscope
• das Stethoskop • el estetoscopio
• lo stetoscopio

cuff • le manchon
• die Luftmanschette
• el manguito • il manicotto

appointment	medical examination
le rendez-vous	l'examen médical
der Termin	die Untersuchung
la cita	el examen médico
l'appuntamento	la visita medica
surgery	inoculation
le cabinet	l'inoculation
das Sprechzimmer	die Impfung
la consulta	la vacunación
l'ambulatorio	la vaccinazione
waiting room	thermometer
la salle d'attente	le thermomètre
der Warteraum	das Thermometer
la sala de espera	el termómetro
la sala d'attesa	il termometro

I need to see a doctor.
J'ai besoin de voir un médecin.
Ich muss einen Arzt sprechen.
Necesito ver a un médico.
Ho bisogno di consultare un medico.

It hurts here.
J'ai mal ici.
Es tut hier weh.
Me duele aquí.
Ho un dolore qui.

injury • la blessure • die Verletzung • la lesión • la ferita

sling
l'écharpe
die Schlinge
el cabestrillo
la fascia a tracolla

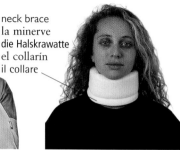

neck brace
la minerve
die Halskrawatte
el collarín
il collare

sprain • l'entorse • die Verstauchung • la torcedura • la slogatura

fracture • la fracture • die Fraktur • la fractura • la frattura

whiplash • le coup du lapin • das Schleudertrauma • el latigazo • il colpo di frusta

cut • la coupure • der Schnitt • el corte • il taglio

graze • l'écorchure • die Abschürfung • la desolladura • l'escorazione

bruise • la contusion • die Prellung • el hematoma • il livido

splinter • l'écharde • der Splitter • la astilla • la scheggia

sunburn • le coup de soleil • der Sonnenbrand • la quemadura de sol • la scottatura

burn • la brûlure • die Brandwunde • la quemadura • l'ustione

bite • la morsure • der Biss • el mordisco • il morso

sting • la piqûre • der Stich • la picadura • la puntura

accident l'accident der Unfall el accidente l'incidente	haemorrhage l'hémorragie die Blutung la hemorragia l'emorragia	concussion la commotion cérébrale die Gehirnerschütterung la conmoción cerebral la commozione cerebrale	Will he/she be all right? Est-ce qu'il/elle va se remettre? Wird er/sie es gut überstehen? ¿Se pondrá bien? Si rimetterà?
emergency l'urgence der Notfall la urgencia l'emergenza	blister l'ampoule die Blase la ampolla la vescica	head injury le traumatisme crânien die Kopfverletzung el traumatismo craneal la ferita alla testa	Please call an ambulance. Appelez une ambulance s'il vous plaît. Rufen Sie bitte einen Krankenwagen. Por favor llame a una ambulancia. Chiami un'ambulanza, per favore.
wound la blessure die Wunde la herida la ferita	poisoning l'empoisonnement die Vergiftung la intoxicación l'avvelenamento	electric shock le choc électrique der elektrische Schlag la descarga eléctrica la scossa elettrica	Where does it hurt? Où avez-vous mal? Wo haben Sie Schmerzen? ¿Dónde le duele? Dove le fa male?

first aid • les premiers secours • die erste Hilfe • los primeros auxilios • il pronto soccorso

ointment • la pommade • die Salbe • la pomada • la pomata

plaster • le pansement • das Pflaster • la tirita • il cerotto

safety pin
l'épingle de sûreté
die Sicherheitsnadel
el imperdible
la spilla da balia

bandage
le bandage
die Bandage
la venda
la benda

painkillers
les analgésiques
die Schmerztabletten
los analgésicos
gli antidolorifici

antiseptic wipe
la serviette antiseptique
das Desinfektionstuch
la toallita antiséptica
la salvietta antisettica

tweezers
la pince fine
die Pinzette
las pinzas
le pinzette

scissors
les ciseaux
die Schere
las tijeras
le forbici

antiseptic
l'antiseptique
das Antiseptikum
el desinfectante
il disinfettante

first aid box • la trousse de premiers secours • der Erste-Hilfe-Kasten • el botiquín • la cassetta di pronto soccorso

gauze • la gaze
• die Gaze
• la gasa
• la garza

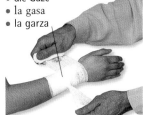

dressing • le pansement • der Verband • el vendaje • la bendatura

splint • l'attelle • die Schiene • la tablilla • la stecca

adhesive tape
• le sparadrap
• das Leukoplast
• el esparadrapo
• il nastro adesivo

resuscitation • la réanimation • die Wiederbelebung • la re-animación • la rianimazione

shock	pulse	choke (v)	Can you help?
le choc	le pouls	étouffer	Est-ce que vous pouvez m'aider?
der Schock	der Puls	ersticken	Können Sie mir helfen?
el shock	el pulso	ahogarse	¿Me puede ayudar?
lo shock	le pulsazioni	soffocare	Può aiutarmi?
unconscious	breathing	sterile	Do you know first aid?
sans connaissance	la respiration	stérile	Pouvez-vous donner les soins d'urgence?
bewusstlos	die Atmung	steril	Beherrschen Sie die Erste Hilfe?
inconsciente	la respiración	estéril	¿Sabe primeros auxilios?
privo di sensi	la respirazione	sterile	Sa dare pronto soccorso?

hospital • l'hôpital • das Krankenhaus • el hospital • l'ospedale

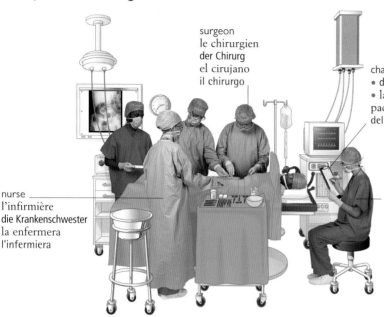

surgeon
le chirurgien
der Chirurg
el cirujano
il chirurgo

chart • la courbe
• das Narkoseprotokoll
• la gráfica del
paciente • la scheda
del paziente

blood test • l'analyse de sang
• die Blutuntersuchung • el
análisis de sangre • l'analisi
del sangue

nurse
l'infirmière
die Krankenschwester
la enfermera
l'infermiera

anaesthetist
l'anesthésiste
die Anästhesistin
la anestesista
l'anestetista

injection • l'injection
• die Spritze • la inyección
• l'iniezione

operating theatre • la salle d'opération • der Operationssaal • el quirófano
• la sala operatoria

trolley • le chariot • die
fahrbare Liege • la camilla
• la lettiga

call button • le bouton d'appel
• der Rufknopf • el timbre • il
pulsante di chiamata

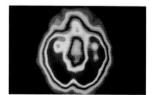

x-ray • la radio • die
Röntgenaufnahme • la
radiografía • la radiografia

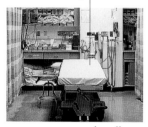

emergency room • la salle
des urgences • die Notaufnahme
• la sala de urgencias • la sala
emergenze

ward • la salle • das
Patientenzimmer • la planta
• il reparto

wheelchair • la chaise
roulante • der Rollstuhl
• la silla de ruedas • la sedia
a rotelle

scan • la scanographie
• der CT-Scan • la tomografia
• la tomografia

operation	discharged	visiting hours	maternity ward	intensive care unit
l'opération	renvoyé	les heures de visite	la maternité	le service de soins intensifs
die Operation	entlassen	die Besuchszeiten	die Entbindungsstation	die Intensivstation
l'intervención	dado de alta	las horas de visita	la sala de maternidad	la unidad de cuidados intensivos
l'operazione	dimesso	l'orario delle visite	il reparto maternità	il reparto di cura intensiva
admitted	clinic	children's ward	private room	outpatient
admis	la clinique	la pédiatrie	la chambre privée	le malade en consultation externe
aufgenommen	die Klinik	die Kinderstation	das Privatzimmer	der ambulante Patient
ingresado	la clínica	la sala de pediatría	la habitación privada	el paciente externo
ricoverato	la clinica	il reparto pediatrico	la camera privata	il paziente esterno

departments • les services • die Abteilungen • los servicios • i reparti

ENT • l'O.R.L.
• die HNO-Abteilung
• la otorrinolaringología
• l'otorinolaringologia

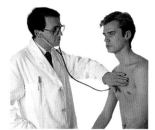

cardiology • la cardiologie
• die Kardiologie • la
cardiología • la cardiologia

orthopedia • l'orthopédie
• die Orthopädie • la
ortopedia • l'ortopedia

gynaecology • la gynécologie
• die Gynäkologie • la
ginecología • la ginecologia

physiotherapy • la
kinésithérapie • die
Physiotherapie • la fisioterapia
• la fisioterapia

dermatology • la dermatologie
• die Dermatologie • la
dermatología • la dermatologia

paediatrics • la pédiatrie
• die Kinderheilkunde • la
pediatría • la pediatria

radiology • la radiologie
• die Radiologie • la radiología
• la radiologia

surgery • la chirurgie
• die Chirurgie • la cirugía
• la chirurgia

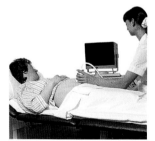

maternity • la maternité
• die Entbindungsstation • la
maternidad • la maternità

psychiatry • la psychiatrie
• die Psychiatrie • la
psiquiatría • la psichiatria

ophthalmology
• l'ophtalmologie
• die Augenheilkunde • la
oftalmología • l'oftalmologia

neurology	urology	plastic surgery	pathology	result
la neurologie	l'urologie	la chirurgie esthétique	la pathologie	le résultat
die Neurologie	die Urologie	die plastische Chirurgie	die Pathologie	das Ergebnis
la neurología	la urología	la cirugía plástica	la patología	el resultado
la neurologia	l'urologia	la chirurgia plastica	la patologia	il risultato
oncology	endocrinology	referral	test	consultant
l'oncologie	l'endocrinologie	l'orientation d'un patient	l'analyse	le spécialiste
die Onkologie	die Endokrinologie	die Überweisung	die Untersuchung	der Facharzt
la oncología	la endocrinología	el volante	el análisis	el especialista
l'oncologia	l'endocrinologia	mandare da uno specialista	l'analisi	lo specialista

dentist • le dentiste • der Zahnarzt • el dentista • il dentista

tooth • la dent • der Zahn • el diente • il dente

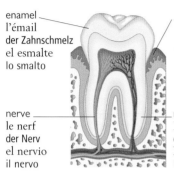

enamel
l'émail
der Zahnschmelz
el esmalte
lo smalto

gum
la gencive
das Zahnfleisch
la encía
la gengiva

nerve
le nerf
der Nerv
el nervio
il nervo

root
la racine
die Zahnwurzel
la raíz
la radice

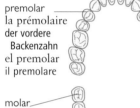

premolar
la prémolaire
der vordere
 Backenzahn
el premolar
il premolare

incisor
l'incisive
der Schneidezahn
el incisivo
l'incisivo

molar
la molaire
der Backenzahn
la muela
il molare

canine
la canine
der Eckzahn
el colmillo
il canino

toothache la rage de dents die Zahnschmerzen el dolor de muelas il mal di denti	drill la fraise der Bohrer el torno del dentista il trapano
plaque la plaque der Zahnbelag la placa bacteriana la placca	dental floss le fil dentaire die Zahnseide el hilo dental il filo dentale
decay la carie die Karies la caries la carie	extraction l'extraction die Extraktion la extracción l'estrazione
filling le plombage die Zahnfüllung el empaste l'otturazione	crown la couronne die Krone la corona la corona

check-up • la visite de contrôle • der Check-up • la revisión • il controllo

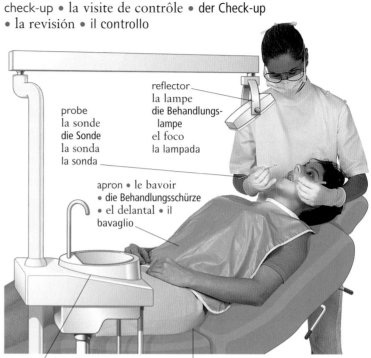

probe
la sonde
die Sonde
la sonda
la sonda

reflector
la lampe
die Behandlungs-
 lampe
el foco
la lampada

apron • le bavoir
• die Behandlungsschürze
• el delantal • il
bavaglio

basin
le crachoir
das Spuckbecken
el lavabo
la sputacchiera

dentist's chair
le fauteuil de dentiste
der Patientenstuhl
el sillón del dentista
la poltrona del dentista

floss (v) • utiliser le fil
dentaire • mit
Zahnseide reinigen
• usar el hilo dental
• usare il filo dentale

brush (v) • brosser
• bürsten • cepillarse
los dientes • spazzolare

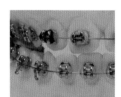

brace • l'appareil
dentaire • die
Zahnspange • el
aparato corrector •
l'apparecchio correttore

dental x-ray • la radio
dentaire • die Röntgen-
aufnahme • los rayos x
dentales • la radio-
grafia dentale

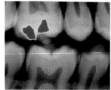

x-ray film • la radio
• das Röntgenbild
• la radiografía • la
lastra radiografica

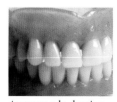

dentures • le dentier
• die Zahnprothese
• la dentadura postiza
• la dentiera

optician • l'opticien • der Augenoptiker • el óptico • l'ottico

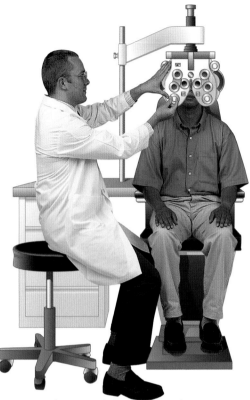

case
l'étui
das Futteral
la funda
la custodia

lens
le verre
das Glas
el cristal
la lente

frame
la monture
das Brillengestell
la montura
la montatura

glasses • les lunettes • die Brille
• las gafas • gli occhiali

sunglasses • les lunettes de soleil
• die Sonnenbrille • las gafas de sol
• gli occhiali da sole

cleaning fluid
la solution nettoyante
das Reinigungsmittel
el líquido limpiador
la soluzione per la pulizia

disinfectant solution
la solution désinfectante
das Desinfektionsmittel
la solución desinfectante
la soluzione disinfettante

lens case
l'étui à lentilles
der Kontaktlinsenbehälter
el estuche para las lentillas
la custodia per le lenti

eye test • l'examen de la vue • der Sehtest
• el examen de ojos • l'esame della vista

contact lenses • les lentilles de contact • die Kontaktlinsen • las lentes de
contacto • le lenti a contatto

eye • l'œil • das Auge • el ojo • l'occhio

eyebrow
le sourcil
die Augenbraue
la ceja
il sopracciglio

pupil
la pupille
die Pupille
la pupila
la pupilla

iris • l'iris • die Iris
• el iris • l'iride

lens
le cristallin
die Linse
el cristalino
la lente

cornea • la cornée
• die Hornhaut • la
córnea • la cornea

eyelid
la paupière
das Lid
el párpado
la palpebra

eyelash
le cil
die Wimper
la pestaña
il ciglio

retina
la rétine
die Netzhaut
la retina
la retina

optic nerve
le nerf optique
der Sehnerv
el nervio óptico
il nervo ottico

vision	astigmatism
la vue	l'astigmatisme
die Sehkraft	der Astigmatismus
la vista	el astigmatismo
la vista	l'astigmatismo
diopter	long sight
la dioptrie	la presbytie
die Dioptrie	die Weitsichtigkeit
la dioptría	la hipermetropía
la diottria	la presbiopia
tear	short sight
la larme	la myopie
die Träne	die Kurzsichtigkeit
la lágrima	la miopía
la lacrima	la miopia
cataract	bifocal
la cataracte	bifocal
der graue Star	Bifokal-
la catarata	bifocal
la cataratta	bifocale

pregnancy • la grossesse • die Schwangerschaft • el embarazo • la gravidanza

nurse
l'infirmière
die Krankenschwester
la enfermera
l'infermiera

pregnancy test • le test de grossesse • der Schwangerschaftstest • la prueba del embarazo • il test di gravidanza

scan
l'échographie
die Ultraschallaufnahme
la ecografía
l'ecografia

umbilical cord
le cordon ombilical
die Nabelschnur
el cordón umbilical
il cordone ombelicale

placenta
le placenta
die Plazenta
la placenta
la placenta

cervix
le col de l'utérus
der Gebärmutterhals
el cuello uterino
la cervice

uterus
l'utérus
die Gebärmutter
el útero
l'utero

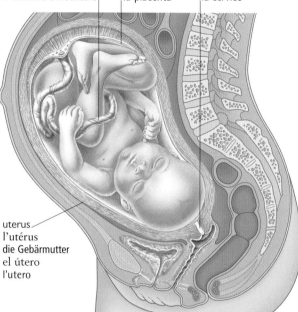

ultrasound • les ultrasons • der Ultraschall • la ecografia • l'ultrasuono

foetus • le fœtus • der Fetus • el feto • il feto

ovulation	antenatal	amniotic fluid	dilation	stitches	breech
l'ovulation	prénatal	le liquide amniotique	la dilatation	les points de suture	par le siège
der Eisprung	vorgeburtlich	das Fruchtwasser	die Erweiterung	die Naht	Steiß-
la ovulación	prenatal	el líquido amniótico	la dilatación	los puntos	de nalgas
l'ovulazione	prenatale	il liquido amniotico	la dilatazione	i punti	podalico
conception	trimester	amniocentesis	epidural	delivery	premature
la conception	le trimestre	l'amniocentèse	la péridurale	l'accouchement	prématuré
die Empfängnis	das Trimester	die Amniozentese	die Periduralanästhesie	die Entbindung	vorzeitig
la concepción	el trimestre	la amniocentesis	la epidural	el parto	prematuro
la concezione	il trimestre	l'amniocentesi	l'epidurale	il parto	prematuro
pregnant	embryo	contraction	caesarean section	birth	gynaecologist
enceinte	l'embryon	la contraction	la césarienne	la naissance	le gynécologue
schwanger	der Embryo	die Wehe	der Kaiserschnitt	die Geburt	der Gynäkologe
embarazada	el embrión	la contracción	la cesárea	el nacimiento	el ginecólogo
incinta	l'embrione	la contrazione	il taglio cesareo	la nascita	il ginecologo
expectant	womb	break waters (v)	episiotomy	miscarriage	obstetrician
enceinte	l'utérus	perdre les eaux	l'épisiotomie	la fausse couche	l'obstétricien
schwanger	die Gebärmutter	das Fruchtwasser geht ab	der Dammschnitt	die Fehlgeburt	der Geburtshelfer
encinta	la matriz	romper aguas	la episiotomía	el aborto espontáneo	el tocólogo
in stato interessante	il grembo	rompere le acque	l'episiotomia	l'aborto spontaneo	l'ostetrico

english • français • deutsch • español • italiano

childbirth • la naissance • die Geburt • el parto • il parto

drip • la perfusion • die Tropfinfusion • el gotero • la fleboclisi

midwife
la sage-femme
die Hebamme
la matrona
l'ostetrica

monitor
le moniteur
der Infusomat
el monitor
il monitor

catheter
le cathéter
der Katheter
el catéter
il catetere

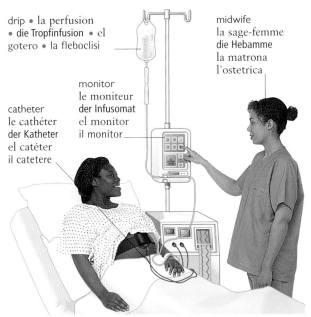

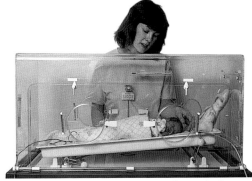

incubator • la couveuse • der Brutkasten • la incubadora • l'incubatrice

scales
le pèse-bébé
die Waage
la báscula
la bilancia

induce labour (v) • déclencher l'accouchement • die Geburt einleiten • provocar el parto • il travaglio indotto

birth weight • le poids de naissance • das Geburtsgewicht • el peso al nacer • il peso alla nascita

forceps • le forceps • die Geburtszange • el fórceps • il forcipe

ventouse cup • la ventouse • die Saugglocke • la ventosa • la ventosa

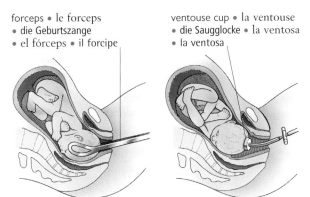

assisted delivery • l'accouchement assisté • die assistierte Entbindung • el parto asistido • il parto assistito

nursing • l'allaitement • das Stillen • la lactancia • l'allattamento

breast pump • la pompe à lait • die Milchpumpe • el sacaleches • la pompa da seno

nursing bra • le soutien-gorge d'allaitement • der Stillbüstenhalter • el sujetador para la lactancia • il reggiseno da allattamento

identity tag • le bracelet d'identité • das Namensbändchen • la pulsera de identificación • la targhetta d'identità

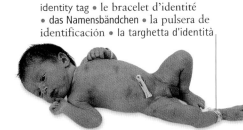

newborn baby • le nouveau-né • das Neugeborene • el recién nacido • il neonato

breastfeed (v) • donner le sein • stillen • dar el pecho • allattare al seno

pads • les coussinets • die Einlagen • los discos protectores • le coppe

alternative therapy • les thérapies alternatives • die Alternativtherapien • las terapias alternativas • le terapie alternative

teacher
le maître
der Lehrer
el profesor
l'allenatore

massage • le massage
• die Massage • el masaje
• il massaggio

shiatsu • le shiatsu
• das Shiatsu • el shiatsu
• lo shiatsu

yoga • le yoga • das Yoga • el yoga • lo yoga

mat
le tapis
die Matte
la colchoneta
il tappetino

chiropractic • la chiropractie
• die Chiropraktik • la
quiropráctica • la chiropratica

osteopathy • l'ostéopathie
• die Osteopathie • la
osteopatía • l'osteopatia

reflexology • la réflexologie •
die Reflexzonenmassage • la
reflexología • la riflessologia

meditation • la méditation
• die Meditation • la
meditación • la meditazione

counsellor • le conseiller
• der Berater • el terapeuta
• l'assistente socio-psicologico

reiki • le reiki • das Reiki
• el reiki • il reiki

acupuncture • l'acuponcture
• die Akupunktur • la
acupuntura • l'agopuntura

group therapy • la thérapie de groupe • die Gruppentherapie
• la terapia de grupo • la terapia di gruppo

ayurveda • la médecine
ayurvédique • das Ayurveda
• la medicina ayurvédica •
la medicina aiurvedica

hypnotherapy
• l'hypnothérapie
• die Hypnotherapie • la
hipnoterapia • l'ipnositerapia

essential oils • les huiles
essentielles • die ätherischen
Öle • los aceites esenciales
• gli oli essenziali

herbalism • l'herboristerie
• die Kräuterheilkunde • el
herbalismo • l'erbalismo

aromatherapy • l'aromathérapie
• die Aromatherapie • la
aromaterapia • l'aromaterapia

homeopathy • l'homéopathie
• die Homöopathie • la
homeopatía • l'omeopatia

acupressure • l'acupression
• die Akupressur • la
acupresión • l'agopressione

therapist • la thérapeute • die Therapeutin
• la terapeuta • la terapista

psychotherapy • la psychothérapie
• die Psychotherapie • la
psicoterapia • la psicoterapia

crystal healing	naturopathy	relaxation	herb
la guérison par cristaux	la naturopathie	la relaxation	l'herbe
die Kristalltherapie	die Naturheilkunde	die Entspannung	das Heilkraut
la cristaloterapia	la naturopatía	la relajación	la hierba
la cristalloterapia	la naturopatia	il rilassamento	l'erba
hydrotherapy	feng shui	stress	supplement
l'hydrothérapie	le feng shui	le stress	le supplément
die Wasserbehandlung	das Feng Shui	der Stress	die Ergänzung
la hidroterapia	el feng shui	el estrés	el suplemento
l'idroterapia	il feng shui	lo stress	l'integratore

home
la maison
das Haus
la casa
la casa

house • la maison • das Haus • la casa • la casa

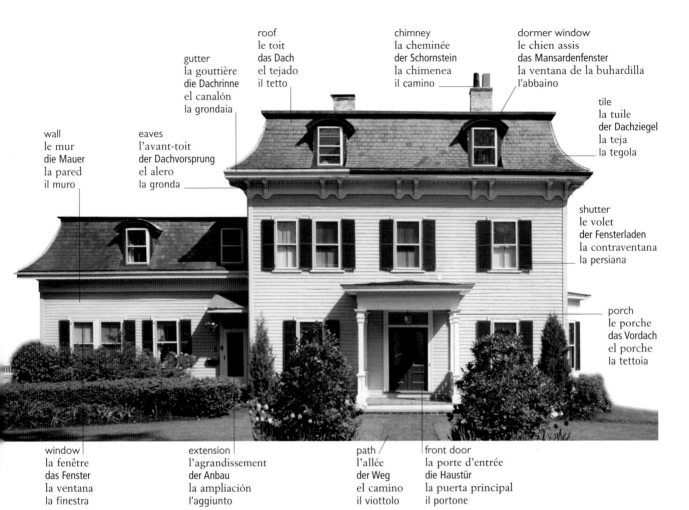

roof
le toit
das Dach
el tejado
il tetto

chimney
la cheminée
der Schornstein
la chimenea
il camino

dormer window
le chien assis
das Mansardenfenster
la ventana de la buhardilla
l'abbaino

gutter
la gouttière
die Dachrinne
el canalón
la grondaia

tile
la tuile
der Dachziegel
la teja
la tegola

wall
le mur
die Mauer
la pared
il muro

eaves
l'avant-toit
der Dachvorsprung
el alero
la gronda

shutter
le volet
der Fensterladen
la contraventana
la persiana

porch
le porche
das Vordach
el porche
la tettoia

window
la fenêtre
das Fenster
la ventana
la finestra

extension
l'agrandissement
der Anbau
la ampliación
l'aggiunto

path
l'allée
der Weg
el camino
il viottolo

front door
la porte d'entrée
die Haustür
la puerta principal
il portone

detached	townhouse	garage	floor	burglar alarm	rent (v)
la maison individuelle	la maison de trois étages	le garage	l'étage	l'alarme	louer
das Einfamilienhaus	das dreistöckige Haus	die Garage	das Stockwerk	die Alarmanlage	mieten
la casa unifamiliar	la casa urbana	el garaje	el piso	la alarma antirrobo	alquilar
la casa unifamiliare	la casa a tre piani	il garage	il piano	l'impianto d'allarme	affittare
semidetached house	bungalow	attic	courtyard	letterbox	rent
la maison mitoyenne	le pavillon	le grenier	la cour	la boîte aux lettres	le loyer
das Doppelhaus	der Bungalow	der Dachboden	der Hof	der Briefkasten	die Miete
la casa adosada	el chalet	la buhardilla	el patio	el buzón	el alquiler
la casa bifamiliare	il bungalow	la soffitta	il cortile	la cassetta della posta	l'affitto
terraced house	basement	room	porch light	landlord	tenant
la maison attenante	le sous-sol	la chambre	la lampe d'entrée	le propriétaire	le locataire
das Reihenhaus	das Kellergeschoss	das Zimmer	die Haustürlampe	der Vermieter	der Mieter
las casas adosadas	el sótano	la habitación	la luz del porche	el propietario	el inquilino
la casa a schiera	il seminterrato	la stanza	la luce del portico	il padrone di casa	l'inquilino

entrance • l'entrée • **der Eingang** • la entrada • l'ingresso

hand rail
la main courante
das Geländer
el pasamanos
la ringhiera

landing
le palier
der Treppenabsatz
el descansillo
il pianerottolo

banister
la rampe
das Treppengeländer
la barandilla
il corrimano

staircase
l'escalier
die Treppe
la escalera
le scale

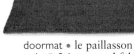

hallway • le vestibule • **die Diele** • el vestíbulo • l'ingresso

doorbell • la sonnette
• **die Türklingel** • el timbre
•il campanello

doormat • le paillasson
• **der Fußabtreter** • el felpudo
• lo zerbino

door knocker • le marteau
de porte • **der Türklopfer**
• la aldaba • il battiporta

door chain • la chaîne de
sûreté • **die Türkette**
• la cadena • la catenella

key • la clef • **der Schlüssel**
• la llave • la chiave

lock • la serrure • **das
Schloss** • la cerradura
• la serratura

bolt • le verrou • **der Türriegel**
• el cerrojo • il chiavistello

flat • l'appartement
• **die Wohnung** • el piso
• l'appartamento

balcony • le balcon
• **der Balkon** • el balcón
• il balcone

block of flats • l'immeuble
• **der Wohnblock** • el edificio
• il caseggiato

intercom • l'interphone
• **die Sprechanlage** • el interfono
• il citofono

lift • l'ascenseur • **der Fahrstuhl**
• el ascensor • l'ascensore

internal systems • les systèmes domestiques • die Hausanschlüsse • las instalaciones internas • i sistemi interni

radiator • le radiateur • der Heizkörper • el radiador • il termosifone

blade • l'aile • der Flügel • la hoja • la pala

fan • le ventilateur • der Ventilator • el ventilador • il ventilatore

heater • l'appareil de chauffage • der Heizofen • la estufa • la stufa

convector heater • le convecteur • der Heizlüfter • el calentador de convección • il termoventilatore

---

electricity • l'électricité • die Elektrizität • la electricidad • l'elettricità

filament
le filament
der Glühfaden
el filamento
il filamento

bayonet fitting • le culot à baïonette • die Bajonettfassung • el portalámparas de bayoneta • l'attacco a baionetta

light bulb • l'ampoule • die Glühlampe • la bombilla • la lampadina

earthing • la mise à la terre • die Erdung • la toma de tierra • la messa a terra

pin • la broche • der Pol • la clavija • il polo

plug • la prise • der Stecker • el enchufe macho • la spina

neutral • neutre • neutral • neutro • neutro

live • sous tension • geladen • con corriente • in tensione

wires • les fils • die Leitung • los cables • i fili

---

voltage	fuse	socket	direct current	transformer
la tension	le fusible	la prise de courant	le courant continu	le transformateur
die Spannung	die Sicherung	die Steckdose	der Gleichstrom	der Transformator
el voltaje	el fusible	el enchufe hembra	la corriente continua	el transformador
la tensione	il fusibile	la presa	la corrente continua	il trasformatore
amp	fuse box	switch	electricity meter	mains supply
l'ampère	la boîte à fusibles	l'interrupteur	le compteur d'électricité	le réseau d'électricité
das Ampère	der Sicherungskasten	der Schalter	der Stromzähler	das Stromnetz
el amperio	la caja de los fusibles	el interruptor	el contador de la luz	el suministro de electricidad
l'ampere	la valvoliera	l'interruttore	il contatore dell'ellettricità	la rete ellettricità
power	generator	alternating current	power cut	
le courant	la génératrice	le courant alternatif	la coupure de courant	
der Strom	der Generator	der Wechselstrom	der Stromausfall	
la corrriente eléctrica	el generador	la corriente alterna	el corte de luz	
l'elettricità	il generatore	la corrente alternata	l'interruzione di ellettricità	

---

english • français • deutsch • español • italiano

plumbing • la plomberie • die Installation • la fontanería • l'impianto idraulico

inlet • l'arrivée • die Zuleitung • la toma • l'entrata

outlet • la sortie • der Auslass • la salida • l'uscita

pressure valve • la soupape de sûreté • das Sicherheitsventil • la válvula de la presión • la valvola della pressione

insulation l'isolation die Isolierung el aislante l'isolamento

overflow pipe • le trop-plein • der Überlauf • el tubo de desagüe • il tubo di troppopieno

tank le réservoir der Kessel el depósito il serbatoio

drain cock • le robinet de purge • der Ablasshahn • la llave del desagüe • il rubinetto di scarico

water chamber • la chambre d'eau • die Wasserkammer • el depósito del agua • il serbatoio dell'acqua

thermostat le thermostat der Thermostat el termostato il termostato

gas burner • le brûleur à gaz • der Gasbrenner • el quemador • il bruciatore a gas

heating element la résistance das Heizelement la resistencia l'elemento riscaldante

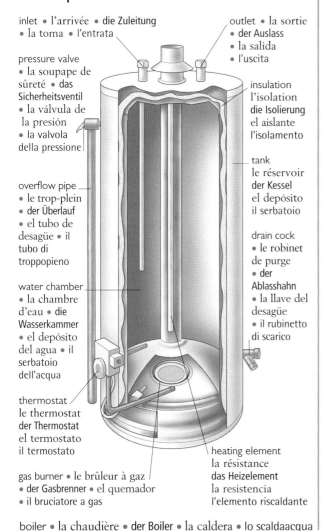

boiler • la chaudière • der Boiler • la caldera • lo scaldaacqua

sink • l'évier • die Spüle • el fregadero • l'acquaio

tap • le robinet • der Hahn • el grifo • il rubinetto

lever • la manette • der Hebel • la palanca • la leva

gasket le joint die Dichtung la junta la guarnizione

supply pipe la conduite d'amenée die Zuleitung la toma del agua il tubo dell'acqua

shutoff valve • le robinet de sectionnement • der Absperrhahn • la llave de paso • il rubinetto di chiusura

waste disposal unit • le broyeur d'ordures • der Müllschlucker • el triturador de basuras • il macinatore di rifiuti

drain • le tuyau d'écoulement • der Abfluss • el desagüe • lo scarico

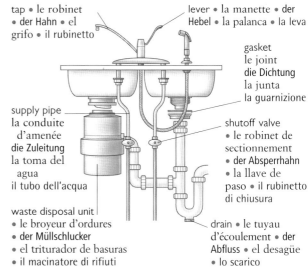

water closet • les W.-C. • das WC • el retrete • il water

float ball • le flotteur • der Schwimmer • el flotador • il galleggiante

cistern • la chasse-d'eau • der Spülkasten • la cisterna • la cassetta

seat • le siège • der Toilettensitz • la tapa • il sedile

bowl la cuvette das Becken la taza la tazza

waste pipe • le tuyau d'écoulement • das Abflussrohr • el desagüe • il tubo di scarico

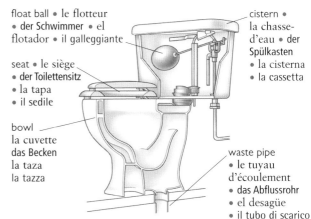

waste disposal • l'enlèvement de déchets • die Abfallentsorgung • la eliminación de desechos • lo smaltimento dei rifiuti

bottle la bouteille die Flasche la botella la bottiglia

recycling bin • la boîte à déchets recyclables • der Recyclingbehälter • el cubo para reciclar • il secchio di riciclaggio

lid le couvercle der Deckel la tapa il coperchio

pedal la pédale der Trethebel el pedal il pedale

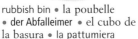

rubbish bin • la poubelle • der Abfalleimer • el cubo de la basura • la pattumiera

sorting unit • la boîte de tri • die Abfallsortiereinheit • el armario para clasificar la basura • l'unità di smistamento

organic waste • les déchets bios • der Bio-Abfall • los desperdicios orgánicos • i rifiuti organici

living room • le salon • das Wohnzimmer • el cuarto de estar • il salotto

painting
le tableau
das Gemälde
el cuadro
il quadro

frame
le cadre
der Bilderrahmen
el marco
la cornice

lamp
la lampe
die Lampe
la lámpara
la lampada

wall light
l'applique
die Wandlampe
el aplique
l'applique

clock
la pendule
die Uhr
el reloj
l'orologio

ceiling
le plafond
die Decke
el techo
il soffitto

cabinet
la vitrine
die Vitrine
el armario
l'armadietto

sofa
le canapé
das Sofa
el sofá
il divano

cushion
le coussin
das Sofakissen
el cojín
il cuscino

coffee table
la table basse
der Couchtisch
la mesa de centro
il tavolino

floor
le sol
der Fußboden
el suelo
il pavimento

62

mirror
le miroir
der Spiegel
el espejo
lo specchio

vase
le vase
die Vase
el jarrón
il vaso

mantelpiece
la tablette de cheminée
der Kaminsims
la repisa de la chimenea
la mensola del caminetto

curtain • le rideau • der Vorhang • la cortina • la tenda

net curtain • le brise-bise • die Gardine • el visillo • la tendina

fireplace
la cheminée
der Kamin
la chimenea
il caminetto

screen
le garde-feu
das Kamingitter
el biombo
il parafuoco

candle
la bougie
die Kerze
la vela
la candela

venetian blind • le store vénitien • die Jalousie • el estor de láminas • la veneziana

roller blind • le store • das Rollo • el estor • la persiana

moulding • la moulure • der Stuckrahmen • la moldura • la cornice

armchair • le fauteuil • der Sessel • el sillón • la poltrona

bookshelf
la bibliothèque
das Bücherregal
la estantería
la libreria

sofabed
le canapé-lit
die Bettcouch
el sofá-cama
il divano letto

rug
le tapis
der Teppich
la alfombra
il tappeto

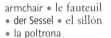

study • le bureau • das Arbeitszimmer • el despacho • lo studio

dining room • la salle à manger • das Esszimmer • el comedor • la sala da pranzo

pepper
le poivre
der Pfeffer
la pimienta
il pepe

salt
le sel
das Salz
la sal
il sale

table
la table
der Tisch
la mesa
il tavolo

crockery
la vaisselle
das Geschirr
la vajilla
i piatti

cutlery
les couverts
das Besteck
los cubiertos
le posate

chair
la chaise
der Stuhl
la silla
la sedia

back
le dossier
die Rückenlehne
el respaldo
lo schienale

seat
le siège
die Sitzfläche
el asiento
il sedile

leg
le pied
das Bein
la pata
la gamba

lay the table (v)	place mat	lunch	full	host	Can I have some more, please?
mettre la table	le napperon	le déjeuner	rassasié	l'hôte	Puis-je en prendre, s'il vous plaît?
den Tisch decken	das Set	das Mittagessen	satt	der Gastgeber	Könnte ich bitte noch ein bisschen haben?
poner la mesa	el mantel individual	la comida	lleno	el anfitrión	¿Puedo repetir, por favor?
apparecchiare	la tovaglia individuale	il pranzo	sazio	il padrone di casa	Posso averne ancora, per favore?
serve (v)	tablecloth	dinner	portion	hostess	I've had enough, thank you.
servir	la nappe	le dîner	la portion	l'hôtesse	Non merci, j'en ai eu assez.
servieren	die Tischdecke	das Abendessen	die Portion	die Gastgeberin	Ich bin satt, danke.
servir	el mantel	la cena	la ración	la anfitriona	Estoy lleno, gracias.
servire	la tovaglia	la cena	la porzione	la padrona di casa	Ne ho avuto abbastanza, grazie.
eat (v)	breakfast	hungry	meal	guest	That was delicious.
manger	le petit déjeuner	(avoir) faim	le repas	l'invité	C'était délicieux.
essen	das Frühstück	hungrig	die Mahlzeit	der Gast	Das war lecker.
comer	el desayuno	hambriento	la comida	el invitado	Estaba buenísimo.
mangiare	la colazione	affamato	il pasto	l'ospite	Era squisito.

crockery and cutlery • la vaisselle et les couverts • das Geschirr und das Besteck
• la vajilla y los cubiertos • le stovigle e le posate

teaspoon • la cuiller à café
• der Teelöffel • la cucharilla
de café • il cucchiaino

mug • la grande tasse
• der Becher • la taza
• la tazza

coffee cup • la tasse à
café • die Kaffeetasse
• la taza de café
• la tazzina da caffé

teacup • la tasse à thé
• die Teetasse • la taza
de té • la tazza da té

plate • l'assiette
• der Teller • el plato
• il piatto

bowl • le bol • die
Schüssel • el bol
• la ciotola

wine glass • le verre à vin
• das Weinglas • la copa de
vino • il calice da vino

tumbler
le verre
das Wasserglas
el vaso
il bicchiere

cafetière • la cafetière
• die Cafetière • la cafetera
de émbolo • la caffettiera

teapot • la théière
• die Teekanne • la
tetera • la teiera

jug • le pot
• der Krug • la jarra
• la brocca

egg cup • le coquetier
• der Eierbecher • la
huevera • il portauovo

glassware • la verrerie
• die Glaswaren • la
cristalería • la cristalleria

napkin ring
le rond de serviette
der Serviettenring
el servilletero
il portatovagliolo

side plate
l'assiette à dessert
der Beilagenteller
el plato del pan
il piattino

dinner plate
l'assiette plate
der Essteller
el plato llano
il piatto piano

soup bowl
l'assiette à soupe
der Suppenteller
el plato hondo
il piatto fondo

soup spoon • la cuiller à
soupe • der Suppenlöffel
• la cuchara sopera • il
cucchiaio da minestra

napkin
la serviette
die Serviette
la servilleta
il tovagliolo

fork • la fourchette
• die Gabel • el tenedor
• la forchetta

spoon
la cuiller
der Löffel
la cuchara
il cucchiaio

knife
le couteau
das Messer
el cuchillo
il coltello

place setting • le couvert • das Gedeck • el cubierto • il coperto

kitchen • la cuisine • die Küche • la cocina • la cucina

shelves
l'étagère
das Küchenregal
los estantes
le mensole

splashback
le revêtement
der Spritzschutz
el frente de la cocina
il pannello di protezione

tap
le robinet
der Wasserhahn
el grifo
il rubinetto

sink
l'évier
das Spülbecken
el fregadero
il lavandino

drawer
le tiroir
die Schublade
el cajón
il cassetto

extractor
la hotte
der Dunstabzug
el extractor
la cappa

ceramic hob • la table
de cuisson céramique
• das Glaskeramikkochfeld
• la placa vitrocerámica
• il fornello di ceramica

worktop
le plan de travail
die Arbeitsfläche
la encimera
il piano di lavoro

oven
le four
der Backofen
el horno
il forno

cabinet
le placard
der Küchenschrank
el armario
l'armadietto

appliances • les appareils ménagers • die Küchengeräte • los electrodomésticos • gli elettrodomestici

microwave oven • le micro-ondes
• die Mikrowelle • el horno
microondas • il forno a microonde

kettle • la bouilloire
électrique • der
Wasserkocher • el
hervidor • il bollitore

toaster • le grille-
pain • der Toaster
• el tostador • il
tostapane

mixing bowl
le bol du mixeur
die Mixerschüssel
el cuenco mezclador
il recipiente

blade
la lame
das Messer
la cuchilla
la lama

food processor • le robot
ménager • die
Küchenmaschine • el robot
de cocina • il miscelatore

lid
le couvercle
der Deckel
la tapa
il coperchio

blender • le mixeur
• der Mixer • la
licuadora • il frullatore

dishwasher • le lave-
vaisselle • die Spülmaschine
• el friegaplatos • la
lavastoviglie

ice maker
• le freezer
• das Eisfach
• la máquina
de los cubitos
• il fabbrica-
ghiaccio

refrigerator
le réfrigérateur
der Kühlschrank
el frigorífico
il frigorifero

shelf
la clayette
der Rost
el estante
la mensola

freezer
le congélateur
das Gefrierfach
el congelador
il freezer

crisper • le bac
à légumes
• das Gemüsefach
• el cajón de las
verduras • il
cassetto per la
verdura

hob	freeze (v)
la table de cuisson	congeler
das Kochfeld	einfrieren
la placa	congelar
la piastra	congelare
draining board	defrost (v)
l'égouttoir	décongeler
das Abtropfbrett	auftauen
el escurridor	descongelar
il gocciolatoio	scongelare
burner	steam (v)
le brûleur	cuire à la vapeur
der Brenner	dämpfen
el quemador	cocer al vapor
il fornello	cuocere al vapore
rubbish bin	sauté (v)
la poubelle	faire sauter
der Mülleimer	anbraten
el cubo de basura	saltear
la pattumiera	rosolare

fridge-freezer • le réfrigérateur-congélateur • der Gefrier-Kühlschrank
• el frigorífico congelador • il frigocongelatore

cooking • la cuisine • das Kochen • cocinar • cucinare

peel (v) • éplucher
• schälen • pelar
• sbucciare

slice (v) • couper
• schneiden • cortar
• affettare

grate (v) • râper
• reiben • rallar
• grattugiare

pour (v) • verser
• gießen • echar
• versare

mix (v) • mélanger
• verrühren • mezclar
• mescolare

whisk (v) • battre
• schlagen • batir
• sbattere

boil (v) • bouillir
• kochen • hervir
• bollire

fry (v) • frire
• braten • freír
• friggere

roll (v) • étaler à rouleau •
ausrollen • extender con el
rodillo • spianare

stir (v) • remuer
• rühren • remover
• rimestare

simmer (v) • mijoter
• köcheln lassen
• cocer a fuego lento
• cuocere a fuoco lento

poach (v) • pocher
• pochieren • escalfar
• affogare

bake (v) • cuire au
four • backen • cocer
al horno • cuocere
al forno

roast (v) • rôtir
• braten • asar
• arrostire

grill (v) • griller
• grillen • asar a la
parrilla • cuocere
sulla griglia

kitchenware • les ustensiles de cuisine • die Küchengeräte • los utensilios de cocina • gli utensili da cucina

chopping board
• la planche à hacher
• das Hackbrett
• la tabla para cortar
• il tagliere

bread knife • le couteau à pain • das Brotmesser
• el cuchillo de sierra
• il coltello da pane

kitchen knife
• le couteau de cuisine
• das Küchenmesser
• el cuchillo de cocina
• il coltello da cucina

cleaver • le fendoir
• das Hackmesser
• el hacha de cocina
• la mannaia

knife sharpener
• l'aiguisoir • der Messer-schärfer • el afilador
• l'affilacoltelli

meat tenderizer
• l'attendrisseur à viande • der Fleischklopfer
• el mazo de cocina
• il martello

skewer • la broche • der Spieß • el pincho
• lo spiedino

peeler • l'épluche-légume • der Schäler
• el mondador • il pelapatate

apple corer
• le vide-pomme
• der Apfelstecher
• el descorazonador
• il cavatorsoli

grater • la râpe
• die Reibe • el ralladore • la grattugia

pestle
le pilon
der Stößel
la mano de mortero
il pestello

mortar • le mortier
• der Mörser • el mortero • il mortaio

masher • le presse-purée • der Kartoffel-stampfer • el mazo para puré de patatas
• lo schiacciapatate

can opener • l'ouvre-boîte • der Dosenöffner
• el abrelatas
• l'apriscatole

bottle opener
• l'ouvre-bouteille
• der Flaschenöffner
• el abrebotellas
• l'apribottiglie

garlic press • le presse-ail • die Knoblauchpresse
• el prensaajos • lo spremiaglio

serving spoon
• la cuiller à servir
• der Servierlöffel • la cuchara de servir • il cucchiaio da portata

fish slice • la pelle à poisson • der Pfannenwender
• la espátula • la paletta forata

colander • la passoire
• das Sieb • el escurridor • lo scolapasta

spatula • la spatule
• der Spachtel • la espátula • la spatola

wooden spoon • la cuiller en bois • der Holzlöffel • la cuchara de madera • il cucchiaio di legno

slotted spoon
• l'écumoire
• der Schaumlöffel
• la espumadera • il cucchiaio perforato

ladle • la louche
• der Schöpflöffel • el cucharón • il mestolo

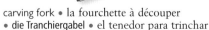

carving fork • la fourchette à découper
• die Tranchiergabel • el tenedor para trinchar
• il forchettone

scoop • la cuiller à glace
• der Portionierer • la cuchara para helado
• il cucchiaio dosatore

whisk • le fouet
• der Schneebesen
• las varillas
• la frusta

sieve • la passoire
• das Sieb • el colador
• il colino

lid • le couvercle • der Deckel
• la tapa • il coperchio

non-stick • anti-adhérent
• antihaftbeschichtet
• antiadherente • antiaderente

frying pan • la poêle
• die Bratpfanne • la
sartén • la padella

saucepan • la casserole
• der Kochtopf • el cazo
• la pentola

grill pan • le gril • das
Grillpfanne • la parrilla
• la padella per grigliare

wok • le wok • der
Wok • el wok • il wok

earthenware dish • le fait-
tout • der Schmortopf • la
cazuela de barro • la
casseruola di terracotta

glass • en verre • Glas-
• de cristal • di vetro

ovenproof • allant au four
• feuerfest • resistente al
horno • pirofilo

mixing bowl • le grand
bol • die Rührschüssel
• el cuenco • la scodella

soufflé dish • le moule à
soufflé • die Souffléform
• el molde para suflé
• lo stampo per soufflé

gratin dish • le plat à
gratin • die Auflaufform
• la fuente para gratinar
• lo stampo per sformati

ramekin • le ramequin
• das Auflaufförmchen
• el molde individual
• lo stampo

casserole dish • la
cocotte • die Kasserolle
• la cazuela
• la casseruola

baking cakes • la pâtisserie • das Kuchenbacken • la repostería • la cottura dei dolci

scales • la balance
• die Haushaltswaage
• la báscula de cocina
• la bilancia

measuring jug • le
pichet gradué • der
Messbecher • la jarra
graduada • il misurino

cake tin • le moule à
gâteaux • die
Kuchenform • el molde
para bizcocho • lo
stampo per dolci

pie tin • la tourtière
• die Pastetenform
• el molde redondo
• lo stampo per torte

flan tin • le moule à
tarte • die Obstkuchen-
form • el molde de tarta
• lo stampo per dolci

pastry brush • le pinceau à pâtisserie
• der Backpinsel • la brocha de cocina
• il pennello da cucina

rolling pin • le rouleau pâtissier • das Nudelholz
• el rodillo de cocina • il mattarello

piping bag • la poche à douille • der
Spritzbeutel • la manga pastelera • la
tasca da pasticciere

muffin tray • le moule à
muffins • die Törtchen-
form • el molde para
magdalenas • la teglia
per pasticcini

baking tray • la plaque
à gâteaux • das
Kuchenblech • la
bandeja de horno
• la piastra da forno

cooling rack • la grille
de refroidissement
• das Abkühlgitter • la
rejilla • la gratella

oven glove • le gant
isolant • der
Topfhandschuh • la
manopla de cocina
• il guanto da forno

apron • le tablier
• die Schürze • el
delantal • il grembiule

bedroom • la chambre • das Schlafzimmer • el dormitorio • la camera da letto

wardrobe
l'armoire
der Kleiderschrank
el armario
l'armadio

bedside lamp
la lampe de chevet
die Nachttischlampe
la lámpara de la mesilla
la lampadina

headboard
la tête de lit
das Kopfende
el cabecero
la testata

bedside table
la table de nuit
der Nachttisch
la mesilla de noche
il comodino

chest of drawers
la commode
die Kommode
la cómoda
il cassettone

drawer
le tiroir
die Schublade
el cajón
il cassetto

bed
le lit
das Bett
la cama
il letto

mattress
le matelas
die Matratze
el colchón
il materasso

bedspread
le couvre-lit
die Tagesdecke
la colcha
il copriletto

pillow
l'oreiller
das Kopfkissen
la almohada
il guanciale

hot-water bottle
• la bouillotte • die
Wärmflasche • la bolsa
de agua caliente • la
borsa dell'acqua calda

clock radio • le radio-
réveil • der Radiowecker
• el radiodespertador
• la radiosveglia

alarm clock • le réveil
• der Wecker • el
despertador • la
sveglia

box of tissues • la boîte
de kleenex • die
Papiertaschentuchschachtel
• la caja de pañuelos
de papel • la scatola
di fazzolettini

coat hanger • le cintre
• der Kleiderbügel • la
percha • la gruccia

bed linen • le linge de lit • die Bettwäsche
• la ropa de cama • le lenzuola

mirror
le miroir
der Spiegel
el espejo
lo specchio

dressing table
la coiffeuse
der Frisiertisch
el tocador
la toeletta

floor
le sol
der Fußboden
el suelo
il pavimento

pillowcase
la taie d'oreiller
der Kissenbezug
la funda de la almohada
la federa

sheet
le drap
das Bettlaken
la sábana
il lenzuolo

valance
la frange de lit
der Volant
el cubrecanapé
il volant

duvet
la couette
die Bettdecke
el edredón
la coperta da letto

quilt
l'édredon
die Steppdecke
la colcha
la trapunta

blanket
la couverture
die Decke
la manta
la coperta

single bed	footboard	insomnia	wake up (v)	set the alarm (v)
le lit simple	le pied de lit	l'insomnie	se réveiller	mettre le réveil
das Einzelbett	das Fußende	die Schlaflosigkeit	aufwachen	den Wecker stellen
la cama individual	el pie de la cama	el insomnio	despertarse	poner el despertador
il letto singolo	i piedi del letto	l'insonnia	svegliarsi	mettere la sveglia
double bed	spring	go to bed (v)	get up (v)	snore (v)
le grand lit	le ressort	se coucher	se lever	ronfler
das Doppelbett	die Sprungfeder	ins Bett gehen	aufstehen	schnarchen
la cama de matrimonio	el muelle	acostarse	levantarse	roncar
il letto matrimoniale	la molla	andare a letto	alzarsi	russare
electric blanket	carpet	go to sleep (v)	make the bed (v)	built-in wardrobe
la couverture chauffante	le tapis	s'endormir	faire le lit	l'armoire encastrée
die Heizdecke	der Teppich	einschlafen	das Bett machen	der Einbauschrank
la manta eléctrica	la alfombra	dormirse	hacer la cama	el armario empotrado
la termocoperta	il tappeto	addormentarsi	fare il letto	l'armadio a muro

bathroom • la salle de bain • das Badezimmer • el cuarto de baño • la stanza da bagno

towel rail
le porte-serviettes
der Handtuchhalter
il toallero
il portasciugamani

shower door
la porte de douche
die Duschtür
la puerta de la ducha
la porta della doccia

cold tap
le robinet d'eau froide
der Kaltwasserhahn
el grifo de agua fría
il rubinetto dell'acqua fredda

hot tap
le robinet d'eau chaude
der Heißwasserhahn
el grifo de agua caliente
il rubinetto dell'acqua calda

shower head
le pommeau de douche
der Duschkopf
la alcachofa de la ducha
il soffione della doccia

washbasin
le lavabo
das Waschbecken
el lavabo
il lavandino

shower
la douche
die Dusche
la ducha
la doccia

plug
la bonde
der Stöpsel
el tapón
il tappo

drain
le tuyau d'écoulement
der Abfluss
el desagüe
lo scolo

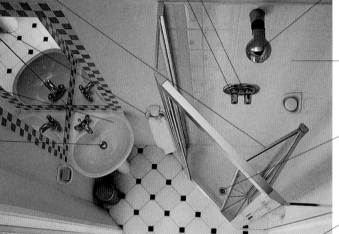

toilet seat
le siège des toilettes
der Toilettensitz
la tapa del wáter
il sedile

toilet
les toilettes
die Toilette
el wáter
il water

toilet brush
la brosse
die Toilettenbürste
la escobilla del wáter
la spazzola da water

bathtub • la baignoire
• die Badewanne • la bañera
• la vasca

bidet • le bidet • das Bidet
• el bidé • il bidè

medicine cabinet
la pharmacie de ménage
die Hausapotheke
el botiquín
l'armadietto dei medicinali

bath mat
le tapis de bain
die Badematte
la alfombrilla de baño
lo scendibagno

toilet roll
le rouleau de papier hygiénique
die Rolle Toilettenpapier
el rollo de papel higiénico
la carta igienica

shower curtain
le rideau de douche
der Duschvorhang
la cortina de ducha
la tenda da doccia

take a shower (v)
prendre une douche
duschen
ducharse
farsi la doccia

take a bath (v)
prendre un bain
baden
bañarse
farsi il bagno

dental hygiene • l'hygiène dentaire • die Zahnpflege
• la higiene dental • l'igiene dentale

toothbrush • la brosse à
dents • die Zahnbürste
• el cepillo de dientes
• lo spazzolino da denti

toothpaste • le dentifrice
• die Zahnpasta • la pasta
de dientes • il dentifricio

dental floss
le fil dentaire
die Zahnseide
el hilo dental
il filo interdentale

mouthwash • l'eau dentifrice
• das Mundwasser • el
enjuague bucal • il colluttorio

loofah
le luffa
der Luffaschwamm
la esponja de luffa
la luffa

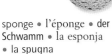

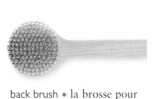

sponge • l'éponge • der
Schwamm • la esponja
• la spugna

pumice stone • la pierre
ponce • der Bimsstein • la
piedra • la pietra pomice

back brush • la brosse pour
le dos • die Rückenbürste
• el cepillo para la espalda
• la spazzola

deodorant • le déodorant
• das Deo • el desodorante
• il deodorante

soap dish
le porte-savon
die Seifenschale
la jabonera
il portasapone

shower gel
le gel douche
das Duschgel
el gel de ducha
la docciaschiuma

soap • le savon • die Seife
• el jabón • il sapone

face cream • la crème pour
le visage • die Gesichtscreme
• la crema para la cara
• la crema per il viso

bubble bath • le bain
moussant • das Schaumbad
• el gel de baño
• il bagnoschiuma

hand towel
la serviette
das Handtuch
la toalla de lavabo
l'asciugamano piccolo

bath towel
la serviette de bain
das Badetuch
la toalla de baño
l'asciugamano grande

towels • les serviettes • die
Handtücher • las toallas • gli
asciugamani

body lotion • la lotion pour le corps
• die Körperlotion • la lócion para el
cuerpo • la lozione per il corpo

talcum powder • le talc
• der Körperpuder • los
polvos de talco • il talco

bathrobe • le peignoir
• der Bademantel • el
albornoz • l'accappatoio

shaving • le rasage • das Rasieren • el afeitado • la rasatura

electric razor
le rasoir électrique
der Elektrorasierer
la máquina de afeitar
il rasoio elettrico

razor blade
la lame de rasoir
die Rasierklinge
la hoja de afeitar
la lametta

shaving foam • la mousse à
raser • der Rasierschaum
• la espuma de afeitar
• la schiuma da barba

disposable razor • le rasoir
jetable • der Einwegrasierer
• la maquinilla de afeitar
• il rasoio usa e getta

aftershave • l'after-shave
• das Rasierwasser • el
aftershave • il dopobarba

nursery • la chambre d'enfants • das Kinderzimmer • la habitación de los niños • la camera dei bambini

baby care • les soins de bébé • die Säuglingspflege • el cuidado del bebé • l'igiene del neonato

nappy rash cream • la crème pour l'érythème • die Wundsalbe • la crema protectora • la pomata antirossore

wet wipe • la serviette humide • das Pflegetuch • la toallita húmeda • la salviettina umidificata

sponge
l'éponge
der Schwamm
la esponja
la spugna

baby bath • la baignoire en plastique • die Babywanne • la bañera de plástico • la vaschetta

potty • le pot • das Töpfchen • el orinal • il vasino

changing mat • le matelas à langer • die Wickelmatte • el cambiador • il materassino

sleeping • le coucher • das Schlafen • la hora de dormir • la dormita

sheet
le drap
das Laken
la sábana
il lenzuolo

blanket • la couverture • die Decke • la manta • la coperta

mobile
le mobile
das Mobile
el móvil
il mobile

bars
les barreaux
die Gitterstäbe
los barrotes
le sbarre

fleece • la couverture laineuse • das Babyfell • el vellón • la felpa

bedding • la literie • das Bettzeug • la ropa de cama • le lenzuola

bumper
le protège-barreaux
der Kopfschutz
la chichonera
il paracolpi

mattress • le matelas • die Matratze • el colchón • il materasso

rattle • le hochet • die Rassel • el sonajero • il sonaglio

moses basket • le moïse • das Körbchen • el moisés • il portabebè

cot • le lit d'enfant • das Kinderbett • la cuna • il lettino

playing • le jeu • das Spielen • los juegos • il gioco

doll • la poupée • die Puppe • la muñeca • la bambola

soft toy • le jouet en peluche • das Kuscheltier • el peluche • il peluche

doll's house • la maison de poupée • das Puppenhaus • la casa de muñecas • la casa delle bambole

playhouse • la maison pliante • das Spielhaus • la casa de juguete • la casa da gioco

teddy bear • l'ours en peluche • der Teddy • el oso de peluche • l'orsacchiotto

toy
le jouet
das Spielzeug
el juguete
il giocattolo

ball
la balle
der Ball
la pelota
la palla

toy basket • le panier à jouets • der Spielzeugkorb • el cesto de los juguetes • il cesto dei giocattoli

playpen • le parc • der Laufstall • el parque • il box

safety • la sécurité • die Sicherheit • la seguridad • la sicurezza

child lock • la serrure de sécurité • die Kindersicherung • el cierre de seguridad • la sicura per bambini

baby monitor • le moniteur • die Babysprechanlage • el escuchabebés • la trasmittente

stair gate • la barrière d'escalier • das Treppengitter • la barrera de seguridad • lo sbarramento

eating • le manger • das Essen • la comida • il pasto

high chair • la chaise haute • der Kinderstuhl • la trona • il seggiolone

teat • la tétine • der Sauger • la tetina • la tettarella

drinking cup
la tasse
der Schnabelbecher
la taza
la tazza per bere

bottle • le biberon • die Babyflasche • el biberón • il biberon

going out • la sortie • das Ausgehen • el paseo • la passeggiata

pushchair • la poussette • die Kinderkarre • la silla de paseo • il passeggino

hood
la capote
das Verdeck
la capota
la capote

pram • le landau • der Kinderwagen • el cochecito de bebé • la carrozzina

carrycot • le couffin • das Tragebettchen • el capazo • la culla portatile

nappy
la couche
die Windel
el pañal
il pannolino

changing bag • le sac • die Babytasche • la bolsa del bebé • la borsa dei ricambi

baby sling • le porte-bébé • die Babytrageschlinge • la mochila porta-bebé • il marsupio

utility room • la buanderie • der Allzweckraum • el lavadero • la lavanderia

laundry • le linge • die Wäsche • la colada • il bucato

dirty washing
le linge sale
die schmutzige Wäsche
la ropa sucia
i panni sporchi

clean clothes
le linge propre
die saubere Wäsche
la ropa limpia
i vestiti puliti

laundry basket • le panier à linge • der Wäschekorb • el cesto de la colada • il cesto della biancheria sporca

washing machine • le lave-linge • die Waschmaschine • la lavadora • la lavatrice

washer-dryer • le lave-linge séchant • der Waschautomat mit Trockner • la lavadora secadora • il lavasciuga

tumble dryer • le sèche-linge • der Trockner • la secadora • l'asciugabiancheria

linen basket • le panier à linge • der Wäschekorb • el cesto de la ropa de plancha • il cesto della biancheria pulita

clothes line
la corde à linge
die Wäscheleine
la cuerda para tender la ropa
la corda per stendere il bucato

clothes peg
la pince à linge
die Wäscheklammer
la pinza para la ropa
la molletta

iron • le fer à repasser • das Bügeleisen • la plancha • il ferro da stiro

dry (v) • sécher • trocknen • secar • asciugare

ironing board • la planche à repasser • das Bügelbrett • la tabla de la plancha • l'asse da stiro

load (v)	spin (v)	iron (v)	How do I operate the washing machine?
charger	essorer	repasser	Comment fonctionne le lave-linge?
füllen	schleudern	bügeln	Wie benutze ich die Waschmaschine?
cargar	centrifugar	planchar	¿Cómo funciona la lavadora?
caricare	centrifugare	stirare	Come funziona la lavatrice?
rinse (v)	spin dryer	fabric conditioner	What is the setting for coloureds/whites?
rincer	l'essoreuse	l'assouplisseur	Quel est le programme pour les couleurs/le blanc?
spülen	die Wäscheschleuder	der Weichspüler	Welches Programm nehme ich für farbige/weiße Wäsche?
aclarar	la centrifugadora	el suavizante	¿Cuál es el programa para la ropa de color/blanca?
sciacquare	la centrifuga	l'ammorbidente	Qual è il programma per i tessuti colorati/bianchi?

cleaning equipment • l'équipement d'entretien • die Reinigungsartikel • el equipo de limpieza • gli accessori per la pulizia

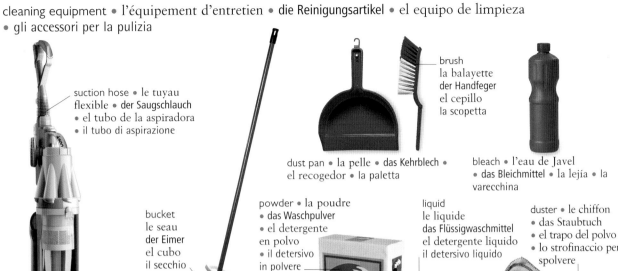

suction hose • le tuyau flexible • der Saugschlauch • el tubo de la aspiradora • il tubo di aspirazione

dust pan • la pelle • das Kehrblech • el recogedor • la paletta

brush la balayette der Handfeger el cepillo la scopetta

bleach • l'eau de Javel • das Bleichmittel • la lejía • la varecchina

bucket le seau der Eimer el cubo il secchio

powder • la poudre • das Waschpulver • el detergente en polvo • il detersivo in polvere

liquid le liquide das Flüssigwaschmittel el detergente liquido il detersivo liquido

duster • le chiffon • das Staubtuch • el trapo del polvo • lo strofinaccio per spolvere

vacuum cleaner • l'aspirateur • der Staubsauger • la aspiradora • l'aspirapolvere

mop • le balai laveur • der Putzmopp • la fregona • la scopa a frange

detergent • le détergent • das Waschmittel • el detergente • il detersivo

polish • la cire • die Politur • la cera • la cera

activities • les activités • die Tätigkeiten • las actividades • le attività

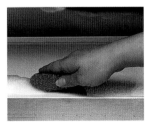

clean (v) • nettoyer • putzen • limpiar • pulire

wash (v) • laver • spülen • fregar • lavare

wipe (v) • essuyer • wischen • pasar la bayeta • asciugare

scrub (v) • laver à la brosse • schrubben • restregar • strofinare

scrape (v) • racler • kratzen • raspar • raschiare

broom le balai der Besen la escoba la scopa

sweep (v) • balayer • fegen • barrer • spazzare

dust (v) • épousseter • Staub wischen • limpiar el polvo • spolverare

polish (v) • cirer • polieren • sacar brillo • lucidare

workshop • l'atelier • die Heimwerkstatt • el taller • il laboratorio

chuck
le mandrin
das Bohrfutter
el cabezal
il mandrino

drill bit
la mèche
der Bohrer
la broca
la punta

battery pack
la pile
die Batterie
la batería
la batteria

jigsaw • la scie sauteuse • die Stichsäge • la sierra de vaivén • il gattuccio

rechargeable drill • la perceuse rechargeable • der Bohrer mit Batteriebetrieb • el taladro inalámbrico • il trapano ricaricabile

electric drill • la perceuse électrique • der Elektrobohrer • el taladro eléctrico • il trapano elettrico

glue gun • le pistolet à colle • die Klebepistole • la pistola para encolar • la pistola per colla

clamp • le serre-joint • die Zwinge • la abrazadera • il morsetto

blade • la lame • das Blatt • la cuchilla • la lama

vice • l'étau • der Schraubstock • el torno de banco • la morsa

sander • la ponceuse • die Schleifmaschine • la lijadora • la levigatrice

circular saw • la scie circulaire • die Kreissäge • la sierra circular • la sega circolare

workbench • l'établi • die Werkbank • el banco de trabajo • il banco da lavoro

wood glue
la colle à bois
der Holzleim
la cola de carpintero
la colla da legno

tool rack
• le porte-outils
• das Werkzeuggestell
• el organizador de las herramientas
• la rastrelliera per gli arnesi

router
la guimbarde
der Grundhobel
la guimbarda
la contornitrice

bit brace
le vilebrequin
die Bohrwinde
el taladro manual
il girabacchino

wood shavings
les copeaux
die Holzspäne
las virutas de madera
i trucioli

extension lead
la rallonge
die Verlängerungsschnur
el alargador
la prolunga

techniques • les techniques • die Techniken • las técnicas • le tecniche

cut (v) • découper • schneiden • cortar • tagliare

saw (v) • scier • sägen • serrar • segare

drill (v) • percer • bohren • taladrar • forare

hammer (v) • marteler • hämmern • clavar con el martillo • martellare

plane (v) • raboter • hobeln • alisar • piallare

turn (v) • tourner • drechseln • tornear • tornire

solder
la soudure
der Lötzinn
el hilo de estaño
la lega per saldatura

carve (v) • sculpter • schnitzen • tallar • intagliare

solder (v) • souder • löten • soldar • saldare

materials • les matériaux • die Materialien • los materiales • i materiali

plywood
le contreplaqué
das Sperrholz
el contrachapado
il compensato

chipboard
l'aggloméré
das Spanholz
el aglomerado
il truciolato

hardboard • l'isorel
• die Hartfaserplatte
• el cartón madera
• il cartone di
fibra compressa

softwood • le
bois tendre •
das Weichholz • la
madera de pino
• il legno dolce

MDF
le médium
die MDF-Platte
el tablero de densidad media
l'MDF

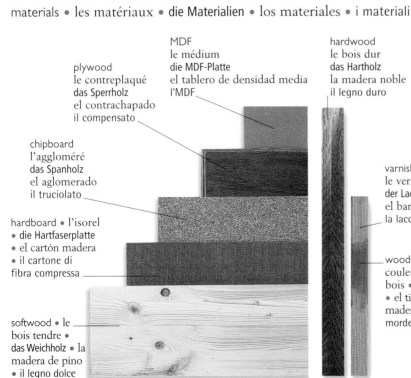

wood • le bois • das Holz • la madera • il legno

hardwood
le bois dur
das Hartholz
la madera noble
il legno duro

varnish
le vernis
der Lack
el barniz
la lacca

woodstain • la
couleur pour
bois • die Beize
• el tinte para
madera • il
mordente

wire
le fil de fer
der Draht
el alambre
il fil di ferro

cable • le câble • das Kabel
• el cable • il cavo

stainless steel
l'inox
der rostfreie Stahl
el acero inoxidable
l'acciaio inossidabile

galvanised
galvanisé
galvanisiert
galvanizado
zincato

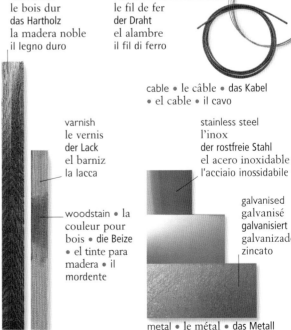

metal • le métal • das Metall
• el metal • il metallo

toolbox • la boîte à outils • der Werkzeugkasten • la caja de las herramientas • la cassetta degli attrezzi

spanner
la clef
der Schraubenschlüssel
la llave de boca
la chiave

adjustable spanner
• la clef à molette
• der verstellbare Schraubenschlüssel • la llave inglesa
• la chiave regolabile

hammer • le marteau
• der Hammer • el martillo
• il martello

needle-nose pliers • la pince plate
• die Flachzange • las tenazas de
alambre • le pinze a punte piatte

socket wrench • la clef à pipe • der Steckschlüssel
• la llave de tubo • la chiave a tubo

screwdriver bits
• les embouts de
tournevis • die
Schraubenziehereinsätze
• los cabezales de
destornillador • le
punte per cacciavite

spirit level
le niveau
die Wasserwaage
el nivel
la livella

washer
le joint
der Dichtungsring
la arandela
la rondella

screwdriver
le tournevis
der Schraubenzieher
el destornillador
il cacciavite

nut
l'écrou
die Mutter
la tuerca
il dado

tape measure • le mètre • das
Metermaß • la cinta métrica
• il metro

knife
le couteau
der Schneider
el cúter
il coltello

bull-nose pliers • la pince universelle
• die Kombinationszange • los alicates
• le pinze tonde

socket • la douille • die Tülle
• el encaje • la bussola

key • la clef • der Schlüssel
• la llave • la chiave

drill bits • les forets • die Bohrer • las brocas • le punte

metal bit • le foret à métaux
• der Metallbohrer • la broca para
metal • la punta per metalli

flat wood bit • le foret à bois plat
• der Flachholzbohrer • la broca para
madera • la punta piana per legno

phillips screwdriver • le tournevis cruciforme
• der Kreuzschlitzschraubenzieher • el
destornillador de estrella • il cacciavite a croce

reamer
l'alésoir
die Reibahle
el escariador
l'alesatore

head • la tête
• der Nagelkopf • la
cabeza • la testa

security bit
le foret de sécurité
der Sicherheitsbohrer
la broca de seguridad
la punta di sicurezza

nail • le clou • der
Nagel • el clavo
• il chiodo

carpentry bits
• les forets de bois
• die Holzbohrer
• las brocas para
madera • le punte
da falegnameria

masonry bit
le foret de maçonnerie
der Mauerwerkbohrer
la broca de albañilería
la punta per muratura

screw • la vis • die
Schraube • el tornillo
• la vite

wire strippers • la pince à dénuder • die Entisolierzange • el pelacables • la pinza spelafilo

wire cutters • la pince coupante • der Drahtschneider • el cortaalambres • la pinza isolata

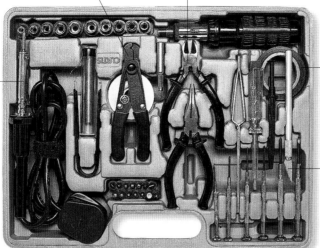

soldering iron
le fer à souder
der Lötkolben
el soldador
il saldatoio

insulating tape
le ruban isolant
das Isolierband
la cinta aislante
il nastro isolante

scalpel
le scalpel
das Skalpell
el escalpelo
lo scalpello

solder
la soudure
der Lötzinn
el hilo de estaño
le lega per saldatura

fretsaw • la scie à chantourner • die Schweifsäge • la sierra de calar • la sega da traforo

tenon saw • la scie à dosseret • die Profilsäge • el serrucho de costilla • la sega per tenoni

safety goggles • les lunettes de sécurité • die Schutzbrille • las gafas de seguridad • gli occhiali protettivi

plane • le rabot • der Hobel • el cepillo • la pialla

handsaw • la scie égoïne • der Fuchsschwanz • el serrucho • il saracco

hand drill • la perceuse manuelle • der Handbohrer • el taladro manual • il trapano manuale

wire wool • la paille de fer • die Stahlwolle • la lana de acero • la lana d'acciaio

mitre block • la boîte à onglets • die Gehrungslade • la caja para cortar en inglete • la cassetta guidalama per ugnature

hacksaw • la scie à métaux • die Metallsäge • la sierra para metales • il seghetto per metalli

wrench • la clef serre-tube • die Rohrzange • los alicates • la chiave inglese

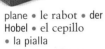

sandpaper • le papier de verre • das Schmirgelpapier • el papel de lija • la carta vetrata

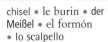

chisel • le burin • der Meißel • el formón • lo scalpello

plunger • la ventouse • der Sauger • el desatascador • lo sturalavandini

file • la lime • die Feile • la lima • la lima

sharpening stone • la pierre à aiguiser • der Wetzstahl • la piedra afiladora • l'affilatore

pipe cutter • le coupe-tube • der Rohrab-schneider • el cortatuberías • il tagliatubi

decorating • la décoration • das Tapezieren • la decoración • il tappezzare

scissors • les ciseaux • die Tapezierschere • las tijeras • le forbici

craft knife • le cutter • das Tapeziermesser • el cúter • il coltello da pacchi

plumb line • le fil à plomb • das Senkblei • la cuerda de plomada • il filo a piombo

scraper • le grattoir • der Spachtel • el raspador • la spatola

decorator
le tapissier décorateur
der Tapezierer
el pintor
il tappeziere

wallpaper
le papier peint
die Tapete
el papel pintado
la carta di parati

stepladder
l'escabeau
die Trittleiter
la escalera de mano
la scala a pioli

wallpaper brush
• la brosse à tapisser
• die Tapezierbürste
• la brocha de empapelador
• la spazzola

pasting table
la table à encoller
der Tapeziertisch
la mesa de encolar
il tavolo da lavoro

pasting brush
la brosse à encoller
die Kleisterbürste
la brocha de encolar
il pennello da colla

wallpaper paste • la colle à tapisser • der Tapetenkleister • la cola para empapelar • la colla da parati

bucket
le seau
der Eimer
el cubo
il secchio

wallpaper (v) • tapisser • tapezieren • empapelar • tappezzare

strip (v) • décoller • abziehen • arrancar • staccare

fill (v) • mastiquer • spachteln • rellenar • stuccare

sand (v) • poncer • schmirgeln • lijar • scartavetrare

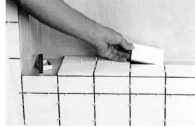

plaster (v) • plâtrer • verputzen • enyesar • intonacare

hang (v) • poser • anbringen • empapelar • incollare

tile (v) • carreler • kacheln • alicatar • piastrellare

english • français • deutsch • español • italiano

roller
le rouleau
der Roller
el rodillo
il rullo

paint tray • le bac à peinture • die Wanne • la bandeja para la pintura • la vaschetta per la vernice

paint • la peinture • die Farbe • la pintura • la vernice

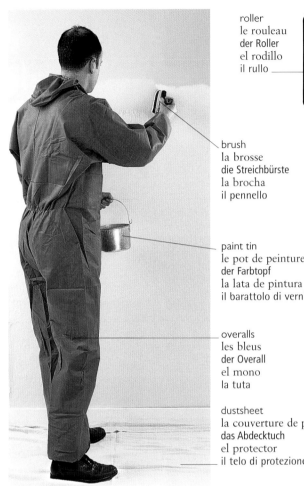

brush
la brosse
die Streichbürste
la brocha
il pennello

paint tin
le pot de peinture
der Farbtopf
la lata de pintura
il barattolo di vernice

sponge • l'éponge • der Schwamm • la esponja • la spugna

masking tape • le papier cache • das Abdeckband • la cinta adhesiva protectora • il nastro adesivo di ricopertura

sandpaper • le papier de verre • das Schmirgelpapier • el papel de lija • la carta vetrata

overalls
les bleus
der Overall
el mono
la tuta

dustsheet
la couverture de protection
das Abdecktuch
el protector
il telo di protezione

turpentine
la térébenthine
das Terpentin
la trementina
la trementina

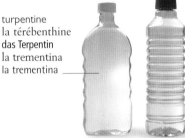

paint (v) • peindre • anstreichen • pintar • dipingere

filler • le mastic • die Spachtelmasse • la masilla • lo stucco

white spirit • le white-spirit • das Verdünnungsmittel • el aguarrás • l'acquaragia

plaster	gloss	embossed paper	undercoat	sealant
le plâtre	brillant	le papier gaufré	la couche de fond	l'enduit
der Gips	Glanz-	das Reliefpapier	die Grundierung	das Versiegelungsmittel
el yeso	con brillo	el papel estampado en relieve	la primera mano	el sellante
il gesso	lucido	la carta a rilievo	la mano di fondo	il sigillante
varnish	mat	lining paper	top coat	solvent
le vernis	mat	le papier d'apprêt	la dernière couche	le solvant
der Lack	matt	das Einsatzpapier	der Deckanstrich	das Lösungsmittel
el barniz	mate	el papel de apresto	la última mano	el disolvente
la vernice trasparente	opaco	la carta di fondo	la mano finale	il solvente
emulsion	stencil	primer	preservative	grout
la peinture mate	le pochoir	l'apprêt	l'agent de conservation	le mastic
die Emulsionsfarbe	die Schablone	die Grundfarbe	der Schutzanstrich	der Fugenkitt
la pintura al agua	la plantilla	la imprimación	el conservante	la masilla
la pittura	lo stampino	la vernice di base	il conservante	il mastice

garden • le jardin • der Garten • el jardín • il giardino

garden styles • les styles de jardin • die Gartentypen • los estilos de jardín • i tipi di giardino

patio garden • le patio • der Patiogarten • la terraza ajardinada • il giardino a patio

formal garden • le jardin à la française • der architektonische Garten • el jardín clásico • il giardino all'italiana

cottage garden • le jardin paysan • der Bauerngarten • el jardín campestre • il giardino all'inglese

herb garden • le jardin d'herbes aromatiques • der Kräutergarten • el jardín de hierbas aromáticas • il giardino di erbe

roof garden • le jardin sur le toit • der Dachgarten • el jardín en la azotea • il giardino pensile

rock garden • la rocaille • der Steingarten • la rocalla • il giardino roccioso

courtyard • la cour • der Hof • el patio • il cortile

water garden • le jardin d'eau • der Wassergarten • el jardín acuático • il giardino acquatico

garden features • les ornements de jardin • die Gartenornamente • los adornos para el jardín • gli ornamenti oggetti per giardini

hanging basket • le panier suspendu • die Blumenampel • la cesta colgante • la fioriera pensile

trellis • le treillis • das Spalier • la espaldera • il graticcio

pergola • la pergola • die Pergola • la pérgola • la pergola

paving
le pavé
die Platten
la terraza
la pavimentazione

path
l'allée
der Weg
el camino
il sentiero

compost heap
le tas de compost
der Komposthaufen
el montón de compost
la concimaia

gate
le portail
das Tor
la puerta
il cancello

flowerbed
le parterre
das Blumenbeet
el parterre
l'aiuola

soil • le sol • der
Boden • la tierra
• il terreno

topsoil • la couche arable
• der Kulturboden • la capa
superior de la tierra • lo
strato superiore di terreno

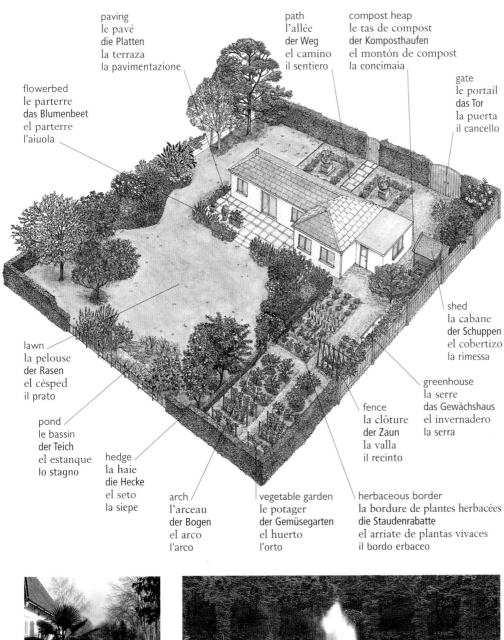

shed
la cabane
der Schuppen
el cobertizo
la rimessa

sand • le sable
• der Sand • la arena
• la sabbia

lawn
la pelouse
der Rasen
el césped
il prato

greenhouse
la serre
das Gewächshaus
el invernadero
la serra

chalk • la chaux • der
Kalk • la creta • la calce

pond
le bassin
der Teich
el estanque
lo stagno

fence
la clôture
der Zaun
la valla
il recinto

hedge
la haie
die Hecke
el seto
la siepe

silt • le vase • der
Schlick • el cieno
• il limo

arch
l'arceau
der Bogen
el arco
l'arco

vegetable garden
le potager
der Gemüsegarten
el huerto
l'orto

herbaceous border
la bordure de plantes herbacées
die Staudenrabatte
el arriate de plantas vivaces
il bordo erbaceo

clay • l'argile • der
Lehm • la arcilla
• l'argilla

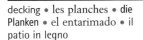

decking • les planches • die
Planken • el entarimado • il
patio in legno

fountain • la fontaine • der Springbrunnen • la fuente • la fontana

garden plants • les plantes de jardin • die Gartenpflanzen • las plantas de jardín • le piante da giardino

types of plants • les genres de plantes • die Pflanzenarten • los tipos de plantas • i tipi di piante

annual • annuel • einjährig • anual • annuale

biennial • bisannuel • zweijährig • bienal • biennale

perennial • vivace • mehrjährig • perenne • perenne

bulb • le bulbe • die Zwiebel • el bulbo • il bulbo

fern • la fougère • der Farn • el helecho • la felce

rush • le jonc • die Binse • el junco • il giunco

bamboo • le bambou • der Bambus • el bambú • il bambù

weeds • les mauvaises herbes • das Unkraut • las malas hierbas • l'erbaccia

herb • l'herbe • das Kraut • la hierba • l'erba aromatica

water plant • la plante aquatique • die Wasserpflanze • la planta acuática • la pianta acquatica

tree • l'arbre • der Baum • el árbol • l'albero

palm • le palmier • die Palme • la palmera • la palma

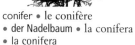

conifer • le conifère • der Nadelbaum • la conífera • la conifera

evergreen • à feuilles persistantes • immergrün • de hoja perenne • sempreverde

deciduous • à feuilles caduques • der Laubbaum • de hoja caduca • a foglie decidue

topiary • la topiaire
• der Formschnitt • las plantas
podadas con formas
• l'arte topiaria

alpine • la plante alpestre
• die Alpenpflanze • la planta
alpestre • le piante da roccia

succulent • la plante grasse
• die Sukkulente • la planta
suculenta • la pianta grassa

cactus • le cactus • der Kaktus
• el cactus • il cactus

potted plant • la plante en pot
• die Topfpflanze • la planta de
tiesto • la pianta in vaso

shade plant • la plante d'ombre
• die Schattenpflanze • la planta de
sombra • la pianta d'ombra

climber
la plante grimpante
die Kletterpflanze
la planta trepadora
la pianta rampicante

flowering shrub
l'arbuste à fleurs
der Zierstrauch
el arbusto de flor
l'arbusto ornamentale

ground cover
la couverture du sol
der Bodendecker
la planta para cubrir
  suelo
la pianta copriterreno

creeper
la plante rampante
die Kriechpflanze
la planta rastrera
la pianta rampicante

ornamental
ornemental
Zier-
ornamental
ornamentale

grass
l'herbe
das Gras
el césped
l'erba

garden tools • les outils de jardin • die Gartengeräte • las herramientas de jardinería • gli attrezzi da giardino

compost • le terreau • die Komposterde • el abono compuesto • il terriccio

seeds • les graines • die Samen • las semillas • i semi

bone meal • la cendre d'os • die Knochenasche • la harina de huesos • la farina di ossa

gravel • le gravier • der Kies • la grava • la ghiaia

lawn rake
le balai à gazon
der Laubrechen
el rastrillo para el césped
la scopa di ferro

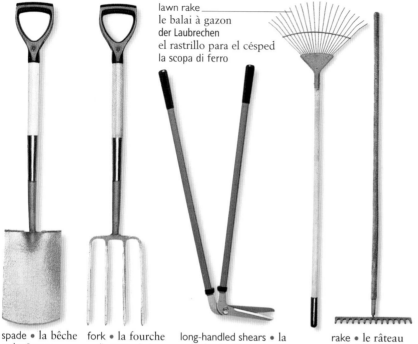

spade • la bêche
• der Spaten
• la pala
• la vanga

fork • la fourche
• die Mistgabel
• la horca
• il forcone

long-handled shears • la grande cisaille • die Schere • la podadera de mango largo • le forbici tagliabordi

rake • le râteau • die Harke • el rastrillo • il rastrello

hoe • la houe • die Hacke • la azada • la zappa

grass bag
le sac à herbe
der Grasfangsack
la bolsa para la hierba
il raccoglierba

motor
le moteur
der Motor
el motor
il motore

handle
le bras
der Griff
el asa
il manico

trug • le panier de jardinier • der Gartenkorb • la cesta de jardinero • il cestello

shield
l'écran de protection
der Schutz
el protector
la protezione

stand
le support
der Ständer
el soporte
il sostegno

trimmer • la tondeuse • der Schneider • el guarnecedor • il tagliabordi

lawnmower • la tondeuse à gazon • der Rasenmäher • el cortacésped • il tosaerba

wheelbarrow • la brouette • die Schubkarre • la carretilla • la carriola

hand fork • la petite fourche • die Handgabel • la horquilla • il forcone

trowel • le déplantoir • die Pflanzschaufel • el desplantador • la paletta

blade
la lame
die Klinge
la hoja
la lama

shears • la cisaille • die Heckenschere • la cizalla • la cesoia per siepi

hand saw • la scie à main • die Handsäge • el serrucho • la sega

secateurs • le sécateur • die Rosenschere • las tijeras de podar • le forbici per potare

seed tray • le germoir • der Setzkasten • el semillero • il semenzaio

pesticide
le pesticide
das Pestizid
el pesticida
il pesticida

gardening gloves
les gants de jardinage
die Gartenhandschuhe
los guantes de jardín
i guanti da giardinaggio

twine
la ficelle
der Zwirn
el hilo de bramante
il fil di ferro

labels
les étiquettes
die Pflanzenschildchen
las etiquetas
le etichette

twist ties
les attaches
die Befestigungen
el alambre
le fettucce

canes
les cannes
die Gartenstöcke
las cañas
le canne

ring ties
les anneaux
die Ringbefestigungen
las anillas
gli anelli

sieve
le tamis
das Sieb
la criba
il setaccio

plant pot
le pot à fleurs
der Blumentopf
la maceta
il vaso da fiori

rubber boots • les bottes • die Gummistiefel • las botas de agua • le galosce

watering • l'arrosage • das Gießen • el riego • l'annaffiare

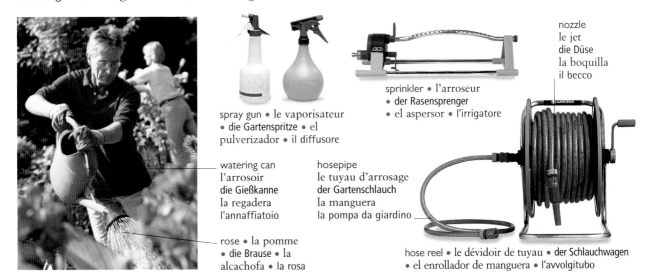

spray gun • le vaporisateur • die Gartenspritze • el pulverizador • il diffusore

watering can
l'arrosoir
die Gießkanne
la regadera
l'annaffiatoio

rose • la pomme • die Brause • la alcachofa • la rosa

sprinkler • l'arroseur • der Rasensprenger • el aspersor • l'irrigatore

hosepipe
le tuyau d'arrosage
der Gartenschlauch
la manguera
la pompa da giardino

nozzle
le jet
die Düse
la boquilla
il becco

hose reel • le dévidoir de tuyau • der Schlauchwagen • el enrollador de manguera • l'avvolgitubo

gardening • le jardinage • die Gartenarbeit • la jardinería • il giardinaggio

lawn
la pelouse
der Rasen
el césped
il prato

flowerbed
le parterre
das Blumenbeet
el parterre
l'aiuola

lawnmower
la tondeuse
der Rasenmäher
el cortacésped
il tosaerba

hedge
la haie
die Hecke
el seto
la siepe

stake
le tuteur
die Stange
la estaca
il bastoncino

mow (*v*) • tondre • mähen • cortar el césped • tagliare l'erba

turf (*v*) • gazonner • mit Rasen bedecken • poner césped • ricoprire di zolle erbose

spike (*v*) • piquer • pikieren • airear el césped • inforcare

rake (*v*) • ratisser • harken • rastrillar • rastrellare

trim (*v*) • tailler • stutzen • podar • potare

dig (*v*) • bêcher • graben • cavar • scavare

sow (*v*) • semer • säen • sembrar • seminare

top dress (*v*) • fumer en surface • mit Kopfdünger düngen • abonar en la superficie • concimare a spandimento

water (*v*) • arroser • gießen • regar • annaffiare

english • français • deutsch • español • italiano

train (v) • palisser • ziehen
• guiar • far crescere

deadhead (v) • enlever les
fleurs fanées • köpfen • quitar
las flores muertas • togliere i
fiori appassiti

spray (v) • asperger • sprühen
• rociar • spruzzare

cane
la canne
der Stock
la caña
la canna

graft (v) • greffer • pfropfen
• injertar • innestare

cutting
la bouture
der Ableger
el esqueje
la propaggine

propagate (v) • propager
• vermehren • propagar
• propagare

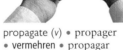
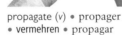

prune (v) • élaguer
• beschneiden • podar
• potare

stake (v) • mettre un tuteur
• hochbinden • apuntalar
• legare a un bastoncino

transplant (v) • transplanter
• umpflanzen • transplantar
• trapiantare

weed (v) • désherber
• jäten • escardar • sarchiare

mulch (v) • pailler • mulchen
• cubrir con pajote •
concimare

harvest (v) • récolter • ernten
• cosechar • raccogliere

cultivate (v)	landscape (v)	fertilize (v)	sieve (v)	organic	seedling	subsoil
cultiver	dessiner	fertiliser	tamiser	biologique	le semis	le sous-sol
züchten	gestalten	düngen	sieben	biologisch	der Sämling	der Untergrund
cultivar	diseñar	abonar	cribar	biológico	el plantón	el subsuelo
coltivare	progettare	concimare	setacciare	biologico	il semenzale	il sottosuolo
tend (v)	pot up (v)	pick (v)	aerate (v)	drainage	fertilizer	weedkiller
soigner	mettre en pot	cueillir	retourner	le drainage	l'engrais	l'herbicide
hegen	eintopfen	pflücken	auflockern	die Entwässerung el	der Dünger	der Unkrautvernichter
cuidar	plantar en tiesto	coger	airear	drenaje	el abono	el herbicida
curare	invasare	cogliere	smuovere	il prosciugamento	il concime	il diserbante

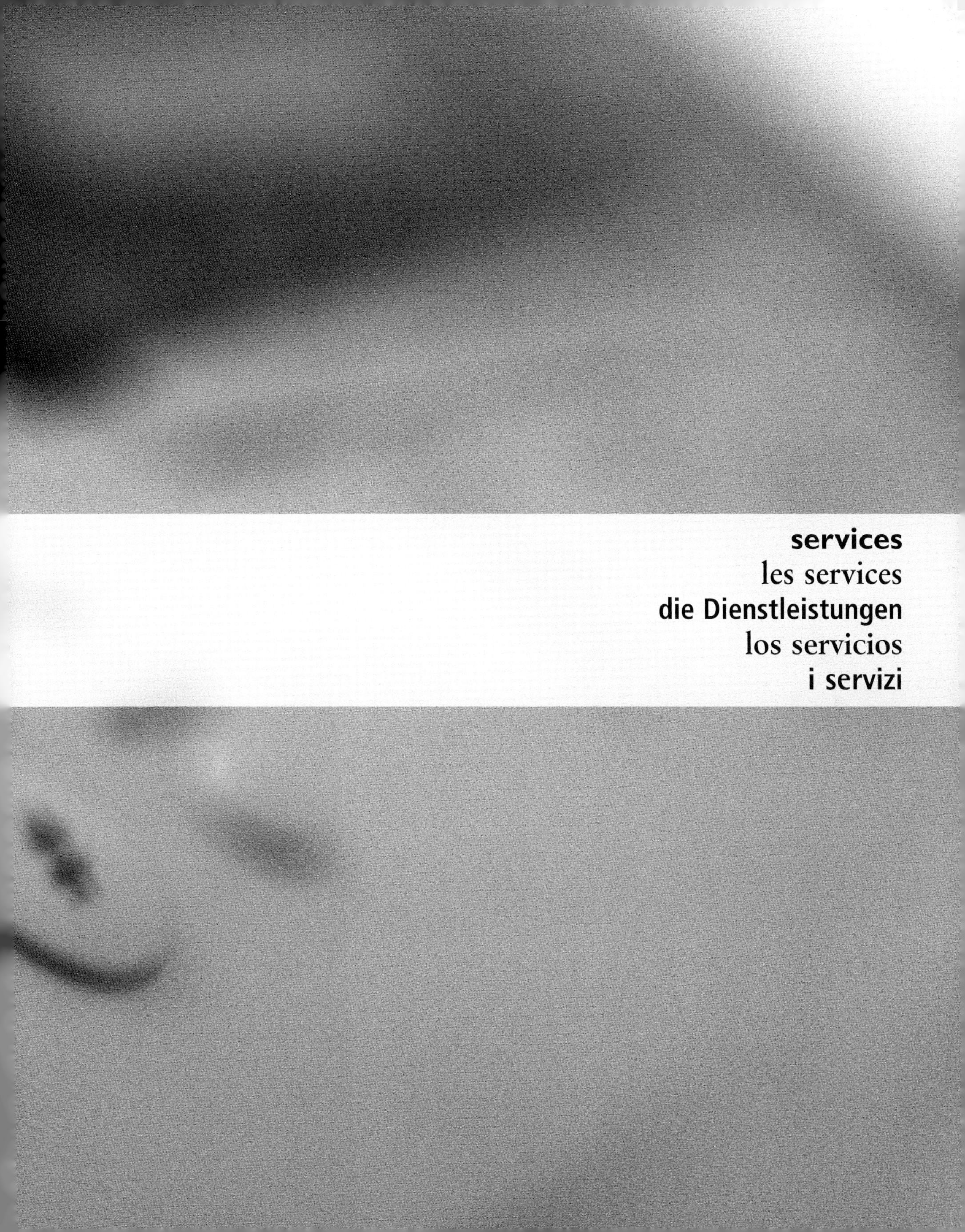

services
les services
die Dienstleistungen
los servicios
i servizi

emergency services • les services d'urgence • die Notdienste • los servicios de emergencia • i servizi di emergenza

ambulance • l'ambulance • der Krankenwagen • la ambulancia • l'ambulanza

stretcher
le brancard
die Tragbahre
la camilla
la barella

ambulance • l'ambulance • der Krankenwagen • la ambulancia • l'ambulanza

paramedic • l'infirmier du SAMU • der Rettungssanitäter • el paramédico • il paramedico

police • la police • die Polizei • la policía • la polizia

badge
le badge
die Kennmarke
la placa
il distintivo

uniform
l'uniforme
die Uniform
el uniforme
l'uniforme

siren
la sirène
die Sirene
la sirena
la sirena

lights
les feux
das Licht
las luces
le luci

police car • la voiture de police • das Polizeiauto • el coche de policía • l'auto della polizia

police station • le poste de police • die Polizeiwache • la comisaría • il posto di polizia

truncheon
la matraque
der Gummiknüppel
la porra
il manganello

gun
le pistolet
die Pistole
la pistola
la pistola

handcuffs
les menottes
die Handschellen
las esposas
le manette

police officer • le policier • der Polizist • el agente de policía • il poliziotto

inspector	burglary	complaint	arrest
l'inspecteur	le cambriolage	la plainte	l'arrestation
der Inspektor	der Einbruchdiebstahl	die Anzeige	die Festnahme
el comisario	el robo	la denuncia	el arresto
il commissario	il furto	la denuncia	l'arresto
detective	assault	investigation	police cell
l'officier de police	l'agression	l'enquête	la cellule
der Detektiv	die Körperverletzung	die Ermittlung	die Polizeizelle
el detective	la agresión	la investigación	la celda
l'investigatore	l'aggressione	l'indagine	la cella
crime	fingerprint	suspect	charge
le crime	les empreintes	le suspect	l'accusation
das Verbrechen	der Fingerabdruck	der Verdächtige	die Anklage
el crimen	la huella dactilar	el sospechoso	los cargos
il reato	l'impronta digitale	il sospetto	l'accusa

fire brigade • les pompiers • die Feuerwehr • los bomberos • i vigili del fuoco

helmet • la casque • der Schutzhelm • el casco • il casco

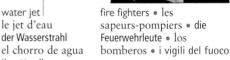

smoke
la fumée
der Rauch
el humo
il fumo

hose
le tuyau
der Schlauch
la manguera
la manichetta
antincendio

cradle
la nacelle
der Auslegerkorb
la cesta
la gabbia

water jet
le jet d'eau
der Wasserstrahl
el chorro de agua
il getto d'acqua

fire fighters • les sapeurs-pompiers • die Feuerwehrleute • los bomberos • i vigili del fuoco

boom
la flèche
der Ausleger
el brazo
il braccio

ladder
l'échelle
die Leiter
la escalera
la scala

cab
la cabine
die Fahrerkabine
la cabina
la cabina

fire • l'incendie • der Brand • el incendio • l'incendio

fire station • le poste d'incendie • die Feuerwache • el parque de bomberos • la caserma dei vigili del fuoco

fire escape • l'escalier de secours • die Feuertreppe • la salida de incendios • la scala d'emergenza

fire engine • la voiture de pompiers • das Löschfahrzeug • el coche de bomberos • l'autopompa

smoke alarm • le détecteur de fumée • der Rauchmelder • el detector de humos • l'allarme antifumo

fire alarm • l'avertisseur d'incendie • der Feuermelder • la alarma contra incendios • il segnalatore d'incendio

axe • la hache • das Beil • el hacha • l'ascia

fire extinguisher • l'extincteur • der Feuerlöscher • el extintor • l'estintore

hydrant • la borne d'incendie • der Hydrant • la boca de agua • l'idrante

---

I need the police/fire brigade/ambulance.
La police/les pompiers/une ambulance, s'il vous plaît.
Die Polizei/die Feuerwehr/einen Krankenwagen, bitte.
Necesito la policía/los bomberos/una ambulancia.
Ho bisogno della polizia/dei vigili del fuoco/di un'ambulanza.

There's a fire at…
Il y a un incendie à…
Es brennt in…
Hay un incendio en…
C'è un incendio a…

There's been an accident.
Il y a eu un accident.
Es ist ein Unfall passiert.
Ha habido un accidente.
C'è stato un incidente.

Call the police!
Appelez la police!
Rufen Sie die Polizei!
¡Llame a la policía!
Chiamate la polizia!

---

bank • la banque • die Bank • el banco • la banca

customer
le client
der Kunde
el cliente
il cliente

window
le guichet
der Schalter
la ventanilla
lo sportello

cashier
le caissier
der Kassierer
el cajero
il cassiere

leaflets
les dépliants
die Broschüren
los folletos
i dépliants

counter
le comptoir
der Schalter
el mostrador
il banco

paying-in slips
les fiches de versement
die Einzahlungsscheine
las hojas de ingreso
i moduli di versamento

debit card
la carte bancaire
die EC-Karte
la tarjeta de débito
la carta di debito

stub
le talon
der Abschnitt
la matriz
la matrice

account number
le numéro de compte
die Kontonummer
el número de cuenta
il numero di conto

signature
la signature
die Unterschrift
la firma
la firma

amount
le montant
der Betrag
el importe
l'importo

bank manager • le directeur
d'agence • der Bankdirektor
• el director de banco
• il direttore di banca

credit card • la carte de
crédit • die Kreditkarte
• la tarjeta de crédito
• la carta di credito

chequebook • le carnet de chèques
• das Scheckheft • el talonario de cheques
• il libretto degli assegni

cheque
le chèque
der Scheck
el cheque
l'assegno

savings	mortgage	payment	pay in (v)	current account
l'épargne	l'hypothèque	le paiement	verser	le compte courant
die Spareinlagen	die Hypothek	die Zahlung	einzahlen	das Girokonto
los ahorros	la hipoteca	el pago	ingresar	la cuenta corriente
i risparmi	l'ipoteca	il pagamento	versare	il conto corrente
tax	overdraft	direct debit	bank transfer	savings account
l'impôt	le découvert	le prélèvement	le virement bancaire	le compte d'épargne
die Steuer	die Kontoüberziehung	der Einzugsauftrag	die Banküberweisung	das Sparkonto
los impuestos	el descubierto	la domiciliación bancaria	la transferencia bancaria	la cuenta de ahorros
l'imposta	lo scoperto	l'addebito diretto	il bonifico bancario	il conto di risparmio
loan	interest rate	withdrawal slip	bank charge	pin number
le prêt	le taux d'intérêt	la fiche de retrait	les frais bancaires	le code secret
das Darlehen	der Zinssatz	das Abhebungsformular	die Bankgebühr	der PIN-Kode
el préstamo	el tipo de interés	el impreso de reintegro	la comisión bancaria	el código pin
il prestito	il tasso d'interesse	il modulo di prelievo	la commissione bancaria	il pin

coin
la pièce
die Münze
la moneda
la moneta

note
le billet
der Schein
el billete
la banconota

screen
l'écran
der Bildschirm
la pantalla
lo schermo

key pad
le clavier
das Tastenfeld
el teclado
la tastiera

card slot
la fente
der Kartenschlitz
la ranura de la tarjeta
la fessura per la carta

money • l'argent • das Geld
• el dinero • il denaro

cash machine • le distributeur • der Geldautomat
• el cajero automático • il bancomat

foreign currency • les devises étrangères • die ausländische Währung • las divisas • la valuta estera

bureau de change • le bureau de change • die Wechselstube • la oficina de cambio • l'ufficio di cambio

traveller's cheque
• le traveller
• der Reisescheck
• el cheque de viaje
• il travel cheque

exchange rate
• le taux de change
• der Wechselkurs
• el tipo de cambio
• il tasso di cambio

cash (v)	shares
encaisser	les actions
einlösen	die Aktien
cobrar	las acciones
incassare	le azioni
denomination	dividends
la valeur	les dividendes
der Nennwert	die Gewinnanteile
el valor nominal	los dividendos
il valore nominale	i dividendi
commission	accountant
la commission	le comptable
die Provision	der Buchhalter
la comisión	el contable
la commissione	il contabile
investment	portfolio
l'investissement	le portefeuille
die Kapitalanlage	das Portefeuille
la inversión	la cartera
l'investimento	il portafoglio
stocks	equity
les titres	le capital
die Wertpapiere	die Stammaktie
los títulos de valores	el patrimonio neto
i titoli	il patrimonio netto

Can I change this please?
Est-ce que je peux changer ça, s'il vous plaît?
Könnte ich das bitte wechseln?
¿Podría cambiar esto por favor?
Potrei cambiare questo, per favore?

What's today's exchange rate?
Quel est le taux de change aujourd'hui?
Wie ist der heutige Wechselkurs?
¿A cuánto está el cambio hoy?
Qual è il tasso di cambio oggi?

finance • la finance • die Geldwirtschaft • las finanzas • la finanza

share price
le prix des actions
der Aktienpreis
el valor de las acciones
il prezzo delle azioni

stockbroker
l'agent de la bourse
der Börsenmakler
el agente de bolsa
il broker

financial advisor • la conseillère financière • die Finanzberaterin • la asesora financiera • la consulente finanziaria

stock exchange • la bourse • die Börse • la bolsa de valores • la borsa

communications • les communications • die Kommunikation • las comunicaciones • le comunicazioni

postal worker
le postier
der Postbeamte
el empleado de correos
l'impiegato delle poste

window
le guichet
der Schalter
la ventanilla
lo sportello

scales
la balance
die Waage
la báscula
la bilancia

counter
le guichet
der Schalter
el mostrador
il banco

post office • la poste • die Post • la oficina de correos • l'ufficio postale

postmark
le tampon de la poste
der Poststempel
el matasellos
il timbro postale

stamp
le timbre
die Briefmarke
el sello
il francobollo

address
l'adresse
die Adresse
la dirección
l'indirizzo

TO: Mr Bradbee de Smyth
BCB DeBaford Road
Borace
SW19 8JL
England

postal code
le code postal
die Postleitzahl
el código postal
il codice di avviamento postale

envelope • l'enveloppe • der Umschlag • el sobre • la busta

postman • le facteur
• der Briefträger • el cartero
• il postino

letter	return address	delivery	fragile	do not bend (v)
la lettre	l'expéditeur	la distribution	fragile	ne pas plier
der Brief	der Absender	die Zustellung	zerbrechlich	nicht falten
la carta	el remite	el reparto	frágil	no doblar
la lettera	il mittente	la consegna	fragile	non piegare
by airmail	signature	postage	mailbag	this way up
par avion	la signature	le tarif d'affranchissement	le sac postal	dessus
per Luftpost	die Unterschrift	die Portokosten	der Postsack	oben
por avión	la firma	el franqueo	la saca postal	hacia arriba
posta aerea	la firma	l'affrancatura	il sacco postale	alto
registered post	collection	postal order	telegram	fax
l'envoi en recommandé	la levée	le mandat postal	le télégramme	le fax
das Einschreiben	die Leerung	die Postanweisung	das Telegramm	das Fax
el correo certificado	la recogida	el giro postal	el telegrama	el fax
la posta raccomandata	la levata della posta	il vaglia postale	il telegramma	il fax

postbox • la boîte aux lettres
• der Briefkasten • el buzón
• la buca delle lettere

letterbox • la boîte aux lettres
• der Hausbriefkasten • el buzón
• la cassetta delle lettere

parcel • le colis • das Paket
• el paquete • il pacco

courier • le service de
messagerie • der Kurierdienst
• el mensajero • il corriere

---

telephone • le téléphone • **das Telefon** • el teléfono • il telefono

handset
le combiné
der Apparat
el auricular
il ricevitore

base station
la base
die Feststation
la base
la base

answering machine
le répondeur
der Anrufbeantworter
el contestador automático
la segreteria telefonica

cordless phone • le téléphone sans fil • **das schnurlose Telefon**
• el teléfono inalámbrico • il telefono senza fili

video phone • le visiophone
• **das Bildtelefon**
• el videoteléfono
• il videotelefono

telephone box • **la cabine
téléphonique** • die Telefonzelle
• la cabina telefónica
• la cabina telefonica

keypad
le clavier
das Tastenfeld
el teclado
la tastiera

mobile phone • le portable
• **das Handy** • el teléfono
móvil • il telefonino

receiver
le combiné
der Hörer
el auricular
il ricevitore

coin return
le rendu de monnaie
die Münzrückgabe
la devolución de las monedas
la restituzione monete

coin phone • le téléphone
à pièces • **der Münzfernsprecher**
• el teléfono de monedas
• il telefono publico a gettoni

card phone • le téléphone
à carte • **das Kartentelefon**
• el teléfono de tarjeta
• il telefono a scheda

---

directory enquiries	answer (v)	operator	Can you give me the number for...?
les renseignements	répondre	le téléphoniste	Pouvez-vous me donner le
die Auskunft	**abheben**	**die Vermittlung**	numéro pour...?
la información telefónica	contestar	el operador	**Können Sie mir die Nummer**
le informazioni telefoniche	rispondere	il centralinista	**für...geben?**
			¿Me podría dar el número de...?
reverse charge call	text message	engaged/busy	Può darmi il numero per...?
le P.C.V.	le texto	occupé	
das R-Gespräch	**die SMS**	**besetzt**	What is the dialling code for...?
la llamada a cobro revertido	el mensaje de texto	comunicando	Quel est l'indicatif pour...?
la chiamata a carico del destinatario	il messaggio di testo	occupato	**Was ist die Vorwahl für...?**
			¿Cuál es el prefijo para llamar
dial (v)	voice message	disconnected	a...?
composer	le message vocal	coupé	Qual'è il prefisso di...?
wählen	**die Sprachmitteilung**	**unterbrochen**	
marcar	el mensaje de voz	cortado	
comporre	il messaggio vocale	interrotto	

---

english • français • deutsch • español • italiano

hotel • l'hôtel • das Hotel • el hotel • l'albergo

lobby • le hall • die Empfangshalle • el vestíbulo • l'ingresso

guest
le client
der Gast
el huésped
l'ospite

room key
la clef de la chambre
der Zimmerschlüssel
la llave de la habitación
la chiave della camera

messages
les messages
die Nachrichten
los mensajes
i messaggi

pigeonhole
le casier
das Fach
la casilla
la casella

receptionist
la réceptionniste
die Empfangsdame
la recepcionista
l'addetta alla ricezione

register
le registre
das Gästebuch
el registro
il registro

counter
le comptoir
der Schalter
el mostrador
il banco

reception • la réception • der Empfang • la recepción • la ricezione

luggage
les bagages
das Gepäck
el equipaje
il bagaglio

trolley
le diable
der Kofferkuli
el carrito
il carrello

porter • le porteur • der Hoteldiener
• el botones • il facchino

lift • l'ascenseur • der Fahrstuhl
• el ascensor • l'ascensore

room number • le numéro de
chambre • die Zimmernummer
• el número de la habitación
• il numero della camera

---

rooms • les chambres • die Zimmer • los habitaciones • le camere

single room • la chambre
simple • das Einzelzimmer
• la habitación individual
• la camera singola

double room • la chambre
double • das Doppelzimmer
• la habitación doble
• la camera doppia

twin room • la chambre à
deux lits • das Zweibettzimmer
• la habitación con dos
camas individuales
• la camera a due letti

private bathroom
• la salle de bain privée
• das Privatbadezimmer
• el cuarto de baño privado
• il bagno privato

---

services • les services • die Dienstleistungen • los servicios • i servizi

breakfast tray • le plateau à petit déjeuner • das Frühstückstablett • la bandeja del desayuno • il vassoio della colazione

maid service • le service de ménage • die Zimmerreinigung • el servicio de limpieza • il servizio di pulizia

laundry service • le service de blanchisserie • der Wäschedienst • el servicio de lavandería • il servizio di lavanderia

room service • le service d'étage • der Zimmerservice • el servicio de habitaciones • il servizio in camera

mini bar • le minibar • die Minibar • el minibar • il minibar

restaurant • le restaurant • das Restaurant • el restaurante • il ristorante

gym • la salle de sport • der Fitnessraum • el gimnasio • la palestra

swimming pool • la piscine • das Schwimmbad • la piscina • la piscina

full board la pension complète die Vollpension la pensión completa la pensione completa	Do you have any vacancies? Avez-vous une chambre de libre? Haben Sie ein Zimmer frei? ¿Tiene alguna habitación libre? Avete una camera libera?	I'd like a room for three nights. Je voudrais une chambre pour trois nuits. Ich möchte ein Zimmer für drei Nächte. Quiero una habitación para tres noches. Vorrei una camera per tre notti.
half board la demi-pension die Halbpension la media pensión la mezza pensione	I have a reservation. J'ai une réservation. Ich habe ein Zimmer reserviert. Tengo una reserva. Ho una prenotazione	What is the charge per night? C'est combien par nuit? Was kostet das Zimmer pro Nacht? ¿Cuánto cuesta la habitación por noche? Quanto costa la camera a notte?
bed and breakfast la chambre avec le petit déjeuner die Übernachtung mit Frühstück la habitación con desayuno incluido il pernottamento e colazione	I'd like a single room. Je voudrais une chambre simple. Ich möchte ein Einzelzimmer. Quiero una habitación individual. Vorrei una camera singola	When do I have to vacate the room? Quand est-ce que je dois quitter la chambre? Wann muss ich das Zimmer räumen? ¿Cuándo tengo que dejar la habitación? Quando devo lasciare la stanza?

shopping
les courses
der Einkauf
las compras
gli acquisti

shopping centre • le centre commercial • das Einkaufszentrum • el centro comercial • il centro commerciale

atrium
l'atrium
das Atrium
el atrio
l'atrio

sign
l'enseigne
das Schild
el letrero
l'insegna

lift
l'ascenseur
der Fahrstuhl
el ascensor
l'ascensore

second floor
le deuxième étage
die zweite Etage
la segunda planta
il secondo piano

first floor
le premier étage
die erste Etage
la primera planta
il primo piano

escalator
l'escalier mécanique
die Rolltreppe
la escalera mecánica
la scala mobile

ground floor
le rez-de-chaussée
das Erdgeschoss
la planta baja
il piano terra

customer
le client
der Kunde
el cliente
il cliente

children's department	customer services	changing rooms	How much is this?
le rayon enfants	le service après-vente	les cabines d'essayage	C'est combien?
die Kinderabteilung	der Kundendienst	die Anprobe	Was kostet das?
la sección infantil	el servicio al cliente	los probadores	¿Cuánto cuesta esto?
il reparto bambini	il servizio clienti	i camerini	Quanto costa questo?
luggage department	store directory	baby changing facilities	May I exchange this?
le rayon bagages	le guide	les soins de bébés	Est-ce que je peux changer ça?
die Gepäckabteilung	die Anzeigetafel	der Wickelraum	Kann ich das umtauschen?
la sección de equipajes	el directorio	el cuarto para cambiar a los bebés	¿Puedo cambiar esto?
il reparto bagagli	la guida al negozio	la stanza di cambio pannolini	Posso cambiare questo?
shoe department	sales assistant	toilets	
le rayon chaussures	le vendeur	les toilettes	
die Schuhabteilung	der Verkäufer	die Toiletten	
la sección de zapatería	el dependiente	los aseos	
il reparto calzature	il commesso	le toilettes	

department store • le grand magasin • **das Kaufhaus** • los grandes almacenes • il grande magazzino

men's wear • les vêtements pour hommes • **die Herrenbekleidung** • la ropa de caballero • l'abbigliamento da uomo

women's wear • les vêtements pour femmes • **die Damenoberbekleidung** • la ropa de señora • l'abbigliamento da donna

lingerie • la lingerie • **die Damenwäsche** • la lencería • la biancheria intima

perfumery • la parfumerie • **die Parfümerie** • la perfumería • la profumeria

beauty • la beauté • **die Schönheitspflege** • los productos de belleza • la bellezza

linen • le linge de maison • **die Wäsche** • la ropa de hogar • la biancheria

home furnishings • l'ameublement • **die Möbel** • el mobiliario para el hogar • l'arredamento per la casa

haberdashery • la mercerie • **die Kurzwaren** • la mercería • la mercerie

kitchenware • la vaisselle • **die Küchengeräte** • el menaje de hogar • gli utensili da cucina

china • la porcelaine • **das Porzellan** • la porcelana • la porcellana

electrical goods • l'électroménager • **die Elektroartikel** • los electrodomésticos • gli articoli elettrodomestici

lighting • l'éclairage • **die Beleuchtung** • la iluminación • l'illuminazione

sports • les articles de sport • **die Sportartikel** • los artículos deportivos • gli articoli sportivi

toys • les jouets • **die Spielwaren** • la juguetería • i giocattoli

stationery • la papeterie • **die Scheibwaren** • la papelería • gli articoli di cartoleria

food hall • l'alimentation • **die Lebensmittelabteilung** • el super-mercado • il reparto alimentari

supermarket • le supermarché • der Supermarkt • el supermercado • il supermercato

aisle • l'allée • der Gang • el pasillo • il passaggio

shelf • l'étàgere • das Warenregal • el estante • lo scaffale

conveyer belt
le tapis roulant
das Förderband
la cinta transportadora
il nastro trasportatore

cashier
le caissier
der Kassierer
el cajero
il cassiere

offers
les promotions
die Angebote
las ofertas
le offerte

checkout • la caisse • die Kasse • la caja • la cassa

customer
le client
der Kunde
el cliente
il cliente

till
la caisse
die Kasse
la caja
la cassa

shopping bag
la sac à provisions
die Einkaufstasche
la bolsa de la compra
la busta della spesa

groceries
les provisions
die Lebensmittel
la compra
la spesa

handle
l'anse
der Henkel
el asa
il manico

trolley • le caddie • der Einkaufswagen • el carro • il carrello

780863 185779

bar code • le code barres • der Strichkode • el código de barras • il codice a barre

basket • le panier • der Einkaufskorb • la cesta • il cestino

scanner • le lecteur optique • der Scanner • el escáner • lo scanner

bakery • la boulangerie
• die Backwaren • la
panadería • il pane

dairy • la crémerie
• die Milchprodukte
• los lácteos • i latticini

breakfast cereals
• les céréales
• die Getreideflocken
• los cereales
• i cereali da colazione

tinned food
• les conserves
• die Konserven
• las conservas
• le conserve

confectionery
• la confiserie
• die Süßwaren • la
confitería • i dolci

vegetables • les
légumes • das Gemüse
• la verdura
• la verdura

fruit • les fruits
• das Obst • la fruta
• la frutta

meat and poultry • la
viande et la volaille •
das Fleisch und das Geflügel
• la carne y las aves
• la carne e il pollame

fish • le poisson
• der Fisch • el
pescado • il pesce

deli • la charcuterie
• die Feinkost • la
charcutería • i salumi

frozen food • les
produits surgelés
• die Tiefkühlkost
• los congelados
• i surgelati

convenience food
• les plats cuisinés
• die Fertiggerichte
• los platos preparados
• i precotti

drinks • les boissons
• die Getränke • las
bebidas • le bibite

household products
• les produits d'entretien
• die Haushaltswaren
• los productos de
limpieza • i casalinghi

toiletries • les articles
de toilette • die
Toilettenartikel • los
artículos de aseo
• i prodotti per il bagno

baby products • les
articles pour bébés
• die Babyprodukte • los
artículos para el bebé
• i prodotti per bambini

electrical goods
• l'électroménager
• die Elektroartikel
• los electrodomésticos
• gli elettrodomestici

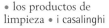
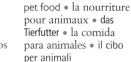

pet food • la nourriture
pour animaux • das
Tierfutter • la comida
para animales • il cibo
per animali

magazines • les magazines • die Zeitschriften
• las revistas • le riviste

chemist • la pharmacie • die Apotheke • la farmacia • la farmacia

dental care
le soin dentaire
die Zahnpflege
el cuidado dental
l'igiene dentale

feminine hygiene
l'hygiène féminine
die Monatshygiene
la higiene femenina
l'igiene femminile

deodorants
les déodorants
die Deos
los desodorantes
i deodoranti

vitamins
les cachets de vitamines
die Vitamintabletten
las vitaminas
le compresse vitaminiche

dispensary
l'officine
die Apotheke
el dispensario
la farmacia

pharmacist
le pharmacien
der Apotheker
el farmacéutico
il farmacista

cough medicine
le médicament pour la toux
das Hustenmedikament
el jarabe para la tos
la medicina per la tosse

herbal remedies
l'herboristerie
Kräuterheilmittel
los remedios de herbolario
i rimedi alle erbe

skin care
les soins de la peau
die Hautpflege
el cuidado de la piel
i prodotti per la pelle

aftersun • l'après-soleil • die After-Sun-Lotion • la loción para después del sol • il doposole

sunscreen • l'écran solaire • die Sonnenschutzcreme • la crema protectora • la crema protettiva solare

sunblock • l'écran total • der Sonnenblocker • la crema protectora total • la crema solare di protezione alta

insect repellent • le produit anti-insecte • das Insektenschutzmittel • el repelente de insectos • l'insettifugo

wet wipe • la serviette humide • das Reinigungstuch • la toallita húmeda • la salviettina umidificata

tissue • le kleenex • das Papiertaschentuch • el pañuelo de papel • il fazzolettino

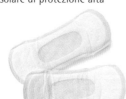

sanitary towel • la serviette hygiénique • die Damenbinde • la compresa • l'assorbente

tampon • le tampon • der Tampon • el tampón • il tampone

panty liner • le protège-slip • die Slipeinlage • el salvaslip • i salvaslip

measuring spoon
la cuiller pour mesurer
der Messlöffel
la cuchara medidora
il cucchiaio misuratore

instructions
le mode d'emploi
die Gebrauchsanweisung
el modo de empleo
le istruzioni

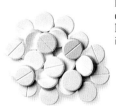

capsule • la capsule • die Kapsel • la cápsula • la pasticca

pill • la pilule • die Tablette • la píldora • la pillola

syrup • le sirop • der Saft • el jarabe • lo sciroppo

inhaler • l'inhalateur • der Inhalierstift • el inhalador • l'inalatore

cream • la crème • die Creme • la crema • la crema

ointment • la pommade • die Salbe • la pomada • la pomata

gel • le gel • das Gel • el gel • il gel

suppository • le suppositoire • das Zäpfchen • el supositorio • la supposta

dropper
le compte-gouttes
der Tropfer
el cuentagotas
il contagocce

needle
l'aiguille
die Nadel
la aguja
l'ago

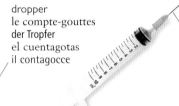

drops • les gouttes • die Tropfen • las gotas • le gocce

syringe • la seringue • die Spritze • la jeringuilla • la siringa

spray • le spray • das Spray • el spray • lo spray

powder • la poudre • der Puder • los polvos • la polvere

iron le fer das Eisen el hierro il ferro	multivitamins le médicament multivitamine das Multivitaminmittel el complejo vitamínico la multivitamina	disposable jetable Wegwerf- desechable monouso	medicine le médicament das Medikament el medicamento la medicina	painkiller l'analgésique das Schmerzmittel el analgésico l'antidolorifico
calcium le calcium das Kalzium el calcio il calcio	side-effects les effets secondaires die Nebenwirkungen los efectos secundarios gli effetti collaterali	soluble soluble löslich soluble solubile	laxative le laxatif das Abführmittel el laxante il lassativo	sedative le sédatif das Beruhigungsmittel el tranquilizante il sedativo
magnesium le magnésium das Magnesium el magnesio il magnesio	expiry date la date d'expiration das Verfallsdatum la fecha de caducidad la data di scadenza	dosage la posologie die Dosierung la dosis il dosaggio	diarrhoea la diarrhée der Durchfall la diarrea la diarrea	sleeping pill le somnifère die Schlaftablette el somnifero il sonnifero
insulin l'insuline das Insulin la insulina l'insulina	travel sickness pills les cachets antinaupathiques die Reisekrankheitstabletten las pastillas para el mareo le pasticche per il mal d'auto	medication la médication die Verordnung la medicación il medicamento	throat lozenge la pastille pour la gorge die Halspastille la pastilla para la garganta la pasticca per la gola	anti-inflammatory l'anti-inflammatoire der Entzündungshemmer el antiinflamatorio l'antinfiammatorio

florist • le fleuriste • das Blumengeschäft • la floristería • il fioraio

flowers
les fleurs
die Blumen
las flores
i fiori

lily
le lis
die Lilie
la azucena
il giglio

acacia
l'acacia
die Akazie
la acacia
l'acacia

carnation
l'œillet
die Nelke
el clavel
il garofano

pot plant
la plante en pot
die Topfpflanze
la maceta
la pianta da vaso

gladiolus
le glaïeul
die Gladiole
el gladiolo
il gladiolo

iris
l'iris
die Iris
el iris
l'iris

daisy
la marguerite
die Margerite
la margarita
la margherita

chrysanthemum
le chrysanthème
die Chrysantheme
el crisantemo
il crisantemo

gypsophila
la gypsophile
das Schleierkraut
la gipsófila
la gipsofila

stocks • la giroflée
• die Levkoje • el alhelí
• la violacciocca

gerbera • le gerbera
• die Gerbera • la
gerbera • la gerbera

foliage • le feuillage
• die Blätter • el follaje
• il fogliame

rose • la rose • die
Rose • la rosa • la rosa

freesia • le freesia
• die Freesie • la fresia
• la fresia

vase • le vase • die Blumenvase • el jarrón • il vaso

orchid • l'orchidée • die Orchidee • la orquídea • l'orchidea

peony • la pivoine • die Pfingstrose • la peonía • la peonia

bunch
la botte
der Strauß
el ramo
il mazzetto

stem
la tige
der Stängel
el tallo
lo stelo

daffodil • la jonquille • die Osterglocke • el narciso • il narciso

bud
le bourgeon
die Knospe
el capullo
il bocciolo

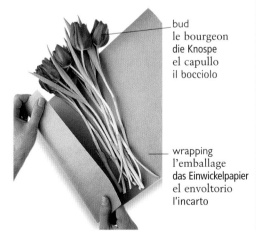

wrapping
l'emballage
das Einwickelpapier
el envoltorio
l'incarto

tulip • la tulipe • die Tulpe • el tulipán • il tulipano

arrangements • les compositions florales • die Blumenarrangements • los arreglos • gli arrangiamenti

ribbon
le ruban
das Band
la cinta
il nastro

bouquet • le bouquet • das Bukett • el ramo • il mazzo di fiori

dried flowers • les fleurs séchées • die Trockenblumen • las flores secas • i fiori secchi

pot-pourri • le pot-pourri • das Potpourri • el popurrí • il pot-pourri

wreath • la couronne • der Kranz • la corona • la corona

garland • la guirlande de fleurs • die Blumengirlande • la guirnalda • la ghirlanda

Can I have a bunch of… please. Je voudrais un bouquet de…, SVP. Ich möchte einen Strauß…, bitte. ¿Me da un ramo de… por favor? Mi dà un mazzo di… per favore?	How long will these last? Elles tiennent combien de temps? Wie lange halten sie? ¿Cuánto tiempo durarán éstas? Quanto dureranno?
Can I have them wrapped? Pouvez-vous les emballer? Können Sie die Blumen bitte einwickeln? ¿Me las puede envolver? Me li può incartare?	Are they fragrant? Est-ce qu'elles sentent bon? Duften sie? ¿Huelen? Sono profumati?
Can I attach a message? Je peux y attacher un message? Kann ich eine Nachricht mitschicken? ¿Puedo adjuntar un mensaje? Posso allegare un messaggio?	Can you send them to….? Pouvez-vous les envoyer à…? Können Sie die Blumen an… schicken? ¿Las puede enviar a…? Li può mandare a…?

newsagent • le marchand de journaux • der Zeitungshändler • el vendedor de periódicos • l'edicola

cigarettes
les cigarettes
die Zigaretten
los cigarrillos
le sigarette

packet of cigarettes
le paquet de cigarettes
das Päckchen Zigaretten
el paquete de tabaco
il pacchetto di sigarette

matches
les allumettes
die Streichhölzer
las cerillas
i fiammiferi

lottery tickets
les billets de loterie
die Lottoscheine
los billetes de lotería
i biglietti della lotteria

stamps
les timbres
die Briefmarken
los sellos
i francobolli

newspaper • le journal
• die Zeitung • el periódico
• il giornale

postcard • la carte postale
• die Postkarte • la tarjeta
postal • la cartolina

comic • la bande dessinée
• das Comicheft • el tebeo
• il giornalino a fumetti

magazine • le magazine
• die Zeitschrift • la revista
• la rivista

---

smoking • fumer • das Rauchen • fumar • fumare

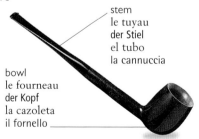

stem
le tuyau
der Stiel
el tubo
la cannuccia

bowl
le fourneau
der Kopf
la cazoleta
il fornello

tobacco • le tabac • der Tabak
• el tabaco • il tabacco

lighter • le briquet • das
Feuerzeug • el mechero
• l'accendino

pipe • la pipe • die Pfeife
• la pipa • la pipa

cigar • le cigare • die Zigarre
• el puro • il sigaro

---

kiosk • le kiosque • der Kiosk • el quiosco • l'edicola

box of chocolates
la boîte de chocolats
die Schachtel Pralinen
la caja de bombones
la scatola di cioccolatini

snack bar
la friandise
die Nascherei
la barrita
lo spuntino

crisps
les chips
die Chips
las patatas fritas
le patatine

sweet shop • la confiserie • das Süßwarengeschäft • la tienda de golosinas
• il negozio di dolciumi

milk chocolate	caramel
le chocolat au lait	le caramel
die Milchschokolade	der Karamell
el chocolate con leche	el caramelo
il cioccolato al latte	il caramello
plain chocolate	truffle
le chocolat noir	la truffe
die Zartbitterschokolade	der Trüffel
el chocolate negro	la trufa
il cioccolato fondente	il tartufo
white chocolate	biscuit
le chocolat blanc	le biscuit
die weiße Schokolade	der Keks
el chocolate blanco	la galleta
il cioccolato bianco	il biscotto
pick and mix	boiled sweets
les bonbons assortis	les bonbons
die bunte Mischung	die Bonbons
las golosinas a granel	los caramelos duros
le caramelle assortite	le caramelle

---

confectionery • la confiserie • die Süßwaren • las golosinas • i dolciumi

chocolate • le chocolat
• die Praline • el bombón
• il cioccolatino

chocolate bar • la tablette de
chocolat • die Tafel Schokolade
• la tableta de chocolate
• la tavoletta di cioccolata

sweets • les bonbons
• die Bonbons • los caramelos
• le caramelle

lollipop • la sucette
• der Lutscher • la piruleta
• il lecca lecca

toffee • le caramel
• das Toffee • el toffee
• la caramella mou

nougat • le nougat • der
Nugat • el turrón • il torrone

marshmallow • la guimauve
• das Marshmallow • la nube
• la caramella gommosa

mint • le bonbon à la menthe
• das Pfefferminz • la pastilla
de menta • la mentina

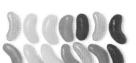

chewing gum • le chewing-
gum • der Kaugummi
• el chicle • la gomma da
masticare

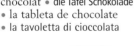

jellybean • la dragée à la
gelée • der Geleebonbon
• el caramelo blando
• la caramella di gelatina

fruit gum • le bonbon au
fruit • der Fruchtgummi
• la gominola • la caramella
alla frutta

licquorice • le réglisse
• die Lakritze • el regaliz
• la liquirizia

other shops • les autres magasins • andere Geschäfte • las otras tiendas • gli altri negozi

baker's • la boulangerie • die Bäckerei • la panadería • il panificio

cake shop • la pâtisserie • die Konditorei • la confitería • la pasticceria

butcher's • la boucherie • die Metzgerei • la carnicería • la macelleria

fishmonger's • la poissonnerie • das Fischgeschäft • la pescadería • la pescheria

greengrocer's • le marchand de légumes • der Gemüseladen • la verdulería • il fruttivendolo

grocer's • l'épicerie • das Lebensmittelgeschäft • el ultra-marinos • il negozio di alimentari

shoe shop • le magasin de chaussures • das Schuhgeschäft • la zapatería • il negozio di calzature

hardware shop • la quincaillerie • die Eisenwaren-handlung • la ferretería • il negozio di ferramenta

antiques shop • le magasin d'antiquités • der Antiquitätenladen • la tienda de antigüedades • il negozio di antiquariato

gift shop • la boutique de cadeaux • der Geschenkartikel-laden • la tienda de regalos • il negozio di articoli da regalo

travel agent's • l'agence de voyage • das Reisebüro • la agencia de viajes • l'agenzia di viaggi

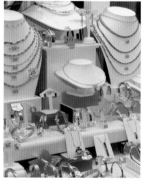

jeweller's • la bijouterie • das Juweliergeschäft • la joyería • la gioielleria

book shop • la librairie
• der Buchladen • la librería
• la libreria

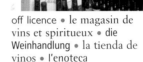

record shop • le magasin de
disques • das Musikgeschäft
• la tienda de discos
• il negozio di dischi

off licence • le magasin de
vins et spiritueux • die
Weinhandlung • la tienda de
vinos • l'enoteca

pet shop • l'animalerie
• die Tierhandlung • la
pajarería • il negozio
di animali

furniture shop • le magasin de
meubles • das Möbelgeschäft
• la tienda de muebles • il
negozio di mobili

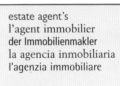

boutique • la boutique
• die Boutique • la boutique
• la boutique

estate agent's l'agent immobilier der Immobilienmakler la agencia inmobiliaria l'agenzia immobiliare	camera shop le magasin d'appareils photos das Fotogeschäft la tienda de fotografía il negozio di articoli fotografici
garden centre la pépinière das Gartencenter el vivero il vivaio	second-hand shop le marchand d'occasion der Gebrauchtwarenhändler la tienda de segunda mano il negozio dell'usato
dry cleaner's le pressing die Reinigung la tintorería la lavanderia	health food shop le magasin bio das Reformhaus la herboristería il negozio di prodotti biologici
launderette la laverie automatique der Waschsalon la lavandería la lavanderia a gettoni	art shop la boutique d'art die Kunsthandlung la tienda de arte il negozio d'arte

tailor's • le tailleur • die
Schneiderei • la sastrería
• la sartoria

hairdresser's • le salon de
coiffure • der Frisiersalon • la
peluquería • il parrucchiere

market • le marché • der Markt • el mercado • il mercato

food
la nourriture
die Nahrungsmittel
los alimentos
il cibo

meat • la viande • das Fleisch • la carne • la carne

lamb
l'agneau
das Lamm
el cordero
l'agnello

butcher
le boucher
der Metzger
el carnicero
il macellaio

meat hook
l'allonge
der Fleischerhaken
el gancho
il gancio

scales
la balance
die Waage
el peso
la bilancia

knife sharpener
le fusil
der Messerschärfer
el afilador
l'affilacoltelli

bacon • le bacon • der Speck • el beicon • la pancetta

sausages • les saucisses • die Würstchen • las salchichas • le salsicce

liver • le foie • die Leber • el hígado • il fegato

pork	venison	offal	free range	red meat
le porc	la venaison	les abats	de ferme	la viande rouge
das Schweinefleisch	das Wild	die Innereien	aus Freilandhaltung	das rote Fleisch
la carne de cerdo	el venado	las asaduras	de granja	la carne roja
la carne di maiale	il cervo	le frattaglie	ruspante	la carne rossa
beef	rabbit	cured	organic	lean meat
le bœuf	le lapin	salé	naturel	la viande maigre
das Rindfleisch	das Kaninchen	getrocknet	biologisch kontrolliert	das magere Fleisch
la carne de vaca	el conejo	curado	biológico	la carne magra
la carne di manzo	il coniglio	messo in salamoia	biologico	la carne magra
veal	tongue	smoked	white meat	cooked meat
le veau	la langue de bœuf	fumé	la viande blanche	la viande cuite
das Kalbfleisch	die Zunge	geräuchert	das weiße Fleisch	der Aufschnitt
la carne de ternera	la lengua	ahumado	la carne blanca	el fiambre
la carne di vitello	la lingua	affumicato	la carne bianca	la carne cotta

cuts • les morceaux de viande • die Fleischsorten • los cortes • i tagli

ham
le jambon
der Schinken
el jamón
il prosciutto

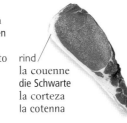

rind
la couenne
die Schwarte
la corteza
la cotenna

slice • la tranche
• die Scheibe • la
loncha • la fetta

rasher • la tranche de
lard • die Speckscheibe
• la loncha de
panceta • la fetta

mince • la viande
hachée • das Hackfleisch
• la carne picada
• la carne macinata

fillet • le filet
• das Filet • el
solomillo • il filetto

rump steak • le rumsteck
• das Rumpsteak • el filete de
contra • la costata di manzo

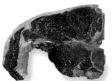

fat
le gras
das Fett
la grasa
il grasso

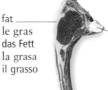

bone
l'os
der Knochen
el hueso
l'osso

kidney
le rognon
die Niere
el riñón
il rognone

sirloin steak • le bifteck
d'aloyau • das Lendensteak
• el entrecot • il filetto di
manzo

rib • la côte de bœuf
• das Rippenstück • la
costilla • la costata

chop • la côtelette
• das Kotelett • la chuleta
• la costoletta

joint • le gigot • die
Keule • la pata de
cordero • il cosciotto

heart • le cœur • das
Herz • el corazón
• il cuore

poultry • la volaille • das Geflügel • las aves • il pollo

skin
la peau
die Haut
la piel
la pelle

breast
le blanc
die Brust
la pechuga
il petto

game
le gibier
das Wildbret
la carne de caza
la cacciagione

leg
la cuisse
das Bein
la pata
la zampa

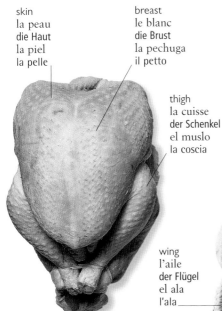

thigh
la cuisse
der Schenkel
el muslo
la coscia

dressed chicken
le poulet préparé
das bratfertige Huhn
el pollo preparado
il pollo preparato

pheasant • le faisan
• der Fasan • el faisán
• il fagiano

quail • la caille • die Wachtel
• la codorniz • la quaglia

wing
l'aile
der Flügel
el ala
l'ala

turkey • la dinde • die Pute
• el pavo • il tacchino

chicken • le poulet • das
Hähnchen • el pollo • il pollo

duck • le canard • die
Ente • el pato • l'anatra

goose • l'oie • die Gans
• la oca • l'oca

fish • le poisson • der Fisch • el pescado • il pesce

peeled prawns
les crevettes décortiquées
die geschälten Garnelen
las gambas peladas
i gamberi sgusciati

red mullet
le rouget barbet
die rote Meerbarbe
el salmonete
la triglia

halibut fillets
les filets de flétan
die Heilbuttfilets
los filetes de fletán
i filetti di ippoglosso

rainbow trout
la truite arc-en-ciel
die Regenbogenforelle
la trucha arco iris
la trota

ice
la glace
das Eis
el hielo
il ghiaccio

skate wings
les ailes de raie
die Rochenflügel
las aletas de raya
le pinne di razza

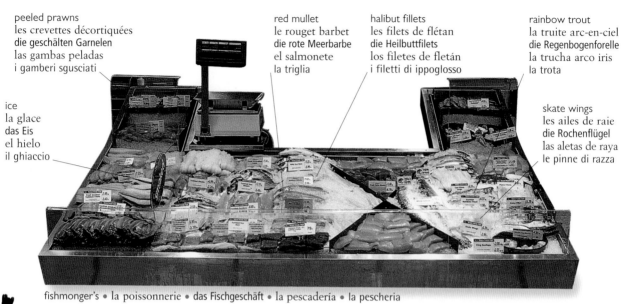

fishmonger's • la poissonnerie • das Fischgeschäft • la pescadería • la pescheria

monkfish • la lotte • der Seeteufel • el rape • la rana pescatrice

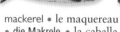

mackerel • le maquereau • die Makrele • la caballa • lo sgombro

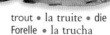

trout • la truite • die Forelle • la trucha • la trota

swordfish • l'espadon • der Schwertfisch • el pez espada • il pesce spada

Dover sole • la sole • die Seezunge • el lenguado • la sogliola

lemon sole • la limande-sole • die Rotzunge • la platija • la sogliola limanda

haddock • l'aiglefin • der Schellfisch • el abadejo • l'eglefino

sardine • la sardine • die Sardine • la sardina • la sardina

skate • la raie • der Rochen • la raya • la razza

whiting • le merlan • der Weißfisch • la pescadilla • il merlango

sea bass • le bar • der Seebarsch • la lubina • la spigola

salmon • le saumon • der Lachs • el salmón • il salmone

cod • la morue • der Kabeljau • el bacalao • il merluzzo

sea bream • la daurade • die Goldbrasse • la dorada • l'abramide

tuna • le thon • der Tunfisch • el atún • il tonno

seafood • les fruits de mer • die Meeresfrüchte • el marisco • i frutti di mare

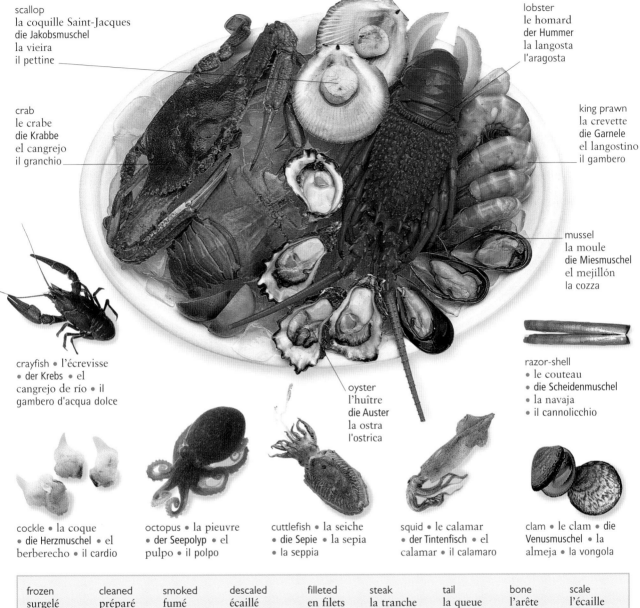

scallop
la coquille Saint-Jacques
die Jakobsmuschel
la vieira
il pettine

lobster
le homard
der Hummer
la langosta
l'aragosta

crab
le crabe
die Krabbe
el cangrejo
il granchio

king prawn
la crevette
die Garnele
el langostino
il gambero

mussel
la moule
die Miesmuschel
el mejillón
la cozza

crayfish • l'écrevisse
• der Krebs • el
cangrejo de río • il
gambero d'acqua dolce

razor-shell
• le couteau
• die Scheidenmuschel
• la navaja
• il cannolicchio

oyster
l'huître
die Auster
la ostra
l'ostrica

cockle • la coque
• die Herzmuschel • el
berberecho • il cardio

octopus • la pieuvre
• der Seepolyp • el
pulpo • il polpo

cuttlefish • la seiche
• die Sepie • la sepia
• la seppia

squid • le calamar
• der Tintenfisch • el
calamar • il calamaro

clam • le clam • die
Venusmuschel • la
almeja • la vongola

frozen	cleaned	smoked	descaled	filleted	steak	tail	bone	scale
surgelé	préparé	fumé	écaillé	en filets	la tranche	la queue	l'arête	l'écaille
tiefgefroren	gesäubert	geräuchert	entschuppt	filetiert	die Schnitte	der Schwanz	die Gräte	die Schuppe
congelado	limpio	ahumado	sin escamas	en filetes	la rodaja	la cola	la espina	la escama
congelato	pulito	affumicato	desquamato	a filetti	la trancia	la coda	la spina	la squama

fresh	salted	skinned	boned	fillet	loin	Will you clean it for me?
frais	salé	sans peau	sans arêtes	le filet	la longe	Pouvez-vous le préparer pour moi?
frisch	gesalzen	enthäutet	entgrätet	das Filet	die Lende	Können Sie ihn mir fertig zubereiten?
fresco	salado	sin piel	sin espinas	el filete	el lomo	¿Me lo puede limpiar?
fresco	salato	spellato	spinato	il filetto	il lombo	Me lo pulisce?

vegetables 1 • les légumes 1 • das Gemüse 1 • las verduras 1 • la verdura 1

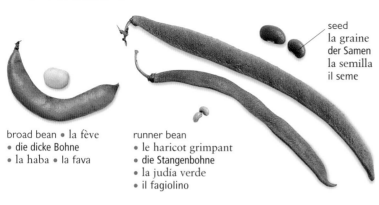

seed
la graine
der Samen
la semilla
il seme

broad bean • la fève
• die dicke Bohne
• la haba • la fava

runner bean
• le haricot grimpant
• die Stangenbohne
• la judía verde
• il fagiolino

French bean • le
haricot vert • die
grüne Bohne • la judía
verde • il fagiolino

garden pea • le petit
pois • die grüne Erbse
• el guisante • il pisello

pod
la gousse
die Schote
la vaina
il baccello

bean sprout • le germe
de soja • die
Sojabohnensprosse
• los brotes de soja
• il germoglio di soia

bamboo • le bambou
• der Bambus • el
bambú • il bambù

okra • l'okra • die
Okra • el quingombó
• l'okra

sweetcorn • le maïs
• der Mais • el maíz
dulce • il granturco

chicory • l'endive
• der Chicorée • la
endibia • la cicoria

fennel • le fenouil
• der Fenchel • el
hinojo • il finocchio

palm hearts • les cœurs
de palmier • die
Palmherzen • los palmitos
• i cuori di palma

celery • le céleri
• der Stangensellerie
• el apio • il sedano

leaf	floret	tip	organic	Do you sell organic vegetables?
la feuille	la fleurette	la pointe	biologique	Est-ce que vous vendez des légumes bios?
das Blatt	das Röschen	die Spitze	biologisch	Verkaufen Sie Biogemüse?
la hoja	la cabezuela	la punta	biológico	¿Vende verduras biológicas?
la foglia	il germoglio	la punta	biologico	Vendete verdure biologiche?
stalk	kernel	heart	plastic bag	Are these grown locally?
le trognon	le grain	le cœur	le sac en plastique	Est-ce qu'ils sont cultivés dans la région?
der Strunk	der Kern	das Herz	die Plastiktüte	Werden sie in dieser Gegend angebaut?
el tallo	el pipo	el centro	la bolsa de plástico	¿Son productos regionales?
lo stelo	il nocciolo	il cuore	la busta di plastica	Sono prodotti della zona?

rocket • la roquette • **die Rauke** • la rúcola • la rucola

watercress • le cresson • **die Brunnenkresse** • el berro • il crescione

radicchio • le radicchio • **der Radicchio** • el radicchio • il radicchio

brussel sprout • le chou de Bruxelles • **der Rosenkohl** • la col de bruselas • il cavolino di Bruxelles

swiss chard • la bette • **der Mangold** • la acelga • la bietola

kale • le chou frisé • **der Grünkohl** • la col rizada • il cavolo verde

sorrel • l'oseille • **der Sauerampfer** • la acedera • l'acetosa

endive • la chicorée • **die Endivie** • la escarola • l'indivia

dandelion • le pissenlit • **der Löwenzahn** • el diente de león • il dente di leone

spinach • les épinards • **der Spinat** • las espinacas • gli spinaci

kohlrabi • le chou-rave • **der Kohlrabi** • el colinabo • il cavolo rapa

pak-choi • le chou chinois • **der Chinakohl** • la col china • la bieta

lettuce • la laitue • **der grüne Salat** • la lechuga • la lattuga

broccoli • le brocoli • **der Brokkoli** • el brócoli • il broccolo

cabbage • le chou • **der Kohl** • el repollo • il cavolo

spring greens • le chou précoce • **der Frühkohl** • la berza • la verza

---

vegetables 2 • les légumes 2 • das Gemüse 2 • las verduras 2 • le verdure 2

cauliflower
le chou-fleur
der Blumenkohl
la coliflor
il cavolfiore

artichoke
l'artichaut
die Artischocke
la alcachofa
il carciofo

radish
le radis
das Radieschen
el rábano
il ravanello

potato
la pomme
de terre
die Kartoffel
la patata
la patata

turnip
le navet
die Rübe
el nabo
la rapa

onion
l'oignon
die Zwiebel
la cebolla
la cipolla

pepper
le poivron
die Paprika
el pimiento
il peperone

chilli • le piment • die Peperoni
• la guindilla • il peperoncino

marrow
la courge
der Gartenkürbis
el calabacín gigante
la zucca

cherry tomato	celeriac	frozen	bitter	Can I have one kilo of potatoes please?
la tomate cerise	le céleri	surgelé	amer	Puis-je avoir un kilo de pommes de
die Kirschtomate	der Sellerie	tiefgefroren	bitter	terre s'il vous plaît?
el tomate cherry	el apio-nabo	congelado	amargo	Könnte ich bitte ein Kilo Kartoffeln
il pomodorino	il sedano rapa	congelato	amaro	haben?
				¿Me da un kilo de patatas, por
carrot	taro root	raw	firm	favor?
la carotte	le taro	cru	ferme	Mi dà un chilo di patate per favore?
die Karotte	die Tarowurzel	roh	fest	
la zanahoria	la raíz del taro	crudo	duro	What's the price per kilo?
la carota	la radice di taro	crudo	sodo	C'est combien le kilo?
				Was kostet ein Kilo?
breadfruit	water chestnut	hot (spicy)	flesh	¿Cuánto vale el kilo?
le fruit de l'arbre à pain	la châtaigne d'eau	épicé	la pulpe	Quanto costa al chilo?
die Brotfrucht	die Wasserkastanie	scharf	das Fleisch	
el fruto del pan	la castaña de agua	picante	la pulpa	What are those called?
il frutto dell'albero del pane	la castagna d'acqua	piccante	la polpa	Ils s'appellent comment?
				Wie heißen diese?
new potato	cassava	sweet	root	¿Cómo se llaman ésos?
la pomme de terre nouvelle	le manioc	sucré	la racine	Quelli come si chiamano?
die neue Kartoffel	der Maniok	süß	die Wurzel	
la patata nueva	la mandioca	dulce	la raíz	
la patata novella	la cassava	dolce	la radice	

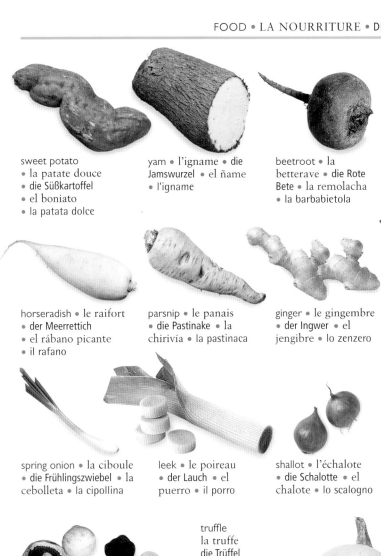

sweet potato
• la patate douce
• die Süßkartoffel
• el boniato
• la patata dolce

yam • l'igname • die
Jamswurzel • el ñame
• l'igname

beetroot • la
betterave • die Rote
Bete • la remolacha
• la barbabietola

swede • le rutabaga
• die Kohlrübe • el
nabo sueco • la rapa
svedese

Jerusalem artichoke
• le topinambour
• der Topinambur
• el topinambur
• il topinambur

horseradish • le raifort
• der Meerrettich
• el rábano picante
• il rafano

parsnip • le panais
• die Pastinake • la
chirivía • la pastinaca

ginger • le gingembre
• der Ingwer • el
jengibre • lo zenzero

aubergine • l'aubergine
• die Aubergine
• la berenjena
• la melanzana

tomato • la tomate
• die Tomate • el tomate
• il pomodoro

spring onion • la ciboule
• die Frühlingszwiebel • la
cebolleta • la cipollina

leek • le poireau
• der Lauch • el
puerro • il porro

shallot • l'échalote
• die Schalotte • el
chalote • lo scalogno

clove
la gousse
die Zehe
el diente
lo spicchio

garlic • l'ail • der
Knoblauch • el ajo
• l'aglio

truffle
la truffe
die Trüffel
la trufa
il tartufo

mushroom • le champignon
• der Pilz • el champiñón
• il fungo

cucumber
• le concombre
• die Gurke • el
pepino • il cetriolo

courgette • la
courgette • die Zucchini
• el calabacín
• la zucchina

butternut squash • la
courge musquée • der
Butternusskürbis • la calabaza
butternut • la zucca

acorn squash • la courge
gland • der Eichelkürbis
• la calabaza bellota
• la zucca a ghianda

pumpkin • la
citrouille • der Kürbis
• la calabaza
• la zucca

fruit 1 • le fruit 1 • das Obst 1 • la fruta 1 • la frutta 1

citrus fruit • les agrumes • die Zitrusfrüchte
• los cítricos • gli agrumi

orange • l'orange
• die Orange • la naranja
• l'arancio

clementine • la clémentine
• die Klementine • la mandarina
clementina • la clementina

pith
• la peau
blanche
• die weiße
Haut • la
médula
• la scorza
interna

ugli fruit • le tangelo • die
Tangelo • el ugli • il mapo

grapefruit • le pamplemousse
• die Grapefruit • el pomelo
• il pompelmo

segment
le quartier
die Rippe
el gajo
lo spicchio

tangerine • la mandarine
• die Mandarine • la mandarina
il mandarino

satsuma • la satsuma
• die Satsuma • la mandarina
satsuma • il satsuma

zest
le zeste
die Schale
la cáscara
la buccia

lime • le citron vert
• die Limone • la lima
• la limetta

lemon • le citron • die Zitrone
• el limón • il limone

kumquat • le kumquat
• die Kumquat • el kumquat
• l'arancino cinese

stoned fruit • les fruits à noyau • das Steinobst
• la fruta con hueso • la frutta con nocciolo

peach • la pêche • der Pfirsich
• el melocotón • la pesca

nectarine • la nectarine
• die Nektarine • la nectarina
• la pesca noce

apricot • l'abricot
• die Aprikose
• el albaricoque
• l'albicocca

plum • la prune
• die Pflaume
• la ciruela
• la prugna

cherry • la cerise
• die Kirsche • la
cereza • la ciliegia

apple • la pomme • der Apfel
• la manzana • la mela

pear • la poire • die Birne
• la pera • la pera

basket of fruit • la corbeille de fruits • der Obstkorb
• la cesta de fruta • il cestino di frutta

berries and melons • les fruits rouges et les melons • das Beerenobst und die
Melonen • las bayas y los melones • i frutti di bosco e i meloni

strawberry • la fraise
• die Erdbeere • la fresa
• la fragola

raspberry • la framboise
• die Himbeere • la frambuesa
• il lampone

melon • le melon
• die Melone • el melón
• il melone

grapes • les raisins
• die Weintrauben • la uva
• l'uva

blackberry • la mûre
• die Brombeere • la mora
• la mora

redcurrant • la groseille
• die Johannisbeere • la
grosella • il ribes rosso

cranberry • la canneberge
• die Preiselbeere • el arándano
rojo • il mirtillo rosso

blackcurrant • le cassis
• die schwarze Johannisbeere
• la grosella negra
• il ribes nero

rind
l'écorce
die Schale
la cáscara
la buccia

seed
le pépin
der Kern
la pepita
il seme

flesh
la pulpe
das Fruchtfleisch
la pulpa
la polpa

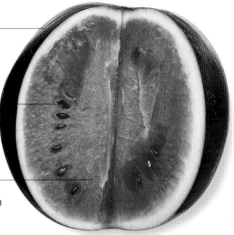

blueberry • la myrtille
• die Heidelbeere •
el arándano • il mirtillo

white currant • la groseille
blanche • die weiße
Johannisbeere • la grosella
blanca • il ribes bianco

watermelon • la pastèque • die Wassermelone • la sandía
• l'anguria

loganberry • la loganberry
• die Loganbeere • la frambuesa
de Logan • la mora-lampone

gooseberry • la groseille à
maquereau • die Stachelbeere
• la grosella espinosa
• l'uva spina

rhubarb	sour	crisp	seedless	Are they ripe?
la rhubarbe	aigre	croquant	sans pépins	Est-ce qu'ils sont mûrs?
der Rhabarber	sauer	knackig	kernlos	Sind sie reif?
el ruibarbo	amargo	fresco	sin pepitas	¿Están maduros?
il rabarbaro	amaro	croccante	senza semi	Sono maturi?
fibre	fresh	rotten	juice	Can I try one?
la fibre	frais	pourri	le jus	Je peux goûter?
die Faser	frisch	faul	der Saft	Könnte ich eine probieren?
la fibra	fresco	podrido	el zumo	¿Puedo probar uno?
la fibra	fresco	marcio	il succo	Posso assaggiarne uno?
sweet	juicy	pulp	core	How long will they keep?
sucré	juteux	la pulpe	le trognon	Ils se gardent combien de temps?
süß	saftig	das Fruchtmark	das Kerngehäuse	Wie lange halten sie sich?
dulce	jugoso	la pulpa	el corazón	¿Hasta cuándo durarán?
dolce	succoso	la polpa	il torsolo	Per quanto tempo si mantengono?

fruit 2 • les fruits 2 • das Obst 2 • la fruta 2 • la frutta 2

mango
la mangue
die Mango
el mango
il mango

pineapple
l'ananas
die Ananas
la piña
l'ananas

avocado
l'avocat
die Avocado
el aguacate
l'avocado

papaya
la papaye
die Papaya
la papaya
la papaia

peach
la pêche
der Pfirsich
el melocotón
la pesca

lychee
le litchi
die Litschi
el lichi
il litchi

pip
le pépin
der Kern
la pepita
il seme

kiwifruit
le kiwi
die Kiwi
el kiwi
il kiwi

cape gooseberry
le physalis
die Kapstachelbeere
el alquequenje
l'alchechengi

skin
la peau
die Schale
la piel
la buccia

quince • le coing • die Quitte • el membrillo • la mela cotogna

passion fruit • le fruit de la passion • die Passionsfrucht • el maracuyá • il frutto della passione

banana • la banane • die Banane • el plátano • la banana

guava • la goyave • die Guave • la guayaba • la guaiava

pomegranate • la grenade • der Granatapfel • la granada • il melograno

persimmon • le kaki • die Persimone • el caqui • il cachi

feijoa • le feijoa • die Feijoa • la feijoa • il feijoa

prickly pear • la figue de Barbarie • die Kaktusfeige • el higo chumbo • il fico d'india

starfruit • la carambole • die Sternfrucht • la carambola • la carambola

mangosteen • le mangoustan • die Mangostane • el mangostán • la mangostina

nuts and dried fruit • les noix et les fruits secs • die Nüsse und das Dörrobst • los frutos secos • le noci e la frutta secca

pine nut • le pignon
• die Piniennuss
• el piñón • il pinolo

pistachio • la pistache
• die Pistazie • el
pistacho • il pistacchio

cashewnut • la noix
de cajou • die
Cashewnuss • el
anacardo • l'anacardio

peanut • la cacahouète
• die Erdnuss • el
cacahuete • l'arachide

hazelnut • la noisette
• die Haselnuss
• la avellana
• la nocciola

brazilnut • la noix du
Brésil • die Paranuss
• la nuez de Brasil
• la mandorla brasiliana

pecan • la noix
pacane • die Pecannuss
• la pacana • il pecan

almond • l'amande
• die Mandel • la
almendra • la mandorla

walnut • la noix • die
Walnuss • la nuez
• la noce

chestnut • le marron
• die Esskastanie • la
castaña • la castagna

shell
la coquille
die Schale
la cáscara
il guscio

macadamia
• le macadamia
• die Macadamianuss
• la macadamia
• la macadamia

fig • la figue • die Feige
• el higo • il fico

date • la datte
• die Dattel • el dátil
• il dattero

prune • le pruneau
• die Backpflaume
• la ciruela pasa
• la prugna secca

flesh
la chair
das Fruchtfleisch
la pulpa
la polpa

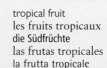

sultana • le raisin de
Smyrne • die Sultanine
• la pasa sultana
• l'uva sultanina

raisin • le raisin sec
• die Rosine • la pasa
• l'uvetta

currant • le raisin de
Corinthe • die Korinthe
• la pasa de Corinto
• l'uva passa

coconut • la noix de
coco • die Kokosnuss
• el coco • la noce di
cocco

green	hard	kernel	salted	roasted	tropical fruit	shelled
vert	dur	l'amande	salé	grillé	les fruits tropicaux	décortiqué
grün	hart	der Kern	gesalzen	geröstet	die Südfrüchte	geschält
verde	duro	la almendra	salado	tostado	las frutas tropicales	pelado
verde	duro	il nocciolo	salato	arrostito	la frutta tropicale	sgusciato
ripe	soft	desiccated	raw	seasonal	candied fruit	whole
mûr	mou	séché	cru	de saison	le fruit confit	complet
reif	weich	getrocknet	roh	Saison-	die kandierten Früchte	ganz
maduro	blando	desecado	crudo	de temporada	la fruta escarchada	entero
maturo	morbido	essiccato	crudo	stagionale	la frutta candita	intero

grains and pulses • les céréales et les légumes secs • die Getreidearten und die Hülsenfrüchte • los cereales y las legumbres • le granaglie e i legumi secchi

grains • les céréales • das Getreide • los granos • le granaglie

wheat • le blé • der Weizen • el trigo • il grano

oats • l'avoine • der Hafer • la avena • l'avena

barley • l'orge • die Gerste • la cebada • l'orzo

millet • le millet • die Hirse • el mijo • il miglio

corn • le maïs • der Mais • el maíz • il mais

quinoa • le quinoa • die Reismelde • la quinoa • la quinoa

seed	fresh	easy cook
la graine	frais	facile à cuisiner
der Samen	frisch	leicht zu kochen
la semilla	fresco	de fácil cocción
il seme	fresco	cottura facile
husk	fragranced	wholegrain
la balle	parfumé	complet
die Hülse	aromatisch	Vollkorn-
la cáscara	perfumado	integral
il baccello	profumato	integrale
kernel	cereal	long-grain
le grain	la céréale	à grains longs
der Kern	die Getreideflocken	Langkorn-
el grano	los cereales	largo
il seme	il cereale	a chiccho lungo
dry	soak (v)	short-grain
sec	laisser tremper	à grains ronds
trocken	einweichen	Rundkorn-
seco	poner a remojo	corto
secco	mettere a bagno	a chiccho corto

rice • le riz • der Reis • el arroz • il riso

white rice • le riz blanc • der weiße Reis • el arroz largo • il riso bianco

brown rice • le riz complet • der Naturreis • el arroz integral • il riso integrale

wild rice • le riz sauvage • der Wildreis • el arroz salvaje • il riso selvatico

pudding rice • le riz rond • der Milchreis • el arroz redondo • il riso a latte

processed grains • les céréales traitées • die verarbeiteten Getreidearten • los granos procesados • i cereali trattati

couscous • le couscous • der Kuskus • el cuscús • il cuscus

cracked wheat • le blé écrasé • das Weizenschrot • el trigo partido • il grano spezzato

semolina • la semoule • der Grieß • la sémola • la semola

bran • le son • die Kleie • el salvado • la crusca

english • français • deutsch • español • italiano

beans and peas • les haricots et les pois • die Bohnen und die Erbsen • las alubias y los guisantes • i fagioli e i piselli

butter beans • les gros haricots blancs • die Mondbohnen • las alubias blancas • i fagioli cannellini

haricot beans • les haricots blancs • die weißen Bohnen • las alubias blancas pequeñas • i fagioli bianchi

red kidney beans • les haricots rouges • die roten Bohnen • las alubias rojas • i fagioli di Spagna

aduki beans • les adzukis • die Adzuki-bohnen • las alubias moradas • i fagioli aduki

broad beans • les fèves • die Saubohnen • las habas • le fave

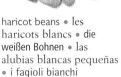

soya beans • les graines de soja • die Sojabohnen • las semillas de soja • i semi di soia

black-eyed beans • les haricots à œil noir • die Teparybohnen • las alubias de ojo negro • i fagioli dall'occhio nero

pinto beans • les haricots pinto • die Pintobohnen • las alubias pintas • i fagioli borlotti

mung beans • les haricots mung • die Mungbohnen • las alubias mung • i fagioli mung

flageolet beans • les flageolets • die französischen Bohnen • las alubias flageolet • i fagioli nani

brown lentils • les lentilles • die braunen Linsen • la lenteja castellana • le lenticchie marroni

red lentils • les lentilles rouges • die roten Linsen • la lenteja roja • le lenticchie rosse

green peas • les petits pois • die grünen Erbsen • los guisantes tiernos • i piselli

chick peas • les pois chiches • die Kichererbsen • los garbanzos • i ceci

split peas • les pois cassés • die getrockneten Erbsen • los guisantes secos • i piselli spaccati

seeds • les graines • die Körner • las semillas • i semi

pumpkin seed • la graine de potiron • der Kürbiskern • la pipa de calabaza • il seme di zucca

mustard seed • le grain de moutarde • das Senfkorn • la mostaza en grano • il seme di mostarda

caraway • la graine de carvi • der Kümmel • la alcaravea • il seme di carvi

sesame seed • la graine de sésame • das Sesamkorn • la semilla de sésamo • il seme di sesamo

sunflower seed • la graine de tournesol • der Sonnenblumenkern • la pipa de girasol • il seme di girasole

herbs and spices • les herbes et les épices • die Kräuter und Gewürze • las hierbas y las especias • le erbe aromatiche e le spezie

spices • les épices • die Gewürze • las especias • le spezie

vanilla • la vanille • die Vanille • la vainilla • la vaniglia

nutmeg • la noix de muscade • die Muskatnuss • la nuez moscada • la noce moscata

mace • le macis • die Muskatblüte • la macis • il macis

turmeric • le curcuma • die Kurkuma • la cúrcuma • la curcuma

cumin • le cumin • der Kreuzkümmel • el comino • il cumino

bouquet garni le bouquet garni die Kräutermischung el bouquet garni il mazzetto odoroso

allspice • le poivre de la Jamaïque • der Piment • la pimienta de Jamaica • il pepe della Giamaica

peppercorn • le grain de poivre • das Pfeffer- korn • la pimienta en grano • il grano di pepe

fenugreek • le fenugrec • der Bockshornklee • la alholva • il fieno greco

chilli • le piment • der Chili • la guindilla • il peperoncino rosso

whole en morceaux ganz entero intero

crushed écrasé zerstoßen machacado tritato

saffron • le safran • der Safran • el azafrán • lo zafferano

cardamom • la cardamome • der Kardamom • el cardamono • il cardamomo

curry powder • la poudre de curry • das Currypulver • el curry en polvo • la polvere di curry

ground en poudre gemahlen molido macinato

paprika • le paprika • der Paprika • el pimentón • la paprica

flakes en flocons geraspelt laminado a scaglie

garlic • l'ail • der Knoblauch • el ajo • l'aglio

herbs • les herbes • die Kräuter • las hierbas • le erbe aromatiche

sticks
les bâtons
die Stangen
las ramas
i bastoncini

cinnamon • la cannelle
• der Zimt • la canela
• la cannella

lemon grass
• la citronnelle
• das Zitronengras • la
citronela • la citronella

cloves • le clou de
girofle • die
Gewürznelke • los clavos
• i chiodi di garofano

star anise • l'anis
étoilé • der Sternanis
• el anís estrellado
• l'anice stellato

ginger • le gingembre
• der Ingwer • el
jengibre • lo zenzero

fennel • le fenouil • der
Fenchel • el hinojo • il
finocchio

chives • la ciboulette
• der Schnittlauch • el
cebollino • l'erba
cipollina

tarragon • l'estragon
• der Estragon • el
estragón • il
dragoncello

oregano • l'origan
• der Oregano • el
orégano • l'origano

fennel seeds
les graines de fenouil
die Fenchelsamen
las semillas de hinojo
i semi di finocchio

mint • la menthe • die
Minze • la menta
• la menta

marjoram • la
marjolaine • der
Majoran • la mejorana
• la maggiorana

coriander • la coriandre
• der Koriander • el
cilantro • il coriandolo

bay leaf • la feuille de
laurier • das Lorbeerblatt
• el laurel • l'alloro

thyme • le thym • der
Thymian • el tomillo
• il timo

basil • le basilic • das
Basilikum • la albahaca
• il basilico

dill • l'aneth • der Dill
• el eneldo • l'aneto

parsley • le persil • die
Petersilie • el perejil
• il prezzemolo

sage • la sauge • der
Salbei • la salvia
• la salvia

rosemary • le romarin
• der Rosmarin • el
romero • il rosmarino

bottled foods • les aliments en bouteilles • die Nahrungsmittel in Flaschen • los alimentos embotellados • i cibi imbottigliati

walnut oil • l'huile de noix • das Walnussöl • el aceite de nueces • l'olio di noce

grapeseed oil • l'huile de pépins de raisin • das Traubenkernöl • el aceite de semillas de uva • l'olio di semi d'uva

cork
le bouchon
der Korken
el corcho
il tappo

sunflower oil • l'huile de tournesol • das Sonnenblumenöl • el aceite de girasol • l'olio di semi di girasole

almond oil • l'huile d'amande • das Mandelöl • el aceite de almendras • l'olio di mandorla

sesame seed oil • l'huile de sésame • das Sesamöl • el aceite de sésamo • l'olio di sesamo

hazelnut oil • l'huile de noisette • das Haselnussöl • el aceite de avellanas • l'olio di noccioline

olive oil • l'huile d'olive • das Olivenöl • el aceite de oliva • l'olio d'oliva

herbs • les herbes • die Kräuter • las hierbas • le erbe aromatiche

flavoured oil • l'huile parfumée • das aromatische Öl • el aceite aromatizado • l'olio aromatizzato

oils • les huiles • die Öle • los aceites • gli oli

sweet spreads • les produits à tartiner • der süße Aufstrich • las confituras • le confetture

jar • le pot • das Glas • el tarro • il barattolo

honeycomb • le gâteau de miel • der Wabenhonig • el panal • il favo

set honey
le miel solide
der feste Honig
la miel compacta
il miele condensato

lemon curd • la pâte à tartiner au citron • der Zitronenaufstrich • la crema de limón • la crema al limone

raspberry jam • la confiture de framboises • die Himbeerkonfitüre • la mermelada de frambuesa • la marmellata di lamponi

marmalade • la confiture d'oranges • die Orangenmarmelade • la mermelada de naranja • la marmellata di agrumi

clear honey • le miel liquide • der flüssige Honig • la miel líquida • il miele sciolto

maple syrup • le sirop d'érable • der Ahornsirup • el jarabe de arce • lo sciroppo d'acero

condiments and spreads • les condiments • die Würzen • los condimentos • condimenti e cibi da spalmare

cider vinegar
le vinaigre de cidre
der Apfelweinessig
el vinagre de sidra
l'aceto di sidro

balsamic vinegar
le vinaigre balsamique
der Gewürzessig
el vinagre balsámico
l'aceto balsamico

bottle
la bouteille
die Flasche
la botella
la bottiglia

English mustard
• la moutarde anglaise
• der englische Senf
• la mostaza inglesa
• la senape

mayonnaise • la mayonnaise
• die Majonäse • la mahonesa
• la maionese

ketchup • le ketchup
• der Ketschup • el
ketchup • il ketchup

French mustard • la
moutarde française
• der französische Senf
• la mostaza francesa
• la senape francese

chutney • le chutney
• das Chutney
• el chutney
• il chutney

malt vinegar
• le vinaigre de malt
• der Malzessig • el
vinagre de malta
• l'aceto di malto

wine vinegar
• le vinaigre de vin
• der Weinessig
• el vinagre de vino
• l'aceto di vino

sauce • la sauce
• die Soße
• la salsa
• la salsa

wholegrain mustard
• la moutarde en
grains • der grobe Senf
• la mostaza en grano
• la senape con semi

vinegar • le vinaigre • der Essig • el vinagre • l'aceto

---

sealed jar • le bocal
scellé • das Einmachglas
• el tarro hermético
• il barattolo a chiusura
ermetica

peanut butter • le beurre
de cacahouètes • die
Erdnussbutter • la mante-
quilla de cacahuete
• il burro di arachidi

chocolate spread • la pâte
à tartiner au chocolat
• der Schokoladenaufstrich
• la crema de cacao • la
cioccolata spalmabile

preserved fruit
• les fruits en bocaux
• das eingemachte Obst
• la fruta en conserva
• la conserva di frutta

vegetable oil l'huile végétale das Pflanzenöl el aceite vegetal l'olio vegetale	rapeseed oil l'huile de colza das Rapsöl el aceite de colza l'olio di colza
corn oil l'huile de maïs das Maiskeimöl el aceite de maíz l'olio di mais	cold-pressed oil l'huile pressée à froid das kaltgepresste Öl el aceite de presión en frío l'olio spremuto a freddo
groundnut oil l'huile d'arachide das Erdnussöl el aceite de cacahuete l'olio di arachide	

---

dairy produce • les produits laitiers • die Milchprodukte • los productos lácteos • i latticini

cheese • le fromage • der Käse • el queso • il formaggio

grated cheese
le fromage râpé
der geriebene Käse
el queso rallado
il formaggio grattugiato

rind
la croûte
die Rinde
la corteza
la crosta

semi-hard cheese
le fromage à pâte pressée non cuite
der mittelharte Käse
el queso semicurado
il formaggio semiduro

hard cheese • le fromage à pâte pressée
cuite • der Hartkäse • el queso curado
• il formaggio duro

cream cheese • le
fromage à la crème
• der Rahmkäse • el
queso cremoso
• il formaggio
cremoso

cottage cheese • le
cottage • der Hütten-
käse • el queso cottage
• il formaggio fresco
tipo fiocchi di latte

blue cheese
• le bleu • der
Blauschimmelkäse
• el queso azul
• il formaggio tipo
gorgonzola

semi-soft cheese • le
fromage à pâte semi-
molle • der halbfeste Käse
• el queso cremoso
semicurado • il
formaggio semimorbido

soft cheese • le fromage à pâte
molle • der Weichkäse • el queso
cremoso • il formaggio morbido

fresh cheese • le fromage frais • der Frischkäse
• el queso fresco • il formaggio fresco

---

milk • le lait • die Milch • la leche • il latte

whole milk
le lait entier
die Vollmilch
la leche entera
il latte intero

semi-skimmed milk
le lait demi-écrémé
die Halbfettmilch
la leche semidesnatada
il latte parzialmente scremato

skimmed milk
le lait écrémé
die Magermilch
la leche desnatada
il latte scremato

milk carton
le carton de lait
die Milchtüte
el cartón de leche
la busta di latte

goat's milk • le
lait de chèvre
• die Ziegenmilch •
la leche de cabra
• il latte di capra

condensed milk
le lait condensé
die Kondensmilch
la leche condensada
il latte condensato

cow's milk • le lait de vache • die Kuhmilch • la leche de vaca • il latte di mucca

butter • le beurre • die Butter
• la mantequilla • il burro

margarine • la margarine
• die Margarine • la margarina
• la margarina

cream • la crème • die Sahne
• la nata • la panna

single cream • la crème allégée
• die fettarme Sahne • la nata
ligera • la panna liquida

double cream
• la crème épaisse
• die süße Sahne
• la nata para montar
• la panna densa

whipped cream
• la crème fouettée
• die Schlagsahne
• la nata montada
• la panna montata

sour cream • la crème
fraîche • die saure
Sahne • la nata agria
• la panna acida

yoghurt • le yaourt
• der Jogurt • el yogur
• lo yogur

ice-cream • la glace
• das Eis • el helado
• il gelato

eggs • les œufs • die Eier • los huevos • le uova

yolk
le jaune d'œuf
das Eigelb
la yema
il tuorlo

egg white
le blanc d'œuf
das Eiweiß
la clara
l'albume

shell
la coquille
die Eierschale
la cáscara
il guscio

egg cup
le coquetier
der Eierbecher
la huevera
il porta uovo

hen's egg • l'œuf de
poule • das Hühnerei
• el huevo de
gallina • l'uovo
di gallina

duck egg • l'œuf de
cane • das Entenei
• el huevo de pato
• l'uovo di anatra

goose egg • l'œuf
d'oie • das Gänseei
• el huevo de oca
• l'uovo d'oca

quail egg • l'œuf de caille
• das Wachtelei • el huevo de
codorniz • l'uovo di quaglia

boiled egg • l'œuf à la coque • das gekochte Ei
• el huevo pasado por agua • l'uovo alla coque

pasteurized	fat free	salted	sheep's milk	lactose	milkshake
pasteurisé	sans matières grasses	salé	le lait de brebis	le lactose	le milk-shake
pasteurisiert	fettfrei	gesalzen	die Schafmilch	die Laktose	der Milchshake
pasteurizado	sin grasa	salado	la leche de oveja	la lactosa	el batido
pastorizzato	senza grassi	salato	il latte di pecora	il lattosio	il frullato
unpasteurized	powdered milk	unsalted	buttermilk	homogenised	frozen yoghurt
non pasteurisé	le lait en poudre	non salé	le babeurre	homogénéisé	le yaourt surgelé
unpasteurisiert	das Milchpulver	ungesalzen	die Buttermilch	homogenisiert	der gefrorene Jogurt
sin pasteurizar	la leche en polvo	sin sal	el suero de la leche	homogeneizado	el yogur helado
non pastorizzato	il latte in polvere	senza sale	il latte fermentato	omogeneizzato	lo yogurt gelato

breads and flours • les pains et la farine • das Brot und das Mehl • el pan y las harinas • il pane e le farine

sliced bread
le pain tranché
das Scheibenbrot
el pan en rebanadas
il pane affettato

poppy seeds
les graines de pavot
der Mohn
las semillas de amapola
i semi di papavero

rye bread
le pain de seigle
das Roggenbrot
el pan de centeno
il pane di segale

baguette
la baguette
das Baguette
la baguette
la baguette

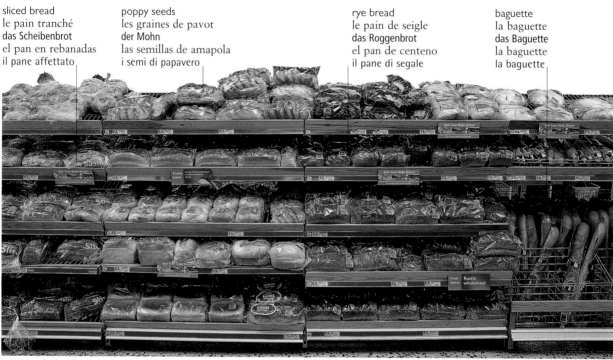

bakery • la boulangerie • die Bäckerei • la panadería • il panificio

---

making bread • faire du pain • Brot backen • haciendo pan • fare il pane

white flour • la farine blanche • das Weizenmehl • la harina blanca • la farina bianca

brown flour • la farine complète • das Roggenmehl • la harina morena • la farina integrale

wholemeal flour • la farine brute • das Vollkornmehl • la harina integral • la farina integrale

yeast • la levure • die Hefe • la levadura • il lievito

dough
la pâte
der Teig
la masa
la pasta

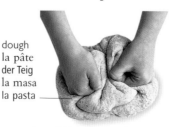

sift (v) • tamiser • sieben • cribar • setacciare

mix (v) • mélanger • verrühren • mezclar • mescolare

knead (v) • pétrir • kneten • amasar • impastare

bake (v) • faire cuir au four • backen • hornear • cuocere al forno

crust
la croûte
die Kruste
la corteza
la crosta

loaf
le pain
der Laib
la hogaza
il filone

slice
la tranche
die Scheibe
la rebanada
la fetta

white bread • le pain blanc
• das Weißbrot • el pan
blanco • il pane bianco

brown bread • le pain bis
• das Graubrot • el pan
moreno • il pane nero

wholemeal bread • le pain de
son • das Vollkornbrot • el pan
integral • il pane integrale

granary bread • le pain
complet • das Mehrkornbrot
• el pan multicereales
• il pane di granaio

corn bread • le pain de maïs
• das Maisbrot • el pan de
maíz • il pane di mais

soda bread • le pain à la
bicarbonate de soude
• das Sodabrot • el pan al
bicarbonato sódico • il pane
lievitato con bicarbonato di sodio

sourdough bread • le pain au
levain • das Sauerteigbrot
• el pan de masa madre
• il pane aspro

flatbread • le pain plat
• das Fladenbrot • el pan sin
levadura • la schiacciata

bagel • le petit pain américain
• das Hefebrötchen • la rosca
• la ciambella

bap • le petit pain rond • das
weiche Brötchen • el bollo • il
panino

roll • le petit pain • das
Brötchen • el panecillo
• il filoncino

fruit bread • le pain aux
raisins secs • das Früchtebrot
• el plumcake • il pane alla
frutta

seeded bread • le pain aux
graines • das Körnerbrot • el pan
con semillas • il pane con semi

naan bread • le naan
• der Naan • el naan
• il naan

pitta bread • le pita
• das Pitabrot • el pan de
pita • la pita

crispbread • le biscuit
scandinave • das Knäckebrot
• el pan crujiente • i crackers

self-raising flour la farine avec la levure das Mehl mit Backpulver la harina con levadura la farina autolievitante	plain flour la farine sans levure das Mehl ohne Backpulver la harina sin levadura la farina semplice	prove (v) lever gehen lassen levar lievitare	breadcrumbs la chapelure das Paniermehl el pan rallado le briciole	slicer la machine à couper der Brotschneider el rebanador l'affettatrice
strong flour la farine traitée das angereicherte Mehl la harina para pan la farina per il pane	rise (v) se lever aufgehen subir crescere	glaze (v) glacer glasieren glasear glassare	flute la flûte das Stangenweißbrot la barra il filoncino	baker le boulanger der Bäcker el panadero il panettiere

cakes and desserts • les gâteaux et les desserts • Kuchen und Nachspeisen • la repostería • i dolci e i dessert

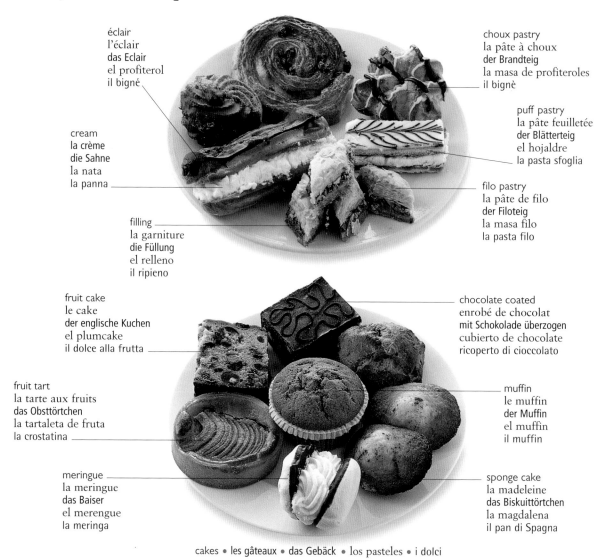

éclair
l'éclair
das Eclair
el profiterol
il bigné

choux pastry
la pâte à choux
der Brandteig
la masa de profiteroles
il bignè

puff pastry
la pâte feuilletée
der Blätterteig
el hojaldre
la pasta sfoglia

cream
la crème
die Sahne
la nata
la panna

filo pastry
la pâte de filo
der Filoteig
la masa filo
la pasta filo

filling
la garniture
die Füllung
el relleno
il ripieno

fruit cake
le cake
der englische Kuchen
el plumcake
il dolce alla frutta

chocolate coated
enrobé de chocolat
mit Schokolade überzogen
cubierto de chocolate
ricoperto di cioccolato

fruit tart
la tarte aux fruits
das Obsttörtchen
la tartaleta de fruta
la crostatina

muffin
le muffin
der Muffin
el muffin
il muffin

meringue
la meringue
das Baiser
el merengue
la meringa

sponge cake
la madeleine
das Biskuittörtchen
la magdalena
il pan di Spagna

cakes • les gâteaux • das Gebäck • los pasteles • i dolci

crème patisserie	bun	pastry	rice pudding	May I have a slice please?
la crème pâtissière	le petit gâteau	la pâte	le riz au lait	Est-ce que je peux avoir une
die Konditorcreme	das Teilchen	der Teig	der Milchreis	tranche s'il vous plaît?
la crema pastelera	el bollo	la masa	el arroz con leche	Könnte ich bitte ein Stück haben?
la crema pasticcera	la pastina	la pasta	il budino di riso	¿Puedo tomar un trozo?
				Posso avere una fetta?
chocolate cake	custard	slice	celebration	
le gâteau au chocolat	la crème anglaise	la tranche	la fête	
die Schokoladentorte	der Vanillepudding	das Stück	die Feier	
el pastel de chocolate	las natillas	el trozo	la celebración	
la torta al cioccolato	la crema	la fetta	la festa	

english • français • deutsch • español • italiano

chocolate chips • les pépites de chocolat • die Schokoladenstückchen • las pepitas de chocolate • i pezzettini di cioccolato

sponge fingers
les boudoirs
die Löffelbiskuits
las soletillas
i savoiardi

florentine
• le florentine
• der Florentiner
• la florentina
• il biscotto alle noci

trifle • le diplomate • das Trifle • el trifle • la zuppa inglese

biscuits • les biscuits • die Kekse • las galletas • i biscotti

mousse • la mousse • die Mousse • la mousse • il mousse

sorbet • le sorbet • das Sorbet • el sorbete • il sorbetto

cream pie • la tarte à la crème • die Sahnetorte • el pastel de nata • la torta alla crema

crème caramel • la crème caramel • der Karamellpudding • el flan • il crème caramel

celebration cakes • les gâteaux de fête • die festlichen Kuchen • las tartas para celebraciones • le torte per celebrazioni

top tier
l'étage supérieur
der obere Kuchenteil
el último piso
il piano superiore

ribbon
le ruban
das Band
la cinta
il nastro

decoration
la décoration
die Dekoration
la decoración
la decorazione

birthday candles
les bougies d'anniversaire
die Geburtstagskerzen
las velas de cumpleaños
le candeline

blow out (v)
souffler
ausblasen
apagar
soffiare

bottom tier
l'étage inférieur
der untere Kuchenteil
el primer piso
il piano inferiore

icing
le glaçage
der Zuckerguss
la alcorza
la glassa

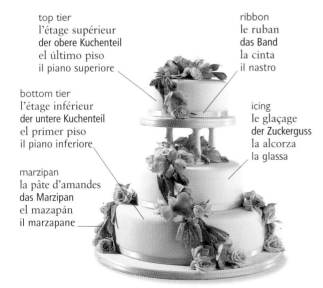

marzipan
la pâte d'amandes
das Marzipan
el mazapán
il marzapane

wedding cake • le gâteau de mariage • die Hochzeitstorte • la tarta nupcial • la torta nuziale

birthday cake • le gâteau d'anniversaire • der Geburtstagskuchen • la tarta de cumpleaños • la torta di compleanno

delicatessen • la charcuterie • die Feinkost • la charcutería • la salumeria

spicy sausage
le saucisson piquant
die pikante Wurst
el fiambre picante
la salsiccia piccante

vinegar
le vinaigre
der Essig
el vinagre
l'aceto

flan • la quiche • die
Quiche • la quiche
• los formato

oil
l'huile
das Öl
el aceite
l'olio

uncooked meat
la viande non cuite
das frische Fleisch
la carne fresca
la carne cruda

counter
le comptoir
die Theke
el mostrador
il banco

salami • le salami
• die Salami • el salami
• il salame

pepperoni • le pepperoni
• die Peperoniwurst
• el salchichón
• il salame piccante

pâté • le pâté • die Pastete
• el paté • il pâté

mozzarella • la mozzarella
• der Mozzarella • la
mozzarella • la mozzarella

brie • le brie • der Brie
• el brie • il brie

goat's cheese • le fromage de
chèvre • der Ziegenkäse • el
queso de cabra • il formaggio
di capra

cheddar • le cheddar • der
Cheddar • el cheddar • il
cheddar

parmesan • le parmesan
• der Parmesan • el
parmesano • il parmigiano

camembert • le camembert
• der Camembert • el
camembert • il camembert

rind
la croûte
die Rinde
la corteza
la scorza

edam • l'édam • der Edamer
• el queso de bola • l'edam

manchego • le manchego
• der Manchego • el
manchego • il manchego

pies • les pâtés en croûte
• die Fleischpasteten
• los pasteles de carne
• i pasticci di carne

black olive
l'olive noire
die schwarze Olive
la aceituna negra
l'oliva nera

chili
le piment
die Peperoni
la guindilla
il peperoncino

sauce
la sauce
die Soße
la salsa
la salsa

bread roll
le petit pain
das Brötchen
el panecillo
il panino

cooked meat
la viande cuite
der Aufschnitt
el fiambre
la carne cotta

green olive
l'olive verte
die grüne Olive
la aceituna verde
l'oliva verde

sandwich counter • le comptoir sandwichs • die Sandwichtheke
• el mostrador de bocadillos • la paninoteca

ham • le jambon
• der Schinken
• el jamón
• il prosciutto

smoked fish • le poisson
fumé • der Räucherfisch
• el pescado ahumado
• il pesce affumicato

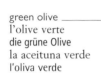

capers • les câpres • die
Kapern • las alcaparras
• i capperi

chorizo • le chorizo
• die Chorizo • el chorizo
• il chorizo

stuffed olive • l'olive fourrée
• die gefüllte Olive • la aceituna
rellena • le olive ripiene

prosciutto • le prosciutto
• der Prosciutto • el jamón
serrano • il prosciutto crudo

in oil • à l'huile • in Öl • en aceite • sott'olio

in brine • en saumure • in Lake • en salmuera • in salamoia

marinated • mariné • mariniert • adobado • marinato

salted • salé • gepökelt • salado • salato

smoked • fumé • geräuchert • ahumado • affumicato

cured • séché • getrocknet • curado • trattato

Take a number please.
Prenez un numéro, s'il vous plaît.
Nehmen Sie bitte eine Nummer.
Coja un número, por favor.
Prenda un numero, per favore.

Can I try some of that please?
Est-ce que je peut goûter un peu de ça, s'il vous plaît?
Kann ich bitte etwas davon probieren?
¿Puedo probar un poco de eso?
Posso assaggiare un po' di quello, per favore?

May I have six slices of that please?
Je voudrais six tranches, s'il vous plaît.
Ich hätte gerne sechs Scheiben davon, bitte.
¿Me pone seis lonchas de aquél?
Mi dia sei fette di quello, per favore?

drinks • les boissons • die Getränke • las bebidas • le bevande

water • l' eau • das Wasser • el agua • l'acqua

bottled water
l'eau en bouteille
das Flaschenwasser
el agua embotellada
l'acqua in bottiglia

sparkling
gazeux
mit Kohlensäure
con gas
frizzante

tap water • l'eau du robinet
• das Leitungswasser • el agua
de grifo • l'acqua dal rubinetto

still
non gazeux
ohne Kohlensäure
sin gas
senza gas

tonic water • le tonic
• das Tonicwater
la tónica • l'acqua
tonica

soda water • le soda
• das Sodawasser • la
soda • la soda

mineral water • l'eau minérale • das Mineralwasser
• el agua mineral • l'acqua minerale

hot drinks • les boissons chaudes • die heißen Getränke • las bebidas calientes • le bevande calde

teabag • le sachet de thé
• der Teebeutel • la bolsita
de té • la bustina di tè

loose leaf tea •
les feuilles de thé
• die Teeblätter
• el té en hoja
• il tè sciolto

tea • le thé • der Tee • el té • il tè

beans • les grains •
die Bohnen • los
granos • i chicchi

ground coffee
le café moulu
der gemahlene Kaffee
el café molido
il caffè macinato

coffee • le café • der Kaffee • el café • il caffè

hot chocolate • le
chocolat chaud • die
heiße Schokolade • el
chocolate caliente
• il cioccolato caldo

malted drink • la
boisson maltée • das
Malzgetränk • la bebida
malteada • la bevanda
al malto

soft drinks • les boissons non alcoolisées • die alkoholfreien Getränke • los refrescos • le bibite

straw • la paille
• der Strohhalm • la
pajita • la cannuccia

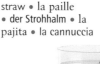

tomato juice • le jus de
tomate • der Tomatensaft
• el zumo de tomate
• il succo di pomodoro

grape juice • le jus de
raisin • der Traubensaft
• el mosto • il succo
d'uva

lemonade • la limonade
• die Limonade • la
limonada • la
limonata

orangeade • l'orangeade
• die Orangenlimonade
• la naranjada
• la spremuta d'arancia

cola • le coca
• die Cola • la cola
• la coca

alcoholic drinks • les boissons alcoolisées • die alkoholischen Getränke • las bebidas alcohólicas • le bevande alcoliche

can
la boîte
die Dose
la lata
la lattina

gin • le gin • der Gin • la ginebra • il gin

beer • la bière • das Bier • la cerveza • la birra

cider • le cidre • der Apfelwein • la sidra • il sidro

bitter • la bière anglaise • das halbdunkle Bier • la cerveza amarga • la birra amara

stout • la bière brune • das Altbier • la cerveza negra • la birra scura

vodka • la vodka • der Wodka • el vodka • la vodka

whisky • le whisky • der Whisky • el whisky • il whisky

rum • le rhum • der Rum • el ron • il rum

brandy • le brandy • der Weinbrand • el brandy • il brandy

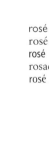

dry • sec • trocken • seco • secco

rosé
rosé
rosé
rosado
rosé

white
blanc
weiß
blanco
bianco

red
rouge
rot
tinto
rosso

port • le porto • der Portwein • el vino de Oporto • il porto

sherry • le sherry • der Sherry • el vino de jerez • lo sherry

campari • le campari • der Campari • el campari • il campari

liqueur • la liqueur • der Likör • el licor • il liquore

tequila • la téquila • der Tequila • el tequila • la tequila

champagne • le champagne • der Champagner • el champán • lo champagne

wine • le vin • der Wein • el vino • il vino

eating out
sortir manger
auswärts essen
comer fuera
mangiare fuori

café • le café • das Café • la cafetería • il caffè

umbrella
le parasol
der Sonnenschirm
la sombrilla
l'ombrellone

awning
le store
die Markise
el toldo
la tenda

menu
le menu
die Speisekarte
la carta
il menù

terrace café • la terrasse de café • das Terrassencafé
• la terraza • il bar con terrazza

waiter
le serveur
der Kellner
el camarero
il cameriere

coffee machine
le percolateur
die Kaffeemaschine
la cafetera
la macchina del caffè

table
la table
der Tisch
la mesa
il tavolo

pavement café • la terrasse de café • das Straßencafé
• la cafetería con terraza • il bar all'aperto

snack bar • le snack • die Snackbar • el bar • lo snack bar

---

coffee • le café • der Kaffee • el café • il caffè

white coffee
le crème
der Milchkaffee
el café con leche
il caffè macchiato

black coffee
le noir
der schwarze Kaffee
el café solo
il caffè nero

cocoa powder
le chocolat en poudre
das Kakaopulver
el cacao en polvo
la polvere di cacao

froth
la mousse
der Schaum
la espuma
la schiuma

filter coffee • le café filtre • der
Filterkaffee • el café americano
• il caffè filtrato

espresso • l'expresso
• der Espresso • el café
solo • il caffè

cappuccino • le cappuccino
• der Cappuccino • el
cappuccino • il cappuccino

iced coffee • le café glacé
• der Eiskaffee • el café helado
• il caffè freddo

tea • le thé • der Tee • el té • il tè

herbal tea
la tisane
der Kräutertee
la infusión
il tè alle erbe

camomile tea • la camomille • der
Kamillentee • la manzanilla • la camomilla

green tea • le thé vert • der grüne Tee
• el té verde • il tè verde

tea with milk • le thé au
lait • der Tee mit Milch
• el té con leche • il tè
con latte

black tea • le thé
nature • der schwarze
Tee • el té
• il tè nero

tea with lemon • le thé
au citron • der Tee mit
Zitrone • el té con
limón • il tè al limone

mint tea • l'infusion de
menthe • der Pfefferminztee
• la menta poleo • il tè
alla menta

iced tea • le thé
glacé • der Eistee
• el té con hielo
• il tè freddo

juices and milkshakes • les jus et milk-shakes • die Säfte und Milchshakes • los zumos y los batidos • le spremute e i frappé

chocolate milkshake
le milk-shake au chocolat
der Schokoladenmilchshake
el batido de chocolate
il frappé al cioccolato

strawberry milkshake
le milk-shake à la fraise
der Erdbeermilchshake
el batido de fresa
il frappé alle fragole

orange juice • le
jus d'orange • der
Orangensaft • el
zumo de naranja
• il succo d'arancia

apple juice • le jus
de pomme • der
Apfelsaft • el zumo
de manzana • il
succo di mela

pineapple juice
• le jus d'ananas
• der Ananassaft
• el zumo de piña
• il succo d'ananas

tomato juice • le jus
de tomate • der
Tomatensaft • el zumo
de tomate • il succo
di pomodoro

coffee milkshake
le milk-shake au café
der Kaffeemilchshake
el batido de café
il frappé al caffè

food • la nourriture • das Essen • la comida • il cibo

brown bread
le pain bis
das Graubrot
el pan integral
il pane integrale

scoop
la boule
die Kugel
la bola
la pallina

toasted sandwich • le sandwich grillé
• das getoastete Sandwich • el sandwich
tostado • il tramezzino tostato

salad • la salade • der Salat
• la ensalada • l'insalata

ice cream • la glace
• das Eis • el helado
• il gelato

pastry • la pâtisserie
• das Gebäck • el bollo
• la pasta

bar • le bar • die Bar • el bar • il bar

glasses	optic	till	bartender	beer tap	coffee machine
les verres	la mesure	la caisse	le barman	la pompe à biere	le percolateur
die Gläser	das Maß	die Kasse	der Barkeeper	der Zapfhahn	die Kaffeemaschine
los vasos	el medidor	la caja	el camarero	el grifo de cerveza	la máquina del café
i bicchieri	il misurino	la cassa	il barista	la spina	la macchina da caffè

ice bucket	bar stool	ashtray	coaster		bar counter
le seau à glace	le tabouret de bar	le cendrier	le dessous de verre		le comptoir
der Eiskübel	der Barhocker	der Aschenbecher	der Untersetzer		die Theke
la champanera	el taburete	el cenicero	el posavasos		la barra
il portaghiaccio	lo sgabello	il posacenere	il sottobicchiere		il banco

bottle opener
l'ouvre-bouteille
der Flaschenöffner
el abrebotellas
l'apribottiglie

lever
le levier
der Hebel
la palanca
la leva

tongs
les pinces
die Eiszange
las pinzas
le pinze

stirrer
l'agitateur
der Cocktailrührer
el agitador
il miscelatore

measure
le verre gradué
der Messbecher
el medidor
il misurino

corkscrew • le tire-bouchon • der Korkenzieher
• el sacacorchos • il cavatappi

cocktail shaker • le shaker à cocktails • der Cocktailshaker
• la coctelera • lo shaker

english • français • deutsch • español • italiano

pitcher
le pichet
der Krug
la jarra
la brocca

ice cube
le glaçon
der Eiswürfel
el cubito de hielo
il cubetto di ghiaccio

gin and tonic • le gin tonic
• der Gin Tonic • el gin tonic
• il gin tonic

scotch and water • le scotch
à l'eau • der Scotch mit Wasser
• el whiskey escocés con
agua • il whisky con acqua

rum and coke • le rhum coca
• der Rum mit Cola • el cuba-
libre • il rum con coca cola

vodka and orange • la vodka
à l'orange • der Wodka mit
Orangensaft • el vodka con
naranja • la vodka all'arancia

martini • le martini
• der Martini • el martini
• il martini

cocktail • le cocktail
• der Cocktail • el cóctel
• il cocktail

wine • le vin • der Wein
• el vino • il vino

beer • la bière • das Bier
• la cerveza • la birra

ice and lemon
citron et glaçons
Eis und Zitrone
con hielo y limón
con ghiaccio e limone

single
simple
einfach
sencillo
singolo

double
double
doppelt
doble
doppio

a shot • un coup • ein Schuss
• un chupito • un bicchiere

measure • la mesure • das
Maß • la medida • la misura

without ice • sans glaçons
• ohne Eis • sin hielo • liscio

with ice • avec des glaçons
• mit Eis • con hielo • con
ghiaccio

---

bar snacks • les amuse-gueule • die Knabbereien • los aperitivos • gli stuzzichini

almonds
les amandes
die Mandeln
las almendras
le mandorle

cashewnuts
les noix de cajou
die Cashewnüsse
los anacardos
gli anacardi

peanuts
les cacahouètes
die Erdnüsse
los cacahuetes
le noccioline americane

crisps • les chips • die Kartoffelchips
• las patatas fritas • le patatine

nuts • les noix • die Nüsse • los frutos secos
• le noccioline

olives • les olives • die Oliven
• las aceitunas • le olive

---

restaurant • le restaurant • das Restaurant • el restaurante • il ristorante

non-smoking section
• la partie non-
fumeurs • der Nicht-
raucherbereich • la zona
de no fumadores • la
zona non fumatori

napkin
la serviette
die Serviette
la servilleta
il tovagliolo

commis chef
le commis
der Hilfskoch
el ayudante del chef
l'aiuto cuoco

table setting
le couvert
das Gedeck
el cubierto
il coperto

chef
le chef de cuisine
der Küchenchef
el chef
il cuoco

glass
le verre
das Glas
la copa
il bicchiere

tray
le plateau
das Tablett
la bandeja
il vassoio

kitchen • la cuisine • die Küche • la cocina
• la cucina

waiter • le garçon • der Kellner
• el camarero • il cameriere

lunch menu	specials	price	tip	buffet	customer
le menu du déjeuner	les spécialités	le prix	le pourboire	le buffet	le client
das Mittagsmenü	die Spezialitäten	der Preis	das Trinkgeld	das Buffet	der Kunde
el menú de la comida	los platos del día	el precio	la propina	el buffet	el cliente
il menù del pranzo	i piatti del giorno	il prezzo	la mancia	il buffet	il cliente
evening menu	à la carte	bill	service included	smoking section	salt
le menu du soir	à la carte	l'addition	service compris	la partie fumeurs	le sel
das Abendmenü	à la carte	die Rechnung	Bedienung inbegriffen	der Raucherbereich	das Salz
el menú de la cena	a la carta	la cuenta	servicio incluido	la zona de fumadores	la sal
il menù della cena	a la carte	il conto	servizio compreso	la zona fumatori	il sale
wine list	sweet trolley	receipt	service not included	bar	pepper
la carte des vins	le chariot à desserts	le reçu	service non compris	le bar	le poivre
die Weinkarte	der Dessertwagen	die Quittung	ohne Bedienung	die Bar	der Pfeffer
la carta de vinos	el carrito de los postres	la factura	servicio no incluido	el bar	la pimienta
la lista dei vini	il carrello dei dolci	la ricevuta	servizio non compreso	il bar	il pepe

english • français • deutsch • español • italiano

menu • la carte • die Speisekarte
• la carta • il menù

child's meal • le menu
d'enfant • die Kinderportion
• el menú para niños
• il menù per bambini

order (v) • commander • bestellen • pedir
• ordinare

pay (v) • payer • bezahlen • pagar • pagare

courses • les plats • die Gänge • los platos • le portate

apéritif • l'apéritif • der
Aperitif • el aperitivo
• l'aperitivo

starter • l'entrée • die
Vorspeise • el entrante
• l'antipasto

soup • la soupe
• die Suppe • la sopa
• la minestra

main course • le plat principal
• das Hauptgericht • el plato principal
• il piatto principale

side order • l'accompagnement
• die Beilage • el acompañamiento
• il contorno

fork
la fourchette
die Gabel
el tenedor
la forchetta

coffee spoon
la cuiller à café
der Kaffeelöffel
la cucharilla de café
il cucchiaino da caffè

dessert • le dessert • der Nachtisch
• el postre • il dessert

coffee • le café • der Kaffee
• el café • il caffè

A table for two please.
Une table pour deux, s'il vous plaît.
Einen Tisch für zwei Personen, bitte.
Una mesa para dos, por favor.
Un tavolo per due, per favore.

Can I see the menu/winelist please?
La carte/la carte des vins, s'il vous plaît.
Die Speisekarte/Weinkarte, bitte.
¿Podría ver la carta/lista de vinos, por favor?
Posso vedere il menù\la lista dei vini, per favore?

Is there a fixed price menu?
Avez-vous un menu à prix fixe?
Haben Sie ein Tagesmenü?
¿Hay menú del día?
C'è un menù a prezzo fisso ?

Do you have any vegetarian dishes?
Avez vous des plats végétariens?
Haben Sie vegetarische Gerichte?
¿Tiene platos vegetarianos?
Avete dei piatti vegetariani ?

Could I have the bill/a receipt please?
L'addition/un reçu, s'il vous plaît.
Könnte ich bitte die Rechnung/eine Quittung haben?
¿Me podría traer la cuenta/un recibo?
Posso avere il conto\una ricevuta per favore?

Can we pay separately?
Est-ce qu'on peut payer séparément?
Können wir getrennt zahlen?
¿Podemos pagar por separado?
Possiamo pagare separatamente?

Where are the toilets, please?
Où sont les toilettes, s'il vous plaît?
Wo sind die Toiletten, bitte?
¿Dónde están los servicios, por favor?
Dove sono i bagni per favore?

english • français • deutsch • español • italiano

fast food • la restauration rapide • der Schnellimbiss • la comida rápida • il fast food

straw
la paille
der Strohhalm
la pajita
la cannuccia

burger
le hamburger
der Hamburger
la hamburguesa
l'hamburger

soft drink
la boisson non-alcoolisée
das alkoholfreie Getränk
el refresco
la bibita

french fries
les frites
die Pommes frites
las patatas fritas
le patate fritte

paper napkin
la serviette en papier
die Papierserviette
la servilleta de papel
il tovagliolo di carta

tray
le plateau
das Tablett
la bandeja
il vassoio

burger meal • le hamburger avec des frites • der Hamburger mit Pommes frites • la hamburguesa con patatas fritas • il hamburger con patate fritte

pizza • la pizza • die Pizza • la pizza • la pizza

price list • le tarif • die Preisliste • la lista de precios • il listino

canned drink
la boisson en boîte
das Dosengetränk
la lata de bebida
la bibita in lattina

pizza parlour
la pizzeria
die Pizzeria
la pizzería
la pizzeria

burger bar
le restaurant rapide
die Imbissstube
la hamburguesería
il fastfood

menu
la carte
die Speisekarte
la carta
il menù

eat-in
manger sur place
hier essen
para comer en el local
mangiare sul posto

take-away
à emporter
zum Mitnehmen
para llevar
da portar via

re-heat (v)
réchauffer
aufwärmen
recalentar
riscaldare

tomato sauce
le ketchup
der Tomatenketschup
el ketchup
il ketchup

Can I have that to go please?
À emporter, s'il vous plaît.
Ich möchte das mitnehmen.
¿Me lo pone para llevar?
Me lo dà da portar via?

Do you deliver?
Est-ce que vous livrez à domicile?
Liefern Sie ins Haus?
¿Entregan a domicilio?
Consegnate a domicilio?

home delivery • la livraison à domicile • die Lieferung ins Haus • la entrega a domicilio • la consegna a domicilio

street stall • le marchand de hot-dogs • der Imbissstand • el puesto callejero • il venditore ambulante

hamburger • le hamburger • der Hamburger • la hamburguesa • l'hamburger

bun
le petit pan
das Brötchen
el bollo
il panino

chicken burger • le hamburger au poulet • der Chickenburger • la hamburguesa de pollo • l'hamburger di pollo

veggie burger • le hamburger végétarien • der vegetarische Hamburger • la hamburguesa vegetariana • l'hamburger vegetariano

mustard
la moutarde
der Senf
la mostaza
la senape

sausage
la saucisse
die Wurst
la salchicha
il wurstel

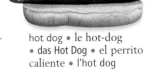

hot dog • le hot-dog • das Hot Dog • el perrito caliente • l'hot dog

sandwich • le sandwich • das Sandwich • el bocadillo • il tramezzino

club sandwich • le sandwich mixte • das Klubsandwich • el club sandwich • il tramezzino a strati

open sandwich • le canapé • das belegte Brot • el sandwich abierto • il tramezzino aperto

filling
la garniture
die Füllung
el relleno
il ripieno

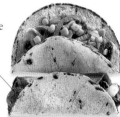

wrap • le taco • das gefüllte Fladenbrot • el taco • la piadina

sauce
la sauce
die Soße
la salsa
la salsa

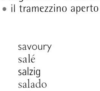

savoury
salé
salzig
salado
salato

sweet
sucré
süß
dulce
dolce

kebab • le kébab • der Kebab • el pincho moruno • il kebab

chicken nuggets • les beignets de poulet • die Hähnchenstückchen • los nuggets de pollo • i bocconcini di pollo

crêpes • les crêpes • die Crêpes • los crepes • le crespelle

topping
la garniture
der Pizzabelag
los ingredientes
il condimento

fish and chips • le poisson avec des frites • der Bratfisch mit Pommes frites • el pescado y las patatas fritas • il pesce con patatine

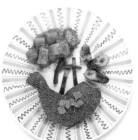

ribs • les côtes • die Rippen • las costillas • le costolette

fried chicken • le poulet frit • das gebratene Hähnchen • el pollo frito • il pollo fritto

pizza • la pizza • die Pizza • la pizza • la pizza

breakfast • le petit déjeuner • das Frühstück • el desayuno • la colazione

milk
le lait
die Milch
la leche
il latte

cereal
les céréales
die Getreideflocken
los cereales
i cereali

jam
la confiture
die Konfitüre
la mermelada
la marmellata

dried fruit
les fruit secs
das Dörrobst
los frutos secos
la frutta secca

ham
le jambon
der Schinken
el jamón
il prosciutto

cheese
le fromage
der Käse
el queso
il formaggio

crispbread
le biscuit scandinave
das Knäckebrot
la galleta de centeno
il pane biscottato

breakfast buffet • le buffet du petit déjeuner • das Frühstücks-
buffet • el bufet de desayuno • il buffet della colazione

marmalade
la confiture d'oranges
die Orangenmarmelade
la mermelada de naranja
la marmellata di agrumi

pâté
le pâté
die Pastete
el paté
il pâté

butter
le beurre
die Butter
la mantequilla
il burro

fruit juice
le jus de fruit
der Obstsaft
el zumo de frutas
il succo di frutta

coffee
le café
der Kaffee
el café
il caffè

croissant
le croissant
das Croissant
el croissant
il cornetto

hot chocolate
le chocolat chaud
der Kakao
el chocolate caliente
la cioccolata calda

tea
le thé
der Tee
el té
il tè

breakfast table • la table du petit déjeuner • der Frühstückstisch
• la mesa del desayuno • il tavolo della colazione

drinks • les boissons • die Getränke • las bebidas
• le bevande

tomato
la tomate
die Tomate
el tomate
il pomodoro

black pudding
le boudin
die Blutwurst
la morcilla
il sanguinaccio

toast
le toast
der Toast
la tostada
il pane tostato

sausage
la saucisse
das Würstchen
la salchicha
la salsiccia

fried egg
l'œuf sur le plat
das Spiegelei
el huevo frito
l'uovo al tegamino

bacon
le bacon
der Frühstücksspeck
el beicon
la pancetta

brioche • la brioche • **die Brioche** • el pan dulce francés • la brioche

bread • le pain • **das Brot** • el pan • il pane

English breakfast • le petit déjeuner anglais • **das englische Frühstück** • el desayuno inglés • la colazione all'inglese

yolk
le jaune d'œuf
das Eigelb
la yema
il tuorlo

kippers • les kippers • **die Räucherheringe** • los arenques ahumados • le aringhe affumicate

french toast • le pain perdu • **die armen Ritter** • la torrija • il pane fritto all'uovo

boiled egg • l'œuf à la coque • **das gekochte Ei** • el huevo pasado por agua • l'uovo alla coque

scrambled eggs • les œufs brouillés • **das Rührei** • los huevos revueltos • le uova strapazzate

cream
la crème
die Sahne
la nata
la panna

fruit yoghurt
le yaourt aux fruits
der Früchtejogurt
el yogur de frutas
lo yogurt alla frutta

pancakes • les crêpes • **die Pfannkuchen** • los crepes • le crêpes

waffles • les gaufres • **die Waffeln** • los gofres • i waffle

porridge • le porridge • **der Haferbrei** • las gachas de avena • il porridge

fresh fruit • les fruits • **das Obst** • la fruta fresca • la frutta fresca

dinner • le repas • die Hauptmahlzeit • la comida principal • la cena

soup • le potage • die Suppe • la sopa • la minestra

broth • le bouillon • die Brühe • el caldo • il brodo

stew • le ragoût • der Eintopf • el guiso • lo stufato

curry • le curry • das Curry • el curry • il curry

roast • le rôti • der Braten • el asado • l'arrosto

pie • la tourte • die Pastete • el pastel • il pasticcio

soufflé • le soufflé • das Soufflé • el soufflé • il soufflé

kebab • le chiche-kébab • das Schaschlik • el pincho • lo spiedino

meatballs • les boulettes de viande • die Fleischklöße • las albóndigas • le polpette

omelette • l'omelette • das Omelett • la tortilla • la frittata

noodles • les nouilles • die Nudeln • los tallarines • i taglierini

stir fry • le sauté • das Pfannengericht • el salteado • la frittura

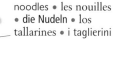

pasta • les pâtes • die Nudeln • la pasta • la pasta

rice • le riz • der Reis • el arroz • il riso

mixed salad • la salade composée • der gemischte Salat • la ensalada mixta • l'insalata mista

green salad • la salade verte • der grüne Salat • la ensalada de lechuga • l'insalata verde

dressing • la vinaigrette • die Salatsoße • el aliño • il condimento

techniques • la préparation • die Zubereitung • las técnicas • i metodi

stuffed • farci • **gefüllt**
• relleno • ripieno

in sauce • en sauce • **in Soße**
• en salsa • al sugo

grilled • grillé • **gegrillt** • a la
plancha • alla griglia

marinated • mariné
• **mariniert** • adobado
• marinato

poached • poché
• **pochiert** • escalfado
• affogato

mashed • en purée • **püriert**
• en puré • passato

baked • cuit • **gebacken**
• cocido en el horno
• cotto al forno

pan fried • sauté • **kurzgebraten**
• a la plancha
• fritto in padella

fried • frit • **gebraten** • frito
• fritto

pickled • macéré • **eingelegt**
• en vinagre • sottaceto

smoked • fumé • **geräuchert**
• ahumado • affumicato

deep fried • frit • **frittiert**
• frito • fritto

in syrup • au sirop • **in Saft**
• en almíbar • allo sciroppo

dressed • assaisonné
• **angemacht** • aliñado
• condito

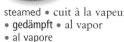

steamed • cuit à la vapeur
• **gedämpft** • al vapor
• al vapore

cured • séché • **getrocknet**
• curado • seccato

study
l'étude
das Lernen
el estudio
lo studio

school • l'école • die Schule • el colegio • la scuola

teacher
l'institutrice
die Lehrerin
la profesora
l'insegnante

blackboard
le tableau
die Tafel
la pizarra
la lavagna

classroom • la salle de classe • das Klassenzimmer
• el aula • l'aula

schoolboy • l'écolier • der
Schuljunge • el colegial • lo scolaro

pupil
l'élève
der Schüler
el alumno
l'alunno

school uniform
l'uniforme
die Schuluniform
el uniforme
la divisa scolastica

desk
le pupitre
das Pult
el pupitre
il banco

school bag
le cartable
die Schultasche
la cartera
la cartella

chalk
la craie
die Kreide
la tiza
il gesso

schoolgirl • l'écolière
• das Schulmädchen
• la colegiala • la scolara

history	art	physics
l'histoire	l'art	la physique
die Geschichte	die Kunst	die Physik
la historia	el arte	la física
la storia	l'arte	la fisica
geography	music	chemistry
la géographie	la musique	la chimie
die Erdkunde	die Musik	die Chemie
la geografía	la música	la química
la geografia	la musica	la chimica
literature	maths	biology
la littérature	les mathématiques	la biologie
die Literatur	die Mathematik	die Biologie
la literatura	las matemáticas	la biología
la letteratura	la matematica	la biologia
languages	science	physical education
les langues	les sciences	l'éducation physique
die Sprachen	die Naturwissenschaft	der Sport
los idiomas	la ciencia	la educación física
le lingue	la scienza	l'educazione fisica

activities • les activités • die Aktivitäten • las actividades • le attività

read (v) • lire • lesen • leer
• leggere

write (v) • écrire • schreiben
• escribir • scrivere

spell (v) • épeler
• buchstabieren • deletrear
• sillabare

draw (v) • dessiner • zeichnen
• dibujar • disegnare

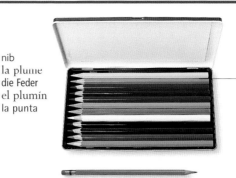

colouring pencil
le crayon de couleur
der Buntstift
el lápiz de colores
la matita colorata

nib
la plume
die Feder
el plumín
la punta

pencil sharpener
le taille-crayon
der Anspitzer
el sacapuntas
il temperamatite

overhead projector • le
rétroprojecteur • der
Overheadprojektor • el proyector
• la lavagna luminosa

pen • le stylo • der Füller
• el bolígrafo • la penna

pencil • le crayon • der
Bleistift • el lápiz • la matita

notebook • le cahier • das Heft
• el cuaderno • il quaderno

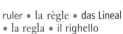

rubber • la gomme • der
Radiergummi • la goma de
borrar • la gomma

textbook • le livre • das Schulbuch • el libro de texto
• il libro di testo

pencil case • la trousse
• das Federmäppchen
• el estuche • l'astuccio

ruler • la règle • das Lineal
• la regla • il righello

question (v) • questionner
• fragen • preguntar
• domandare

answer (v) • répondre
• antworten • contestar
• rispondere

discuss (v) • discuter
• diskutieren • discutir
• discutere

learn (v) • apprendre • lernen
• aprender • imparare

head teacher	answer	grade
le directeur	la réponse	la note
der Schulleiter	die Antwort	die Note
el director	la respuesta	la nota
il preside	la risposta	il livello
lesson	homework	year
la leçon	les devoirs	la classe
die Stunde	die Hausaufgabe	die Klasse
la clase	los deberes	el curso
la lezione	i compiti	la classe
take notes (v)	essay	dictionary
prendre des notes	la rédaction	le dictionnaire
Notizen machen	der Aufsatz	das Wörterbuch
tomar apuntes	la redacción	el diccionario
prendere appunti	il tema	il dizionario
question	examination	encyclopedia
la question	l'examen	l'encyclopédie
die Frage	die Prüfung	das Lexikon
la pregunta	el examen	la enciclopedia
la domanda	l'esame	l'enciclopedia

maths • les mathématiques • die Mathematik • las matemáticas • la matematica

shapes • les formes • die Formen • las formas • le forme

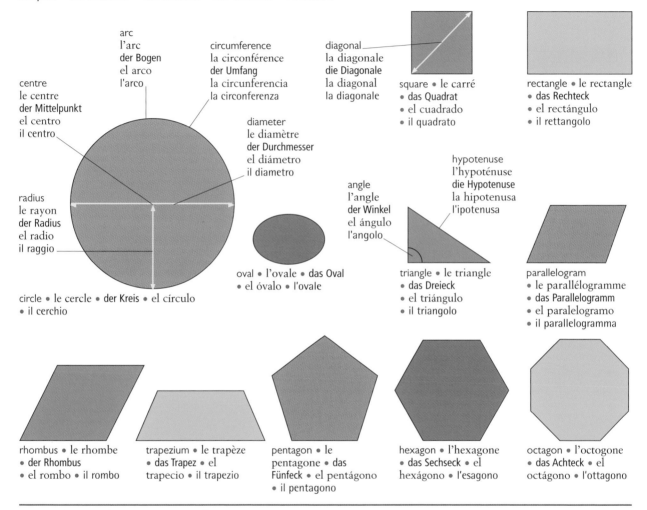

arc
l'arc
der Bogen
el arco
l'arco

circumference
la circonférence
der Umfang
la circunferencia
la circonferenza

diagonal
la diagonale
die Diagonale
la diagonal
la diagonale

square • le carré
• das Quadrat
• el cuadrado
• il quadrato

rectangle • le rectangle
• das Rechteck
• el rectángulo
• il rettangolo

centre
le centre
der Mittelpunkt
el centro
il centro

diameter
le diamètre
der Durchmesser
el diámetro
il diametro

hypotenuse
l'hypoténuse
die Hypotenuse
la hipotenusa
l'ipotenusa

radius
le rayon
der Radius
el radio
il raggio

angle
l'angle
der Winkel
el ángulo
l'angolo

oval • l'ovale • das Oval
• el óvalo • l'ovale

triangle • le triangle
• das Dreieck
• el triángulo
• il triangolo

parallelogram
• le parallélogramme
• das Parallelogramm
• el paralelogramo
• il parallelogramma

circle • le cercle • der Kreis • el círculo
• il cerchio

rhombus • le rhombe
• der Rhombus
• el rombo • il rombo

trapezium • le trapèze
• das Trapez • el
trapecio • il trapezio

pentagon • le
pentagone • das
Fünfeck • el pentágono
• il pentagono

hexagon • l'hexagone
• das Sechseck • el
hexágono • l'esagono

octagon • l'octogone
• das Achteck • el
octágono • l'ottagono

---

solids • les solides • die Körper • los cuerpos geométricos • i solidi

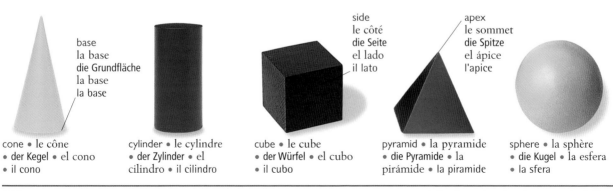

base
la base
die Grundfläche
la base
la base

side
le côté
die Seite
el lado
il lato

apex
le sommet
die Spitze
el ápice
l'apice

cone • le cône
• der Kegel • el cono
• il cono

cylinder • le cylindre
• der Zylinder • el
cilindro • il cilindro

cube • le cube
• der Würfel • el cubo
• il cubo

pyramid • la pyramide
• die Pyramide • la
pirámide • la piramide

sphere • la sphère
• die Kugel • la esfera
• la sfera

---

lines • les lignes • die Linien • las líneas • le linee

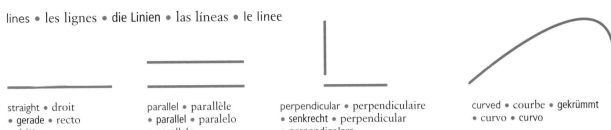

straight • droit
• gerade • recto
• dritto

parallel • parallèle
• parallel • paralelo
• parallelo

perpendicular • perpendiculaire
• senkrecht • perpendicular
• perpendicolare

curved • courbe • gekrümmt
• curvo • curvo

measurements • les mesures • die Maße • las medidas • le misure

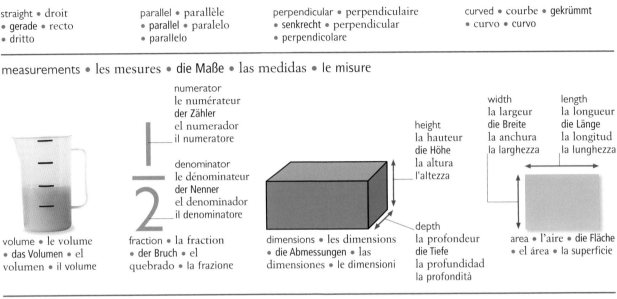

volume • le volume
• das Volumen • el
volumen • il volume

numerator
le numérateur
der Zähler
el numerador
il numeratore

denominator
le dénominateur
der Nenner
el denominador
il denominatore

fraction • la fraction
• der Bruch • el
quebrado • la frazione

dimensions • les dimensions
• die Abmessungen • las
dimensiones • le dimensioni

height
la hauteur
die Höhe
la altura
l'altezza

depth
la profondeur
die Tiefe
la profundidad
la profondità

width
la largeur
die Breite
la anchura
la larghezza

length
la longueur
die Länge
la longitud
la lunghezza

area • l'aire • die Fläche
• el área • la superficie

equipment • l'équipement • die Ausrüstung • los materiales • l'attrezzatura

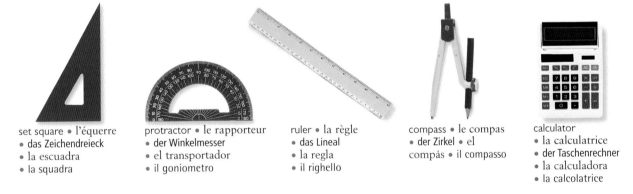

set square • l'équerre
• das Zeichendreieck
• la escuadra
• la squadra

protractor • le rapporteur
• der Winkelmesser
• el transportador
• il goniometro

ruler • la règle
• das Lineal
• la regla
• il righello

compass • le compas
• der Zirkel • el
compás • il compasso

calculator
• la calculatrice
• der Taschenrechner
• la calculadora
• la calcolatrice

geometry	plus	times	equals	add (v)	multiply (v)	equation
la géométrie	plus	fois	égale(nt)	additionner	multiplier	l'équation
die Geometrie	plus	mal	gleich	addieren	multiplizieren	die Gleichung
la geometría	más	multiplicado por	igual a	sumar	multiplicar	la ecuación
la geometria	più	moltiplicato per	uguale	sommare	moltiplicare	l'equazione
arithmetic	minus	divided by	count (v)	subtract (v)	divide (v)	percentage
l'arithmétique	moins	divisé par	compter	soustraire	diviser	le pourcentage
die Arithmetik	minus	geteilt durch	zählen	subtrahieren	dividieren	der Prozentsatz
la aritmética	menos	dividido por	contar	restar	dividir	el porcentaje
l'aritmetica	meno	diviso per	contare	sottrarre	dividere	la percentuale

science • la science • die Wissenschaft • las ciencias • la scienza

laboratory • le laboratoire
• das Labor • el laboratorio
• il laboratorio

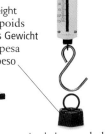

scales • la balance • die
Laborwaage • la báscula
• la bilancia

weight
le poids
das Gewicht
la pesa
il peso

spring balance • la balance
à ressort • die Federwaage
• la balanza de muelle
• la bilancia a molla

crucible • le creuset
• der Tiegel • el crisol
• il crogiolo

bunsen burner
le bec Bunsen
der Bunsenbrenner
el mechero Bunsen
il becco Bunsen

tripod • le trépied
• der Dreifuß • el trípode
• il treppiede

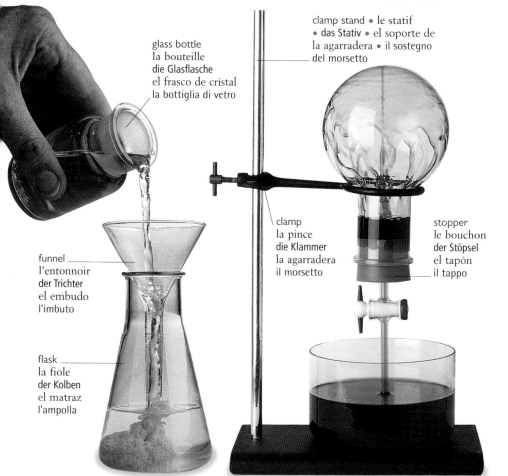

glass bottle
la bouteille
die Glasflasche
el frasco de cristal
la bottiglia di vetro

clamp stand • le statif
• das Stativ • el soporte de
la agarradera • il sostegno
del morsetto

clamp
la pince
die Klammer
la agarradera
il morsetto

stopper
le bouchon
der Stöpsel
el tapón
il tappo

funnel
l'entonnoir
der Trichter
el embudo
l'imbuto

flask
la fiole
der Kolben
el matraz
l'ampolla

test tube
l'éprouvette
das Reagenzglas
el tubo de ensayo
la provetta

rack • le support • das Gestell
• el soporte • la rastrelliera

timer • le chronomètre • der
Zeitmesser • el cronómetro
• il cronometro

petri dish • la boîte de Pétri
• die Petrischale • la cápsula
de Petri • la capsula di Petri

experiment • l'expérience • der Versuch • el experimento • l'esperimento

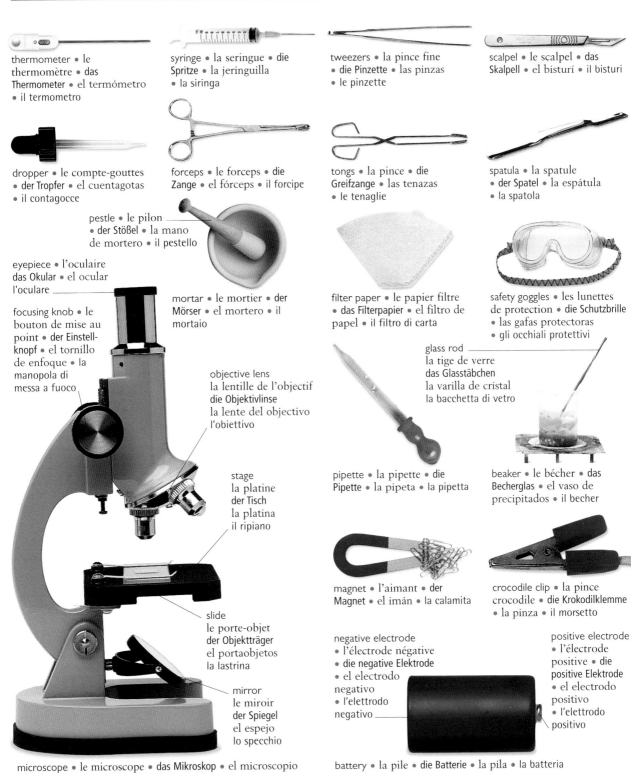

thermometer • le thermomètre • das Thermometer • el termómetro • il termometro

syringe • la seringue • die Spritze • la jeringuilla • la siringa

tweezers • la pince fine • die Pinzette • las pinzas • le pinzette

scalpel • le scalpel • das Skalpell • el bisturí • il bisturi

dropper • le compte-gouttes • der Tropfer • el cuentagotas • il contagocce

forceps • le forceps • die Zange • el fórceps • il forcipe

tongs • la pince • die Greifzange • las tenazas • le tenaglie

spatula • la spatule • der Spatel • la espátula • la spatola

pestle • le pilon • der Stößel • la mano de mortero • il pestello

eyepiece • l'oculaire das Okular • el ocular l'oculare

focusing knob • le bouton de mise au point • der Einstell-knopf • el tornillo de enfoque • la manopola di messa a fuoco

mortar • le mortier • der Mörser • el mortero • il mortaio

filter paper • le papier filtre • das Filterpapier • el filtro de papel • il filtro di carta

safety goggles • les lunettes de protection • die Schutzbrille • las gafas protectoras • gli occhiali protettivi

objective lens la lentille de l'objectif die Objektivlinse la lente del objectivo l'obiettivo

glass rod la tige de verre das Glasstäbchen la varilla de cristal la bacchetta di vetro

stage la platine der Tisch la platina il ripiano

pipette • la pipette • die Pipette • la pipeta • la pipetta

beaker • le bécher • das Becherglas • el vaso de precipitados • il becher

magnet • l'aimant • der Magnet • el imán • la calamita

crocodile clip • la pince crocodile • die Krokodilklemme • la pinza • il morsetto

slide le porte-objet der Objektträger el portaobjetos la lastrina

negative electrode • l'électrode négative • die negative Elektrode • el electrodo negativo • l'elettrodo negativo

positive electrode • l'électrode positive • die positive Elektrode • el electrodo positivo • l'elettrodo positivo

mirror le miroir der Spiegel el espejo lo specchio

microscope • le microscope • das Mikroskop • el microscopio • il microscopio

battery • la pile • die Batterie • la pila • la batteria

college • l'enseignement supérieur • die Hochschule • la enseñanza superior • l'università

admissions
le secrétariat
das Sekretariat
el negociado
l'ufficio iscrizioni

refectory
le restaurant universitaire
die Mensa
el comedor universitario
la mensa

health centre
le service de santé
die Gesundheitsfürsorge
el centro de salud
l'ambulatorio

sports field
• le terrain de sport
• der Sportplatz
• el campo de deportes • il campo sportivo

hall of residence
• la résidence universitaire •
das Studentenheim
• el colegio mayor • la casa dello studente

catalogue
le catalogue
der Katalog
el catálogo
il catalogo

campus • le campus • der Campus • el campus • il campus

library card	enquiries	renew (v)
la carte de lecteur	les renseignements	renouveler
der Leserausweis	die Auskunft	verlängern
la tarjeta de la biblioteca	la información	renovar
il tesserino	il banco informazioni	rinnovare
reading room	borrow (v)	book
la salle de lecture	emprunter	le livre
der Lesesaal	ausleihen	das Buch
la sala de lecturas	coger prestado	el libro
la sala di lettura	prendere in prestito	il libro
reading list	reserve (v)	title
les ouvrages recommandés	réserver	le titre
die Literaturliste	vorbestellen	der Titel
la lista de lecturas	reservar	el título
la lista dei libri	prenotare	il titolo
return date	loan	aisle
la date de retour	le prêt	le couloir
das Rückgabedatum	die Ausleihe	der Gang
la fecha de devolución	el préstamo	el pasillo
la data di restituzione	il prestito	la corsia

loans desk • le service de prêt • die Ausleihe • el mostrador de préstamos • il banco prestiti

librarian
la bibliothécaire
die Bibliothekarin
la bibliotecaria
la bibliotecaria

bookshelf
les rayons
das Bücherregal
la estantería
lo scaffale

periodical
le périodique
das Periodikum
la publicación periódica
il periodico

journal
la revue
die Zeitschrift
la revista
la rivista

library • la bibliothèque • die Bibliothek • la biblioteca • la biblioteca

undergraduate • l'étudiant
• **der Student** • el estudiante
• lo studente universitario

lecturer • l'assistant
• **der Dozent** • el profesor
• il docente

graduate • la licenciée
• **die Graduierte** • la
licenciada • la laureata

robe • la robe • **die
Robe** • la toga • la toga

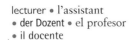

lecture theatre • la salle de cours • **der Hörsaal** • el anfiteatro
• l'aula

graduation ceremony • la cérémonie de la remise des diplômes
• **die Graduierungsfeier** • la ceremonia de graduación
• la consegna delle lauree

schools • les écoles • **die Fachhochschulen** • las escuelas • le scuole

model
le modèle
das Modell
la modelo
la modella

art college • l'école des beaux arts
• **die Kunsthochschule** • la escuela de
Bellas Artes • la scuola d'arte

music school • le Conservatoire
• **die Musikhochschule** • el conservatorio
• il conservatorio

dance academy • l'école de danse
• **die Tanzakademie** • la academia
de danza • l'accademia di danza

scholarship	research	dissertation	medicine	economics
la bourse	la recherche	la dissertation	la medecine	les sciences économiques
das Stipendium	**die Forschung**	**die Examensarbeit**	**die Medizin**	**die Wirtschaftswissenschaft**
la beca	la investigación	la tesina	la medicina	las ciencias económicas
la borsa di studio	la ricerca	la dissertazione	la medicina	l'economia
diploma	masters	department	zoology	politics
le diplôme	la maîtrise	l'U.F.R.	la zoologie	les sciences politiques
das Diplom	**der Magister**	**der Fachbereich**	**die Zoologie**	**die Politologie**
el diploma	el máster	el departamento	la zoología	las ciencias políticas
il diploma	il master	il dipartimento	la zoologia	la politica
degree	doctorate	law	physics	literature
la licence	le doctorat	le droit	la physique	la littérature
der akademische Grad	**die Promotion**	**die Rechtswissenschaft**	**die Physik**	**die Literaturwissenschaft**
el título universitario	el doctorado	el derecho	la física	la literatura
la laurea	il dottorato	il diritto	la fisica	la letteratura
postgraduate	thesis	engineering	philosophy	history of art
de troisième cycle	la thèse	les études d'ingénieur	la philosophie	l'histoire d'art
postgradual	**die Dissertation**	**das Ingenieurwesen**	**die Philosophie**	**die Kunstgeschichte**
de posgrado	la tesis	la ingeniería	la filosofía	la historia del arte
di perfezionamento	la tesi	l'ingegneria	la filosofia	la storia dell'arte

work
le travail
die Arbeit
el trabajo
il lavoro

office 1 • le bureau 1 • das Büro 1 • la oficina 1 • l'ufficio 1

office • le bureau • das Büro • la oficina • l'ufficio

computer
l'ordinateur
der Computer
el ordenador
il computer

monitor
le moniteur
der Bildschirm
la pantalla
il monitor

desktop organizer
le porte-crayons
der Stifthalter
el portabolígrafos
il portapenne

file
le classeur
der Ordner
la carpeta
la cartellina

in-tray
la corbeille arrivée
die Ablage für Eingänge
la bandeja de entrada
il vassoio per gli arrivi

out-tray
la corbeille départ
die Ablage für Ausgänge
la bandeja de salida
il vassoio per le partenze

keyboard
le clavier
die Tastatur
el teclado
la tastiera

notebook
le carnet
das Notizbuch
el cuaderno
il blocco

telephone
le téléphone
das Telefon
el teléfono
il telefono

label
l'étiquette
das Schild
la etiqueta
l'etichetta

desk
le bureau
der Schreibtisch
el escritorio
la scrivania

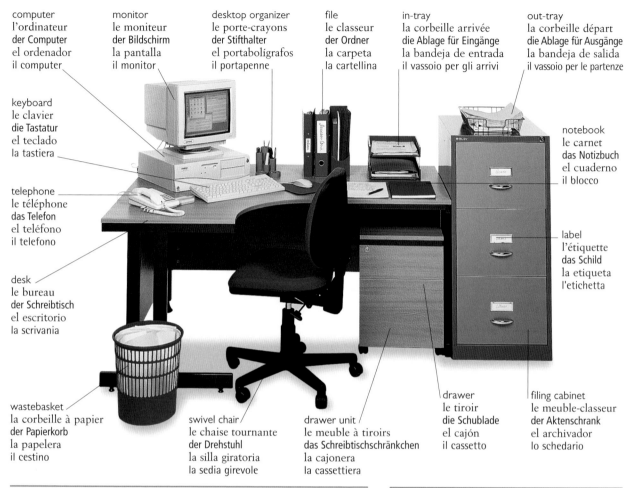

wastebasket
la corbeille à papier
der Papierkorb
la papelera
il cestino

swivel chair
le chaise tournante
der Drehstuhl
la silla giratoria
la sedia girevole

drawer unit
le meuble à tiroirs
das Schreibtischschränkchen
la cajonera
la cassettiera

drawer
le tiroir
die Schublade
el cajón
il cassetto

filing cabinet
le meuble-classeur
der Aktenschrank
el archivador
lo schedario

---

office equipment • l'équipement de bureau • die Büroausstattung • el equipo de oficina • l'apparecchiature da ufficio

paper tray
le magasin à papier
der Papierbehälter
la bandeja para el papel
la contenitore per la carta

paper guide
le guide
die Papierführung
la guía
la guida

fax
le fax
das Fax
el fax
il fax

printer • l'imprimante • der Drucker • la impresora • la stampante

fax machine • le fax • das Faxgerät • el fax • il fax

print (v) imprimer drucken imprimir stampare	enlarge (v) agrandir vergrößern ampliar ingrandire
copy (v) photocopier kopieren fotocopiar copiare	reduce (v) réduire verkleinern reducir ridurre

I need to make some copies.
J'ai besoin de faire des photocopies.
Ich möchte fotokopieren.
Necesito hacer unas fotocopias.
Devo fare delle copie.

office supplies • les fournitures de bureau • der Bürobedarf • los materiales de oficina • gli articoli di cancelleria

letterhead • l'en-tête
• der Geschäftsbogen
• el membrete
• la carta intestata

compliments slip
la fiche compliments
der Empfehlungszettel
la nota con saludos
il foglietto di omaggio

envelope • l'enveloppe
• der Briefumschlag
• el sobre • la busta

box file
le dossier-classeur
der Aktenordner
el archivador
il classificante

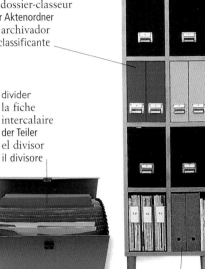

divider
la fiche
intercalaire
der Teiler
el divisor
il divisore

clipboard • le
clipboard • das
Klemmbrett • la tablilla
con sujetapapeles
• il portablocco con
fermaglio

note pad • le bloc-
notes • der Notizblock
• el bloc de apuntes
• il blocco per appunti

tab • l'étiquette • der
Kartenreiter • el rótulo
• l'etichetta

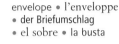

hanging file • le
dossier suspendu
• der Hängeordner • el
archivador suspendido
• la cartella sospesa

concertina file • le
porte-dossiers • der
Fächerordner • la carpeta
de acordeón • il
portacarte a fisarmonica

lever arch file
• le classeur à levier
• der Ringordner
• la carpeta de anillas
• il raccoglitore

staples
les agrafes
die Klammern
las grapas
i punti

sticky tape • le scotch
• der Tesafilm • el papel
celo • il nastro adesivo

ink pad
le tampon encreur
das Stempelkissen
la almohadilla de la tinta
il tampone di inchiostro

personal organizer
• l'agenda • der
Terminkalender • la
agenda • l'agenda

stapler • l'agrafeuse
• der Hefter
• la grapadora
• la cucitrice

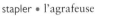

tape dispenser • le
dévidoir de scotch
• der Tesafilmhalter • el
soporte del papel celo
• il dispenser

hole punch • le
perforateur • der Locher
• la perforadora
• il perforatore

rubber stamp • le
cachet • der Stempel
• el sello • il timbro

rubber band
• l'élastique • das
Gummiband • la goma
elástica • l'elastico

bulldog clip • la pince
à dessin • die Papier-
klammer • el sujeta-
papeles • la molletta

paper clip • le
trombone • die Büro-
klammer • el clip
• la graffetta

drawing pin
la punaise
die Reißzwecke
la chincheta
la puntina

notice board • le panneau d'affichage
• die Pinnward • el corcho • il tabellone

office 2 • le bureau 2 • das Büro 2 • la oficina 2 • l'ufficio 2

flipchart
le tableau à feuilles mobiles
das Flipchart
la pizarra blanca
il poster scorrevole

minutes
le compte rendu
das Protokoll
el acta
il verbale

easel
le chevalet
das Gestell
el caballete
il cavalletto

report
le rapport
der Bericht
el informe
la relazione

manager
le gérant
der Manager
el gerente
il direttore

proposal
la proposition
das Angebot
la propuesta
la proposta

executive
le cadre
der leitende Angestellte
el ejecutivo
il dirigente

meeting • le réunion • die Sitzung • la reunión • la riunione

meeting room	attend (v)
la salle de conférence	assister à
der Sitzungsraum	teilnehmen
la sala de reuniones	asistir
la sala da riunione	partecipare
agenda	chair (v)
l'ordre du jour	présider
die Tagesordnung	den Vorsitz führen
el orden del día	presidir
l'ordine del giorno	presiedere

What time is the meeting?
La conférence est à quelle heure?
Um wie viel Uhr ist die Sitzung?
¿A qué hora es la reunión?
A che ora è la riunione?

What are your office hours?
Quelles sont vos heures de bureau?
Welche sind Ihre Geschäftszeiten?
¿Cuál es su horario de oficina?
Qual è il vostro orario di lavoro?

projector
le projecteur
der Projektor
el proyector
la lavagna luminosa

speaker
le conférencier
der Sprecher
el conferenciante
il relatore

presentation • la présentation • die Präsentation • la presentación • la presentazione

business • les affaires • das Geschäft • los negocios • gli affari

laptop
le portable
der Laptop
el ordenador portátil
il computer portabile

notes
les notes
die Notizen
los apuntes
gli appunti

businessman
l'homme d'affaires
der Geschäftsmann
el hombre de negocios
l'uomo di affari

businesswoman
la femme d'affaires
die Geschäftsfrau
la mujer de negocios
la donna di affari

business lunch • le déjeuner d'affaires • das Arbeitsessen • la comida de negocios • il pranzo di affari

business trip • le voyage d'affaires • die Geschäftsreise • el viaje de negocios • il viaggio di affari

appointment
le rendez-vous
der Termin
la cita
l'appuntamento

palmtop
l'ordinateur de poche
der Palmtop
el PDA
il palmtop

diary • l'agenda • der Terminkalender • la agenda • l'agenda

client • le client • der Kunde • el cliente • il cliente

managing director • le directeur général • der Geschäftsfürer • el director general • l'amministratore delegato

business deal • le contrat • das Geschäftsabkommen • el acuerdo de negocios • l'accordo di affari

company la société die Firma la empresa l'azienda	staff le personnel das Personal el personal il personale	accounts department la comptabilité die Buchhaltung el departamento de contabilidad l'ufficio contabilità	legal department le service du contentieux die Rechtsabteilung el departamento legal l'ufficio legale
head office le siège social die Zentrale la oficina central la sede	payroll le livre de paie die Lohnliste la nómina il libro paga	marketing department le service marketing die Marketingabteilung el departamento de márketing l'ufficio marketing	customer service department le service après-vente die Kundendienstabteilung el departamento de atención al cliente l'ufficio di assistenza al cliente
branch la succursale die Zweigstelle la sucursal la succursale	salary le salaire das Gehalt el sueldo lo stipendio	sales department le service des ventes die Verkaufsabteilung el departamento de ventas l'ufficio vendite	personnel department le service de ressources humaines die Personalabteilung el departamento de recursos humanos l'ufficio del personale

computer • l'ordinateur • der Computer • el ordenador • il computer

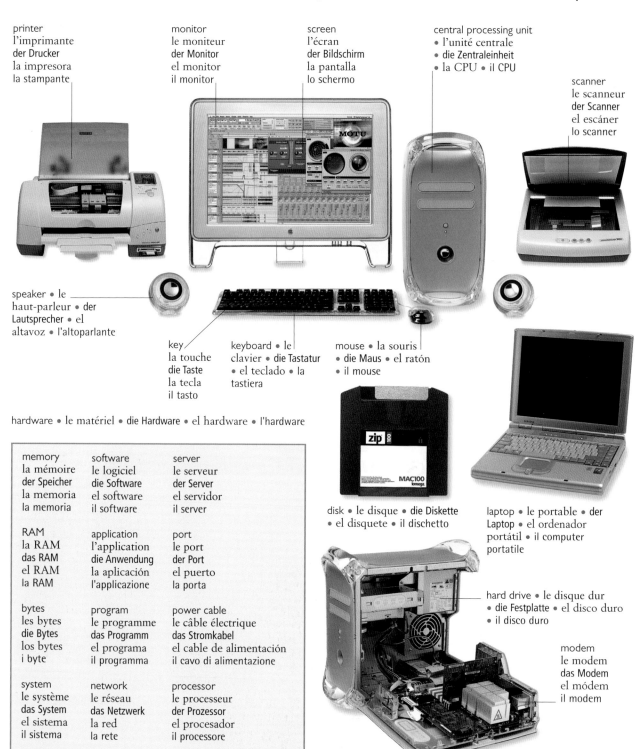

printer
l'imprimante
der Drucker
la impresora
la stampante

monitor
le moniteur
der Monitor
el monitor
il monitor

screen
l'écran
der Bildschirm
la pantalla
lo schermo

central processing unit
• l'unité centrale
• die Zentraleinheit
• la CPU • il CPU

scanner
le scanneur
der Scanner
el escáner
lo scanner

speaker • le
haut-parleur • der
Lautsprecher • el
altavoz • l'altoparlante

key
la touche
die Taste
la tecla
il tasto

keyboard • le
clavier • die Tastatur
• el teclado • la
tastiera

mouse • la souris
• die Maus • el ratón
• il mouse

hardware • le matériel • die Hardware • el hardware • l'hardware

memory	software	server
la mémoire	le logiciel	le serveur
der Speicher	die Software	der Server
la memoria	el software	el servidor
la memoria	il software	il server
RAM	application	port
la RAM	l'application	le port
das RAM	die Anwendung	der Port
el RAM	la aplicación	el puerto
la RAM	l'applicazione	la porta
bytes	program	power cable
les bytes	le programme	le câble électrique
die Bytes	das Programm	das Stromkabel
los bytes	el programa	el cable de alimentación
i byte	il programma	il cavo di alimentazione
system	network	processor
le système	le réseau	le processeur
das System	das Netzwerk	der Prozessor
el sistema	la red	el procesador
il sistema	la rete	il processore

disk • le disque • die Diskette
• el disquete • il dischetto

laptop • le portable • der
Laptop • el ordenador
portátil • il computer
portatile

hard drive • le disque dur
• die Festplatte • el disco duro
• il disco duro

modem
le modem
das Modem
el módem
il modem

zip
MAC100
Iomega.

desktop • le bureau • das Desktop • el escritorio • il desktop

menubar
la barre de menus
der Menübalken
la barra del menú
la barra del menu

toolbar • la barre
d'outils • die
Werkzeugleiste • la
barra de acceso
• la barra degli
strumenti

wallpaper • le
papier peint • der
Bildschirmhintergrund
• el fondo de
pantalla • lo sfondo

font • la police • die Schriftart
• la fuente • il carattere

icon • l'icône
• das Symbol • el
icono • l'icona

scrollbar • la barre de
défilement • der
Scrollbalken • la barra de
desplazamiento • la
barra di scorrimento

window • la fenêtre
• das Fenster • la
ventana • la finestra

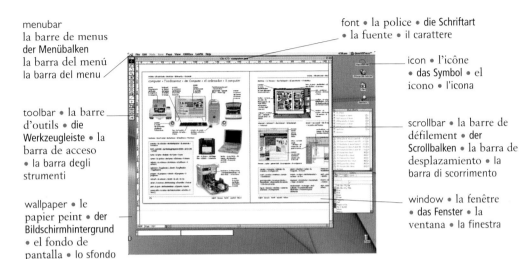

file • le fichier • die
Datei • el fichero
• il file

folder • le dossier
• der Ordner • la
carpeta • la cartella

trash • la poubelle
• der Papierkorb • la
papelera • il cestino

internet • l'internet • das Internet • el internet
• Internet

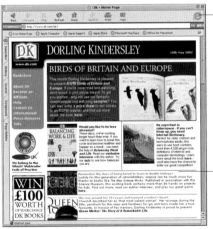

browser
le navigateur
der Browser
el navegador
il browser

inbox • la boîte de
réception • der Post-
eingang • la bandeja
de entrada • la
posta in arrivo

website
le site web
die Website
el sitio web
il sito web

browse (v) • naviguer • browsen • navegar • la navigazione

email • le courrier électronique • die E-Mail
• el correo electrónico • la posta elettronica

email address • l'adresse de courrier électronique
• die E-Mail-Adresse • la dirección de correo
electrónico • l'indirizzo di posta elettronica

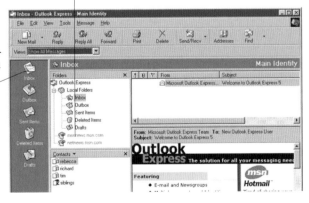

connect (v)	service provider	log on (v)	download (v)	send (v)	save (v)
connecter	le fournisseur d'accès	entrer	télécharger	envoyer	sauvegarder
verbinden	der Serviceprovider	einloggen	herunterladen	senden	sichern
conectar	el proveedor de servicios	entrar	bajar	enviar	guardar
collegare	il fornitore di servizi	collegarsi	scaricare	spedire	salvare
instal (v)	email account	on-line	attachment	receive (v)	search (v)
installer	le compte de courrier électronique	en ligne	le document attaché	recevoir	chercher
installieren	das E-Mail-Konto	online	der Anhang	erhalten	suchen
instalar	la cuenta de correo	en línea	el documento adjunto	recibir	buscar
installare	l'account di posta elettronica	in rete	l'allegato	ricevere	cercare

media • les médias • die Medien • los medios de comunicación • i mass media

television studio • le studio de télévision • das Fernsehstudio • el estudio de televisión • lo studio televisivo

presenter
le présentateur
der Moderator
el presentador
il presentatore

light
l'éclairage
die Beleuchtung
el foco
la lampada

set
le plateau
die Studioeinrichtung
el plató
il set

camera
la caméra
die Kamera
la cámara
la telecamera

camera crane
la grue de caméra
der Kamerakran
la grúa de la cámara
il carrello della telecamera

cameraman
le cameraman
der Kameramann
el cámara
il cameraman

channel	documentary	press	soap	cartoon	live
la chaîne	le documentaire	la presse	le feuilleton	le dessin animé	en direct
der Kanal	der Dokumentarfilm	die Presse	die Seifenoper	der Zeichentrickfilm	live
el canal	el documental	la prensa	la telenovela	los dibujos animados	en directo
il canale	il documentario	la stampa	la telenovela	il cartone animato	in diretta

programming	news	television series	game show	prerecorded	broadcast (v)
la programmation	les nouvelles	la série télévisée	le jeu télévisé	en différé	émettre
die Programmgestaltung	die Nachrichten	die Fernsehserie	die Spielshow	vorher aufgezeichnet	senden
la programación	las noticias	la serie televisiva	el concurso	en diferido	emitir
la programmazione	il telegiornale	le serie televisiva	il gioco a premi	in differita	trasmettere

english • français • deutsch • español • italiano

interviewer • l'interviewer
• der Interviewer
• el entrevistador
• l'intervistatore

reporter • la reporter
• die Reporterin • la reportera
• la cronista

autocue • le télésouffleur
• der Teleprompter • el
autocue • il gobbo

newsreader • la présentatrice
• die Nachrichtensprecherin • la
presentadora de las noticias
• la presentatrice

actors •les acteurs • die
Schauspieler • los actores
• gli attori

sound boom • la perche • der
Mikrofongalgen • la jirafa
• la giraffa

clapper board • la claquette
• die Klappe • la claqueta
• il ciac

film set • le décor de cinéma
• das Set • el plató de rodaje
• il set

radio • la radio • das Radio • la radio • la radio

mixing desk
le pupitre de mixage
das Mischpult
la mesa de mezclas
il tavolo di missaggio

microphone
le microphone
das Mikrofon
el micrófono
il microfono

sound technician
l'ingénieur du son
der Tonmeister
el técnico de sonido
il tecnico del suono

recording studio • le studio d'enregistrement • das Tonstudio
• el estudio de grabación • lo studio di registrazione

radio station	short wave
la station de radio	les ondes courtes
die Rundfunkstation	die Kurzwelle
la estación de radio	la onda corta
il canale radiofonico	l'onda corta
DJ	medium wave
le D.J.	les ondes moyennes
der DJ	die Mittelwelle
el DJ	la onda media
il DJ	l'onda media
broadcast	frequency
l'émission	la fréquence
die Sendung	die Frequenz
la emisión	la frecuencia
la trasmissione	la frequenza
wavelength	volume
la longueur d'ondes	le volume
die Wellenlänge	die Lautstärke
la longitud de onda	el volumen
la lunghezza d'onda	il volume
long wave	tune (v)
les grandes ondes	régler
die Langwelle	einstellen
la onda larga	sintonizar
l'onda lunga	sintonizzare

law • le droit • das Recht • el derecho • la legge

court officer
l'huissier de tribunal
der Gerichtsdiener
el alguacil
la guardia

witness
le témoin
der Zeuge
el testigo
il testimone

judge • le juge • der Richter
• el juez • il giudice

lawyer
l'avocat
der Rechtsanwalt
el abogado
l'avvocato

jury
le jury
die Geschworenen
el jurado
la giuria

jury box
le banc des jurés
die Geschworenenbank
la tribuna del jurado
il banco della giuria

courtroom • la salle de tribunal • der Gerichtssaal
• la sala del tribunal • l'aula del tribunale

prosecution • l'accusation
• die Staatsanwaltschaft • la
acusación • il pubblico ministero

court official • le greffier
• der Protokollführer • el
auditor • il protocollista

lawyer's office le cabinet das Anwaltsbüro el bufete lo studio dell'avvocato	summons l'assignation die Vorladung la citación la citazione	writ l'acte judiciaire die Verfügung la orden judicial l'ordine	court case la cause das Gerichtsverfahren el juicio il procedimento
legal advice le conseil juridique die Rechtsberatung la asesoría jurídica la consulenza legale	statement la déposition die Aussage la declaración la dichiarazione	court date la date du procès der Gerichtstermin la fecha del juicio la data di comparizione	charge l'accusation die Anklage el cargo l'imputazione
client le client der Klient el cliente il cliente	warrant le mandat der Haftbefehl la orden de arresto il mandato	plea le plaidoyer das Plädoyer el alegato la petizione	accused l'accusé der Angeklagte el acusado l'accusato

stenographer
le sténographe
der Gerichtsstenograf
la taquígrafa
lo stenografo

suspect
le suspect
der Verdächtige
el sospechoso
la persona suspetta

criminal
le criminel
der Straftäter
el criminal
il criminale

defendant • l'accusé
• der Angeklagte • el
acusado • l'imputato

defence • la défense • die
Verteidigung • la defensa
• la difesa

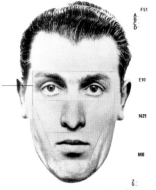

photofit • le portrait-robot
• das Phantombild • el retrato
robot • l'indekit

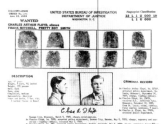

criminal record • le casier judiciare
• das Strafregister • los ante-
cedentes • il casellario giudiziale

prison guard • le gardien de prison
• der Gefängniswärter • el funcionario
de prisiones • la guardia carceraria

cell • la cellule • die
Gefängniszelle • la celda
• la cella

prison • la prison • das Gefängnis
• la cárcel • il carcere

evidence	guilty	bail	I want to see a lawyer.
la preuve	coupable	la caution	Je voudrais voir un avocat.
das Beweismittel	schuldig	die Kaution	Ich möchte mit einem Anwalt sprechen.
la prueba	culpable	la fianza	Quiero ver a un abogado.
la prova	colpevole	la cauzione	Voglio vedere un avvocato.
verdict	acquitted	appeal	Where is the courthouse?
le verdict	acquitté	l'appel	Où est le palais de justice?
das Urteil	freigesprochen	die Berufung	Wo ist das Gericht?
el veredicto	absuelto	la apelación	¿Dónde está el juzgado?
il verdetto	assolto	il ricorso	Dov'è il palazzo di giustizia?
innocent	sentence	parole	Can I post bail?
innocent	la condamnation	la liberté conditionnelle	Est-ce que je peux verser la caution?
unschuldig	das Strafmaß	die Haftentlassung auf Bewährung	Kann ich die Kaution leisten?
inocente	la sentencia	la libertad condicional	¿Puedo pagar la fianza?
innocente	la sentenza	la libertà per buona condotta	Posso versare una cauzione?

farm 1 • la ferme 1 • der Bauernhof 1 • la granja 1 • la fattoria 1

farmland
les terres cultivées
das Ackerland
las tierras de labranza
il terreno agricolo

farmyard
la cour de ferme
der Hof
el corral
l'aia

outbuilding
la dépendence
das Nebengebäude
el cobertizo
il capanno

farmhouse
la maison d'habitation
das Bauernhaus
la casa de labranza
il casolare

field
le champ
das Feld
el campo
il campo

barn
la grange
die Scheune
el granero
il granaio

farmer
• le fermier
• der Landwirt
• el agricultor
• l'agricoltore

vegetable plot
le potager
der Gemüsegarten
el huerto
l'orto

hedge
la haie
die Hecke
el seto
la siepe

gate
la barrière
das Tor
la puerta
il cancello

fence
la clôture
der Zaun
la cerca
il recinto

pasture
le pré
die Weide
el pasto
il pascolo

livestock
les bestiaux
das Vieh
el ganado
il bestiame

cultivator
le cultivateur
der Kultivator
el cultivador
l'aratro

tractor • le tracteur • der Traktor • el tractor • il trattore

combine harvester • la moissonneuse-batteuse
• der Mähdrescher • la cosechadora • la mietitrebbiatrice

english • français • deutsch • español • italiano

types of farm • les exploitations agricoles • die landwirtschaftlichen Betriebe • los tipos de granja • i tipi di fattoria

crop • la culture • die
Feldfrucht • la cosecha
• il prodotto dei campi

flock • le troupeau
• die Herde • el rebaño
• il gregge

arable farm • la ferme de
culture • der Ackerbaubetrieb
• la granja agrícola
• l'azienda agricola

dairy farm • la ferme laitière
• der Betrieb für Milchproduktion
• la vaquería • il caseificio

sheep farm • la ferme d'élevage
de moutons • die Schaffarm
• la granja de ganado ovino
• l'allevamento di pecore

poultry farm • la ferme
d'aviculture • die Hühnerfarm
• la granja avícola • lo
stabilimento avicolo

vine • la vigne • der Wein-
stock • la viña • la vigna

pig farm • la ferme d'élevage
porcin • die Schweinefarm
• la granja de ganado porcino
• l'allevamento di maiali

fish farm • le centre de
pisciculture • die Fischzucht
• la piscifactoría
• il vivaio ittico

fruit farm • l'exploitation
fruitière • der Obstbau
• la granja de frutales
• la frutticoltura

vineyard • la vigne
• der Weinberg • el viñedo
• il vigneto

actions • les activités • die Tätigkeiten • las actividades • le attività

furrow
le sillon
die Furche
el surco
il solco

plough (v) • labourer
• pflügen • arar • arare

sow (v) • semer • säen
• sembrar • seminare

milk (v) • traire • melken
• ordeñar • mungere

feed (v) • donner à manger
• füttern • dar de comer
• dar da mangiare

herbicide	herd	trough
l'herbicide	le troupeau	l'auge
das Herbizid	die Herde	der Trog
el herbicida	la manada	el comedero
l'erbicida	la mandria	la mangiatoia
pesticide	silo	plant (v)
le pesticide	le silo	planter
das Pestizid	das Silo	pflanzen
el pesticida	el silo	plantar
il pesticida	il silo	piantare

water (v) • arroser
• bewässern • regar • irrigare

harvest (v) • récolter • ernten
• cosechar • raccogliere

farm 2 • la ferme 2 • der Bauernhof 2 • la granja 2 • la fattoria 2

crops • les cultures • die Feldfrüchte • las cosechas • li prodotti dei campi

wheat • le blé • der Weizen
• el trigo • il grano

corn • le maïs • der Mais
• el maíz • il granturco

barley • l'orge • die Gerste
• la cebada • l'orzo

rapeseed • le colza •
der Raps • la colza • la colza

sunflower • le tournesol
• die Sonnenblume • el girasol
• il girasole

bale • la balle
• der Ballen • la
bala • la balla

hay • le foin • das Heu
• el heno • il fieno

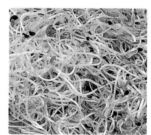

alfalfa • la luzerne
• die Luzerne • la alfalfa
• l'alfalfa

tobacco • le tabac • der
Tabak • el tabaco • il tabacco

rice • le riz • der Reis
• el arroz • il riso

tea • le thé • der Tee • el té
• il tè

coffee • le café • der Kaffee
• el café • il caffè

flax • le lin • der Flachs
• el lino • il lino

sugarcane • la canne à sucre
• das Zuckerrohr • la caña de
azúcar • la canna da zucchero

cotton • le coton • die
Baumwolle • el algodón
• il cotone

scarecrow • l'épouvantail
• die Vogelscheuche
• el espantapájaros
• lo spaventapasseri

livestock • le bétail • das Vieh • el ganado • il bestiame

piglet • le porcelet • das Ferkel • el lechón • il maialino

calf
le veau
das Kalb
el ternero
il vitello

pig • le cochon • das Schwein • el cerdo • il maiale

cow • la vache • die Kuh • la vaca • la mucca

bull • le taureau • der Stier • el toro • il toro

sheep • le mouton • das Schaf • la oveja • la pecora

kid
le chevreau
das Zicklein
el cabrito
il capretto

foal
le poulain
das Fohlen
el potro
il puledro

lamb • l'agneau • das Lamm • el cordero • l'agnello

goat • la chèvre • die Ziege • la cabra • la capra

horse • le cheval • das Pferd • el caballo • il cavallo

donkey • l'âne • der Esel • el burro • l'asino

chick • le poussin • das Küken • el polluelo • il pulcino

duckling
le caneton
das Entenküken
el patito
l'anatroccolo

chicken • le poulet • das Huhn • la gallina • la gallina

cockerel • le coq • der Hahn • el gallo • il gallo

turkey • le dindon • der Truthahn • el pavo • il tacchino

duck • le canard • die Ente • el pato • l'anatra

stable • l'écurie • der Stall • el establo • la stalla

pen • l'enclos • der Pferch • el redil • il recinto

chicken coop • le poulailler • der Hühnerstall • el gallinero • il pollaio

pigsty • la porcherie • der Schweinestall • la pocilga • il porcile

construction • la construction • der Bau • la construcción • la costruzione

scaffolding • l'échafaudage
das Gerüst • el andamio
• l'impalcatura

pallet
la palette
die Palette
el palet
il pallet

ladder
l'échelle
die Leiter
la escalera
la scala

window
la fenêtre
das Fenster
la ventana
la finestra

rafter • le chevron
• der Dachsparren • la viga
del tejado • la trave

building site • le chantier • die Baustelle • la obra • il cantiere

fork-lift truck
le chariot de levage
der Gabelstapler
la carretilla elevadora
il carrello elevatore

lintel
le linteau
der Sturz
el dintel
l'architrave

wall
le mur
die Mauer
la pared
il muro

girder
la poutre
der Träger
la viga
la trave

hard hat • le casque de
sécurité • der Schutzhelm
• el casco • il casco

toolbelt • la ceinture à outils
• der Werkzeuggürtel • el cinturón
de las herramientas • la cintura
per gli attrezzi

beam
la poutre
der Balken
la viga de madera
la trave

cement
le ciment
der Zement
el cemento
il cemento

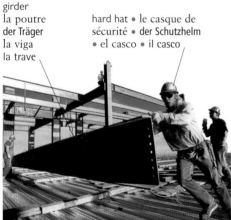

build (v) • construire • bauen • construir
• costruire

builder • le maçon • der
Bauarbeiter • el albañil
• il muratore

cement mixer • la bétonnière • die
Betonmischmaschine • la hormigonera
• la betoniera

materials • les matériaux • das Material • los materiales • i materiali

brick • la brique • der Ziegelstein • el ladrillo • il mattone

timber • le bois • das Bauholz • la madera • il legno

roof tile • la tuile • der Dachziegel • la teja • la tegola

concrete block • le bloc de béton • der Betonblock • el bloque de hormigón • il blocco di calcestruzzo

tools • les outils • die Werkzeuge • las herramientas • gli attrezzi

mortar • le mortier • der Mörtel • la argamasa • la malta

trowel • la truelle • die Kelle • la paleta • la cazzuola

spirit level • le niveau à bulle • die Wasserwaage • el nivel • la livella

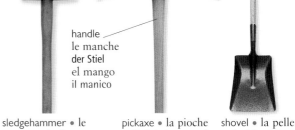

handle
le manche
der Stiel
el mango
il manico

sledgehammer • le marteau de forgeron • der Vorschlaghammer • el mazo • la mazza

pickaxe • la pioche • die Spitzhacke • el pico • il piccone

shovel • la pelle • die Schaufel • la pala • la pala

machinery • les machines • die Maschinen • la maquinaria • i macchinari

roller • le rouleau compresseur • die Walze • la apisonadora • il rullo compressore

dumper truck • le tombereau • der Kipper • el camión volquete • il camion con cassone ribaltabile

support • le support • die Stütze • el soporte • il supporto

hook
le crochet
der Haken
el gancho
il gancio

crane • la grue • der Kran • la grúa • la gru

roadworks • les travaux • die Straßenarbeiten • las obras • i lavori stradali

tarmac
le macadam goudronné
der Asphalt
el asfalto
l'asfalto

cone
le cône
der Leitkegel
el cono
il birillo

pneumatic drill • le marteau-piqueur • der Pressluftbohrer • el martillo neumático • il martello pneumatico

resurfacing
le revêtement
der Neubelag
el revestimiento
la riasfaltatura

mechanical digger • la pelle mécanique • der Bagger • la excavadora • l'escavatrice meccanica

occupations 1 • les professions 1 • die Berufe 1 • las profesiones 1 • i mestieri 1

carpenter • le menuisier
• der Schreiner • el carpintero
• il falegname

electrician • l'électricien
• der Elektriker • el electricista
• l'elettricista

plumber • le plombier
• der Klempner • el fontanero
• l'idraulico

builder • le maçon
• der Maurer • el albañil
• il muratore

gardener • le jardinier
• der Gärtner • el jardinero
• il giardiniere

vacuum cleaner
l'aspirateur
der Staubsauger
la aspiradora
l'aspirapolvere

cleaner • le nettoyeur • der
Gebäudereiniger • el empleado
de la limpieza • l'addetto alle
pulizie

mechanic • le mécanicien
• der Mechaniker • el mecánico
• il meccanico

butcher • le boucher
• der Metzger • el carnicero
• il macellaio

scissors
les ciseaux
die Schere
las tijeras
le forbici

hairdresser • le coiffeur
• der Friseur • el peluquero
• il parrucchiere

fishmonger • la marchande
de poissons • die Fischhändlerin
• la pescadera
• la pescivendola

greengrocer • le marchand
de légumes • der
Gemüsehändler • el frutero
• il fruttivendolo

florist • la fleuriste
• die Floristin • la florista
• la fioraia

barber • le coiffeur
• der Friseur • el barbero
• il barbiere

jeweller • le bijoutier
• der Juwelier • el joyero
• il gioielliere

shop assistant • l'employée de
magasin • die Verkäuferin • la
dependienta • la commessa

estate agent • l'agent immobilier • die Immobilienmaklerin • la agente inmobiliaria • l'agente immobiliare

optician • l'opticien • der Optiker • el óptico • l'ottico

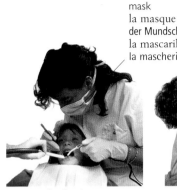

dentist • la dentiste • die Zahnärztin • la dentista • la dentista

mask
la masque
der Mundschutz
la mascarilla
la mascherina

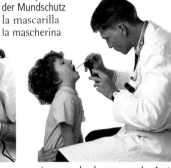

doctor • le docteur • der Arzt • el médico • il medico

pharmacist • la pharmacienne • die Apothekerin • la farmacéutica • la farmacista

nurse • l'infirmière • die Krankenschwester • la enfermera • l'infermiera

vet • la vétérinaire • die Tierärztin • la veterinaria • la veterinaria

farmer • le fermier • der Landwirt • el agricultor • l'agricoltore

fisherman • le pêcheur • der Fischer • el pescador • il pescatore

machine-gun
• la mitrailleuse
• das Maschinen-
gewehr
• la metralleta
• la mitragliatrice

uniform
l'uniforme
die Uniform
el uniforme
la divisa

identity badge
• le badge
• das Abzeichen
• la placa de
identificación
• il distintivo

security guard • le garde • der Wächter • el guardia de seguridad • la guardia di sicurezza

sailor • le marin • der Seemann • el marinero • il marinaio

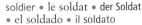

soldier • le soldat • der Soldat • el soldado • il soldato

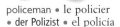

policeman • le policier • der Polizist • el policía • il poliziotto

fireman • le pompier • der Feuerwehrmann • el bombero • il vigile del fuoco

occupations 2 • les professions 2 • die Berufe 2 • las profesiones 2 • i mestieri 2

model
la maquette
das Modell
la maqueta
il modello

lawyer • l'avocat • der Rechtsanwalt • el abogado • l'avvocato

accountant • le comptable • der Buchhalter • el contable • il contabile

architect • l'architecte • der Architekt • el arquitecto • l'architetto

scientist • le scientifique • der Wissenschaftler • el científico • lo scienziato

teacher • l'institutrice • die Lehrerin • la profesora • l'insegnante

librarian • le bibliothécaire • der Bibliothekar • el bibliotecario • il bibliotecario

receptionist • la réceptionniste • die Empfangsdame • la recepcionista • l'addetta al ricevimento

mailbag
le sac postal
die Posttasche
la cartera
la borsa

postman • le facteur • der Briefträger • el cartero • il postino

bus driver • le conducteur de bus • der Busfahrer • el conductor de autobús • l'autista

lorry driver • le camionneur • der Lastwagenfahrer • el camionero • il camionista

taxi driver • le chauffeur de taxi • der Taxifahrer • el taxista • il tassista

pilot • le pilote • der Pilot • el piloto • il pilota

air stewardess • l'hôtesse de l'air • die Flugbegleiterin • la azafata • l'assistente di volo

travel agent • l'agent de voyages • die Reisebürokauffrau • la agente de viajes • l'agente di viaggio

chef's hat
• la toque
• die Kochmütze
• el gorro de cocinero
• il cappello

chef • le chef • der Koch • el cocinero• il cuoco

tutu
le tutu
das Ballettröckchen
el tutú
il tutù

musician • le musicien
• der Musiker • el músico
• il musicista

dancer • la danseuse
• die Tänzerin • la bailarina
• la ballerina

actor • le comédien
• der Schauspieler • el actor
• l'attore

singer • la chanteuse
• die Sängerin • la cantante
• la cantante

waitress • la serveuse
• die Kellnerin • la camarera
• la cameriera

barman • le barman
• der Barkeeper • el camarero
• il barista

sportsman • le sportif
• der Sportler • el deportista
• l'atleta

sculptor • le sculpteur
• der Bildhauer • el escultor
• lo scultore

notes
les notes
die Notizen
las notas
gli appunti

painter • la peintre
• die Malerin • la pintora
• la pittrice

photographer • le
photographe • der Fotograf
• el fotógrafo • il fotografo

newsreader • le présentateur
• der Nachrichtensprecher • el
presentador • il presentatore

journalist • le journaliste
• der Journalist • el periodista
• il giornalista

editor • la rédactrice
• die Redakteurin • la
redactora • la redattrice

designer • la dessinatrice
• die Designerin • la diseñadora
• la disegnatrice

seamstress • la couturière
• die Damenschneiderin
• la modista • la sarta

tailor • le couturier • der
Schneider • el sastre • il sarto

transport
le transport
der Verkehr
el transporte
i trasporti

roads • les routes • die Straßen • las carreteras • le strade

motorway
l'autoroute
die Autobahn
la autopista
l'autostrada

toll booth
le poste de péage
die Mautstelle
la cabina de peaje
il casello

road markings
les signalisations
die Straßenmarkierungen
las señales horizontales
la segnaletica orizzontale

slip road
la bretelle d'accès
die Zufahrtsstraße
la vía de acceso
lo svincolo

one-way
à sens unique
Einbahn-
de sentido único
a senso unico

divider
l'îlot directionnel
die Verkehrsinsel
la línea divisoria
la linea divisoria

junction
le carrefour
die Kreuzung
el cruce
lo svincolo

traffic light
les feux
die Verkehrsampel
el semáforo
il semaforo

inside lane • la file
de droite • die rechte
Spur • el carril para
el tráfico lento
• la corsia interna

middle lane
la voie centrale
die mittlere Spur
el carril central
la corsia centrale

outside lane
la voie de
dépassement
die Überholspur
el carril de
adelantamiento
la corsia di sorpasso

exit ramp
la bretelle de sortie
die Ausfahrt
la vía de salida
l'uscita

traffic
la circulation
der Verkehr
el tráfico
il traffico

flyover
l'autopont
die Überführung
el paso elevado
il cavalcavia

hard shoulder
l'accotement stabilisé
der Seitenstreifen
el arcén
la corsia d'emergenza

underpass
le passage inférieur
die Unterführung
el paso subterráneo
il sottopassaggio

lorry
le camion
der Lastwagen
el camión
il camion

central reservation
le terre-plein
der Mittelstreifen
la mediana
lo spartitraffico

emergency phone • le téléphone de secours • die Notrufsäule • el teléfono de emergencia • il telefono per emergenze

disabled parking • le parking réservé aux personnes handicapées • der Behindertenparkplatz • el aparcamiento para discapacitados • il parcheggio per disabili

traffic jam • l'embouteillage • der Verkehrsstau • el atasco • l'ingorgo

pedestrian crossing
• le passage clouté
• der Fußgängerüberweg
• el paso de peatones
• il passaggio pedonale

map
la carte
die Landkarte
el mapa
la mappa

parking meter • le parc-mètre • die Parkuhr
• el parquímetro
• il parchimetro

traffic policeman
• l'agent de la circulation
• der Verkehrspolizist
• el policía de tráfico
• il vigile urbano

roundabout	reverse (v)	tow away (v)
le rond-point	faire marche arrière	remorquer
der Kreisverkehr	rückwärts fahren	abschleppen
la rotonda	dar marcha atrás	remolcar
la rotatoria	fare marcia indietro	rimorchiare
diversion	drive (v)	dual carriageway
la déviation	conduire	la route à quatre voies
die Umleitung	fahren	die Schnellstraße
el desvío	conducir	la autovía
la deviazione	guidare	la superstrada
park (v)	roadworks	Is this the road to...?
garer	les travaux	C'est la route pour...?
parken	die Straßenbaustelle	Ist dies die Straße nach...?
aparcar	las obras	¿Es ésta la carretera para...?
parcheggiare	i lavori stradali	È questa la strada per ...?
overtake (v)	crash barrier	Where can I park?
doubler	la glissière de sécurité	Où peut-on se garer?
überholen	die Leitplanke	Wo kann ich parken?
adelantar	la valla protectora	¿Dónde se puede aparcar?
sorpassare	il guardrail	Dove posso parcheggiare?

road signs • les panneaux routiers • die Verkehrsschilder • las señales de tráfico • i cartelli stradali

no entry • sens interdit • keine Einfahrt
• prohibido el paso
• ingresso vietato

speed limit • la limitation de vitesse • die Geschwindig-keitsbegrenzung • el límite de velocidad • il limite di velocità

hazard • danger
• Gefahr • peligro
• pericolo

no stopping
• arrêt interdit
• Halten verboten
• prohibido parar
• sosta vietata

no right turn • interdit de tourner à droite
• rechts abbiegen verboten
• no torcer a la derecha
• svolta a destra vietata

bus • le bus • der Bus • el autobús • l'autobus

driver's seat
le siège du conducteur
der Fahrersitz
el asiento del conductor
il sedile dell'autista

handrail
la poignée
der Haltegriff
la barandilla
la maniglia

automatic door
la porte automatique
die Automatiktür
la puerta automática
la porta a soffietto

front wheel
la roue avant
das Vorderrad
la rueda delantera
la ruota anteriore

luggage hold
le compartiment à bagages
das Gepäckfach
el maletero
il bagagliaio

door • la porte • die Tür • la puerta • la porta

coach • le car • der Reisebus • el autocar • il pullman

---

types of buses • les types de bus • die Bustypen • los tipos de autobuses • i tipi di autobus

route number
le numéro de bus
die Liniennummer
el número de ruta
il numero del percorso

driver
le conducteur
der Fahrer
el conductor
l'autista

double-decker bus • le bus à deux étages • der Doppeldecker • el autobús de dos pisos • l'autobus a due piani

tram • le tramway • die Straßenbahn • el tranvía • il tram

trolley bus • le trolleybus • der Omnibus • el trolebús • il filobus

school bus • le bus scolaire • der Schulbus • el autobús escolar • lo scuolabus

stop button • le bouton
d'arrêt • der Halteknopf
• el botón de parada
• il pulsante di chiamata

rear wheel
la roue arrière
das Hinterrad
la rueda trasera
la ruota posteriore

window
la fenêtre
das Fenster
la ventanilla
il finestrino

bus ticket • le ticket
• der Fahrschein
• el billete de autobús
• il biglietto

bell • la sonnette
• die Klingel
• el timbre
• il campanello

bus station • la gare routière
• der Busbahnhof • la estación de autobuses
• l'autostazione

bus stop • l'arrêt de
bus • die Bushaltestelle
• la parada de
autobús • la fermata
dell'autobus

fare	wheelchair access
le prix du ticket	l'accès aux handicapés
der Fahrpreis	der Rollstuhlzugang
la tarifa	la rampa para sillas de ruedas
la tariffa	l'accesso per sedie a rotelle
timetable	bus shelter
l'horaire	l'abribus
der Fahrplan	das Wartehäuschen
el horario	la marquesina
l'orario	la pensilina

Do you stop at…?	Which bus goes to…?
Vous stoppez à…?	C'est quel bus pour aller à…?
Halten Sie am…?	Welcher Bus fährt nach…?
¿Para usted en…?	¿Qué autobús va a…?
Ferma a…?	Qual è l'autobus per…?

minibus • le minibus • der Kleinbus
• el microbús • il pulmino

tourist bus • le bus de touristes • der Touristenbus • el autobús turístico
• il pullman turistico

shuttle bus • la navette • der Zubringer
• el autobús de enlace • la navetta

car 1 • la voiture 1 • das Auto 1 • el coche 1 • l'automobile 1

exterior • l'extérieur • das Äußere • el exterior • l'esterno

wing mirror
le rétroviseur
der Seitenspiegel
el retrovisor exterior
lo specchietto laterale

windscreen
le pare-brise
die Windschutzscheibe
el parabrisas
il parabrezza

rearview mirror
le rétroviseur
der Rückspiegel
el espejo retrovisor
lo specchietto retrovisore

windscreen wiper
l'essuie-glace
der Scheibenwischer
el limpiaparabrisas
il tergicristallo

door
la porte
die Autotür
la puerta
lo sportello

bonnet
le capot
die Motorhaube
el capó
il cofano

boot
le coffre
der Kofferraum
el maletero
il bagagliaio

indicator
le clignotant
der Blinker
el intermitente
la freccia

licence plate
la plaque d'immatriculation
das Nummernschild
la matrícula
la targa

bumper
le pare-chocs
die Stoßstange
el parachoques
il paraurti

headlight
le phare
der Scheinwerfer
el faro
il faro

wheel
la roue
das Rad
la rueda
la ruota

tyre
le pneu
der Reifen
el neumático
il pneumatico

luggage
les bagages
das Gepäck
el equipaje
i bagagli

roofrack • la galerie • der
Dachgepäckträger • la baca
• il portabagagli

tailgate • le hayon
• die Hecktür • la puerta del
maletero • il portellone

seat belt • la ceinture de
sécurité • der Sicherheitsgürtel
• el cinturón de seguridad
• la cintura di sicurezza

child seat • le siège d'enfant
• der Kindersitz • la silla para
niños • il seggiolino

types • les modèles • die Wagentypen • los modelos • i tipi

small car • la petite voiture • der Kleinwagen • el utilitario • l'auto piccola

hatchback • la berline à hayon • die Fließhecklimousine • el coche de cinco puertas • l'auto a cinque porte

saloon • la berline • die Limousine • la berlina • la berlina

estate • le break • der Kombiwagen • el coche ranchera • l'auto familiare

convertible • la décapotable • das Kabriolett • el coche descapotable • la cabriolet

sports car • le cabriolet sport • das Sportkabriolett • el coche deportivo • l'auto sportiva

people carrier • la voiture à six places • die Großraum-limousine • el monovolumen • la monovolume

four-wheel drive • la quatre-quatre • der Geländewagen • el todoterreno • il fuoristrada

vintage • la voiture d'époque • der Oldtimer • el coche de época • l'auto d'epoca

limousine • la limousine • die Limousine • la limusina • la limousine

petrol station • la station-service • die Tankstelle • la gasolinera • la stazione di servizio

petrol pump
la pompe
die Zapfsäule
el surtidor
la pompa di benzina

price
le tarif
der Benzinpreis
el precio
il prezzo

forecourt
l'aire de stationnement
der Tankstellenplatz
la zona de abastecimiento
l'area di stazionamento

air supply
le compresseur
das Druckluftgerät
la bomba del aire
il distributore di aria compressa

oil	leaded	car wash
l'huile	avec plomb	le lave-auto
das Öl	verbleit	die Autowaschanlage
el aceite	con plomo	el lavadero de coches
l'olio	con piombo	l'autolavaggio
petrol	diesel	antifreeze
l'essence	le diesel	l'antigel
das Benzin	der Diesel	das Frostschutzmittel
la gasolina	el diesel	el anticongelante
la benzina	il diesel	l'antigelo
unleaded	garage	screenwash
sans plomb	le garage	le lave-glace
bleifrei	die Werkstatt	die Scheibenwaschmittel
sin plomo	el taller	el líquido limpiaparabrisas
senza piombo	il garage	il detergente per vetri

Fill the tank, please.
Le plein, s'il vous plaît.
Voll tanken, bitte.
Lleno por favor.
Il pieno per favore.

car 2 • la voiture 2 • das Auto 2 • el coche 2 • l'automobile 2

interior • l'intérieur • die Innenausstattung • el interior • l'interno

back seat	armrest	headrest	door lock	handle
le siège arrière	l'accoudoir	le repose-tête	le verrouillage	la poignée
der Rücksitz	die Armstütze	die Kopfstütze	die Türverriegelung	der Türgriff
el asiento trasero	el reposabrazos	el reposacabezas	el pestillo	el tirador
il sedile posteriore	il bracciolo	il poggiatesta	la sicura	la maniglia

two-door	four-door	automatic	brake	accelerator
à deux portes	à quatre portes	automatique	le frein	l'accélérateur
zweitürig	viertürig	mit Automatik	die Bremse	das Gaspedal
de dos puertas	de cuatro puertas	automático	el freno	el acelerador
a due porte	a quattro porte	automatico	il freno	l'acceleratore
three-door	manual	ignition	clutch	air conditioning
à trois portes	manuel	l'allumage	l'embrayage	la climatisation
dreitürig	mit Handschaltung	die Zündung	die Kupplung	die Klimaanlage
de tres puertas	manual	el encendido	el embrague	el aire acondicionado
a tre porte	manuale	l'accensione	la frizione	l'aria condizionata

Can you tell me the way to…?
Pouvez-vous m'indiquer la route pour…?
Wie komme ich nach…?
¿Me puede decir cómo se va a…?
Può indicarmi la strada per…?

Where is the car park?
Où est le parking?
Wo ist hier ein Parkplatz?
¿Dónde hay un parking?
Dov'è il parcheggio?

Can I park here?
On peut se garer ici?
Kann ich hier parken?
¿Se puede aparcar aquí?
Posso parcheggiare qui?

english • français • deutsch • español • italiano

controls • les commandes • die Armaturen • los controles • i comandi

steering wheel
le volant
das Lenkrad
el volante
il volante

horn
le klaxon
die Hupe
el claxon
il clacson

dashboard
le tableau de bord
das Armaturenbrett
el salpicadero
il cruscotto

hazard lights
les feux de détresse
die Warnlichter
las luces de emergencia
le luci intermittenti

satellite navigation
le navigateur par satellite
das GPS-System
la navegación por satélite
la navigazione via satellite

left-hand drive • la conduite à gauche • die Linkssteuerung • el volante a la izquierda • la guida a sinistra

temperature gauge
le thermomètre
die Temperaturanzeige
el indicador de temperatura
l'indicatore della temperatura

rev counter
le compte-tours
der Drehzahlmesser
el cuentarrevoluciones
il contagiri

speedometer
le compteur
der Tachometer
el velocímetro
il tachimetro

fuel gauge
la jauge d'essence
die Kraftstoffanzeige
el testigo de nivel de gasolina
l'indicatore del carburante

car stereo
la stéréo
die Autostereoanlage
el equipo estéreo
l'autoradio

lights switch
l'interrupteur feux
der Lichtschalter
el mando de luces
l'interruttore per le luci

heater controls
la manette de chauffage
der Heizungsregler
los mandos de la calefacción
i comandi per il riscaldamento

odometer
l'odomètre
der Kilometerzähler
el cuentakilómetros
il contachilometri

gearstick
le levier de vitesses
der Schalthebel
la palanca de cambio
la leva del cambio

air bag
l'airbag
der Airbag
el airbag
l'airbag

right-hand drive • la conduite à droite • die Rechtssteuerung
• el volante a la derecha • la guida a destra

car 3 • la voiture 3 • das Auto 3 • el coche 3 • l'automobile 3

mechanics • la mécanique • die Mechanik • la mecánica • la meccanica

screen wash reservoir
le réservoir de lave-glace
der Scheibenputzmittelbehälter
el depósito del limpiaparabrisas
il serbatoio del liquido lavavetri

dipstick
la jauge d'huile
der Ölmessstab
la varilla del nivel del aceite
l'indicatore di livello dell'olio

air filter
le filtre à air
der Luftfilter
el filtro del aire
il filtro dell'aria

brake fluid reservoir
le réservoir de liquide de frein
der Bremsflüssigkeitsbehälter
el depósito del líquido de frenos
il serbatoio del liquido per i freni

battery
la batterie
die Batterie
la batería
la batteria

bodywork
la carrosserie
die Karosserie
la chapa
la carrozzeria

sunroof
le toit ouvrant
das Schiebedach
el techo solar
il tetto scorrevole

coolant reservoir • le réservoir
de liquide de refroidissement
• der Kühlmittelbehälter
• el depósito del líquido
refrigerante • il serbatoio per il
liquido refrigerante

cylinder head
la culasse
der Zylinderkopf
la culata
la testa del cilindro

pipe
le tuyau
das Rohr
el tubo
il tubo

radiator
le radiateur
der Kühler
el radiador
il radiatore

fan
le ventilateur
der Ventilator
el ventilador
il ventilatore

engine
le moteur
der Motor
el motor
il motore

hubcap
l'enjoliveur
die Radkappe
el tapacubo
il copriruota

gearbox
la boîte de vitesses
das Getriebe
la caja de cambios
la scatola del cambio

transmission
la transmission
die Transmission
la transmisión
la trasmissione

driveshaft
l'arbre de transmission
die Kardanwelle
el eje de la transmisión
l'albero di trasmissione

puncture • la crevaison • die Reifenpanne • el pinchazo • la foratura

spare tyre
la roue de secours
das Ersatzrad
la rueda de repuesto
la ruota di scorta

wrench
la manivelle
der Radschlüssel
la llave
la chiave

wheel nuts
les écrous de roue
die Radmuttern
las tuercas de la rueda
i bulloni della ruota

jack
le cric
der Wagenheber
el gato
il cric

change a wheel (v) • changer une roue • ein Rad wechseln
• cambiar una rueda • cambiare una ruota

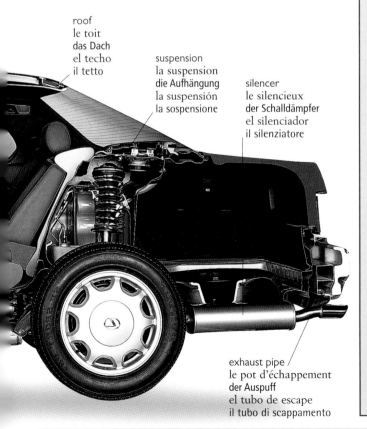

roof
le toit
das Dach
el techo
il tetto

suspension
la suspension
die Aufhängung
la suspensión
la sospensione

silencer
le silencieux
der Schalldämpfer
el silenciador
il silenziatore

exhaust pipe
le pot d'échappement
der Auspuff
el tubo de escape
il tubo di scappamento

car accident l'accident de voiture der Autounfall el accidente de coche l'incidente stradale	cam belt la courroie de cames der Nockenriemen la correa del distribución la cinghia della camma
breakdown la panne die Panne la avería la panna	turbocharger le turbocompresseur der Turbolader el turboalimentador il tubocompressore
insurance l'assurance die Versicherung el seguro l'assicurazione	distributor le distributeur der Verteiler el distribuidor il distributore
tow truck la dépanneuse der Abschleppwagen la grúa il carro attrezzi	idle running marche à vide Leerlauf el ralentí corsa a vuoto
mechanic le mécanicien der Mechaniker el mecánico il meccanico	chassis le châssis das Chassis el chasis il telaio
tyre pressure la pression des pneus der Reifendruck la presión del neumático la pressione dei pneumatici	handbrake le frein à main die Handbremse el freno de mano il freno a mano
fuse box le porte-fusibles der Sicherungskasten la caja de fusibles la scatola dei fusibili	alternator l'alternateur die Lichtmaschine el alternador l'alternatore
spark plug la bougie die Zündkerze la bujía la candela d'accensione	I've broken down. Ma voiture est en panne. Ich habe eine Panne. Tengo una avería. Sono in panne.
fan belt la courroie de ventilateur der Keilriemen la correa del ventilador la cinghia della ventilatore	My car won't start. Ma voiture ne démarre pas. Mein Auto springt nicht an. Mi coche no arranca. La mia macchina non parte.
petrol tank le réservoir d'essence der Benzintank el depósito de gasolina il serbatoio della benzina	

motorbike • la moto • das Motorrad • la motocicleta • la motocicletta

indicator
le clignotant
der Blinker
el intermitente
la freccia

speedometer • le compteur • der Tachometer • el cuentakilómetros • il contachilometri

brake
le frein
die Bremse
el freno
il freno

helmet
le casque
der Motorradhelm
el casco
il casco

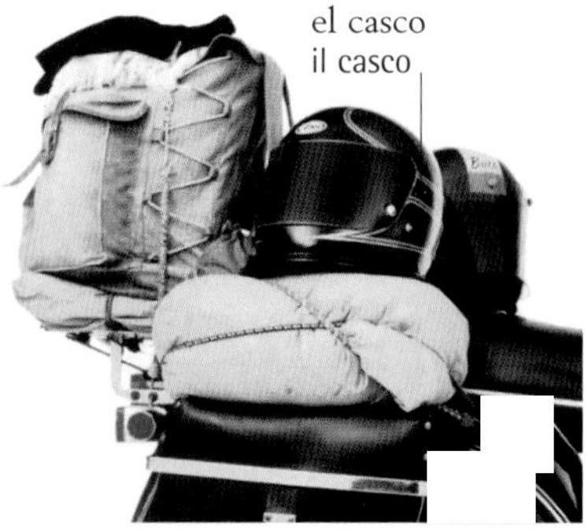

horn
le klaxon
die Hupe
el claxon
il clacson

clutch
l'embrayage
die Kupplung
el embrague
la frizione

throttle
l'accélérateur
der Gashebel
el acelerador
l'acceleratore

controls • les commandes • die Steuerung • los controles • i comandi

carrier • le porte-bagages • der Gepäckträger • el portaequipaje • il portabagagli

reflector
le réflecteur
das Katzenauge
el reflectante
il riflettore

pillion
le siège arrière
der Soziussitz
el asiento trasero
il sellino posteriore

seat
la selle
der Sitz
el asiento
il sedile

engine
le moteur
der Motor
el motor
il motore

fuel tank
le réservoir d'essence
der Kraftstofftank
el depósito de gasolina
il serbatoio

tail light
le feu arrière
das Rücklicht
la luz trasera
il fanale posteriore

exhaust pipe
le pot d'échappement
das Auspuffrohr
el tubo de escape
il tubo di scappamento

silencer
le silencieux
der Auspufftopf
el silenciador
il silenziatore

oil tank
le réservoir d'huile
der Ölsumpf
el depósito del aceite
il serbatoio dell'olio

gearbox
la boîte de vitesses
das Getriebe
la caja de cambios
la scatola del cambio

air filter
le filtre d'air
der Luftfilter
el filtro del aire
il filtro dell'aria

visor
la visière
das Visier
la visera
la visiera

leathers
le vêtement en cuir
der Lederanzug
el traje de cuero
la tuta di pelle

reflector strap
la bande fluorescente
der Leuchtstreifen
la cinta reflectante
la fascia rifrangente

knee pad
la genouillère
der Knieschützer
la rodillera
il paraginocchio

clothing • les vêtements • die Kleidung • el equipo • l'abbigliamento

headlight
le phare
der Scheinwerfer
el faro
il proiettore

suspension
la suspension
die Aufhängung
la suspensión
l'ammortizzatore

mudguard
le garde-boue
das Schutzblech
el guardabarros
il parafango

brake pedal
la pédale de frein
das Bremspedal
el pedal de los frenos
il pedale del freno

axle
l'essieu
die Achse
el eje
l'asse

tyre
le pneu
der Reifen
el neumático
il pneumatico

types • les types • die Typen • los tipos
• i tipi

racing bike • la moto de course • die Rennmaschine
• la moto de carreras • la moto da corsa

windshield • le pare-brise
• die Windschutzscheibe • el
parabrisas • il parabrezza

tourer • la moto routière • der Tourer • la moto
de carretera • la moto da turismo

dirt bike • la moto tout-terrain • das Geländemotorrad
• la moto de cross • la moto da cross

stand • la béquille • der
Motorradständer • el soporte
• il cavalletto

scooter • le scooter • der Roller • el escúter • la vespa

bicycle • la bicyclette • das Fahrrad • la bicicleta • la bicicletta

tandem • le tandem • das Tandem
• el tándem • il tandem

racing bike • le vélo de
course • das Rennrad
• la bicicleta de carreras
• la bicicletta da corsa

mountain bike • le vélo tout-
terrain • das Mountainbike
• la bicicleta de montaña
• la mountain bike

saddle
la selle
der Sattel
el sillín
il sellino

seat post
le tube porte-selle
die Sattelstütze
el soporte del sillín
il tubo reggisella

frame
le cadre
der Rahmen
el cuadro
il telaio

water bottle
la bouteille d'eau
die Wasserflasche
la botella del agua
la borraccia

brake
le frein
die Felgenbremse
el freno
il freno

hub
le moyeu
die Nabe
el eje
il mozzo

gears
les vitesses
die Gänge
las marchas
le marce

rim
la jante
die Felge
la llanta
il cerchione

tyre
le pneu
der Reifen
la cubierta
il pneumatico

chain
la chaîne
die Fahrradkette
la cadena
la catena

cog
la roue dentée
das Zahnrad
el diente de la rueda
la ruota dentata

pedal
la pédale
das Pedal
el pedal
il pedale

touring bike • le vélo de
randonnée • das Tourenfahrrad
• la bicicleta de paseo
• la bicicletta da turismo

road bike • le vélo de ville
• das Straßenrad • la bicicleta
de carretera • la bicicletta
da strada

helmet
le casque
der Fahrradhelm
el casco
il casco

cycle lane • la piste cyclable • der Fahrradweg
• el carril de bicicletas • la pista ciclabile

crossbar
la barre
die Stange
el tubo superior
la canna

handlebar
le guidon
die Lenkstange
el manillar
il manubrio

gear lever
le levier de vitesse
der Schalthebel
la palanca de cambio
la leva del cambio

brake lever
le levier de frein
der Bremsgriff
la palanca de frenos
la leva del freno

fork
la fourche
die Gabel
la horquilla
la forcella

spoke
le rayon
die Speiche
el radio
il raggio

wheel
la roue
das Rad
la rueda
la ruota

valve
la valve
das Ventil
la válvula
la valvola

tread
la bande de roulement
das Reifenprofil
la banda de rodadura
il battistrada

tyre lever • le
démonte-pneu
• der Reifenschlüssel
• la palanca de la
llanta • la leva
per il pneumatico

patch
la rustine
der Flicken
el parche
la toppa

repair kit • la boîte d'outils • der Reparaturkasten
• el kit de reparaciones • il kit per riparazioni

key
la clef
der Schlüssel
la llave
la chiave

pump • la pompe • die
Luftpumpe • la bomba
• la pompa

lock • l'antivol • das
Fahrradschloss • el candado
• il lucchetto

inner tube • la chambre à air
• der Schlauch • la cámara
• la camera d'aria

child seat • le siège d'enfant
• der Kindersitz • la silla de
niño • il seggiolino
per bambino

lamp	kickstand	brake block	basket	toe clip	change gear (v)
le phare	la béquille	le patin de frein	le panier	le cale-pied	changer de vitesse
die Fahrradlampe	der Fahrradständer	die Bremsbacke	der Korb	der Rennbügel	schalten
el faro	la patilla de apoyo	el taco del freno	la cesta	el calzapié	cambiar de marcha
il fanale	il cavalletto	la ganascia	il cestello	il fermapiedi	cambiare marcia
rear light	stabilisers	cable	dynamo	toe strap	brake (v)
le feu arrière	les roues d'entraînement	le câble	la dynamo	la lanière	freiner
das Rücklicht	die Stützräder	das Kabel	der Dynamo	der Riemen	bremsen
el faro trasero	las ruedas de apoyo	el cable	la dinamo	la correa del calzapié	frenar
il fanale posteriore	le rotelle	il cavo	la dinamo	il cinghietto	frenare
reflector	bike rack	sprocket	puncture	pedal (v)	cycle (v)
le cataphote	la galerie à vélo	le pignon	la crevaison	pédaler	faire du vélo
der Rückstrahler	der Fahrradträger	das Kettenzahnrad	die Reifenpanne	treten	Rad fahren
el reflectante	la baca para bicicletas	el piñón	el pinchazo	pedalear	ir en bicicleta
il catarifrangente	il posteggio per bici	il dente	la foratura	pedalare	andare in bici

train • le train • der Zug • el tren • il treno

carriage
la voiture
der Wagen
el vagón
il vagone

platform
le quai
der Bahnsteig
el andén
il binario

trolley
le caddie
der Kofferkuli
el carrito
il carrello

platform number
le numéro de voie
die Gleisnummer
el número de andén
il numero del binario

commuter
le voyageur
der Pendler
el viajero de
cercanías
il pendolare

train station • la gare • der Bahnhof • la estación de tren • la stazione ferroviaria

---

types of train • les types de trains • die Zugtypen • los tipos de tren • i tipi di treno

engine
la locomotive
die Lokomotive
la locomotora
la locomotiva

driver's cab
la cabine du conducteur
der Führerstand
la cabina del conductor
la cabina del conducente

rail
le rail
die Schiene
el raíl
la rotaia

steam train • le train à vapeur
• die Dampflokomotive • el tren de vapor
• il treno a vapore

diesel train • le train diesel • die Diesellokomotive • el tren diesel • il treno diesel

electric train • le train électrique
• die Elektrolokomotive • el tren eléctrico
• il treno elettrico

high-speed train • le train à grande vitesse
• der Hochgeschwindigkeitszug • el tren de
alta velocidad • il treno ad alta velocità

monorail • le monorail • die
Einschienenbahn • el monorraíl
• la monorotaia

underground train • le métro
• die U-Bahn • el metro
• la metropolitana

tram • le tram • die Straßenbahn
• el tranvía • il tram

freight train • le train de marchandises
• der Güterzug • el tren de mercancías
• il treno merci

luggage rack • le porte-bagages • die Gepäckablage • el portaequipajes • il portabagagli

window
la fenêtre
das Zugfenster
la ventanilla
il finestrino

door
la porte
die Tür
la puerta
la porta

track
la voie ferrée
das Gleis
la vía
il binario

seat
le siège
der Sitz
el asiento
il sedile

ticket barrier • le portillon • die Eingangssperre • la barrera • la barriera

compartment • le compartiment • das Abteil • el compartimento • lo scompartimento

public address system
le haut-parleur
der Lautsprecher
la megafonía
il sistema di altoparlanti

timetable
l'horaire
der Fahrplan
el horario
l'orario

41213
KUPONG 7.00 kr

ticket • le billet • die Fahrkarte • el billete • il biglietto

dining car • la voiture-restaurant • der Speisewagen • el vagón restaurante • il vagone ristorante

concourse • le hall de gare • die Bahnhofshalle • el vestíbulo • l'atrio

sleeping compartment • le compartiment-couchettes • das Schlafabteil • el compartimento de cochecama • lo scompartimento a cuccette

rail network	underground map	ticket office	live rail
le réseau ferroviaire	le plan de métro	le guichet	le rail conducteur
das Bahnnetz	der U-Bahnplan	der Fahrkartenschalter	die Strom führende Schiene
la red ferroviaria	el plano del metro	la taquilla	el rail electrificado
la rete ferroviaria	la mappa della metropolitana	la biglietteria	il binario elettrificato
inter-city train	delay	ticket inspector	signal
le rapide	le retard	le contrôleur	le signal
der Intercity	die Verspätung	der Schaffner	das Signal
el tren intercity	el retraso	el revisor	la señal
il treno intercity	il ritardo	il controllore	il segnale
rush hour	fare	change (v)	emergency lever
l'heure de pointe	le prix	changer	la manette de secours
die Stoßzeit	der Fahrpreis	umsteigen	der Notbremse
la hora punta	el precio del billete	cambiar	el freno de emergencia
l'ora di punta	la tariffa	cambiare	la leva di emergenza

aircraft • l'avion • das Flugzeug • el avión • l'aeroplano

airliner • l'avion de ligne • das Verkehrsflugzeug • el avión de pasajeros • l'aereo di linea

nose
le nez
der Bug
el morro
il muso

cockpit
le cockpit
das Cockpit
la cabina de pilotaje
la cabina di pilotaggio

engine
le réacteur
das Triebwerk
el motor
il motore

fuselage
le fuselage
der Rumpf
el fuselaje
la fusoliera

wing
l'aile
die Tragfläche
el ala
l'ala

tail
la queue
das Heck
la cola
la coda

rudder
la gouverne
das Seitenruder
el timón
il timone

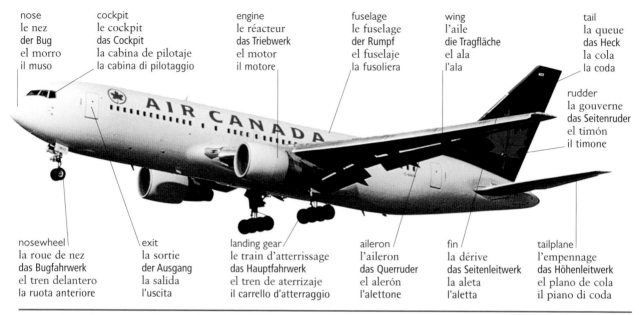

nosewheel
la roue de nez
das Bugfahrwerk
el tren delantero
la ruota anteriore

exit
la sortie
der Ausgang
la salida
l'uscita

landing gear
le train d'atterrissage
das Hauptfahrwerk
el tren de aterrizaje
il carrello d'atterraggio

aileron
l'aileron
das Querruder
el alerón
l'alettone

fin
la dérive
das Seitenleitwerk
la aleta
l'aletta

tailplane
l'empennage
das Höhenleitwerk
el plano de cola
il piano di coda

cabin • la cabine • die Kabine • la cabina • la cabina

emergency exit
la sortie de secours
der Notausgang
la salida de emergencia
l'uscita di emergenza

flight attendant
l'hôtesse de l'air
die Flugbegleiterin
la azafata de vuelo
l'assistente di volo

overhead locker
le casier à bagages
das Gepäckfach
el compartimento portaequipajes
il compartimento portabagagli

air vent
le ventilateur
die Luftdüse
el ventilador
la ventola per l'aria

window
le hublot
das Fenster
la ventanilla
il finestrino

reading light
la liseuse
die Leselampe
la luz de lectura
la luce di lettura

seat
le siège
der Sitz
el asiento
il sedile

row
la rangée
die Reihe
la fila
la fila

armrest
l'accoudoir
die Armlehne
el apoyabrazos
il bracciolo

aisle
le couloir
der Gang
el pasillo
il corridoio

tray-table
la tablette
der Klapptisch
la bandeja
il tavolo pieghevole

seat back
le dossier
die Rückenlehne
el respaldo
lo schienale

english • français • deutsch • español • italiano

microlight • l'U.L.M. • das Ultraleichtflugzeug • el ultraligero • l'aereo ultraleggero

glider • le planeur • das Segelflugzeug • el planeador • l'aliante

biplane • le biplan • der Doppeldecker • el biplano • il biplano

propeller
l'hélice
der Propeller
la hélice
l'elica

hot-air balloon • la montgolfière • der Heißluftballon • el globo aerostático • la mongolfiera

light aircraft • l'avion léger • das Leichtflugzeug • la avioneta • l'aereo leggero

sea plane • l'hydravion • das Wasserflugzeug • el hidroavión • l'idrovolante

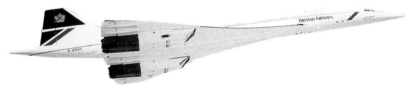

private jet • le jet privé • der Privatjet • el jet privado • l'aereo privato

supersonic jet • l'avion supersonique • das Uberschallflugzeug • el avión supersónico • l'aereo supersonico

rotor blade
la pale de rotor
das Rotorblatt
el aspa
la lama rotante

missile
le missile
die Rakete
el misil
il missile

helicopter • l'hélicoptère • der Hubschrauber • el helicóptero • l'elicottero

bomber • le bombardier • das Bombenflugzeug • el avión de bombardeo • il bombardiere

fighter plane • le chasseur • das Jagdflugzeug • el caza • l'aereo da caccia

pilot	take off (v)	land (v)	economy class	hand luggage
le pilote	décoller	atterrir	la classe économique	les bagages à main
der Pilot	starten	landen	die Economyclass	das Handgepäck
el piloto	despegar	aterrizar	la clase turista	el equipaje de mano
il pilota	decollare	atterrare	la classe economica	il bagaglio a mano
co-pilot	fly (v)	altitude	business class	seat belt
le copilote	voler	l'altitude	la classe affaires	la ceinture de sécurité
der Kopilot	fliegen	die Höhe	die Businessclass	der Sicherheitsgurt
el copiloto	volar	la altitud	la clase preferente	el cinturón de seguridad
il copilota	volare	la quota	la business class	la cintura di sicurezza

airport • l'aéroport • der Flughafen • el aeropuerto • l'aeroporto

apron
l'aire de stationnement
das Vorfeld
la plataforma de estacionamiento
l'area di stazionamento

baggage trailer
le porte-bagages
der Gepäckanhänger
el remolque del equipaje
il carrello portabagagli

terminal
le terminal
der Terminal
la terminal
il terminale

service vehicle
le véhicule de service
das Versorgungsfahrzeug
el vehículo de servicio
il veicolo di servizio

walkway
la passerelle
die Fluggastbrücke
la pasarela
il passaggio pedonale

airliner • l'avion de ligne • das Verkehrsflugzeug • el avión de línea • l'aereo di linea

runway la piste die Start- und Landebahn la pista la pista	flight number le numéro de vol die Flugnummer el número de vuelo il numero del volo	carousel le tapis roulant das Gepäckband la cinta transportadora il nastro trasportatore	holiday les vacances der Urlaub las vacaciones la vacanza
international flight le vol international der Auslandsflug el vuelo internacional il volo internazionale	immigration l'immigration die Passkontrolle el control de pasaportes il controllo passaporti	security la sécurité die Sicherheitsvorkehrungen la seguridad la sicurezza	book a flight (v) faire une réservation de vol einen Flug buchen reservar un vuelo prenotare un volo
domestic flight le vol domestique der Inlandsflug el vuelo nacional il volo nazionale	customs la douane der Zoll la aduana la dogana	X-ray machine la machine de rayons x die Gepäckröntgenmaschine la máquina de rayos x l'apparecchio a raggi x	check in (v) enregistrer einchecken facturar fare il check-in
connection la correspondance die Flugverbindung la conexión la coincidenza	excess baggage l'excédent de bagages das Übergepäck el exceso de equipaje il bagaglio in eccedenza	holiday brochure la brochure de vacances der Urlaubsprospekt el folleto de viajes l'opuscolo vacanze	control tower la tour de contrôle der Kontrollturm la torre de control la torre di controllo

hand luggage
les bagages à main
das Handgepäck
el equipaje de mano
il bagaglio a mano

luggage
les bagages
das Gepäck
el equipaje
il bagaglio

trolley
le chariot
der Kofferkuli
el carro
il carrello

check-in desk • l'enregistrement des bagages • der Abfertigungsschalter • el mostrador de facturación • il banco accettazione

visa
le visa
das Visum
el visado
il visto

passport • le passeport • der Pass • el pasaporte • il passaporto

boarding pass
la carte d'embarquement
die Bordkarte
la tarjeta de embarque
la carta d'imbarco

passport control • le contrôle de passeports • die Passkontrolle • el control de pasaportes • il controllo passaporti

ticket • le billet • das Flugticket • el billete • il biglietto

gate number • le numéro de la porte d'embarquement • die Gatenummer • el número de puerta de embarque • il numero dell'uscita

departures
les départs
der Abflug
las salidas
le partenze

departure lounge • la salle de départ • die Abflughalle • la sala de embarque • la sala delle partenze

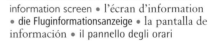

destination
la destination
das Reiseziel
el destino
la destinazione

arrivals
les arrivées
die Ankunft
las llegadas
gli arrivi

information screen • l'écran d'information • die Fluginformationsanzeige • la pantalla de información • il pannello degli orari

duty-free shop • la boutique hors taxes • der Duty-free-Shop • la tienda libre de impuestos • il negozio duty free

baggage reclaim • le retrait des bagages • die Gepäckausgabe • la recogida de equipajes • il ricupero bagagli

taxi rank • la station de taxis • der Taxistand • la parada de taxis • il posteggio dei taxi

car hire • la location de voitures • der Autoverleih • el alquiler de coches • l'autonoleggio

ship • le navire • das Schiff • el barco • la nave

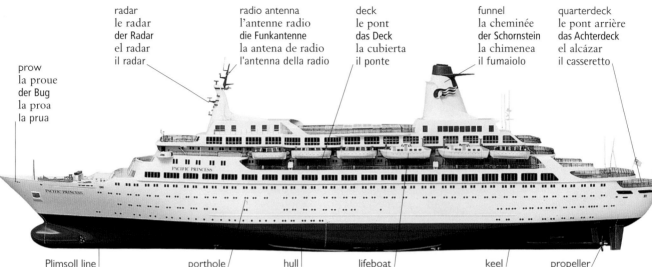

prow
la proue
der Bug
la proa
la prua

radar
le radar
der Radar
el radar
il radar

radio antenna
l'antenne radio
die Funkantenne
la antena de radio
l'antenna della radio

deck
le pont
das Deck
la cubierta
il ponte

funnel
la cheminée
der Schornstein
la chimenea
il fumaiolo

quarterdeck
le pont arrière
das Achterdeck
el alcázar
il casseretto

Plimsoll line
la marque de flottaison
die Höchstlademarke
la línea de flotación
la marca di bordo libero

porthole
le hublot
das Bullauge
el ojo de buey
l'oblò

hull
la coque
der Rumpf
el casco
lo scafo

lifeboat
le canot de sauvetage
das Rettungsboot
el bote salvavidas
la lancia di salvataggio

keel
la quille
der Kiel
la quilla
la chiglia

propeller
l'hélice
die Schiffsschraube
la hélice
l'elica

ocean liner • le paquebot • der Ozeandampfer • el transatlántico • la nave da crociera

bridge • la passerelle de commandement • die Kommandobrücke • el puente • il ponte di comando

engine room • la salle des moteurs • der Maschinenraum • la sala de máquinas • la sala macchine

cabin • la cabine • die Kabine • el camarote • la cabina

galley • la cuisine • die Kombüse • la cocina • la cucina di bordo

dock
le dock
das Dock
el muelle
il bacino

windlass
le guindeau
die Ankerwinde
el cabrestante
il mulinello

port
le port
der Hafen
el puerto
il porto

captain
le capitaine
der Kapitän
el capitán
il capitano

gangway
la passerelle
die Landungsbrücke
la pasarela
la passerella

speedboat
le runabout
das Rennboot
la lancha motora
il motoscafo

anchor
l'ancre
der Anker
el ancla
l'ancora

rowing boat
la barque
das Ruderboot
la barca de remos
la barca a remi

bollard
le bollard
der Poller
el noray
la colonna d'ormeggio

canoe
le canoë
das Kanu
la piragua
la canoa

other ships • autres bateaux • andere Schiffe • otras embarcaciones • altre imbarcazioni

ferry • le ferry • die Fähre • el ferry • il traghetto

outboard motor
le hors-bord
der Außenbordmotor
el motor fueraborda
il motore fuoribordo

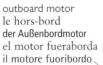

inflatable dinghy • le dinghy pneumatique • das Schlauchboot • la zodiac • il gommone

hydrofoil • l'hydroptère • das Tragflügelboot • el hidrodeslizador • l'aliscafo

yacht • le yacht • die Jacht • el yate • lo yacht

catamaran • le catamaran • der Katamaran • el catamarán • il catamarano

tug boat • le remorqueur • der Schleppdampfer • el remolcador • il rimorchiatore

hovercraft • l'aéroglisseur • das Luftkissenboot • el aerodeslizador • l'hovercraft

container ship • le navire porte-conteneurs • das Containerschiff • el buque portacontenedores • la nave porta-container

rigging
le gréement
die Takelung
las jarcias
il sartiame

sailboat • le voilier • das Segelboot • el velero • la barca a vela

hold
la cale
der Frachtraum
la bodega
la stiva

freighter • le cargo • das Frachtschiff • el buque de carga • la nave da trasporto

oil tanker • le pétrolier • der Öltanker • el barco petrolero • la petroliera

aircraft carrier • le porte-avions • der Flugzeugträger • el portaaviones • la portaerei

battleship • le navire de guerre • das Kriegsschiff • el barco de guerra • la nave da guerra

conning tower
le kiosque
der Kommandoturm
la falsa torre
la torretta di comando

submarine • le sous-marin • das U-Boot • el submarino • il sottomarino

port • le port • der Hafen • el puerto • il porto

warehouse
l'entrepôt
das Warenlager
el almacén
il magazzino

crane
la grue
der Kran
la grúa
la gru

fork-lift truck
le chariot élévateur
der Gabelstapler
la carretilla elevadora
il carrello elevatore

access road
la route d'accès
die Zufahrtsstraße
la carretera de acceso
la strada di accesso

customs house
le bureau des douanes
das Zollamt
la oficina de aduanas
l'ufficio della dogana

container
le conteneur
der Container
el contenedor
il container

dock
le dock
das Dock
la dársena
il bacino

quay
le quai
der Kai
el muelle
la banchina

cargo
la cargaison
die Fracht
la carga
il carico

ferry terminal
le terminal de ferrys
der Fährterminal
la terminal del ferry
il terminale dei traghetti

ferry
le ferry
die Fähre
el ferry
il traghetto

ticket office
le guichet
der Fahrkartenschalter
la ventanilla de pasajes
la biglietteria

passenger
le passager
der Passagier
el pasajero
il passeggero

container port • le port de conteneurs • der Containerhafen • el muelle comercial • il porto per container

passenger port • le port de passagers • der Passagier-hafen • el muelle de pasajeros • il porto per passeggeri

english • français • deutsch • español • italiano

net
le filet
das Netz
la red
la rete

fishing boat
le bateau de pêche
das Fischerboot
el barco de pesca
la barca da pesca

mooring
les amarres
die Verankerung
el punto de amarre
l'ormeggio

marina • la marina • die Marina • el puerto deportivo • il porto turistico

fishing port • le port de pêche • der Fischereihafen • el puerto de pesca • il porto da pesca

harbour • le port • der Hafen • el puerto • il porto

pier • l'embarcadère • der Pier • el embarcadero • il molo

jetty • la jetée • der Landungssteg • el espigón • il pontile

shipyard • le chantier naval • die Werft • el astillero • il cantiere navale

lamp
le feu
die Laterne
la lámpara
la luce

lighthouse • le phare • der Leuchtturm • el faro • il faro

buoy • la bouée • die Boje • la boya • la boa

coastguard	dry dock	board (v)
le garde-côte	la cale sèche	embarquer
die Küstenwache	das Trockendock	an Bord gehen
el guardacostas	el dique seco	embarcar
il guardacoste	il bacino di carenaggio	imbarcare
harbour master	moor (v)	disembark (v)
le capitaine de port	mouiller	débarquer
der Hafenmeister	festmachen	von Bord gehen
el capitán del puerto	amarrar	desembarcar
il capitano di porto	ormeggiare	sbarcare
drop anchor (v)	dock (v)	set sail (v)
jeter l'ancre	se mettre à quai	prendre la mer
den Anker werfen	anlegen	auslaufen
fondear	atracar	zarpar
gettare l'ancora	approdare	salpare

sports
les sports
die Sportarten
los deportes
gli sport

American football • le football américain • der Football • el fútbol americano • il football americano

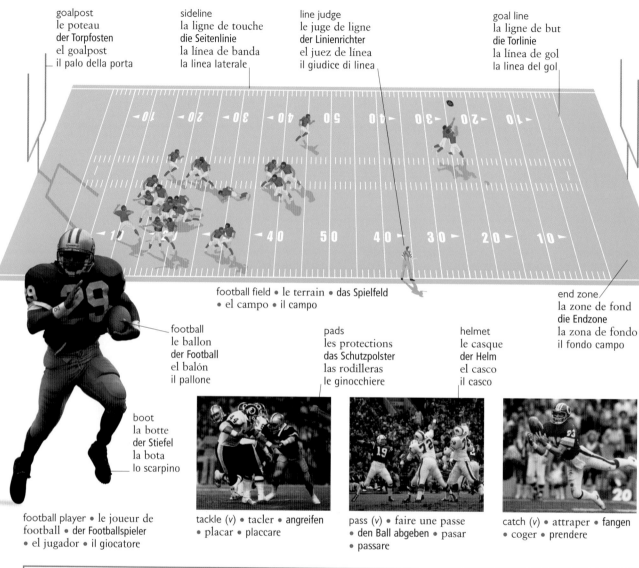

goalpost
le poteau
der Torpfosten
el goalpost
il palo della porta

sideline
la ligne de touche
die Seitenlinie
la línea de banda
la linea laterale

line judge
le juge de ligne
der Linienrichter
el juez de línea
il giudice di linea

goal line
la ligne de but
die Torlinie
la línea de gol
la linea del gol

football field • le terrain • das Spielfeld • el campo • il campo

end zone
la zone de fond
die Endzone
la zona de fondo
il fondo campo

football
le ballon
der Football
el balón
il pallone

pads
les protections
das Schutzpolster
las rodilleras
le ginocchiere

helmet
le casque
der Helm
el casco
il casco

boot
la botte
der Stiefel
la bota
lo scarpino

football player • le joueur de
football • der Footballspieler
• el jugador • il giocatore

tackle (v) • tacler • angreifen
• placar • placcare

pass (v) • faire une passe
• den Ball abgeben • pasar
• passare

catch (v) • attraper • fangen
• coger • prendere

time out le temps mort die Auszeit el tiempo muerto il time-out	team l'équipe die Mannschaft el equipo la squadra	defence la défense die Verteidigung la defensa la difesa	cheerleader la majorette der Cheerleader la animadora la cheerleader	What is the score? Où en est le match? Wie ist der Stand? ¿Cómo van? A quanto stanno?
fumble la prise de ballon maladroite das unsichere Fangen des Balls el mal pase il fumble	attack l'attaque der Angriff el ataque l'attacco	score le score der Spielstand la puntuación il punteggio	touchdown le but der Touchdown el ensayo il touch-down	Who is winning? Qui est-ce qui gagne? Wer gewinnt? ¿Quién va ganando? Chi vince?

rugby • le rugby • das Rugby • el rugby • il rugby

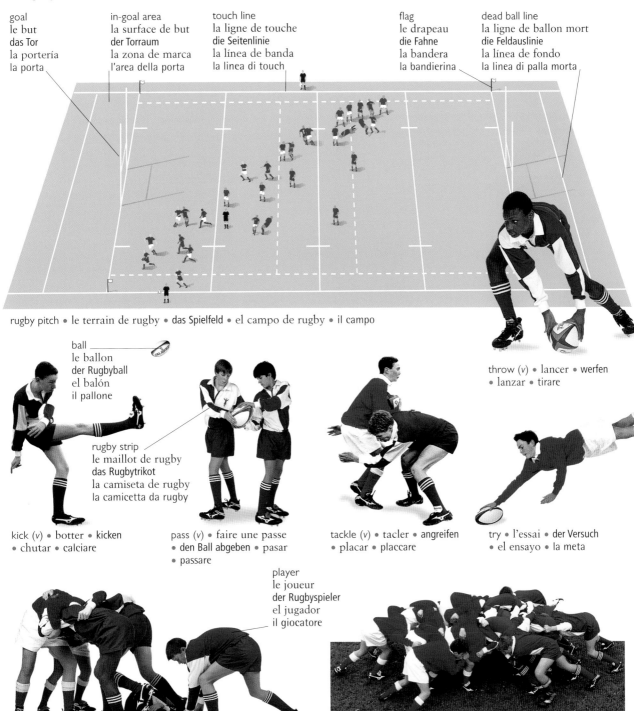

goal
le but
das Tor
la portería
la porta

in-goal area
la surface de but
der Torraum
la zona de marca
l'area della porta

touch line
la ligne de touche
die Seitenlinie
la línea de banda
la linea di touch

flag
le drapeau
die Fahne
la bandera
la bandierina

dead ball line
la ligne de ballon mort
die Feldauslinie
la linea di fondo
la linea di palla morta

rugby pitch • le terrain de rugby • das Spielfeld • el campo de rugby • il campo

ball
le ballon
der Rugbyball
el balón
il pallone

rugby strip
le maillot de rugby
das Rugbytrikot
la camiseta de rugby
la camicetta da rugby

throw (v) • lancer • werfen
• lanzar • tirare

kick (v) • botter • kicken
• chutar • calciare

pass (v) • faire une passe
• den Ball abgeben • pasar
• passare

tackle (v) • tacler • angreifen
• placar • placcare

try • l'essai • der Versuch
• el ensayo • la meta

player
le joueur
der Rugbyspieler
el jugador
il giocatore

ruck • la mêlée ouverte • das offene Gedränge • la abierta • il ruck

scrum • la mêlée • das Gedränge • la melée • la mischia

soccer • le football • der Fußball • el fútbol • il calcio

football
le ballon
der Fußball
el balón
il pallone

forward
l'avant
der Mittelstürmer
el delantero
l'attaccante

referee
l'arbitre
der Schiedsrichter
el árbitro
l'arbitro

centre circle
le cercle central
der Mittelkreis
el círculo central
il centro campo

goalkeeper
le gardien de but
der Torwart
el portero
il portiere

football strip
la tenue
der Dress
la equipación
la divisa

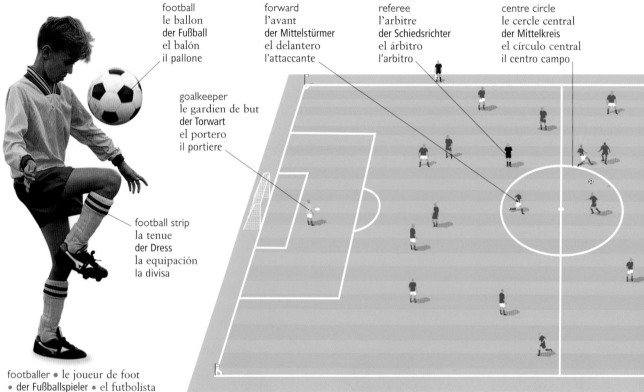

footballer • le joueur de foot
• der Fußballspieler • el futbolista
• il calciatore

football pitch • le terrain • das Fußballfeld • el campo de fútbol • il campo di calcio

goalpost
le poteau
der Torpfosten
el poste
il palo

net
le filet
das Tornetz
la red
la rete

crossbar
la barre transversale
die Querlatte
el larguero
la traversa

dribble (v) • dribbler • dribbeln
• regatear • dribblare

head (v) • faire une tête
• köpfen • rematar de cabeza
• colpire di testa

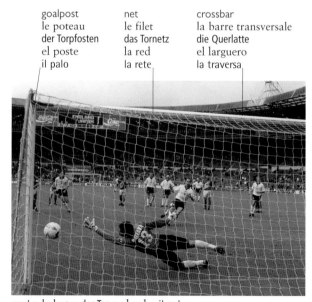

goal • le but • das Tor • el gol • il gol

wall
le mur
die Mauer
la barrera
il muro

free kick • le coup franc • der Freistoß • el tiro libre • il calcio di punizione

penalty area
la surface de réparation
der Strafraum
el área de penalti
l'area di rigore

goal line
la ligne de but
die Torlinie
la linea de fondo
la linea della porta

goal area
la surface de but
der Torraum
el área pequeña
l'area di porta

goal
le but
das Tor
la portería
la porta

defender
le défenseur
der Verteidiger
el defensa
il difensore

linesman
le juge de ligne
der Linienrichter
el juez de línea
il guardialinee

corner flag
le drapeau de coin
die Eckfahne
la bandera de esquina
la bandierina

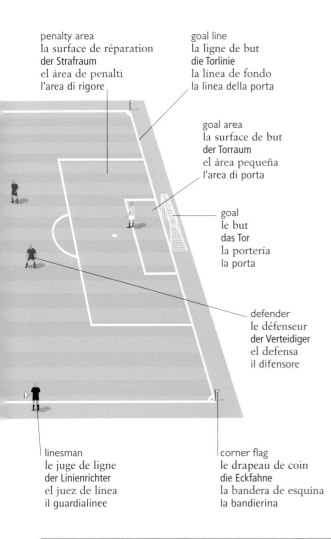

throw-in • la rentrée en touche • der Einwurf • el saque de banda • la rimessa in gioco

kick (v) • botter • kicken • chutar • calciare

pass (v) • faire une passe • den Ball abgeben • hacer un pase • passare

boot
la botte
der Fußballschuh
la bota
lo scarpino

shoot (v) • shooter • schießen • tirar • tirare

save (v) • sauver • halten • hacer una parada • parare

tackle (v) • tacler • angreifen • hacer una entrada • contrastare

stadium le stade das Stadion el estadio lo stadio	foul la faute das Foul la falta il fallo	yellow card le carton jaune die gelbe Karte la tarjeta amarilla il cartellino giallo	league le championnat die Liga la liga il campionato	extra time la prolongation die Verlängerung la prórroga il tempo supplementare
score a goal (v) marquer un but ein Tor schießen marcar un gol segnare	corner le corner der Eckball el córner il calcio d'angolo	off-side l'hors-jeu das Abseits el fuera de juego il fuorigioco	draw l'egalité das Unentschieden el empate il pareggio	substitute le remplaçant der Ersatzspieler el suplente il sostituto
penalty le penalty der Elfmeter el penalti il rigore	red card le carton rouge die rote Karte la tarjeta roja il cartellino rosso	send off l'expulsion der Platzverweis la expulsión l'espulsione	half time la mi-temps die Halbzeit el descanso l'intervallo	substitution le remplacement die Auswechslung la sustitución la sostituzione

hockey • le hockey • das Hockey • el hockey • l'hockey

ice hockey • le hockey sur glace • das Eishockey • el hockey sobre hielo • l'hockey su ghiaccio

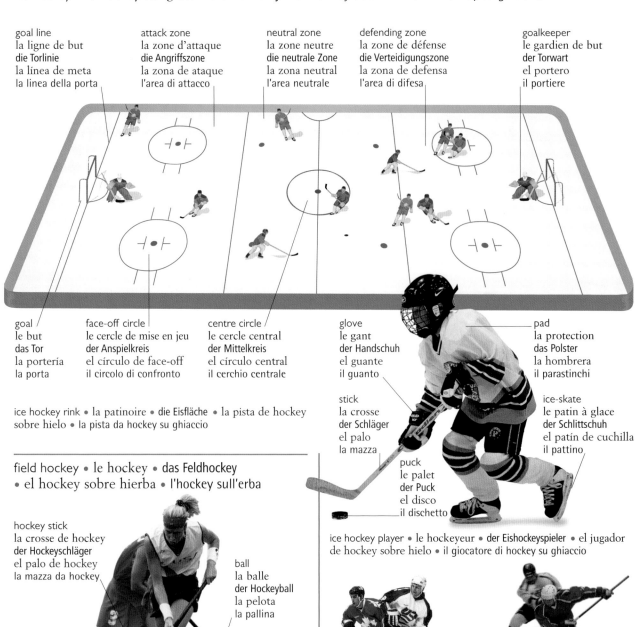

goal line
la ligne de but
die Torlinie
la línea de meta
la linea della porta

attack zone
la zone d'attaque
die Angriffszone
la zona de ataque
l'area di attacco

neutral zone
la zone neutre
die neutrale Zone
la zona neutral
l'area neutrale

defending zone
la zone de défense
die Verteidigungszone
la zona de defensa
l'area di difesa

goalkeeper
le gardien de but
der Torwart
el portero
il portiere

goal
le but
das Tor
la portería
la porta

face-off circle
le cercle de mise en jeu
der Anspielkreis
el círculo de face-off
il circolo di confronto

centre circle
le cercle central
der Mittelkreis
el círculo central
il cerchio centrale

glove
le gant
der Handschuh
el guante
il guanto

pad
la protection
das Polster
la hombrera
il parastinchi

ice hockey rink • la patinoire • die Eisfläche • la pista de hockey
sobre hielo • la pista da hockey su ghiaccio

stick
la crosse
der Schläger
el palo
la mazza

ice-skate
le patin à glace
der Schlittschuh
el patín de cuchilla
il pattino

field hockey • le hockey • das Feldhockey
• el hockey sobre hierba • l'hockey sull'erba

puck
le palet
der Puck
el disco
il dischetto

hockey stick
la crosse de hockey
der Hockeyschläger
el palo de hockey
la mazza da hockey

ball
la balle
der Hockeyball
la pelota
la pallina

ice hockey player • le hockeyeur • der Eishockeyspieler • el jugador
de hockey sobre hielo • il giocatore di hockey su ghiaccio

skate (v) • patiner
• Schlittschuh laufen • patinar
• pattinare

hit (v) • frapper • schlagen
• golpear • colpire

cricket • le cricket • das Kricket • el críquet • il cricket

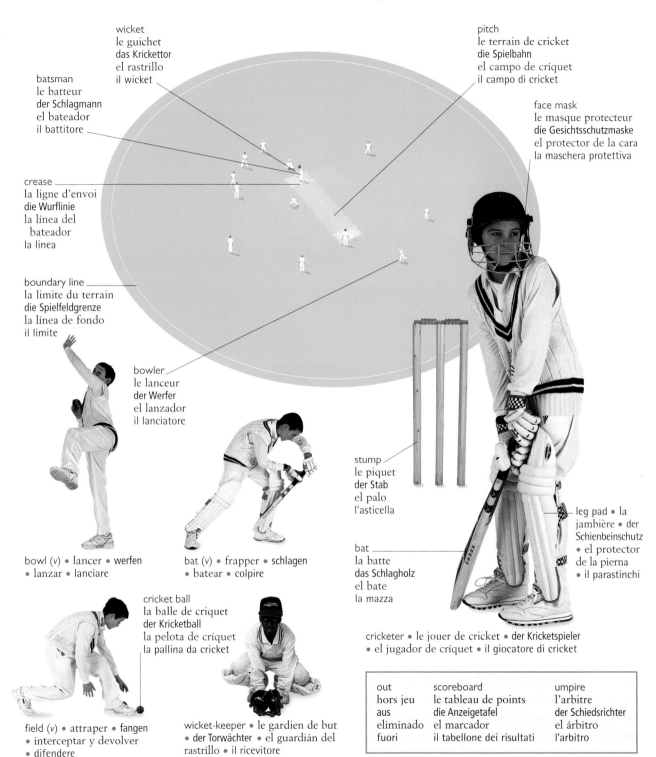

wicket
le guichet
das Krickettor
el rastrillo
il wicket

pitch
le terrain de cricket
die Spielbahn
el campo de críquet
il campo di cricket

batsman
le batteur
der Schlagmann
el bateador
il battitore

face mask
le masque protecteur
die Gesichtsschutzmaske
el protector de la cara
la maschera protettiva

crease
la ligne d'envoi
die Wurflinie
la línea del
 bateador
la linea

boundary line
la limite du terrain
die Spielfeldgrenze
la línea de fondo
il limite

bowler
le lanceur
der Werfer
el lanzador
il lanciatore

stump
le piquet
der Stab
el palo
l'asticella

leg pad • la
jambière • der
Schienbeinschutz
• el protector
de la pierna
• il parastinchi

bat
la batte
das Schlagholz
el bate
la mazza

bowl (v) • lancer • werfen
• lanzar • lanciare

bat (v) • frapper • schlagen
• batear • colpire

cricket ball
la balle de criquet
der Kricketball
la pelota de críquet
la pallina da cricket

cricketer • le jouer de cricket • der Kricketspieler
• el jugador de críquet • il giocatore di cricket

field (v) • attraper • fangen
• interceptar y devolver
• difendere

wicket-keeper • le gardien de but
• der Torwächter • el guardián del
rastrillo • il ricevitore

out	scoreboard	umpire
hors jeu	le tableau de points	l'arbitre
aus	die Anzeigetafel	der Schiedsrichter
eliminado	el marcador	el árbitro
fuori	il tabellone dei risultati	l'arbitro

basketball • le basket • der Basketball • el baloncesto • la pallacanestro

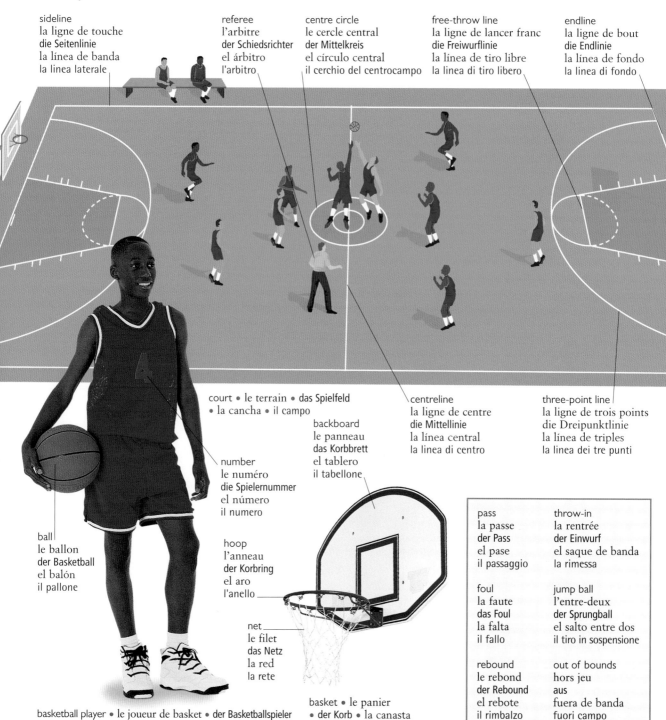

sideline
la ligne de touche
die Seitenlinie
la línea de banda
la linea laterale

referee
l'arbitre
der Schiedsrichter
el árbitro
l'arbitro

centre circle
le cercle central
der Mittelkreis
el círculo central
il cerchio del centrocampo

free-throw line
la ligne de lancer franc
die Freiwurflinie
la línea de tiro libre
la linea di tiro libero

endline
la ligne de bout
die Endlinie
la línea de fondo
la linea di fondo

court • le terrain • **das Spielfeld** • la cancha • il campo

backboard
le panneau
das Korbbrett
el tablero
il tabellone

number
le numéro
die Spielernummer
el número
il numero

centreline
la ligne de centre
die Mittellinie
la línea central
la linea di centro

three-point line
la ligne de trois points
die Dreipunktlinie
la línea de triples
la linea dei tre punti

hoop
l'anneau
der Korbring
el aro
l'anello

ball
le ballon
der Basketball
el balón
il pallone

net
le filet
das Netz
la red
la rete

pass	throw-in
la passe	la rentrée
der Pass	**der Einwurf**
el pase	el saque de banda
il passaggio	la rimessa
foul	jump ball
la faute	l'entre-deux
das Foul	**der Sprungball**
la falta	el salto entre dos
il fallo	il tiro in sospensione
rebound	out of bounds
le rebond	hors jeu
der Rebound	**aus**
el rebote	fuera de banda
il rimbalzo	fuori campo

basketball player • le joueur de basket • **der Basketballspieler** • el jugador de baloncesto • il giocatore di pallacenestro

basket • le panier • **der Korb** • la canasta • il canestro

actions • les actions • die Aktionen • las acciones • le azioni

throw (v) • lancer • werfen • lanzar • tirare

catch (v) • attraper • fangen • coger • acchiappare

shoot (v) • tirer • zielen • tirar • tirare

jump (v) • sauter • springen • saltar • saltare

mark (v) • marquer • decken • marcar • marcare

block (v) • bloquer • blocken • bloquear • bloccare

bounce (v) • faire rebondir • springen lassen • botar • rimbalzare

dunk (v) • faire un dunk • einen Dunk spielen • hacer un mate • segnare

volleyball • le volley • der Volleyball • el voleibol • la pallavolo

block (v)
bloquer
blocken
bloquear
contrastare

net
le filet
das Netz
la red
la rete

dig (v)
faire une manchette
baggern
recibir
difendere

referee
l'arbitre
der Schiedsrichter
el árbitro
l'arbitro

knee support
la genouillère
der Knieschützer
la rodillera
la ginocchiera

court • le terrain • das Spielfeld • la cancha • il campo

baseball • le baseball • der Baseball • el béisbol • il baseball

field • le terrain • das Spielfeld • el campo • il campo

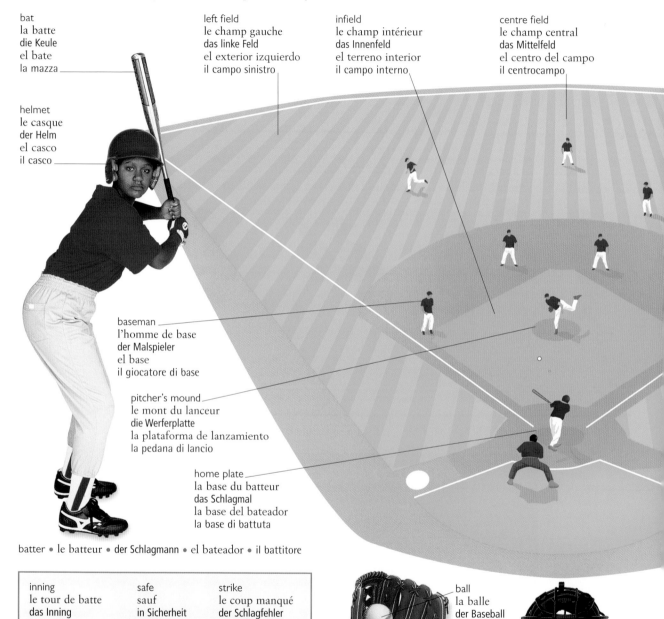

bat
la batte
die Keule
el bate
la mazza

left field
le champ gauche
das linke Feld
el exterior izquierdo
il campo sinistro

infield
le champ intérieur
das Innenfeld
el terreno interior
il campo interno

centre field
le champ central
das Mittelfeld
el centro del campo
il centrocampo

helmet
le casque
der Helm
el casco
il casco

baseman
l'homme de base
der Malspieler
el base
il giocatore di base

pitcher's mound
le mont du lanceur
die Werferplatte
la plataforma de lanzamiento
la pedana di lancio

home plate
la base du batteur
das Schlagmal
la base del bateador
la base di battuta

batter • le batteur • der Schlagmann • el bateador • il battitore

inning	safe	strike
le tour de batte	sauf	le coup manqué
das Inning	in Sicherheit	der Schlagfehler
la entrada	a salvo	el strike
il turno di battuta	salvo	lo strike
run	out	foul ball
le point	hors jeu	la fausse balle
der Lauf	aus	der ungültige Schlag
la carrera	fuera	el fallo
il giro	fuori	il fallo

ball
la balle
der Baseball
la pelota
la palla

mitt • le gant • der Handschuh
• el guante • il guantone

mask • le masque • die
Schutzmaske • la máscara
• la maschera

outfield
le champ extérieur
das Außenfeld
el exterior
il campo esterno

right field
le champ droit
das rechte Feld
el exterior derecho
il campo destro

foul line
la ligne de pénalité
die Foullinie
la línea de falta
la linea di fallo

team
l'équipe
das Team
el equipo
la squadra

dugout
le banc de touche
die Spielerbank
el banquillo
la fossa

catcher • le receveur
• der Fänger • el cátcher
• il ricevitore

pitcher • le lanceur • der
Werfer • el pítcher • il pitcher

actions • les actions • **die Aktionen** • las acciones
• le azioni

throw (v) • lancer • **werfen**
• lanzar • lanciare

catch (v) • attraper • **fangen**
• coger • acchiappare

run (v) • courir • **rennen**
• correr • correre

field (v) • être en défense
• als Fänger spielen • **defender**
• difendere

slide (v)
glisser
rutschen
resbalar
scivolare

tag (v) • courser • **hinterherlaufen** • perseguir • inseguire

pitch (v)
lancer
werfen
lanzar
servire

bat (v)
batter
schlagen
batear
battere

umpire
l'arbitre
der Schiedsrichter
el árbitro
l'arbitro

play (v) • jouer • **spielen** • jugar • giocare

tennis • le tennis • das Tennis • el tenis • il tennis

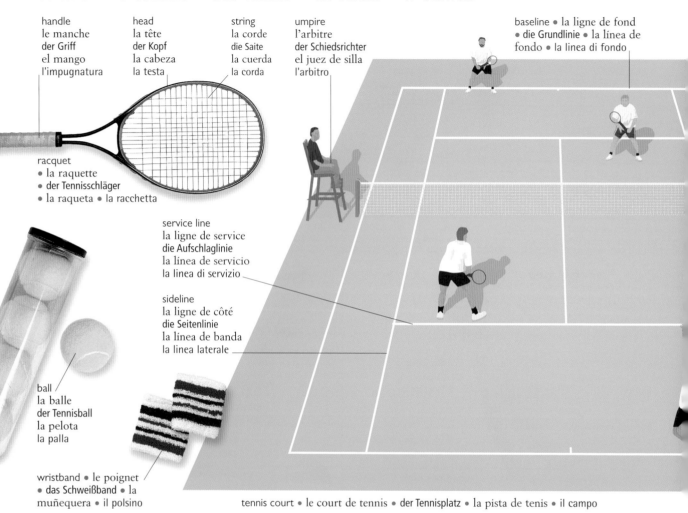

handle
le manche
der Griff
el mango
l'impugnatura

head
la tête
der Kopf
la cabeza
la testa

string
la corde
die Saite
la cuerda
la corda

umpire
l'arbitre
der Schiedsrichter
el juez de silla
l'arbitro

baseline • la ligne de fond
• die Grundlinie • la línea de
fondo • la linea di fondo

racquet
• la raquette
• der Tennisschläger
• la raqueta • la racchetta

service line
la ligne de service
die Aufschlaglinie
la línea de servicio
la linea di servizio

sideline
la ligne de côté
die Seitenlinie
la línea de banda
la linea laterale

ball
la balle
der Tennisball
la pelota
la palla

wristband • le poignet
• das Schweißband • la
muñequera • il polsino

tennis court • le court de tennis • der Tennisplatz • la pista de tenis • il campo

singles	set	deuce	fault	slice	spin
le simple	le set	l'égalité	la faute	le slice	l'effet
das Einzel	der Satz	der Einstand	der Fehler	der Slice	der Spin
el individual	el set	cuarenta iguales	la falta	el golpe cortado	el efecto
il singolare	il set	il parità	il fallo	il taglio	l'avvitamento
doubles	match	advantage	ace	rally	linesman
le double	le match	l'avantage	l'as	l'échange	le juge de ligne
das Doppel	das Match	der Vorteil	das Ass	der Ballwechsel	der Linienrichter
los dobles	el partido	la ventaja	el ace	el peloteo	el juez de línea
il doppio	la partita	il vantaggio	l'asso	il palleggio	il giudice di linea
game	tiebreak	love	dropshot	let!	championship
le jeu	le tiebreak	zéro	l'amorti	net!	le championnat
das Spiel	der Tiebreak	null	der Stoppball	Netz!	die Meisterschaft
el juego	el tiebreak	nada	la dejada	¡red!	el campeonato
il gioco	il tiebreak	a zero	la smorzata	colpo nullo!	il campionato

strokes • les coups • die Schläge • los golpes • i colpi

net
le filet
das Netz
la red
la rete

smash
le smash
der Schmetterball
el smash
la schiacciata

ballboy
le ramasseur de balles
der Balljunge
el recogepelotas
il raccattapalle

serve (v)
servir
aufschlagen
sacar
battere il servizio

tennis shoes
• les tennis
• die Tennisschuhe
• los zapatos de
tenis • le scarpe
da tennis

player • le joueur • der Tennisspieler • el jugador • il giocatore

serve • le service • der
Aufschlag • el servicio
• il servizio

volley • la vollée • der Volley
• la volea • il palleggio

return • le retour • der Return
• el resto • il ritorno

lob • le lob • der Lob
• el lob • il lob

forehand • le coup droit
• die Vorhand • el derecho
• il dritto

backhand • le revers
• die Rückhand • el revés
• il rovescio

racquet games • les jeux de raquette • die Schlägerspiele • los juegos de raqueta • i giochi con la racchetta

shuttlecock
le volant
der Federball
el volante
il volano

bat • la raquette •
der Tischtennisschläger
• la pala • la
racchetta

badminton • le badminton
• das Badminton • el
bádminton • il badminton

table tennis • le tennis de
table • das Tischtennis • el
ping-pong • il ping pong

squash • le squash • das
Squash • el squash • lo
squash

racquetball • le racquetball
• der Racquetball • el
racketball • il racquetball

golf • le golf • das Golf • el golf • il golf

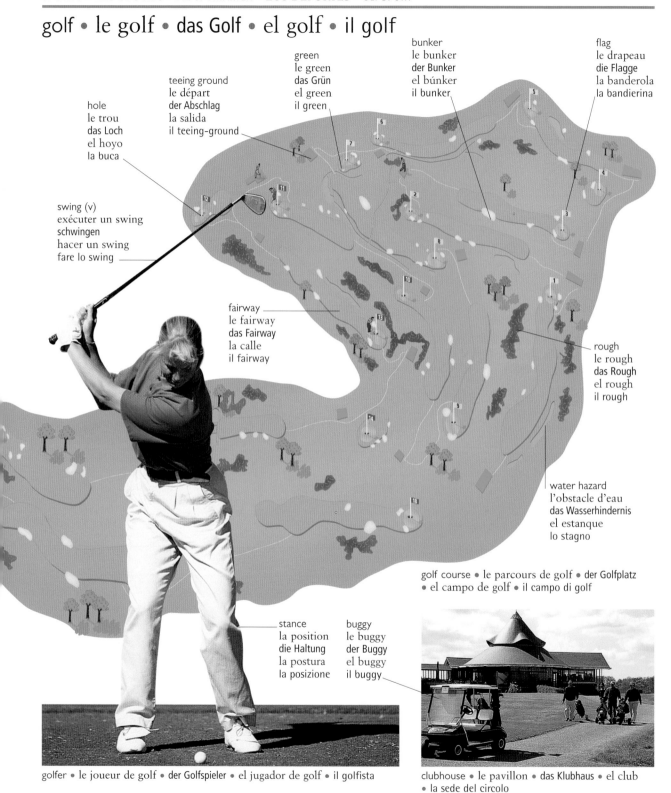

green
le green
das Grün
el green
il green

bunker
le bunker
der Bunker
el búnker
il bunker

flag
le drapeau
die Flagge
la banderola
la bandierina

teeing ground
le départ
der Abschlag
la salida
il teeing-ground

hole
le trou
das Loch
el hoyo
la buca

swing (v)
exécuter un swing
schwingen
hacer un swing
fare lo swing

fairway
le fairway
das Fairway
la calle
il fairway

rough
le rough
das Rough
el rough
il rough

water hazard
l'obstacle d'eau
das Wasserhindernis
el estanque
lo stagno

golf course • le parcours de golf • der Golfplatz
• el campo de golf • il campo di golf

stance
la position
die Haltung
la postura
la posizione

buggy
le buggy
der Buggy
el buggy
il buggy

golfer • le joueur de golf • der Golfspieler • el jugador de golf • il golfista

clubhouse • le pavillon • das Klubhaus • el club
• la sede del circolo

equipment • l'équipement • die Ausrüstung • el equipo • le attrezzature

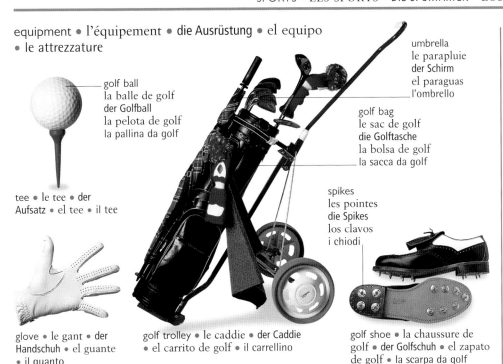

golf ball
la balle de golf
der Golfball
la pelota de golf
la pallina da golf

umbrella
le parapluie
der Schirm
el paraguas
l'ombrello

golf bag
le sac de golf
die Golftasche
la bolsa de golf
la sacca da golf

tee • le tee • der
Aufsatz • el tee • il tee

spikes
les pointes
die Spikes
los clavos
i chiodi

glove • le gant • der
Handschuh • el guante
• il guanto

golf trolley • le caddie • der Caddie
• el carrito de golf • il carrellino

golf shoe • la chaussure de
golf • der Golfschuh • el zapato
de golf • la scarpa da golf

golf clubs • les clubs de golf • die Golfschläger • los palos de golf • le mazze da golf

wood • le bois • das Holz
• el palo de madera
• la mazza di legno

putter • le putter
• der Putter • el putter
• il putter

iron • le fer • das Eisen
• el hierro • la mazza di
ferro

wedge • la cale
• das Wedge • el wedge
• la mazza ricurva

actions • les actions • die Aktionen • las acciones • le azioni

tee-off (v) • partir du
tee • vom Abschlag
spielen • salir •
cominciare la partita

drive (v) • driver
• driven • hacer un
drive • colpire a
distanza

putt (v) • putter
• einlochen • tirar al
hoyo con un putter
• colpire leggermente

chip (v) • cocher
• chippen • hacer
un chip • colpire da
vicino

par	over par	handicap	caddy	stroke	backswing
le par	le over par	le handicap	le caddie	le coup	le swing en arrière
das Par	das Überpar	das Golfhandicap	der Caddie	der Schlag	der Durchschwung
el par	el sobre par	el handicap	el caddie	el golpe	el backswing
il par	l'overpar	l'handicap	il caddy	il colpo	il back-swing
under par	hole in one	tournament	spectators	practice swing	line of play
le under par	le trou en un	le tournoi	les spectateurs	le swing d'essai	la ligne de jeu
das Unterpar	das Hole-in-One	das Golfturnier	die Zuschauer	der Übungsschwung	die Spielbahn
el bajo par	el hoyo en uno	el torneo	los espectadores	el swing de práctica	la línea de juego
l'underpar	la buca in uno	il torneo	gli spettatori	lo swing di pratica	la linea di gioco

athletics • l'athlétisme • die Leichtathletik • el atletismo • l'atletica

lane
le couloir
die Bahn
la calle
la corsia

track
la piste
die Rennbahn
la pista
la pista

finishing line
la ligne d'arrivée
die Ziellinie
la línea de meta
il traguardo

starting line
la ligne de départ
die Startlinie
la línea de salida
la linea di partenza

field • le terrain • das Feld • el campo • il campo

athlete
l'athlète
die Leichtathletin
la atleta
l'atleta

starting blocks
le bloc de départ
der Startblock
los tacos de salida
la pedana di partenza

sprinter • le sprinter
• der Sprinter • el esprinter
• il velocista

discus • le disque
• das Diskuswerfen
• el lanzamiento de disco
• il lancio del disco

shotput • le lancement du
poids • das Kugelstoßen
• el lanzamiento de peso
• il lancio del peso

javelin • le javelot • das
Speerwerfen • el lanzamiento
de jabalina • il lancio del
giavellotto

race	record	photo finish	pole vault
la course	le record	le photo-finish	le saut à la perche
das Rennen	der Rekord	das Fotofinish	der Stabhochsprung
la carrera	el récord	la fotofinish	el salto con pértiga
la gara	il primato	il fotofinish	il salto con l'asta
time	break a record (v)	marathon	personal best
le temps	battre un record	le marathon	le record personnel
die Zeit	einen Rekord brechen	der Marathon	die persönliche Bestleistung
el tiempo	batir un récord	la maratón	la marca personal
il tempo	battere un primato	la maratona	il primato personale

stopwatch • le chronomètre
• die Stoppuhr • el
cronómetro • il cronometro

baton • le bâton
• der Stab • el testigo
• il testimone

crossbar • la barre
• die Latte • el listón
• la sbarra

relay race • le relais • der Staffellauf • la carrera de relevos • la staffetta

high jump • le saut en hauteur • der Hochsprung • el salto de altura • il salto in alto

long jump • le saut en longueur • der Weitsprung • el salto de longitud • il salto in lungo

hurdles • les haies • der Hürdenlauf • la carrera de vallas • la corsa a ostacoli

gymnastics • la gymnastique • das Turnen • la gimnasia • la ginnastica

springboard
le tremplin
das Sprungbrett
el trampolín
la pedana elastica

gymnast
la gymnaste
die Turnerin
la gimnasta
la ginnasta

horse
le cheval
das Pferd
el caballo
il cavallo

somersault • le salto
• der Salto • el salto mortal
• la capriola

beam • la poutre • der Schwebebalken • la barra de equilibrio • la trave

ribbon • le drapeau
• das Gymnastikband
• la cinta • il nastro

mat • le tapis • die Matte • la colchoneta • la pedana

vault • le saut • der Sprung
• el salto • il salto

floor exercises • les exercises au sol • das Bodenturnen • los ejercicios de suelo • la ginnastica a corpo libero

tumble • la cabriole • die Bodenakrobatik • la voltereta • la ruota

rhythmic gymnastics • la gymnastique rythmique • die rhythmische Gymnastik • la gimnasia rítmica • la ginnastica ritmica

horizontal bar	asymmetric bars	rings	medals	silver
la barre fixe	les barres asymétriques	les anneaux	les médailles	l'argent
das Reck	der Stufenbarren	die Ringe	die Medaillen	das Silber
la barra fija	las paralelas asimétricas	las anillas	las medallas	la plata
la sbarra	le sbarre asimmetriche	gli anelli	le medaglie	l'argento
parallel bars	pommel horse	podium	gold	bronze
les barres parallèles	le cheval d'arçons	le podium	l'or	le bronze
der Barren	das Seitpferd	das Siegerpodium	das Gold	die Bronze
las paralelas	el caballo con arcos	el podio	el oro	el bronce
le parallele	il cavallo	il podio	l'oro	il bronzo

combat sports • les sports de combat • der Kampfsport • los deportes de combate • gli sport da combattimento

opponent
l'adversaire
der Gegner
el adversario
l'avversario

glove
le gant
der Handschuh
el guante
il guanto

guard
le protège-tête
der Kopfschutz
el protector
il casco

belt
la ceinture
der Gürtel
el cinturón
la cintura

tae-kwon-do • le taekwondo • das Taekwondo • el taekwondo • il tae kwondo

karate • le karaté • das Karate • el karate • il karate

judo • le judo • das Judo • el yudo • il judo

aikido • l'aïkido • das Aikido • el aikido • l'aikido

mask
le masque
die Maske
la careta
la maschera

sword
le sabre
der Säbel
la espada
la sciabola

kendo • le kendo • das Kendo • el kendo • il kendo

kung fu • le kung-fu • das Kung-Fu • el kung fu • il kung fu

kickboxing • la boxe thaïlandaise • das Kickboxen • el full contact • il kickboxing

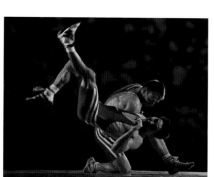

wrestling • la lutte • das Ringen • la lucha libre • la lotta greco-romana

boxing • la boxe • das Boxen • el boxeo • il pugilato

actions • les actions • die Techniken • los movimientos • le mosse

fall • la chute • das Fallen
• la caída • la scivolata

hold • la prise • der Griff
• el agarre • la presa

throw • la projection • der Wurf
• el derribo • la proiezione

pin • l'immobilisation • das Fesseln
• la inmovilización • la caduta

kick • le coup de pied
• der Seitfußstoß • la patada
• il calcio

punch • le coup de poing
• der Stoß • el puñetazo
• il pugno

strike • le coup • der Angriff
• el golpe • il colpo

jump • le saut • der Sprung
• el salto • il salto

block • le blocage • der Block
• la parada • la parata

chop • le coup • der Hieb
• el golpe • il colpo di taglio

boxing ring le ring der Boxring el ring il ring	round le round die Runde el asalto il round	fist le poing die Faust el puño il pugno	black belt la ceinture noire der schwarze Gürtel el cinturón negro la cintura nera	capoeira la capoeira das Capoeira la capoeira la capoeira
boxing gloves les gants de boxe die Boxhandschuhe los guantes de boxeo i guanti	bout le combat der Kampf el combate l'incontro	knock out le knock-out der Knock-out el K.O. il k.o	self defence l'autodéfense die Selbstverteidigung la defensa personal l'autodifesa	sumo wrestling le sumo das Sumo el sumo il sumo
mouth guard le protège-dents der Mundschutz el protector dental il paradenti	sparring l'entraînement das Sparring el entrenamiento l'allenamento	punch bag le punching-bag der Sandsack el saco de arena il sacco	martial arts les arts martiaux die Kampfsportarten las artes marciales le arti marziali	tai-chi le taï chi das Tai Chi el tai-chi il tai-chi

swimming • la natation • der Schwimmsport • la natación • il nuoto

equipment • l'équipement • die Ausrüstung • el equipo • l'attrezzatura

nose clip
la pince pour le nez
die Nasenklemme
la pinza para la nariz
la molletta per il naso

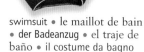

armband • la brassière
• der Schwimmflügel
• los manguitos
• il bracciolo

goggles • les lunettes protectrices
• die Schwimmbrille • las gafas de agua
• gli occhialetti

float • la planche • das
Schwimmbrett • la tabla
• la tavoletta

swimsuit • le maillot de bain
• der Badeanzug • el traje de
baño • il costume da bagno

cap • le bonnet
de natation
• die Badekappe
• el gorro de
baño • la cuffia

lane
le couloir
die Bahn
la calle
la corsia

water
l'eau
das Wasser
el agua
l'acqua

trunks
le slip de bain
die Badehose
el bañador
il costume da
bagno

starting block
le plot de départ
der Startblock
el cajón de salida
il podio di partenza

swimming pool • la piscine • das Schwimmbecken • la piscina • la piscina

springboard
le tremplin
das Sprungbrett
el trampolín
il trampolino

diver
le plongeur
der Springer
el saltador
il tuffatore

swimmer • le nageur • der Schwimmer
• el nadador • il nuotatore

dive (v) • plonger • springen
• saltar • tuffarsi

swim (v) • nager • schwimmen • nadar
• nuotare

turn • le tour • die Wende • el giro
• la giravolta

styles • les styles • die Schwimmstile • los estilos • gli stili

front crawl • le crawl • das Kraulen • el crol • lo stile libero

breaststroke • la brasse • das Brustschwimmen • la braza • la rana

stroke
la nage
der Zug
la brazada
la bracciata

kick
le coup de pied
der Stoß
la patada
la gambata

backstroke • la nage sur le dos • das Rückenschwimmen
• la espalda • il dorso

butterfly • le papillon • der Schmetterling • la mariposa
• la farfalla

scuba diving • la plongée • das Tauchen • el buceo • il nuoto subacqueo

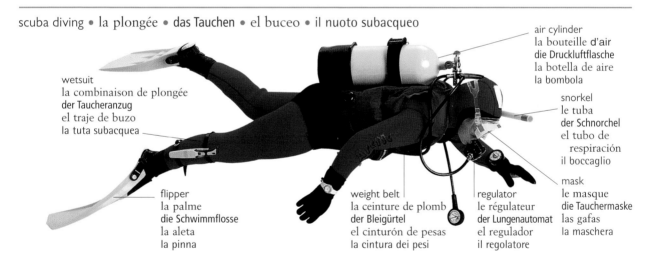

air cylinder
la bouteille d'air
die Druckluftflasche
la botella de aire
la bombola

wetsuit
la combinaison de plongée
der Taucheranzug
el traje de buzo
la tuta subacquea

snorkel
le tuba
der Schnorchel
el tubo de
respiración
il boccaglio

flipper
la palme
die Schwimmflosse
la aleta
la pinna

weight belt
la ceinture de plomb
der Bleigürtel
el cinturón de pesas
la cintura dei pesi

regulator
le régulateur
der Lungenautomat
el regulador
il regolatore

mask
le masque
die Tauchermaske
las gafas
la maschera

dive	racing dive	lockers	water polo	shallow end	cramp
le plongeon	le départ plongé	les casiers	le water-polo	le petit bassin	la crampe
der Sprung	der Startsprung	die Schließfächer	der Wasserball	das flache Ende	der Krampf
el salto	el salto de salida	las taquillas	el waterpolo	la zona poco profunda	el calambre
il tuffo	il tuffo di rincorsa	gli armadietti	la pallanuoto	la parte bassa	il crampo
high dive	tread water (v)	lifeguard	deep end	synchronized swimming	drown (v)
le plongeon de haut vol	nager en chien	le maître nageur	le grand bassin	la nage synchronisée	se noyer
der Turmsprung	Wasser treten	der Bademeister	das tiefe Ende	das Synchronschwimmen	ertrinken
el salto alto	hacer la bicicleta	el socorrista	la zona profunda	la natación sincronizada	ahogarse
il tuffo alto	tenersi a galla	il bagnino	la parte profonda	il nuoto sincronizzato	annegare

sailing • la voile • der Segelsport • la vela • la vela

compass • le compas • der Kompass • la brújula • la bussola

anchor • l'ancre • der Anker • el ancla • l'ancora

mast
le mât
der Mast
el mástil
l'albero

rigging
le gréement
die Takelung
las jarcias
il sartiame

mainsail
la grand-voile
das Großsegel
la vela mayor
la vela maestra

boom
la bôme
der Baum
la botavara
il boma

stern
l'arrière
das Heck
la popa
la poppa

cleat
le taquet
die Klampe
la escotera
la galloccia

sidedeck
le pont de côté
das Seitendeck
la cubierta
il ponte laterale

headsail
la voile d'avant
die Fock
el foque
la vela di prua

bow
l'avant
der Bug
la proa
la prua

tiller
la barre
die Pinne
la caña del timón
la barra

hull
la coque
der Rumpf
el casco
lo scafo

navigate (v) • naviguer • navigieren • navegar • navigare

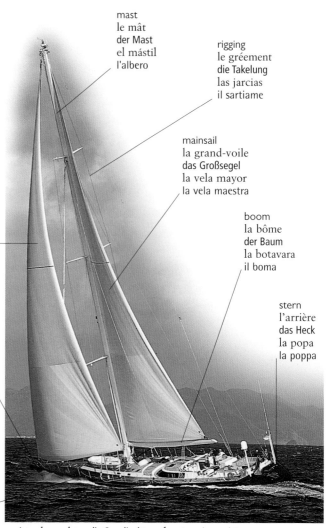

yacht • le yacht • die Segeljacht • el yate • lo yacht

safety • la sécurité • die Sicherheit • la seguridad • la sicurezza

flare • la fusée éclairante • die Leuchtrakete • la bengala • il razzo illuminante

lifebuoy • la bouée de sauvetage • der Rettungsring • el salvavidas • il salvagente

life jacket • le gilet de sauvetage • die Schwimmweste • el chaleco salvavidas • il giubbotto di salvataggio

life raft • le radeau de sauvetage • das Rettungsboot • la balsa salvavidas • la scialuppa di salvataggio

english • français • deutsch • español • italiano

watersports • les sports aquatiques • **der Wassersport** • los deportes acuáticos • gli sport acquatici

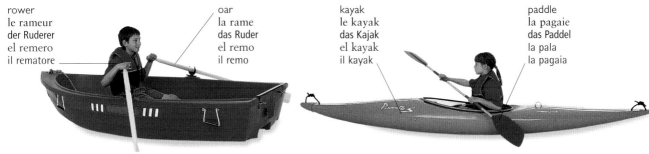

rower
le rameur
der Ruderer
el remero
il rematore

oar
la rame
das Ruder
el remo
il remo

kayak
le kayak
das Kajak
el kayak
il kayak

paddle
la pagaie
das Paddel
la pala
la pagaia

row (v) • ramer • **rudern** • remar • remare

canoeing • le canoë • **der Kanusport** • el piragüismo
• il canottaggio

sail
la voile
das Segel
la vela
la vela

surfboard • la planche • **das Surfbrett** • la tabla de surf •
il surf

ski • le ski • **der Wasserski**
• el esquí aquático • lo sci

windsurfer
le planchiste
der Windsurfer
el windsurfista
il windsurf

surfing • le surf • **das Wellenreiten** • el surfing
• il surfing

waterskiing • le ski nautique
• **das Wasserski** • el esquí
acuático • lo sci d'acqua

speed boating • le moto-
nautisme • **der Schnellbootsport**
• la carrera de motoras
• la corsa in motoscafo

board
la planche
das Surfbrett
la tabla
la tavola

footstrap
la bride
die Fußschlaufe
la cinta para el pie
la presa per il piede

windsurfing • la planche à voile • **das Windsurfing** • el windsurf
• il windsurfing

rafting • le rafting • **das
Rafting** • el rafting • rafting

jet skiing • le jet-ski
• **der Jetski** • la moto
acuática • l'acquascooter

waterskier	crew	wind	surf	sheet	centreboard
le skieur nautique	l'équipage	le vent	l'écume	l'écoute	la dérive
der Wasserskifahrer	die Crew	der Wind	die Brandung	die Schot	das Schwert
el esquiador acuático	la tripulación	el viento	las rompientes	la escota	la orza
lo sciatore d'acqua	l'equipaggio	il vento	la cresta dell'onda	la scotta	il centro della tavola
surfer	tack (v)	wave	rapids	rudder	capsize (v)
le surfeur	louvoyer	la vague	les rapides	le gouvernail	chavirer
der Surfer	kreuzen	die Welle	das Wildwasser	das Ruder	kentern
el surfista	hacer una bordada	la ola	los rápidos	el timón	volcar
il surfista	bordeggiare	l'onda	le rapide	il timone	capovolgersi

horse riding • l'équitation • der Reitsport • la equitación • l'equitazione

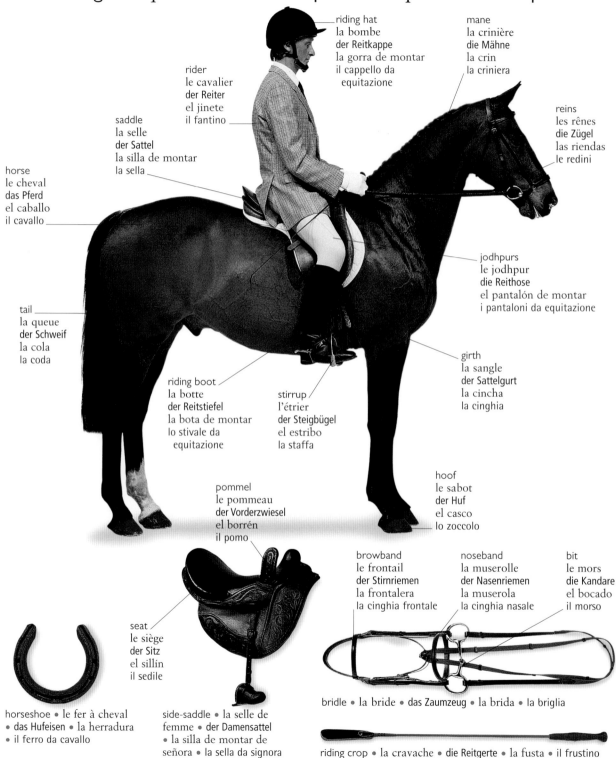

riding hat
la bombe
der Reitkappe
la gorra de montar
il cappello da
equitazione

mane
la crinière
die Mähne
la crin
la criniera

rider
le cavalier
der Reiter
el jinete
il fantino

reins
les rênes
die Zügel
las riendas
le redini

saddle
la selle
der Sattel
la silla de montar
la sella

horse
le cheval
das Pferd
el caballo
il cavallo

jodhpurs
le jodhpur
die Reithose
el pantalón de montar
i pantaloni da equitazione

tail
la queue
der Schweif
la cola
la coda

girth
la sangle
der Sattelgurt
la cincha
la cinghia

riding boot
la botte
der Reitstiefel
la bota de montar
lo stivale da
equitazione

stirrup
l'étrier
der Steigbügel
el estribo
la staffa

hoof
le sabot
der Huf
el casco
lo zoccolo

pommel
le pommeau
der Vorderzwiesel
el borrén
il pomo

browband
le frontail
der Stirnriemen
la frontalera
la cinghia frontale

noseband
la muserolle
der Nasenriemen
la muserola
la cinghia nasale

bit
le mors
die Kandare
el bocado
il morso

seat
le siège
der Sitz
el sillín
il sedile

bridle • la bride • das Zaumzeug • la brida • la briglia

horseshoe • le fer à cheval
• das Hufeisen • la herradura
• il ferro da cavallo

side-saddle • la selle de
femme • der Damensattel
• la silla de montar de
señora • la sella da signora

riding crop • la cravache • die Reitgerte • la fusta • il frustino

events • les courses • die Veranstaltungen • las modalidades • le corse

racehorse • le cheval de course • das Rennpferd • el caballo de carreras • il cavallo da corsa

fence • l'obstacle • das Hindernis • la valla • l'ostacolo

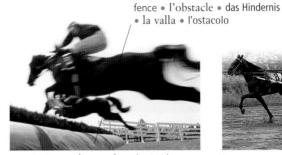

horse race • la course de chevaux • das Pferderennen • la carrera de caballos • la corsa di cavalli

steeplechase • le steeple • das Jagdrennen • la carrera de obstáculos • la corsa a ostacoli

harness race • la course de trot • das Trabrennen • la carrera al trote • la corsa di calessi

rodeo • le rodéo • das Rodeo • el rodeo • il rodeo

showjumping • le jumping • das Springreiten • el concurso de saltos • il concorso di salto a ostacoli

carriage race • la course attelée • das Zweispännerrennen • la carrera de carrozas • la corsa di carrozze

trekking • la randonnée • der Wanderritt • el paseo • l'escursione a cavallo

dressage • le dressage • das Dressurreiten • la doma • il dressage

polo • le polo • das Polo • el polo • il polo

walk	canter	jump	halter	paddock	flat race
le pas	le petit galop	le saut	le licou	l'enclos	la course de plat
der Schritt	der Kanter	der Sprung	das Halfter	die Koppel	das Flachrennen
el paso	el medio galope	el salto	el cabestro	el cercado	la carrera plana
il passo	il piccolo galoppo	il salto	la cavezza	il recinto	la corsa in piano
trot	gallop	groom	stable	arena	racecourse
le trot	le galop	le valet d'écurie	l'écurie	l'arène	le champs de courses
der Trab	der Galopp	der Stallbursche	der Pferdestall	der Turnierplatz	die Rennbahn
el trote	el galope	el mozo de cuadra	la cuadra	el ruedo	el hipódromo
il trotto	il galoppo	lo stalliere	la scuderia	l'arena	l'ippodromo

fishing • la pêche • der Angelsport • la pesca • la pesca

weight • le plomb • das Gewicht • el plomo • il peso

float • le flotteur • die Pose • el flotador • il galleggiante

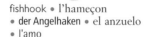

barb
le barbillon
der Widerhaken
la lengüeta
l'uncino

eye
l'œillet
das Öhr
el ojo
l'occhiello

fishhook • l'hameçon • der Angelhaken • el anzuelo • l'amo

lure • l'appât • der Köderhaken • el señuelo • l'esca

bait • l'amorce • der Köder • el cebo • l'esca

fly • la mouche • die Fliege • la mosca • la mosca

landing net • l'épuisette • der Kescher • la red para recoger • la retina

tackle box • la boîte d'équipement • der Spinnerkasten • la caja de aparejos • la scatola degli attrezzi

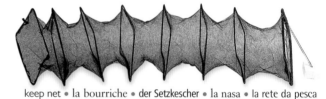

keep net • la bourriche • der Setzkescher • la nasa • la rete da pesca

line
la ligne
die Schnur
el sedal
la lenza

fishing rod
la canne à pêche
die Angelrute
la caña de pescar
la canna da pesca

reel
le moulinet
die Rolle
el carrete
il mulinello

waders
les bottes de pêche
die Watstiefel
las botas altas de goma
gli stivaloni di gomma

angler • le pêcheur • der Angler • el pescador de caña • il pescatore types of fishing • les genres de pêche • die Fischfangarten • los tipos de pesca • i tipi di pesca

freshwater fishing • la pêche en eau douce • das Süßwasserangeln • la pesca en agua dulce • la pesca in acqua dolce

fly fishing • la pêche à la mouche • das Fliegenangeln • la pesca con mosca • la pesca con la mosca

sport fishing • la pêche sportive • das Sportangeln • la pesca deportiva • la pesca sportiva

deep sea fishing • la pêche hauturière • die Hochseefischerei • la pesca de altura • la pesca il alto mare

surfcasting • la pêche au lancer en mer • das Brandungsangeln • la pesca en la orilla • la pesca dalla riva

activities • les activités • die Aktivitäten • las acciones • le attività

cast (v) • lancer • auswerfen • lanzar • lanciare

catch (v) • attraper • fangen • coger • prendere

reel in (v) • ramener • einholen • recoger • tirare con il mulinello

net (v) • prendre au filet • mit dem Netz fangen • coger con la red • pescare con la rete

release (v) • lâcher • loslassen • soltar • rilasciare

bait (v) amorcer ködern cebar adescare	tackle le matériel de pêche die Angelgeräte los aparejos l'attrezzatura	waterproofs l'imperméable die Regenhaut la ropa impermeable l'impermeabile	fishing permit le permis de pêche der Angelschein la licencia de pesca la licenza di pesca	creel le panier de pêche der Fischkorb la nasa la nassa
bite (v) mordre anbeißen picar abboccare	spool le tambour die Rolle el carrete la bobina	pole la perche die Stake la pértiga il palo	marine fishing la pêche maritime die Seefischerei la pesca marítima la pesca in mare	spearfishing la pêche sous-marine das Speerfischen la pesca con arpón la pesca con la fiocina

skiing • le ski • der Skisport • el esquí • lo sci

ski slope • la pente de ski
• der Skihang • la pista de
esquí • la pista da sci

chairlift
le télésiège
der Sessellift
la telesilla
la seggiovia

cable car
la télécabine
der Kabinenlift
el teleférico
la funivia

ski suit
la combinaison de ski
der Skianzug
el traje de esquí
la tuta da sci

ski pole
le bâton de ski
der Skistock
el bastón
il bastone da sci

glove
le gant
der Handschuh
el guante
il guanto

ski run
la piste de ski
die Skipiste
la pista de esquí
la pista da sci

ski boot
la chaussure de ski
der Skistiefel
la bota de esquí
lo scarpone da sci

ski • le ski • der Ski
• el esquí • lo sci

safety barrier
• la barrière de sécurité
• die Sicherheitssperre
• la barrera de seguridad
• la transenna di sicurezza

edge • la carre
• die Kante • el canto
• la lama

skier • la skieuse • die Skiläuferin
• la esquiadora • la sciatrice

tip • la pointe • die Spitze
• la punta • la punta

events • les épreuves • die Disziplinen • las modalidades • le gare

gate • la porte
• das Tor • el poste
• la porta

downhill skiing • la descente
• der Abfahrtslauf
• el descenso • la discesa

slalom • le slalom
• der Slalom • el slalom
• lo slalom

ski jump • le saut
• der Skisprung • el salto
de esquí • il salto

cross-country skiing • le ski de
randonnée • der Langlauf • el
esquí de fondo • lo sci di fondo

winter sports • les sports d'hiver • der Wintersport
• los deportes de invierno • gli sport invernali

goggles • les lunettes
de ski • die Skibrille
• las gafas de nieve
• gli occhiali

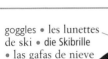

skate
le patin à glace
der Schlittschuh
el patín
il pattino

ice climbing • l'escalade en
glace • das Eisklettern
• la escalada en hielo
• l'arrampicata su ghiaccio

ice-skating • le patinage
• das Eislaufen • el patinaje
sobre hielo • il pattinaggio
su ghiaccio

figure skating • le patinage
artistique • der Eiskunstlauf
• el patinaje artístico
• il pattinaggio artistico

snowboarding
• le surf des neiges
• das Snowboarding • el
snowboard • lo snowboard

bobsleigh • le bobsleigh
• der Bobsport • el bobsleigh
• il bob

luge • la luge • das Rennrodeln
• el luge • lo slittino

alpine skiing le ski alpin die alpine Kombination el esquí alpino lo sci alpino	dog sledding le traîneau à chiens das Hundeschlittenfahren el trineo con perros la corsa su slitta trainata da cani
giant slalom le slalom géant der Riesenslalom el slalom gigante lo slalom gigante	speed skating le patinage de vitesse das Eisschnelllauf el patinaje de velocidad il pattinaggio di velocità
off-piste hors piste abseits der Piste fuera de pista fuoripista	biathlon le biathlon das Biathlon el biatlón il biathlon
curling le curling das Curling el curling il curling	avalanche l'avalanche die Lawine el alud la valanga

snowmobile • l'autoneige
• das Schneemobil • la moto
de nieve • la motoslitta

sledding • la luge • das
Schlittenfahren • ir en trineo
• la corsa su slitta

other sports • les autres sports • die anderen Sportarten • los otros deportes • gli altri sport

glider
le planeur
das Segelflugzeug
el planeador
l'aliante

hang-glider
le deltaplane
der Drachen
el ala delta
il deltaplano

gliding • le vol plané • das Segelfliegen • el vuelo sin motor • il volo a vela

hang-gliding • le deltaplane • das Drachenfliegen • el vuelo con ala delta • il volo in deltaplano

rope
la corde
das Seil
la cuerda
la corda

parachute
le parachute
der Fallschirm
el paracaídas
il paracadute

rock climbing • l'escalade • das Klettern • la escalada • l'arrampicata

parachuting • le parachutisme • das Fallschirmspringen • el paracaidismo • il paracadutismo

paragliding • le parapente • das Gleitschirmfliegen • el parapente • il parapendio

skydiving • le saut en chute libre • das Fallschirmspringen • el paracaidismo en caída libre • il paracadutismo libero

abseiling • le rappel • das Abseilen • el rápel • la cordata

bungee jumping • le saut à l'élastique • das Bungeejumping • el puenting • il bungee jumping

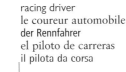

racing driver
le coureur automobile
der Rennfahrer
el piloto de carreras
il pilota da corsa

rally driving • le rallye • das Rallyefahren • el rally • il rally

motor racing • la course automobile • der Rennsport • el automovilismo • l'automobilismo

motorcross • le motocross • das Motocross • el motocross • il motocross

motorbike racing • la course de moto • das Motorradrennen • el motociclismo • il motociclismo

skateboard
la planche à roulettes
das Skateboard
el monopatín
la tavola da skateboard

rollerskate
le patin à roulettes
der Rollschuh
el patín de ruedas
il pattino a rotelle

stick
la crosse
der Lacrosseschläger
el palo
la mazza

mask
le masque
die Maske
la máscara
la maschera

foil
le fleuret
das Florett
el florete
il fioretto

skateboarding • la planche à roulettes • das Skateboard-fahren • montar en monopatín • lo skate board

roller skating • le patinage à roulettes • das Rollschuhfahren • el patinaje sobre ruedas • il pattinaggio a rotelle

lacrosse • le lacrosse • das Lacrosse • el lacrosse • il lacrosse

fencing • l'escrime • das Fechten • la esgrima • la scherma

pin • la quille • der Kegel • el bolo • il birillo

arrow
la flèche
der Pfeil
la flecha
la freccia

bow • l'arc • der Bogen • el arco • l'arco

target • la cible • die Zielscheibe • la diana • il bersaglio

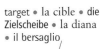

quiver
le carquois
der Köcher
el carcaj
la faretra

archery • le tir à l'arc • das Bogenschießen • el tiro con arco • il tiro con l'arco

target shooting • le tir à cible • das Scheibenschießen • el tiro al blanco • il tiro al bersaglio

bowling ball • la boule de bowling • die Bowlingkugel • la bola • la palla da bowling

bowling • le bowling • das Bowling • la bolera • il bowling

pool • le billard américain • das Poolbillard • el billar americano • il biliardo

snooker • le billard • das Snooker • el snooker • lo snooker

fitness • le conditionnement physique • die Fitness • la forma física • il fitness

gym machine • l'appareil de gym • das Fitnessgerät • la máquina de ejercicios • la macchina per esercizi

bench • le banc • die Bank • el banco • la panca

exercise bike • le vélo d'entraînement • das Trainingsrad • la bicicleta estática • la cyclette

free weights les poids die Gewichte las pesas i manubri

bar la barre die Stange la barra la sbarra

gym • le gymnase • das Fitnesscenter • el gimasio • la palestra

rowing machine • la machine à ramer • die Rudermaschine • la máquina de remos • il vogatore

treadmill • la tapis roulant • das Laufband • la cinta de correr • il tapis roulant

cross trainer • la machine de randonnée • die Langlaufmaschine • la máquina de cross • il cross trainer

personal trainer • l'entraîneuse individuelle • die private Fitnesstrainerin • la entrenadora personal • l'istruttore individuale

step machine • l'escalier d'entraînement • der Stepper • la máquina de step • lo stepper

swimming pool • la piscine • das Schwimmbecken • la piscina • la piscina

sauna • le sauna • die Sauna • la sauna • la sauna

250

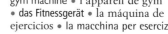
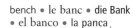
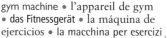

exercises • les exercices • die Übungen • los ejercicios • gli esercizi

stretch • l'étirement • das Strecken • el estiramiento • lo stretching

lunge • la fente en avant • der Ausfallschritt • la flexión con estiramiento • lo stiramento

tights
le collant
die Gymnastikhose
los leotardos
il collant

press-up • la traction • der Liegestütz • la flexión • le flessioni

squat • la flexion de jambes • die Kniebeuge • ponerse en cuclillas • lo squat

sit-up • le redressement assis • das Rumpfheben • el abdominal • gli addominali

dumb bell
l'haltère
die Hantel
la pesa
il manubrio

bicep curl • l'exercice pour les biceps • die Bizepsübung • el ejercicio de bíceps • le alzate con il manubrio

leg press • la traction pour les jambes • der Beinstütz • el empuje de piernas • la pressa per le gambe

chest press • l'exercice pour la poitrine • die Brustübung • los ejercicios pectorales • la pressa per i pettorali

trainers • les baskets • die Trainingsschuhe • las zapatillas • gli scarponcini

weight bar
la barre à poids
die Gewichthantel
la barra de pesas
il bilanciere

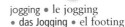

weight training • l'entraînement poids et haltères • das Kraft-training • el levantamiento de pesas • l'addestramento ai pesi

vest
le maillot
das Hemd
la camiseta
la maglietta

jogging • le jogging • das Jogging • el footing • il jogging

aerobics • l'aérobic • das Aerobic • el aerobic • la ginnastica aerobica

train (v) s'entraîner trainieren entrenar allenarsi	jog on the spot (v) jogger sur place auf der Stelle joggen correr en el sitio correre sul posto	extend (v) étendre dehnen estirar stendere	Pilates les exercices Pilates die Pilates-Übungen el pilates il pilates	circuit training l'entraînement en circuit das Zirkeltraining el entrenamiento en circuito l'allemamento in circuito
warm up (v) s'échauffer sich aufwärmen calentar riscaldarsi	flex (v) fléchir beugen flexionar flettere	pull up (v) tirer hochziehen levantar sollevare	boxercise l'aéroboxe die Boxgymnastik la gimnasia prepugilística la ginnastica prepugilistica	skipping le saut à la corde das Seilspringen saltar a la comba saltare con la corda

leisure
le temps libre
die Freizeit
el ocio
il tempo libero

theatre • le théâtre • das Theater • el teatro • il teatro

curtain
le rideau
der Vorhang
el telón
il sipario

wings
les coulisses
die Kulisse
los bastidores
la quinta

set
le décor
das Bühnenbild
el decorado
la scenografia

audience
le public
das Publikum
el público
il pubblico

orchestra
l'orchestre
das Orchester
la orquesta
l'orchestra

stage • la scène • die Bühne • el escenario • il palcoscenico

seat
le fauteuil
der Sitzplatz
la butaca
la poltrona

upper circle
la deuxième galerie
der zweite Rang
la platea alta
la seconda galleria

row
la rangée
die Reihe
la fila
la fila

box
la loge
die Loge
el palco
il palco

circle
la corbeille
der erste Rang
la platea
la galleria

balcony
le balcon
der Balkon
la galería
la balconata

aisle
l'allée
der Gang
el pasillo
il corridoio

stalls
l'orchestre
das Parkett
el patio de
butacas
la platea

seating • les places • die Bestuhlung • los asientos • i posti

play	director	first night
la pièce de théâtre	le metteur en scène	la première
das Theaterstück	der Regisseur	die Premiere
la obra de teatro	el director	el estreno
l'opera teatrale	il regista	la prima
cast	producer	interval
la distribution	le metteur en scène	l'entracte
die Besetzung	der Regisseur	die Pause
el reparto	el director artístico	el descanso
il cast	il produttore	l'intervallo
actor	script	programme
l'acteur	le texte	le programme
der Schauspieler	das Rollenheft	das Programm
el actor	el guión	el programa
l'attore	il copione	il programma
actress	backdrop	orchestra pit
l'actrice	la toile de fond	la fosse d'orchestre
die Schauspielerin	der Prospekt	der Orchestergraben
la actriz	el telón de fondo	el foso de la orquesta
l'attrice	il fondale	la fossa dell'orchestra

english • français • deutsch • español • italiano

concert • le concert • das Konzert • el concierto • il concerto

musical • la comédie musicale • das Musical • el musical • il musical

costume
le costume
das Theaterkostüm
el traje
il costume

ballet • le ballet • das Ballett • el ballet • il balletto

opera • l'opéra • die Oper • la ópera • l'opera

usher le placeur der Platzanweiser el acomodador la maschera	soundtrack la bande sonore der Soundtrack la banda sonora la colonna sonora	I'd like two tickets for tonight's performance. Je voudrais deux billets pour la représentation de ce soir. Ich möchte zwei Karten für die Aufführung heute Abend. Quisiera dos entradas para la sesión de esta noche. Vorrei due biglietti per lo spettacolo di stasera.
classical music la musique classique die klassische Musik la música clásica la musica classica	applaud (v) applaudir applaudieren aplaudir applaudire	
musical score la partition die Noten la partitura la partitura musicale	encore le bis die Zugabe el bis il bis	What time does it start? Ça commence à quelle heure? Um wie viel Uhr beginnt die Aufführung? ¿A qué hora empieza? A che ora inizia?

cinema • le cinéma • das Kino • el cine • il cinema

popcorn
le pop-corn
das Popcorn
las palomitas
il popcorn

box office
la caisse
die Kasse
la taquilla
la biglietteria

lobby
le foyer
das Foyer
el vestíbulo
l'atrio

poster
l'affiche
das Plakat
el cartel
il poster

cinema hall • la salle de cinéma • der Kinosaal • el cine • il cinema

screen • l'écran • die Leinwand • la pantalla • lo schermo

comedy la comédie die Komödie la comedia la commedia	romance la comédie romantique der Liebesfilm la película romántica il film d'amore
thriller le thriller der Thriller la película de suspense il thriller	science fiction film le film de science-fiction der Science-Fiction-Film la película de ciencia ficción il film di fantascienza
horror film le film d'horreur der Horrorfilm la película de miedo il film di orrore	adventure le film d'aventures der Abenteuerfilm la película de aventuras il film di avventura
western le western der Western la película del oeste il western	animated film le film d'animation der Zeichentrickfilm la película de dibujos animados il film di animazione

orchestra • l'orchestre • das Orchester • la orquesta • l'orchestra

strings • les cordes • die Saiteninstrumente • la cuerda • gli strumenti a corda

harp
la harpe
die Harfe
el arpa
l'arpa

conductor
le chef d'orchestre
der Dirigent
el director de orquesta
il direttore di orchestra

double bass
le contrebasse
der Kontrabass
el contrabajo
il contrabbasso

violin
le violon
die Geige
el violín
il violino

podium
le podium
das Podium
el podio
il podio

viola
l'alto
die Bratsche
la viola
la viola

cello
le violoncelle
das Cello
el violoncelo
il violoncello

score
la partition
die Noten
la partitura
lo spartito

treble clef
la clé de sol
der Violinschlüssel
la clave de sol
la chiave di violino

note
la note
die Note
la nota
la nota

staff
la portée
das Liniensystem
el pentagrama
il pentagramma

bass clef
la clé de fa
der Bassschlüssel
la clave de fa
la chiave di basso

Andante

notation • la notation • die Notation • la notación • l'annotazione

piano • le piano • das Klavier • el piano • il pianoforte

overture	sonata	rest	sharp	natural	scale
l'ouverture	la sonate	le silence	la dièse	le bécarre	la gamme
die Ouvertüre	die Sonate	das Pausenzeichen	das Kreuz	das Auflösungszeichen	die Tonleiter
la obertura	la sonata	el silencio	sostenido	becuadro	la escala
l'ouverture	la sonata	la pausa	il diesis	bequadro	la scala
symphony	instruments	pitch	flat	bar	baton
la symphonie	les instruments	le ton	le bémol	la mesure	la baguette
die Symphonie	die Musikinstrumente	die Tonhöhe	das B	der Taktstrich	der Taktstock
la sinfonía	los instrumentos	el tono	bemol	la linea divisoria	la batuta
la sinfonia	gli strumenti	il tono	il bemolle	la battuta	la bacchetta

woodwind • les bois • die Blasinstrumente • el viento-madera • gli strumenti a fiato

piccolo • le piccolo • die Pikkoloflöte • el flautín • l'ottavino

flute • la flûte traversière • die Querflöte • la flauta travesera • il flauto traverso

oboe • le hautbois • die Oboe • el oboe • l'oboe

cor anglais • le cor anglais • das Englischhorn • el corno inglés • il corno inglese

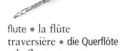

clarinet • la clarinette • die Klarinette • el clarinete • il clarinetto

bass clarinet • la clarinette basse • die Bassklarinette • el clarinete bajo • il clarinetto basso

bassoon • le basson • das Fagott • el fagote • il fagotto

double bassoon • le contrebasson • das Kontrafagott • el contra-fagote • il controfagotto

saxophone • le saxophone • das Saxofon • el saxofón • il sassofono

percussion • la percussion • die Schlaginstrumente • la percusión • la percussione

kettledrum • la timbale • die Kesselpauke • el timbal • il timpano

gong • le gong • der Gong • el gong • il gong

bongos • les bongos • die Bongos • los bongos • i bongo

snare drum • la caisse claire • die kleine Trommel • el tambor pequeño • il tamburo militare

cymbals • les cymbales • das Becken • los platillos • i piatti

tambourine • le tambour • das Tamburin • la pandereta • il tamburino

vibraphone • le vibraphone • das Vibrafon • el vibráfono • il vibrafono

triangle • le triangle • der Triangel • el triángulo • il triangolo

maracas • les maracas • die Maracas • las maracas • i maracas

brass • les cuivres • die Blechblasinstrumente • el viento-metal • gli ottoni

trumpet • la trompette • die Trompete • la trompeta • la tromba

trombone • le trombone • die Posaune • el trombón de varas • il trombone

horn • le cor • das Horn • la trompa • il corno

tuba • le tuba • die Tuba • la tuba • la tuba

concert • le concert • das Konzert • el concierto • il concerto

lead singer
le chanteur
der Leadsänger
el cantante
il cantante

microphone
le microphone
das Mikrofon
el micrófono
il microfono

drummer
le batteur
der Schlagzeuger
el batería
il batterista

guitarist
le guitariste
der Gitarrist
el guitarrista
il chitarrista

fans
les fans
die Fans
los fans
i fans

speaker
le haut-parleur
der Lautsprecher
el altavoz
l'altoparlante

bass guitarist
le bassiste
der Bassgitarrist
el bajo
il bassista

rock concert • le concert de rock • das Rockkonzert • el concierto de rock • il concerto rock

instruments • les instruments • die Instrumente • los instrumentos • gli strumenti

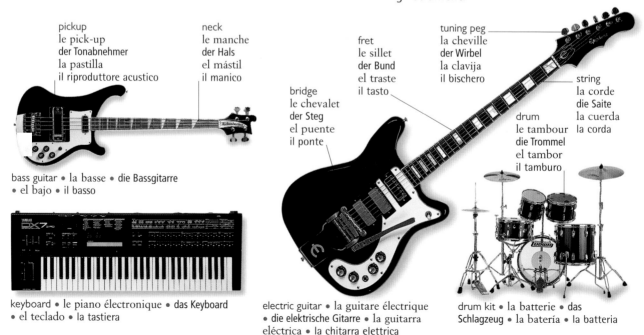

pickup
le pick-up
der Tonabnehmer
la pastilla
il riproduttore acustico

neck
le manche
der Hals
el mástil
il manico

fret
le sillet
der Bund
el traste
il tasto

tuning peg
la cheville
der Wirbel
la clavija
il bischero

bridge
le chevalet
der Steg
el puente
il ponte

string
la corde
die Saite
la cuerda
la corda

drum
le tambour
die Trommel
el tambor
il tamburo

bass guitar • la basse • die Bassgitarre
• el bajo • il basso

keyboard • le piano électronique • das Keyboard
• el teclado • la tastiera

electric guitar • la guitare électrique
• die elektrische Gitarre • la guitarra
eléctrica • la chitarra elettrica

drum kit • la batterie • das
Schlagzeug • la batería • la batteria

musical styles • les styles de musique • die Musikstile • los estilos musicales • gli stili musicali

jazz • le jazz • der Jazz • el jazz • il jazz

blues • le blues • der Blues • el blues • il blues

punk • la musique punk • die Punkmusik • la música punk • il punk

folk music • la musique folk • der Folk • la música folk • la musica folk

pop • la pop • die Popmusik • la música pop • il pop

dance • la dance • die Tanzmusik • la música de baile • la musica da ballo

rap • le rap • der Rap • el rap • il rap

heavy metal • la heavy métal • das Heavymetal • el heavy metal • l'heavy metal

classical music • la musique classique • die klassische Musik • la música clásica • la musica classica

song	lyrics	melody	beat	reggae	country	spotlight
la chanson	les paroles	la mélodie	le beat	le reggae	la country	le projecteur
das Lied	der Text	die Melodie	der Beat	der Reggae	die Countrymusic	der Scheinwerfer
la canción	la letra	la melodía	el ritmo	el reggae	la música country	el foco
la canzone	il testo	la melodia	il ritmo	il reggae	il country	il proiettore

sightseeing • le tourisme • die Besichtigungstour • el turismo • la visita turistica

tourist
le touriste
der Tourist
el turista
il turista

itinerary
l'itinéraire
die Route
el itinerario
l'itinerario

open-top
à impériale
mit offenem Oberdeck
panorámico
scoperto

This is an official London Sightseeing Bus.
LONDON PRIDE

tour guide
la guide
die Fremdenführerin
la guía turística
la guida turistica

tour bus • le bus touristique • der Stadtrundfahrtbus • el autobús turístico • il pullman turistico

statuette • la statuette • die Figur • la estatuilla • la statuina

tourist attraction • l'attraction touristique • die Touristenattraktion • la atracción turística • il luogo d'interesse turistico

guided tour • la tour guidé • die Führung • la visita con guiada • la visita guidata

souvenirs • les souvenirs • die Andenken • los recuerdos • i ricordi

open	guide book	camcorder	left	Where is…?	I'm lost.
ouvert	le guide	le caméscope	à gauche	Où est…?	Je me suis perdu.
geöffnet	der Reiseführer	der Camcorder	links	Wo ist…?	Ich habe mich verlaufen.
abierto	la guía	la cámara de vídeo	la izquierda	¿Dónde está…?	Me he perdido.
aperto	la guida	la videocamera	a sinistra	Dov'è…?	Mi sono perso.
closed	film	camera	right	Can you tell me the way to….?
fermé	la pellicule	l'appareil photo	à droite	Pour aller à…, s'il vous plaît?
geschlossen	der Film	die Kamera	rechts	Können Sie mir sagen, wie ich nach… komme?
cerrado	la película	la máquina fotográfica	la derecha	¿Podría decirme cómo se va a…?
chiuso	la pellicola	la macchina fotografica	a destra	Mi può dire come si arriva a…?
entrance fee	batteries	directions	straight on		
le prix d'entrée	les piles	les directions	tout droit		
das Eintrittsgeld	die Batterien	die Richtungsangaben	geradeaus		
el precio de entrada	las pilas	las indicaciones	recto		
la tariffa d'ingresso	le batterie	le indicazioni	dritto		

attractions • les attractions • die Sehenswürdigkeiten • los lugares de interés • i luoghi d'interesse

painting
le tableau
das Gemälde
el cuadro
il quadro

exhibit
l'objet exposé
das Ausstellungsstück
la muestra
l'oggetto

exhibition • l'exposition
• die Ausstellung • la exposición
• l'esposizione

famous ruin
la ruine célèbre
die berühmte Ruine
la ruina famosa
la rovina famosa

art gallery • le musée d'art
• die Kunstgalerie • la galería
de arte • la galleria d'arte

monument • le monument
• das Monument • el
monumento • il monumento

museum • le musée
• das Museum • el museo
• il museo

historic building • le
monument historique • das
historische Gebäude • el edificio
histórico • l'edificio storico

casino • le casino • das Kasino
• el casino • il casinò

gardens • le parc • der Park
• los jardines • i giardini publici

national park • le parc national • der Nationalpark • el parque
nacional • il parco nazionale

information • l'information • die Information • la información • l'informazione

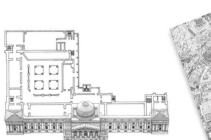

times
les heures
die Zeiten
las horas
gli orari

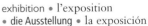

floor plan • le plan
• der Grundriss • la planta
• la pianta del piano

map • le plan • der Stadtplan
• el plano • la mappa

timetable • l'horaire •
der Fahrplan • el horario
• l'orario

tourist information
• l'information touristique
• die Touristeninformation • la
oficina de turismo • l'ufficio
informazioni turistiche

outdoor activities • les activités de plein air • die Aktivitäten im Freien • las actividades al aire libre • le attività all'aria aperta

footpath
le sentier
der Fußweg
el sendero
il sentiero

sundial
le cadran solaire
die Sonnenuhr
el reloj de sol
la meridiana

café
le café
das Café
la cafetería
il caffè

park • le parc • der Park • el parque • il parco

grass
la pelouse
das Gras
la hierba
il prato

bench
le banc
die Bank
el banco
la panchina

formal gardens
les jardins à la française
die Gartenanlagen
los jardines clásicos
il giardino all'italiana

roller coaster
les montagnes russes
die Achterbahn
la montaña rusa
le montagne russe

fairground • la foire
• der Jahrmarkt • las ferias
• il luna park

theme park • le parc
d'attractions • der Vergnügungs-
park • el parque temático
• il parco di divertimenti

safari park • la réserve
• der Safaripark • el safari park
• il parco safari

zoo • le zoo • der Zoo
• el zoo • lo zoo

activities • les activités • die Aktivitäten • las actividades • le attività

cycling • le vélo • das
Radfahren • el ciclismo
• il ciclismo

jogging • le jogging
• das Jogging • el footing
• il footing

skateboarding • la planche à
roulette • das Skateboardfahren
• montar en monopatín
• lo skateboard

rollerblading • le roller
• das Inlinerfahren • el
patinaje • il pattinaggio

bridle path • la piste cavalière
• der Reitweg • el sendero para
caballos • il sentiero per cavalli

hamper • le panier à
pique-nique • der
Picknickkorb • la cesta de
picnic • la cesta

bird watching • l'observation
des oiseaux • das
Vogelbeobachten • la
ornitología • l'ornitologia

horse riding • l'équitation
• das Reiten • la equitación
• l'equitazione

hiking • la randonnée • das
Wandern • el senderismo
• l'escursionismo

picnic • le pique-nique
• das Picknick • el picnic
• il picnic

playground • le terrain de jeux • der Spielplatz • el área de juegos • il parco giochi

sandpit • le bac à sable
• der Sandkasten • el cajón
de arena • il recinto di sabbia

paddling pool • la pataugeoire
• das Planschbecken • la piscina
para niños • la piscina
gonfiabile

swings • la balançoire
• die Schaukel • los columpios
• l'altalena

seesaw • la bascule • die Wippe
• el subibaja • l'altalena a bilico

slide • le toboggan • die Rutsche • el tobogán
• lo scivolo

climbing frame • la cage à poules
• das Klettergerüst • la estructura para
escalar • la struttura per arrampicarsi

beach • la plage • der Strand • la playa • la spiaggia

hotel
l'hôtel
das Hotel
el hotel
l'albergo

beach umbrella
le parasol
der Sonnenschirm
la sombrilla
l'ombrellone

beach hut
la cabine de plage
das Strandhäuschen
la caseta
la cabina

sand
le sable
der Sand
la arena
la sabbia

wave
la vague
die Welle
la ola
l'onda

sea
la mer
das Meer
el mar
il mare

beach bag
le sac de plage
die Strandtasche
la bolsa de playa
la borsa da spiaggia

bikini
le bikini
der Bikini
el bikini
il bikini

sunbathe (v) • prendre un bain de soleil • sonnenbaden • tomar el sol • prendere il sole

lifeguard
le maître nageur
der Rettungsschwimmer
el socorrista
il bagnino

lifeguard tower • la tour de surveillance • der Rettungsturm • el puesto de vigilancia • la torre di sorveglianza

windbreak • le pare-vent • der Windschutz • la red cortaviento • il paravento

promenade • la promenade • die Promenade • el paseo marítimo • il lungomare

deck chair • le transat • der Liegestuhl • la hamaca • la sedia a sdraio

sunglasses • les lunettes de soleil • die Sonnenbrille • las gafas de sol • gli occhiali da sole

sunhat • le chapeau de soleil • der Sonnenhut • el sombrero para el sol • il cappello per il sole

suntan lotion • la lotion solaire • die Sonnenmilch • la crema bronceadora • la crema abbronzante

sunblock • l'écran total • der Sonnenblocker • la crema protectora total • la crema solare di protezione alta

swimsuit
le maillot de bain
der Badeanzug
el bañador
il costume da bagno

spade
la pelle
der Spaten
la pala
la paletta

bucket
le seau
der Eimer
el cubo
il secchiello

beach ball • le ballon de plage • der Wasserball • el balón de playa • il pallone da spiaggia

rubber ring • la bouée • der Schwimmreifen • el flotador • la ciambella

sandcastle
le château de sable
die Sandburg
el castillo de arena
il castello di sabbia

shell
le coquillage
die Muschel
la concha
la conchiglia

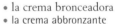

beach towel • la serviette de plage • das Strandtuch • la toalla de playa • l'asciugamano da spiaggia

camping • le camping • das Camping • el camping • il camping

toilets
les toilettes
die Toiletten
los aseos
i bagni

waste disposal
les poubelles
die Mülleimer
el contenedor de la basura
il secchio delle immondizie

shower block
les douches
die Duschen
las duchas
le docce

electric hook-up
le branchement électrique
der Stromanschluss
el punto eléctrico
la presa di corrente

flysheet
le double toit
das Überdach
el doble techo
il telo protettivo

tent peg
le piquet
der Hering
la piqueta
il piolo

guy rope
la corde
die Zeltspannleine
el viento
la corda

caravan
la caravane
der Wohnwagen
la roulotte
la roulotte

campsite • le terrain de camping • der Campingplatz • el camping • il campeggio

camp (v)	pitch	picnic bench	charcoal
camper	l'emplacement	le banc à pique-nique	le charbon de bois
zelten	der Zeltplatz	die Picknickbank	die Holzkohle
acampar	la plaza	la mesa de picnic	el carbón vegetal
campeggiare	il campeggio	il tavolo da picnic	la carbonella
site manager's office	pitch a tent (v)	hammock	firelighter
le bureau du chef	monter une tente	le hamac	l'allume-feu
die Campingplatzverwaltung	ein Zelt aufschlagen	die Hängematte	der Feueranzünder
la oficina del director	montar una tienda	la hamaca	la pastilla para encender
l'ufficio del direttore	piantare una tenda	l'amaca	l'accendifuoco
pitches available	tent pole	camper van	light a fire (v)
les emplacements de libre	le mât	l'autocaravane	allumer un feu
Zeltplätze frei	die Zeltstange	das Wohnmobil	ein Feuer machen
hay plazas libres	el mastil	la autocaravana	encender una hoguera
le piazzole disponibili	il palo	il camper	accendere un fuoco
full	camp bed	trailer	campfire
complet	le lit de camp	la remorque	le feu de camp
voll	das Faltbett	der Anhänger	das Lagerfeuer
completo	el catre de campaña	el remolque	la hoguera
completo	il lettino da campeggio	il rimorchio	il fuoco

frame
le cadre
das Gestänge
la estructura
la struttura

ground sheet
le tapis de sol
der Zeltboden
el suelo aislante
il telo isolante

backpack
le sac à dos
der Rucksack
la mochila
lo zaino

vacuum flask
le thermos
die Thermosflasche
el termo
il thermos

water bottle
la bouteille d'eau
die Wasserflasche
la cantimplora
la borraccia

tent • la tente • das Zelt • la tienda de campaña • la tenda

insect repellent • le spray contre les insectes • der Insektenspray • el repelente de insectos • lo spray insetticida

torch • la lampe torche • die Taschenlampe • la linterna • la torcia

mosquito net
la moustiquaire
das Moskitonetz
la mosquitera
la zanzariera

thermals
les sous-vêtements thermiques
die Thermowäsche
la ropa termoaislante
gli indumenti termici

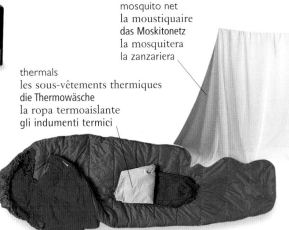

walking boots • les chaussures de marche • die Wanderschuhe • las botas de montaña • le scarpe da escursionismo

waterproofs • l'imperméable • die Regenhaut • la ropa impermeable • gli indumenti impermeabili

sleeping bag • le sac de couchage • der Schlafsack • el saco de dormir • il sacco a pelo

sleeping mat
le tapis de sol
die Schlafmatte
la esterilla
il materassino

camping stove • le réchaud • der Gasbrenner • el hornillo • il fornello a gas

barbecue • le barbecue • der Grill • la barbacoa • la griglia per barbecue

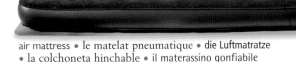

air mattress • le matelat pneumatique • die Luftmatratze • la colchoneta hinchable • il materassino gonfiabile

home entertainment • les distractions à la maison • die Unterhaltungselektronik • el ocio en el hogar • l'elettronica d'intrattenimento

DVD disk • le DVD
• die DVD
• el disco de DVD
• il disco DVD

personal CD player • le
baladeur CD • der Discman
• el discman • il lettore di
CD portatile

mini disk recorder
• l'enregistreur minidisk
• der Minidiskrekorder • la
grabadora de minidisks
• il lettore di mini disk

MP3 player • le baladeur
MP3 • der MP3-Spieler
• el lector de MP3
• il lettore di MP3

DVD player • le lecteur DVD • der
DVD-Spieler • el reproductor de DVD
• il lettore di DVD

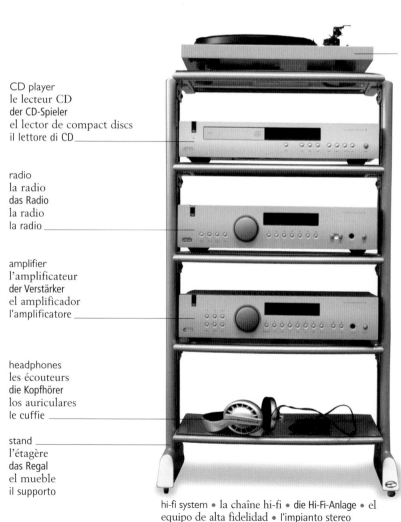

record player
le tourne-disque
der Plattenspieler
el tocadiscos
il giradischi

CD player
le lecteur CD
der CD-Spieler
el lector de compact discs
il lettore di CD

(loud) speaker
le baffle
die Lautsprecherbox
el altavoz
l'altoparlante

radio
la radio
das Radio
la radio
la radio

amplifier
l'amplificateur
der Verstärker
el amplificador
l'amplificatore

speaker stand
le support
der Ständer
el pie del altavoz
il supporto per
l'altoparlante

headphones
les écouteurs
die Kopfhörer
los auriculares
le cuffie

stand
l'étagère
das Regal
el mueble
il supporto

hi-fi system • la chaîne hi-fi • die Hi-Fi-Anlage • el
equipo de alta fidelidad • l'impianto stereo

english • français • deutsch • español • italiano

video tape
la vidéocassette
die Videokassette
la cinta de vídeo
la videocassetta

screen
l'écran
der Bildschirm
la pantalla
lo schermo

eyecup
l'œilleton
das Okular
el adaptador del visor
l'oculare

video recorder • le magnétoscope
• **der Videorekorder** • el aparato de vídeo
• il videoregistratore

camcorder • le caméscope
• **der Camcorder** • la cámara de
vídeo • la videocamera

satellite dish • l'antenne parabolique
• **die Satellitenschüssel** • la antena
parabólica • l'antenna parabolica

widescreen television • la télévision
16/9ème • **der Breitbildfernseher**
• la televisión panorámica
• il televisore a schermo largo

console
la console
die Spielkonsole
la consola
la console

fast forward • l'avance
rapide • **der Vorlauf**
• el avance rápido
• l'avanzamento veloce

pause
la pause
die Pause
la pausa
la pausa

record
• l'enregistrement
• **die Aufnahme**
• el botón para
grabar • la
registrazione

volume
le volume
die Lautstärke
el volumen
il volume

controller
la commande
der Steuerhebel
el mando
il comando

rewind
le retour rapide
der Rücklauf
el botón para rebobinar
il riavvolgimento

play
la lecture
das Abspielen
el play
il play

stop
l'arrêt
der Stop
el stop
lo stop

remote control • la télécommande • **die Fernbedienung**
• el mando a distancia • il telecomando

video game • le jeu vidéo • **das Videospiel** • el videojuego • il videogioco

compact disc	feature film	cable television	pay per view channel	turn the television off (v)
le CD	le film	la télévision par câble	la chaîne à péage	éteindre la télévision
die CD	**der Spielfilm**	**das Kabelfernsehen**	**der Pay-Kanal**	**den Fernseher abschalten**
el compact disc	el largometraje	la televisión por cable	el canal de pago	apagar la televisión
il compact disc	il lungometraggio	la televisione via cavo	il canale a pagamento	spegnere la televisione
cassette tape	advertisement	programme	turn the television on (v)	tune the radio (v)
la cassette	la publicité	le programme	allumer la télévision	régler la radio
die Kassette	**die Werbung**	**das Programm**	**den Fernseher einschalten**	**das Radio einstellen**
la casete	el anuncio	el programa	encender la televisión	sintonizar la radio
l'audiocassetta	la pubblicità	il programma	accendere la televisione	sintonizzare la radio
cassette player	digital	change channel (v)	watch television (v)	stereo
le lecteur cassettes	numérique	changer de chaîne	regarder la télévision	stéréo
der Kassettenrekorder	digital	**den Kanal wechseln**	fernsehen	stereo
el radiocasete	digital	cambiar de canal	ver la televisión	estéreo
il mangianastri	digitale	cambiare canale	guardare la televisione	stereo

photography • la photographie • die Fotografie • la fotografía • la fotografia

frame counter
le compteur de vues
der Zähler
el indicador de fotos
il contafotogrammi

flash
le flash
der Blitz
el flash
il flash

aperture dial
le réglage de l'ouverture
der Blendenregler
la rueda del diafragma
il regolatore di esponsione

filter • le filtre • der Filter • el filtro • il filtro

shutter release
le déclencheur
der Auslöser
el disparador
il pulsante di scatto

lens cap • le bouchon d'objectif • die Schutzkappe • la tapa del objetivo • il copriobiettivo

shutter-speed dial
le réglage du temps de pose
die Zeiteinstellscheibe
la rueda de la velocidad
il regolatore del tempo di esposizione

lens
l'objectif
die Linse
el objetivo
l'obiettivo

SLR camera • l'appareil réflex mono-objectif • die Spiegelreflexkamera • la cámara réflex • la macchina fotografica SLR

flash gun • le flash compact • der Elektronenblitz • el flash electrónico • il lampeggiatore

lightmeter • le posemètre • der Belichtungsmesser • el fotómetro • l'esposimetro

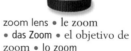

zoom lens • le zoom • das Zoom • el objetivo de zoom • lo zoom

tripod • le trépied • das Stativ • el trípode • il treppiede

---

types of camera • les types d'appareils photo • die Fotoapparattypen • los tipos de cámara • i tipi di macchina fotografica

digital camera • l'appareil numérique • die Digitalkamera • la cámara digital • la macchina fotografica digitale

APS camera • l'appareil photo APS • die Kamera für APS-Film • la cámara APS • la macchina fotografica APS

instant camera • l'appareil instantané • die Sofortbildkamera • la cámara Polaroid • la macchina fotografica instantanea

disposable camera • l'appareil jetable • die Einwegkamera • la cámara desechable • la macchina fotografica usa e getta

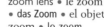
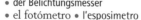

photograph (v) • photographier • fotografieren • fotografiar • fotografare

film spool
le rouleau de pellicule
die Filmspule
el carrete
il rullino

film • la pellicule • der Film
• la película • la pellicola

focus (v) • mettre au point
• einstellen • enfocar • mettere
a fuoco

develop (v) • développer
• entwickeln • revelar
• sviluppare

negative • le négatif • das
Negativ • el negativo • il
negativo

landscape • paysage
• quer • apaisado
• orizzontale

portrait • portrait
• hoch • en formato
vertical • verticale

photograph • la photo • das Foto • la fotografía • la fotografia

photo album • l'album de photos
• das Fotoalbum • el álbum de
fotos • l'album fotografico

photo frame • le cadre de
photo • der Fotorahmen • el
portarretratos • la cornice

---

problems • les problèmes • die Probleme • los problemas • i difetti

underexposed • sous-exposé
• unterbelichtet • subexpuesto
• sottoesposto

overexposed • surexposé
• überbelichtet • sobreexpuesto
• sovraesposto

out of focus • flou • unscharf
• desenfocado • sfocato

red eye • la tache rouge • die
Rotfärbung der Augen • los ojos
rojos • l'occhio rosso

viewfinder	print
le viseur	l'épreuve
der Bildsucher	der Abzug
el visor	la copia
il mirino	la fotografia (sviluppata)
camera case	mat
le sac d'appareil photo	mat
die Kameratasche	matt
la funda de la cámara	mate
l'astuccio	opaco
exposure	gloss
la pose	brilliant
die Belichtung	Hochglanz-
la exposición	con brillo
l'esposizione	lucido
darkroom	enlargement
la chambre noire	l'agrandissement
die Dunkelkammer	die Vergrößerung
el cuarto oscuro	la ampliación
la camera oscura	l'ingrandimento

I'd like this film processed.
Pourriez-vous faire développer cette pellicule?
Könnten Sie diesen Film entwickeln lassen?
Me gustaría revelar este carrete.
Vorrei far sviluppare questo rullino.

---

english • français • deutsch • español • italiano

games • les jeux • die Spiele • los juegos • i giochi

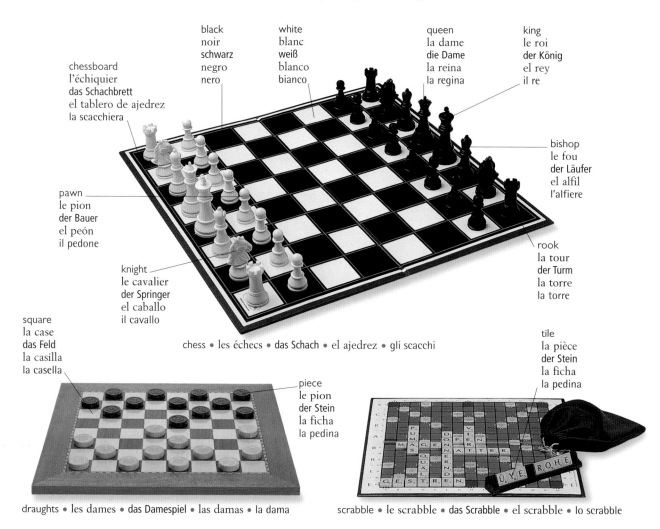

chessboard
l'échiquier
das Schachbrett
el tablero de ajedrez
la scacchiera

black
noir
schwarz
negro
nero

white
blanc
weiß
blanco
bianco

queen
la dame
die Dame
la reina
la regina

king
le roi
der König
el rey
il re

bishop
le fou
der Läufer
el alfil
l'alfiere

pawn
le pion
der Bauer
el peón
il pedone

rook
la tour
der Turm
la torre
la torre

knight
le cavalier
der Springer
el caballo
il cavallo

square
la case
das Feld
la casilla
la casella

chess • les échecs • das Schach • el ajedrez • gli scacchi

tile
la pièce
der Stein
la ficha
la pedina

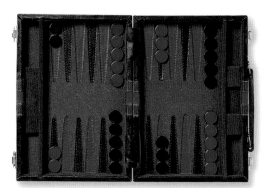

piece
le pion
der Stein
la ficha
la pedina

draughts • les dames • das Damespiel • las damas • la dama

scrabble • le scrabble • das Scrabble • el scrabble • lo scrabble

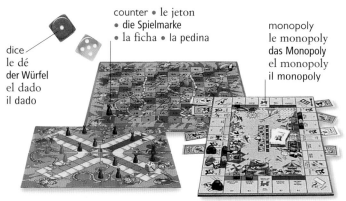

counter • le jeton
• die Spielmarke
• la ficha • la pedina

dice
le dé
der Würfel
el dado
il dado

monopoly
le monopoly
das Monopoly
el monopoly
il monopoly

backgammon • le trictrac • das Backgammon
• el chaquete • il backgammon

board games • les jeux de société • die Brettspiele • los juegos
de mesa • i giochi da tavolo

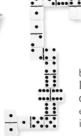

dartboard
la cible
die Dartscheibe
la diana
il bersaglio

bullseye
le mille
das Bull's Eye
el centro
il centro

stamp collecting • la philatélie
• die Briefmarkensammlung
• la filatelia • la filatelia

jigsaw puzzle • le puzzle
• das Puzzle • el puzzle
• il puzzle

dominoes • les dominos
• das Domino • el dominó
• il domino

darts • les fléchettes
• das Darts • los dardos
• le freccette

joker
le joker
der Joker
el comodín
il jolly

jack
le valet
der Bube
la sota
il fante

queen
la dame
die Dame
la reina
la regina

king
le roi
der König
el rey
il re

ace • l'as
• das Ass • el as
• l'asso

diamond
le carreau
das Karo
el diamante
il quadro

spade
le pique
das Pik
la pica
la picca

heart
le cœur
das Herz
el corazón
il cuore

club
le trèfle
das Kreuz
el trébol
il fiore

cards • les cartes • die Karten • las cartas
• le carte

shuffle (v) • battre • mischen
• barajar • mescolare

deal (v) • donner • geben
• dar • distribuire

move	win (v)	loser	point	bridge	Whose turn is it?
le coup	gagner	le perdant	le point	le bridge	C'est à qui de jouer?
der Zug	gewinnen	der Verlierer	der Punkt	das Bridge	Wer ist dran?
el turno	ganar	el perdedor	el punto	el bridge	¿A quién le toca?
la mossa	vincere	il perdente	il punto	il bridge	A chi tocca?
play (v)	winner	game	score	pack of cards	It's your move.
jouer	le gagnant	le jeu	la marque	le jeu de cartes	C'est à toi de jouer.
spielen	der Gewinner	das Spiel	das Spielergebnis	das Kartenspiel	Du bist dran.
jugar	el ganador	la partida	la puntuación	la baraja	Te toca a ti.
giocare	il vincitore	il gioco	il punteggio	il mazzo di carte	Tocca a te.
player	lose (v)	bet	poker	suit	Roll the dice.
le joueur	perdre	le pari	le poker	la couleur	Jette le dé.
der Spieler	verlieren	die Wette	das Poker	die Farbe	Würfle.
el jugador	perder	la apuesta	el póquer	el palo	Tira los dados.
il giocatore	perdere	la scommessa	il poker	il colore	Tira i dadi.

arts and crafts 1 • les arts et métiers 1 • das Kunsthandwerk 1 • las manualidades 1 • arte e artigianato 1

artist
l'artiste peintre
die Künstlerin
la pintora
l'artista

painting
le tableau
das Gemälde
el cuadro
il quadro

easel
le chevalet
die Staffelei
el caballete
il cavalletto

canvas
la toile
die Leinwand
el lienzo
la tela

brush
le pinceau
der Pinsel
el pincel
il pennello

palette
la palette
die Palette
la paleta
la tavolozza

painting • la peinture • die Malerei • la pintura • la pittura

paints • les couleurs • die Farben • las pinturas • la vernice

oil paints • les couleurs à l'huile • die Ölfarben • las pinturas al óleo • i colori ad olio

watercolour paint • la couleur à l'eau • die Aquarellfarbe • las acuarelas • gli acquarelli

pastels • les pastels • die Pastellstifte • los pasteles • i pastelli

acrylic paint • l'acrylique • die Acrylfarbe • la pintura acrílica • i colori acrilici

poster paint • la gouache • die farbe • la témpera • il colore a tempera

colours • les couleurs • die Farben • los colores • i colori

red • rouge • rot • rojo • rosso

blue • bleu • blau • azul • blu

yellow • jaune • gelb • amarillo • giallo

green • vert • grün • verde • verde

orange • orange • orange • naranja • arancione

purple • violet • lila • morado • viola

white • blanc • weiß • blanco • bianco

black • noir • schwarz • negro • nero

grey • gris • grau • gris • grigio

pink • rose • rosa • rosa • rosa

brown • marron • braun • marrón • marrone

indigo • indigo • indigoblau • añil • indaco

other crafts • les autres arts • andere Kunstfertigkeiten • las otras manualidades • altri lavori artigianali

sketch pad
le carnet à croquis
der Skizzenblock
el bloc de dibujo
il blocco per schizzi

sketch
le croquis
die Skizze
el boceto
lo schizzo

ink
l'encre
die Druckfarbe
la tinta
l'inchiostro

pencil
le crayon
der Bleistift
el lápiz
la matita

charcoal
le fusain
der Kohlestift
el carboncillo
il carboncino

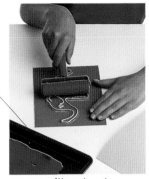

drawing • le dessin • das Zeichnen • el dibujo • il disegno

printing • l'imprimerie • das Drucken • la impresión • la stampa

engraving • la gravure • das Gravieren • el grabado • l'incisione

stone
la pierre
der Stein
la piedra
la pietra

mallet
le maillet
der Schlegel
el mazo
il martello

chisel
le burin
der Meißel
el cincel
lo scalpello

wood
le bois
das Holz
la madera
il legno

modelling tool
la spatule
das Modellierholz
la herramienta para modelar
l'attrezzo per modellare

potter's wheel
le tour de potier
die Töpferscheibe
el torno de alfarero
il tornio da vasaio

clay
l'argile
der Ton
la arcilla
l'argilla

sculpting • la sculpture • die Bildhauerei • la escultura • la scultura

woodworking • la sculpture sur bois • die Holzarbeit • la talla en madera • la falegnameria

glue
la colle
der Klebstoff
la cola
la colla

cardboard
le carton
die Pappe
la cartulina
il cartone

collage • le collage • die Collage • el collage • il collage

pottery • la poterie • die Töpferei • la cerámica • la ceramica

jewellery making • la joaillerie • die Juwelierarbeit • la orfebrería • l'oreficeria

papier-mâché • le papier mâché • das Pappmaschee • el papel maché • la cartapesta

origami • l'origami • das Origami • la papiroflexia • l'origami

model making • le modélisme • der Modellbau • el modelismo • il modellismo

arts and crafts 2 • les arts et métiers 2 • das Kunsthandwerk 2 • las manualidades 2 • arte e artigianato 2

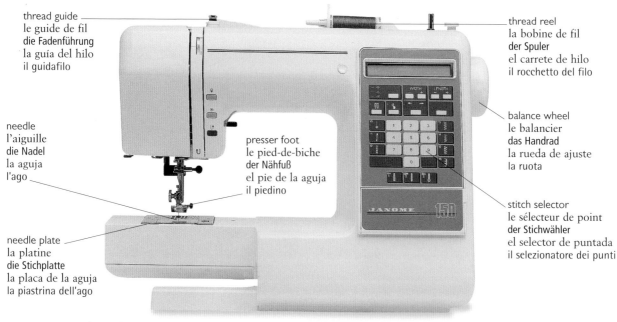

thread guide
le guide de fil
die Fadenführung
la guía del hilo
il guidafilo

thread reel
la bobine de fil
der Spuler
el carrete de hilo
il rocchetto del filo

needle
l'aiguille
die Nadel
la aguja
l'ago

presser foot
le pied-de-biche
der Nähfuß
el pie de la aguja
il piedino

balance wheel
le balancier
das Handrad
la rueda de ajuste
la ruota

needle plate
la platine
die Stichplatte
la placa de la aguja
la piastrina dell'ago

stitch selector
le sélecteur de point
der Stichwähler
el selector de puntada
il selezionatore dei punti

sewing machine • la machine à coudre • die Nähmaschine • la máquina de coser • la macchina da cucire

scissors • les ciseaux • die Schere • las tijeras • le forbici

pattern • le patron • das Schnittmuster • el patrón • il modello

pincushion
la pelote à épingles
das Nadelkissen
el alfiletero
il puntaspilli

pin
l'épingle
die Stecknadel
el alfiler
lo spillo

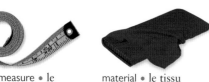

tape measure • le centimètre • das Zentimetermaß • la cinta métrica • il metro

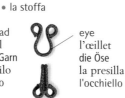

material • le tissu • der Stoff • la tela • la stoffa

sewing basket • la corbeille à couture • der Nähkorb • el costurero • il cestino da lavoro

thread
le fil
das Garn
el hilo
il filo

eye
l'œillet
die Öse
la presilla
l'occhiello

bobbin • la bobine • die Spule • la bobina • la bobina

hook • l'agrafe • der Haken • el corchete • il gancio

thimble • le dé à coudre • der Fingerhut • el dedal • il ditale

tailor's chalk • la craie de tailleur • die Schneiderkreide • el jaboncillo • il gesso

tailor's dummy • le mannequin • die Schneiderpuppe • el maniquí • il manichino

thread (v) • enfiler • einfädeln • enhebrar • infilare

stitch
le point
der Stich
la puntada
il punto

sew (v) • coudre • nähen • coser • cucire

darn (v) • repriser • stopfen • zurcir • rammendare

tack (v) • bâtir • heften • hilvanar • imbastire

cut (v) • couper • schneiden • cortar • tagliare

needlepoint • la tapisserie • die Gobelinstickerei • el bordado en cañamazo • la punta dell'ago

embroidery • la broderie • die Stickerei • el bordado • il ricamo

crochet hook
le crochet
der Häkelhaken
la aguja de ganchillo
l'uncinetto

crochet • le crochet • das Häkeln • el ganchillo • l'uncinetto

macramé • le macramé • das Makramee • el macramé • il macramè

patchwork • le patchwork • das Patchwork • la labor de retales • il patchwork

quilting • le ouatage • das Wattieren • el acolchado • l'imbottire

lace bobbin • le fuseau • der Klöppel • el bolillo • il fuso

lace-making • la dentelle • die Spitzenklöppelei • el encaje de bolillos • la fabbricazione dei merletti

loom • le métier à tisser • der Webstuhl • el telar • il telaio

weaving • le tissage • das Weben • tejer • la tessitura

unpick (v) défaire **auftrennen** descoser scucire	nylon le nylon **das Nylon** el nailon il nailon
fabric le tissu **der Stoff** la tela la tela	silk la soie **die Seide** la seda la seta
cotton le coton **die Baumwolle** el algodón il cotone	designer le styliste **der Modedesigner** el diseñador lo stilista
linen le lin **das Leinen** el lino il lino	fashion la mode **die Mode** la moda la moda
polyester le polyester **das Polyester** el poliéster il poliestere	zip la fermeture éclair **der Reißverschluss** la cremallera la chiusura lampo

knitting needle
l'aiguille à tricoter
die Stricknadel
la aguja de tejer
il ferro da calza

knitting • le tricot • das Stricken • la labor de punto • il lavoro a maglia

wool
la laine
die Wolle
la lana
la lana

skein • l'écheveau • der Strang • la madeja • la matassa

environment
l'environnement
die Umwelt
el medio ambiente
l'ambiente

space • l'espace • der Weltraum • el espacio • lo spazio

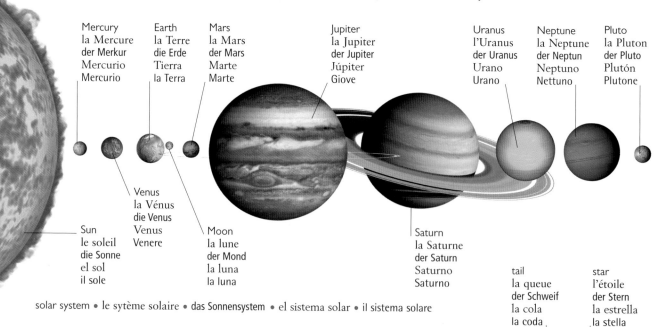

Mercury
la Mercure
der Merkur
Mercurio
Mercurio

Earth
la Terre
die Erde
Tierra
la Terra

Mars
la Mars
der Mars
Marte
Marte

Jupiter
la Jupiter
der Jupiter
Júpiter
Giove

Uranus
l'Uranus
der Uranus
Urano
Urano

Neptune
la Neptune
der Neptun
Neptuno
Nettuno

Pluto
la Pluton
der Pluto
Plutón
Plutone

Venus
la Vénus
die Venus
Venus
Venere

Sun
le soleil
die Sonne
el sol
il sole

Moon
la lune
der Mond
la luna
la luna

Saturn
la Saturne
der Saturn
Saturno
Saturno

tail
la queue
der Schweif
la cola
la coda

star
l'étoile
der Stern
la estrella
la stella

solar system • le sytème solaire • das Sonnensystem • el sistema solar • il sistema solare

galaxy • la galaxie
• die Galaxie • la galaxia
• la galassia

nebula • la nébuleuse
• der Nebelfleck • la nebulosa
• la nebulosa

asteroid • l'astéroïde
• der Asteroid • el asteroide
• l'asteroide

comet • la comète
• der Komet • el cometa
• la cometa

universe
l'univers
das Universum
el universo
l'universo

black hole
le trou noir
das schwarze Loch
el agujero negro
il buco nero

full moon
la pleine lune
der Vollmond
la luna llena
la luna piena

orbit
l'orbite
die Umlaufbahn
la órbita
l'orbita

planet
la planète
der Planet
el planeta
il pianeta

new moon
la nouvelle lune
der Neumond
la luna nueva
la luna nuova

gravity
la pesanteur
die Schwerkraft
la gravedad
la gravità

meteor
le météore
der Meteor
el meteorito
la meteora

crescent moon
le croissant de lune
die Mondsichel
la media luna
la mezzaluna

eclipse • l'éclipse • die Finsternis • el eclipse • l'eclisse

space exploration • l'exploration spatiale • die Weltraumforschung • la exploración espacial • la ricerca spaziale

radar
le radar
der Radar
el radar
il radar

space shuttle
• la navette spatiale
• die Raumfähre
• el transbordador
espacial • lo shuttle

space suit
le scaphandre spatial
der Raumanzug
el traje espacial
la tuta spaziale

thruster
la fusée d'orientation
die Steuerrakete
el propulsor
il reattore

crew hatch • le
sas d'équipage
• die Besatzungs-
luke • la escotilla
• lo sportello
dell'equipaggio

booster
l'accélérateur
der Booster
el lanzacohetes
il lanciarazzi

astronaut • l'astronaute
• der Astronaut • el
astronauta • l'astronauta

lunar module • le module lunaire • die Mondfähre • el módulo
lunar • il modulo lunare

launch pad • la rampe
de lancement
• die Abschussrampe
• la rampa de
lanzamiento
• la rampa
di lancio

launch • le lancement • der
Abschuss • el lanzamiento
• il lancio

satellite • le satellite • der
Satellit • el satélite • il satellite

space station • la station spatiale • die Raumstation • la estación
espacial • la stazione spaziale

astronomy • l'astronomie • die Astronomie • la astronomía • l'astronomia

telescope
le télescope
das Teleskop
el telescopio
il telescopio

tripod
le trépied
das Stativ
el trípode
il treppiede

constellation • la constellation
• das Sternbild • la constelación
• la costellazione

binoculars • les jumelles
• das Fernglas • los prismáticos
• il binocolo

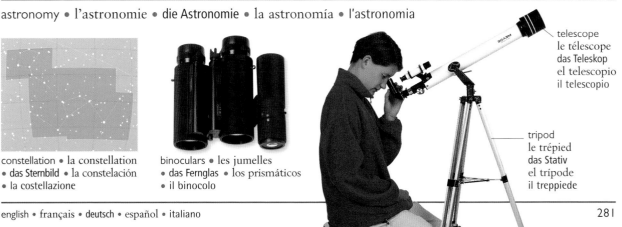

Earth • la terre • die Erde • la Tierra • la Terra

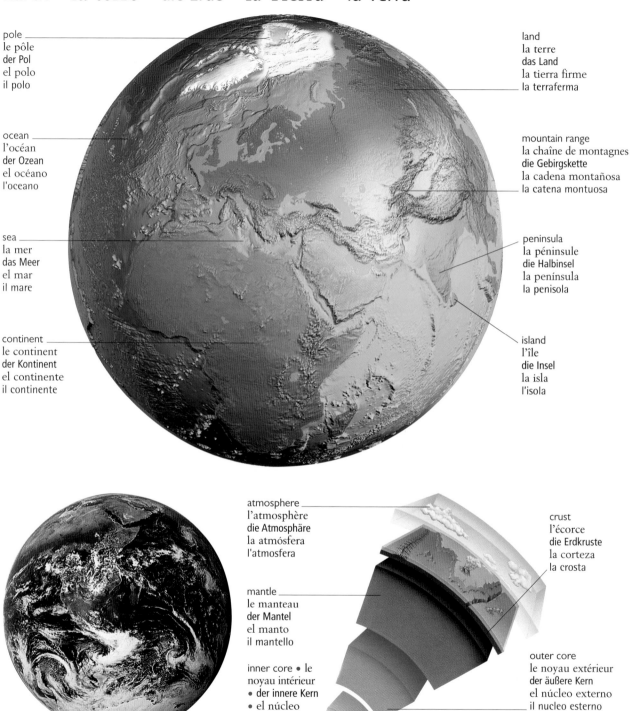

pole
le pôle
der Pol
el polo
il polo

ocean
l'océan
der Ozean
el océano
l'oceano

sea
la mer
das Meer
el mar
il mare

continent
le continent
der Kontinent
el continente
il continente

land
la terre
das Land
la tierra firme
la terraferma

mountain range
la chaîne de montagnes
die Gebirgskette
la cadena montañosa
la catena montuosa

peninsula
la péninsule
die Halbinsel
la península
la penisola

island
l'île
die Insel
la isla
l'isola

atmosphere
l'atmosphère
die Atmosphäre
la atmósfera
l'atmosfera

crust
l'écorce
die Erdkruste
la corteza
la crosta

mantle
le manteau
der Mantel
el manto
il mantello

inner core • le
noyau intérieur
• der innere Kern
• el núcleo
interno • il
nucleo interno

outer core
le noyau extérieur
der äußere Kern
el núcleo externo
il nucleo esterno

planet • la planète • der Planet • el planeta
• il pianeta

section • la section • der Längsschnitt
• la sección • lo spaccato

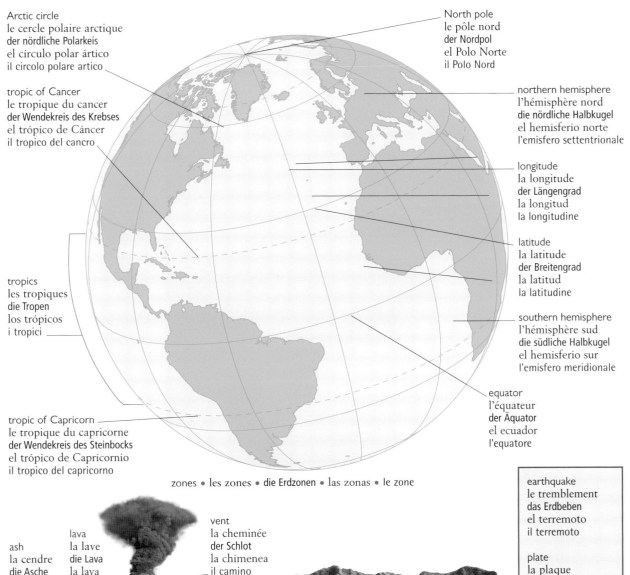

Arctic circle
le cercle polaire arctique
der nördliche Polarkeis
el círculo polar ártico
il circolo polare artico

tropic of Cancer
le tropique du cancer
der Wendekreis des Krebses
el trópico de Cáncer
il tropico del cancro

tropics
les tropiques
die Tropen
los trópicos
i tropici

tropic of Capricorn
le tropique du capricorne
der Wendekreis des Steinbocks
el trópico de Capricornio
il tropico del capricorno

North pole
le pôle nord
der Nordpol
el Polo Norte
il Polo Nord

northern hemisphere
l'hémisphère nord
die nördliche Halbkugel
el hemisferio norte
l'emisfero settentrionale

longitude
la longitude
der Längengrad
la longitud
la longitudine

latitude
la latitude
der Breitengrad
la latitud
la latitudine

southern hemisphere
l'hémisphère sud
die südliche Halbkugel
el hemisferio sur
l'emisfero meridionale

equator
l'équateur
der Äquator
el ecuador
l'equatore

zones • les zones • die Erdzonen • las zonas • le zone

ash
la cendre
die Asche
la ceniza
la cenere

lava
la lave
die Lava
la lava
la lava

vent
la cheminée
der Schlot
la chimenea
il camino

chamber
la chambre
die Kammer
la cámara
la camera

magma • le magma
• das Magma • el
magma • il magma

volcano • le volcan • der Vulkan • el volcán • il vulcano

crater • le cratère • der Krater • el cráter
• il cratere

earthquake
le tremblement
das Erdbeben
el terremoto
il terremoto

plate
la plaque
die Platte
la placa
la zolla

erupt (v)
entrer en éruption
ausbrechen
entrar en erupción
eruttare

tremor
le tremblement
das Beben
el temblor
il tremore

landscape • le paysage • die Landschaft • el paisaje • il paesaggio

mountain
la montagne
der Berg
la montaña
la montagna

slope
la pente
der Hang
la ladera
la pendio

bank
la rive
das Ufer
la orilla
la riva

river
la rivière
der Fluss
el río
il fiume

rapids
les rapides
die Stromschnellen
los rápidos
le rapide

rocks
les rochers
die Felsen
las rocas
le rocce

glacier • le glacier
• der Gletscher • el glaciar
• il ghiacciaio

valley • la vallée • das Tal
• el valle • la valle

hill • la colline • der Hügel
• la colina • la collina

plateau • le plateau
• das Plateau • la meseta
• l'altipiano

gorge • la gorge • die Schlucht
• el desfiladero • la gola

cave • la caverne • die Höhle
• la cueva • la caverna

plain • la plaine • die Ebene
• la llanura • la pianura

desert • le désert • die Wüste
• el desierto • il deserto

forest • la forêt • der Wald
• el bosque • la foresta

wood • le bois • der Wald
• el bosque • il bosco

rainforest • la forêt tropicale
• der Regenwald • la selva
tropical • la foresta pluviale

swamp • le marais • der
Sumpf • el pantano
• la palude

meadow • le pré • die Weide
label • el prado • il pascolo

grassland • la prairie
• das Grasland • la pradera
• la prateria

waterfall • la cascade
• der Wasserfall • la cascada
• la cascata

stream • le ruisseau
• der Bach • el arroyo
• il torrente

lake • le lac • der See
• el lago • il lago

geyser • le geyser • der Geysir
• el géiser • il geyser

coast • la côte • die Küste
• la costa • la costa

cliff • la falaise • die Klippe
• el acantilado • la scogliera

coral reef • le récif de corail
• das Korallenriff • el arrecife
de coral • la barriera corallina

estuary • l'estuaire • die
Flussmündung • el estuario
• l'estuario

weather • le temps • das Wetter • el tiempo • il tempo

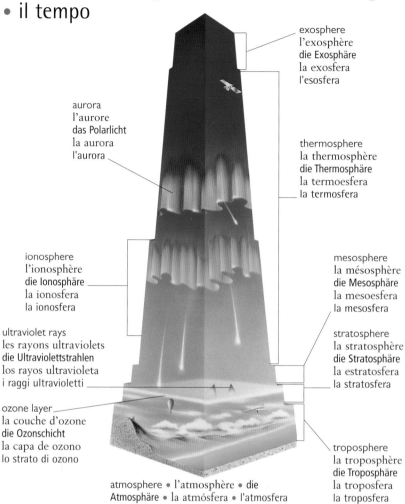

exosphere
l'exosphère
die Exosphäre
la exosfera
l'esosfera

aurora
l'aurore
das Polarlicht
la aurora
l'aurora

thermosphere
la thermosphère
die Thermosphäre
la termoesfera
la termosfera

ionosphere
l'ionosphère
die Ionosphäre
la ionosfera
la ionosfera

mesosphere
la mésosphère
die Mesosphäre
la mesoesfera
la mesosfera

ultraviolet rays
les rayons ultraviolets
die Ultraviolettstrahlen
los rayos ultravioleta
i raggi ultravioletti

stratosphere
la stratosphère
die Stratosphäre
la estratosfera
la stratosfera

ozone layer
la couche d'ozone
die Ozonschicht
la capa de ozono
lo strato di ozono

troposphere
la troposphère
die Troposphäre
la troposfera
la troposfera

atmosphere • l'atmosphère • die
Atmosphäre • la atmósfera • l'atmosfera

sunshine • le soleil • der Sonnenschein
• el sol • la luce del sole

wind • le vent • der Wind
• el viento • il vento

sleet	shower	hot	dry	windy	I'm hot/cold.
la neige fondue	l'averse	(très) chaud	sec	venteux	J'ai chaud/froid.
der Schneeregen	der Schauer	heiß	trocken	windig	Mir ist heiß/kalt.
el aguanieve	el chubasco	caluroso	seco	ventoso	Tengo calor/frío.
il nevischio	il rovescio	caldo	secco	ventoso	Ho caldo/freddo.
hail	sunny	cold	wet	gale	It's raining.
la grêle	ensoleillé	froid	humide	la tempête	Il pleut.
der Hagel	sonnig	kalt	nass	der Sturm	Es regnet.
el granizo	soleado	frío	lluvioso	el temporal	Está lloviendo.
la grandine	soleggiato	freddo	piovoso	la bufera	Sta piovendo.
thunder	cloudy	warm	humid	temperature	It's ... degrees.
le tonnerre	nuageux	chaud	humide	la température	Il fait ... degrés.
der Donner	bewölkt	warm	feucht	die Temperatur	Es sind ... Grad.
el trueno	nublado	cálido	húmedo	la temperatura	Estamos a ... grados.
il tuono	nuvoloso	tiepido	umido	la temperatura	Fa ... gradi.

cloud • le nuage • **die Wolke** • la nube • la nuvola

rain • la pluie • **der Regen** • la lluvia • la pioggia

lightning • l'éclair • **der Blitz** • el relámpago • il fulmine

storm • l'orage • **das Gewitter** • la tormenta • la tempesta

mist • la brume • **der Nebel** • la neblina • la foschia

fog • le brouillard • **der dichte Nebel** • la niebla • la nebbia

rainbow • l'arc-en-ciel • **der Regenbogen** • el arcoiris • l'arcobaleno

snow • la neige • **der Schnee** • la nieve • la neve

frost • le givre • **der Raureif** • la escarcha • la brina

icicle • le glaçon • **der Eiszapfen** • el carámbano • il ghiacciolo

ice • la glace • **das Eis** • el hielo • il ghiaccio

freeze • le gel • **der Frost** • la helada • il gelo

hurricane • l'ouragan • **der Hurrikan** • el huracán • l'uragano

tornado • la tornade • **der Tornado** • el tornado • il tornado

monsoon • la mousson • **der Monsun** • el monzón • il monsone

flood • l'inondation • **die Überschwemmung** • la inundación • l'inondazione

rocks • les roches • das Gestein • las rocas • le rocce

igneous • igné • eruptiv • ígneo • igneo

granite • le granit • der Granit • el granito • il granito

obsidian • l'obsidienne • der Obsidian • la obsidiana • l'ossidiana

basalt • le basalte • der Basalt • el basalto • il basalto

pumice • la pierre ponce • der Bimsstein • la piedra pómez • la pomice

sedimentary • sédimentaire • sedimentär • sedimentario • sedimentario

sandstone • le grès • der Sandstein • la piedra arenisca • l'arenaria

limestone • le calcaire • der Kalkstein • la piedra caliza • la pietra calcarea

chalk • la craie • die Kreide • la tiza • il gesso

flint • le silex • der Feuerstein • el pedernal • la selce

conglomerate • le conglomérat • das Konglomerat • el conglomerado • il conglomerato

coal • le charbon • die Kohle • el carbón • il carbone

metamorphic • métamorphique • metamorph • metamórfico • metamorfico

slate • l'ardoise • der Schiefer • la pizarra • l'ardesia

schist • le schiste • der Schiefer • el esquisto • lo scisto

gneiss • le gneiss • der Gneis • el gneis • lo gneiss

marble • le marbre • der Marmor • el mármol • il marmo

gems • les gemmes • die Edelsteine • las gemas • le gemme

ruby
le rubis
der Rubin
el rubí
il rubino

amethyst
l'améthyste
der Amethyst
la amatista
l'ametista

jet
le jais
der Jett
el azabache
il giaietto

opal
l'opale
der Opal
el ópalo
l'opale

moonstone
la pierre de lune
der Mondstein
la piedra lunar
la lunaria

diamond
le diamant
der Diamant
el diamante
il diamante

garnet
le grenat
der Granat
el granate
il granato

topaz
le topaze
der Topas
el topacio
il topazio

aquamarine
l'aigue-marine
der Aquamarin
la aguamarina
l'acquamarina

jade
le jade
der Jade
el jade
la giada

emerald
l'émeraude
der Smaragd
la esmeralda
lo smeraldo

sapphire
le saphir
der Saphir
el zafiro
lo zaffiro

tourmaline
la toumaline
der Turmalin
la turmalina
la tormalina

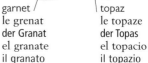

minerals • les minéraux • die Mineralien • los minerales • i minerali

quartz • le quartz • der Quarz • el cuarzo • il quarzo

mica • le mica • der Glimmer • la mica • la mica

sulphur • le soufre • der Schwefel • el azufre • lo zolfo

hematite • l'hématite • der Hämatit • el hematites • l'ematite

calcite • la calcite • der Kalzit • la calcita • la calcite

malachite • la malachite • der Malachit • la malaquita • la malachite

turquoise • la turquoise • der Türkis • la turquesa • il turchese

onyx • l'onyx • der Onyx • el ónice • l'onice

agate • l'agate • der Achat • el ágata • l'agata

graphite • le graphite • der Graphit • el grafito • la grafite

---

metals • les métaux • die Metalle • los metales • i metalli

gold • l'or • das Gold • el oro • l'oro

silver • l'argent • das Silber • la plata • l'argento

platinum • le platine • das Platin • el platino • il platino

nickel • le nickel • das Nickel • el níquel • il nichel

iron • le fer • das Eisen • el hierro • il ferro

copper • le cuivre • das Kupfer • el cobre • il rame

tin • l'étain • das Zinn • el estaño • lo stagno

aluminium • l'aluminium • das Aluminium • el aluminio • l'alluminio

mercury • le mercure • das Quecksilber • el mercurio • il mercurio

zinc • le zinc • das Zink • el zinc • lo zinco

---

animals 1 • les animaux 1 • die Tiere 1 • los animales 1 • gli animali 1

mammals • les mammifères • die Säugetiere • los mamíferos • i mammiferi

rabbit • le lapin
• das Kaninchen
• el conejo • il coniglio

hamster • le hamster
• der Hamster • el
hámster • il criceto

whiskers
les poils
die Schnurrhaare
los bigotes
i baffi

mouse • la souris
• die Maus • el ratón
• il topo

tail
la queue
der Schwanz
la cola
la coda

rat • le rat • die Ratte
• la rata • il ratto

hedgehog • le hérisson
• der Igel • el erizo
• il riccio

squirrel • l'écureuil
• das Eichhörnchen •
la ardilla • lo scoiattolo

bat • la chauve-souris
• die Fledermaus • el
murciélago
• il pipistrello

raccoon • le raton laveur
• der Waschbär • el
mapache • il procione

fox • le renard
• der Fuchs • el zorro
• la volpe

wolf • le loup
• der Wolf • el lobo
• il lupo

puppy
le chiot
der Welpe
el cachorro
il cucciolo

kitten
le chaton
das Kätzchen
el gatito
il gattino

pup
le bébé-phoque
das Junge
la cría
il cucciolo

dog • le chien • der Hund
• el perro • il cane

cat • le chat • die Katze
• el gato • il gatto

otter • la loutre • der Otter
• la nutria • la lontra

seal • le phoque • die Robbe
• la foca • la foca

flipper
la nageoire
die Flosse
la aleta
la pinna

blowhole
l'évent
das Atemloch
el orificio nasal
lo sfiatatoio

dolphin •
le dauphin • der Delfin
• el delfín • il delfino

sea lion • l'otarie
• der Seelöwe • el león
marino • il leone marino

walrus • le morse
• das Walross • la
morsa • il tricheco

whale • la baleine • der Wal
• la ballena • la balena

antler
la ramure
das Geweih
la cornamenta
le corna

mane
la crinière
die Mähne
le crin
la criniera

hump • la bosse
• der Höcker • la
giba • la gobba

hoof
le sabot
der Huf
la pezuña
lo zoccolo

deer • le cerf • der Hirsch
• el ciervo • il cervo

zebra • le zèbre
• das Zebra • la cebra
• la zebra

giraffe • la girafe
• die Giraffe • la jirafa
• la giraffa

camel • le chameau
• das Kamel • el camello
• il cammello

trunk • la trompe • der Rüssel
• la trompa • la proboscide

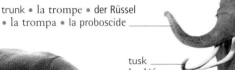

tusk
la défense
der Stoßzahn
el colmillo
la zanna

horn • la corne
• das Horn • el
cuerno • il corno

hippopotamus • le
hippopotame • das Nilpferd
• el hipopótamo
• l'ippopotamo

elephant • l'éléphant
• der Elefant • el elefante
• l'elefante

rhinoceros • le rhinocéros
• das Nashorn • el rinoceronte
• il rinoceronte

tiger • le tigre • der Tiger
• el tigre • il tigre

mane
la crinière
die Mähne
la melena
la criniera

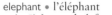

lion • le lion • der Löwe
• el león • il leone

monkey • le singe
• der Affe • el mono
• la scimmia

gorilla • le gorille
• der Gorilla • el gorila
• il gorilla

koala • le koala • der Koalabär
• el koala • il koala

pouch
la poche
der Beutel
la bolsa
il marsupio

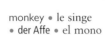

panda • le panda
• der Pandabär
• el oso panda
• il panda

claw
la griffe
die Klaue
la zarpa
l'artiglio

kangaroo • le kangourou
• das Känguru • el canguro
• il canguro

bear • l'ours
• der Bär • el oso
• l'orso

polar bear • l'ours blanc
• der Eisbär • el oso polar
• l'orso polare

animals 2 • les animaux 2 • die Tiere 2 • los animales 2 • gli animali 2

birds • les oiseaux • die Vögel • las aves • gli uccelli

tail
la queue
der Schwanz
la cola
la coda

canary • le canari
• der Kanarienvogel • el
canario • il canarino

sparrow • le moineau
• der Spatz • el gorrión
• il passero

hummingbird • le
colibri • der Kolibri
• el colibrí • il colibri

swallow • l'hirondelle
• die Schwalbe • la
golondrina • la rondine

crow • le corbeau
• die Krähe • el cuervo
• la cornacchia

pigeon • le pigeon
• die Taube • la
paloma • il piccione

woodpecker • le pic
• der Specht • el pájaro
carpintero • il picchio

falcon • le faucon
• der Falke • el halcón
• il falco

owl • la chouette
• die Eule • el búho
• il gufo

gull • la mouette • die
Möwe • la gaviota
• il gabbiano

eagle • l'aigle
• der Adler • el águila
• l'aquila

pelican • le pélican
• der Pelikan • el
pelícano • il pellicano

flamingo • le flamant
• der Flamingo
• el flamenco
• il fiammingo

stork • la cigogne • der
Storch • la cigüeña
• la cicogna

crane • la grue
• der Kranich
• la grulla • la gru

penguin • le pingouin
• der Pinguin • el
pingüino • il pinguino

ostrich • l'autruche
• der Strauß • el
avestruz • lo struzzo

english • français • deutsch • español • italiano

goose • l'oie • die Gans
• la oca • l'oca

swan • le cygne • der Schwan
• el cisne • il cigno

peacock • le paon • der Pfau
• el pavo real • il pavone

pheasant • le faisan
• der Fasan • el
faisán • il fagiano

bill
le bec
der Schnabel
el pico
il becco

turkey • le dindon
• der Truthahn • el pavo
• il tacchino

feather
la plume
die Feder
la pluma
la piuma

wing
l'aile
der Flügel
el ala
l'ala

cockatoo
le cacatoès
der Kakadu
la cacatúa
la cacatua

claw
la griffe
die Kralle
la garra
l'artiglio

parrot • le perroquet
• der Papagei • el loro
• il pappagallo

reptiles • les reptiles • die Reptilien • los reptiles
• i rettili

scales • les écailles
• die Schuppen • las
escamas • le scaglie

alligator • l'alligator • der Alligator • el aligátor
• l'alligatore

lizard • le lézard • die Eidechse
• el lagarto • la lucertola

iguana • l'iguane
• der Leguan • la iguana
• l'iguana

shell
la carapace
der Panzer
el caparazón
il guscio

turtle • la tortue marine
• die Wasserschildkröte • el
galápago • la testuggine

tortoise • la tortue
• die Schildkröte • la tortuga
• la tartaruga

snake • le serpent
• die Schlange
• la serpiente
• il serpente

snout
le museau
die Schnauze
el hocico
il muso

crocodile • le crocodile
• das Krokodil • el
cocodrilo • il coccodrillo

animals 3 • les animaux 3 • die Tiere 3 • los animales 3 • gli animali 3

amphibians • les amphibiens • die Amphibien • los anfibios • gli anfibi

frog • la grenouille • der Frosch • la rana • la rana

toad • le crapaud • die Kröte • el sapo • il rospo

tadpole • le têtard • die Kaulquappe • el renacuajo • il girino

salamander • la salamandre • der Salamander • la salamandra • la salamandra

fish • les poissons • die Fische • los peces • i pesci

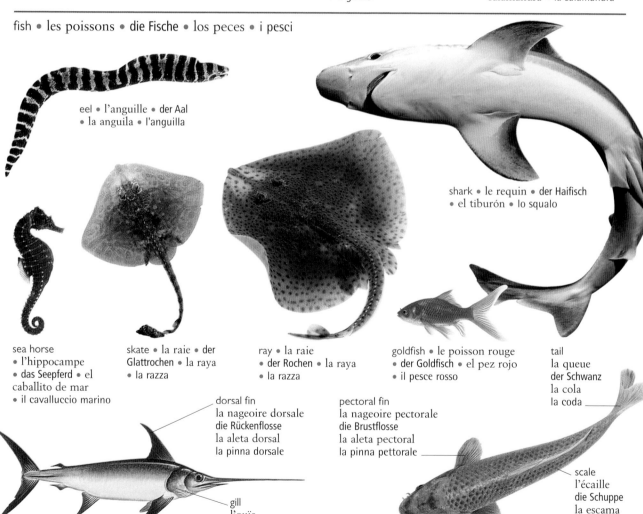

eel • l'anguille • der Aal • la anguila • l'anguilla

shark • le requin • der Haifisch • el tiburón • lo squalo

sea horse • l'hippocampe • das Seepferd • el caballito de mar • il cavalluccio marino

skate • la raie • der Glattrochen • la raya • la razza

ray • la raie • der Rochen • la raya • la razza

goldfish • le poisson rouge • der Goldfisch • el pez rojo • il pesce rosso

tail
la queue
der Schwanz
la cola
la coda

dorsal fin
la nageoire dorsale
die Rückenflosse
la aleta dorsal
la pinna dorsale

pectoral fin
la nageoire pectorale
die Brustflosse
la aleta pectoral
la pinna pettorale

scale
l'écaille
die Schuppe
la escama
la scaglia

swordfish • l'espadon • der Schwertfisch • el pez espada • il pesce spada

gill
l'ouïe
die Kieme
la agalla
la branchia

koi carp • la carpe koi • der Koikarpfen • la carpa koi • la carpa koi

294

english • français • deutsch • español • italiano

invertebrates • les invertébrés • die Wirbellosen • los invertebrados • gli invertebrati

ant • la fourmi • die Ameise • la hormiga • la formica

termite • la termite • die Termite • la termita • la termite

bee • l'abeille • die Biene • la abeja • l'ape

wasp • la guêpe • die Wespe • la avispa • la vespa

beetle • le scarabée • der Käfer • el escarabajo • il coleottero

cockroach • le cafard • der Kakerlak • la cucaracha • lo scarafaggio

moth • le papillon • die Motte • la polilla • la tarma

antenna
l'antenne
der Fühler
la antena
l'antenna

butterfly • le papillon • der Schmetterling • la mariposa • la farfalla

cocoon • le cocon • der Kokon • el capullo • il bozzolo

caterpillar • la chenille • die Raupe • la oruga • il bruco

cricket • le grillon • die Grille • el grillo • il grillo

grasshopper • la sauterelle • die Heuschrecke • el saltamontes • la cavalletta

praying mantis • la mante religieuse • die Gottesanbeterin • la mantis religiosa • la mantide religiosa

sting
le dard
der Stachel
el aquijón
il pungiglione

scorpion • le scorpion • der Skorpion • el escorpión • lo scorpione

centipede • le mille-pattes • der Tausendfüßer • el ciempiés • il millepiedi

dragonfly • la libellule • die Libelle • la libélula • la libellula

fly • la mouche • die Fliege • la mosca • la mosca

mosquito • le moustique • die Stechmücke • el mosquito • la zanzara

ladybird • la coccinelle • der Marienkäfer • la mariquita • la coccinella

spider • l'araignée • die Spinne • la araña • il ragno

slug • la limace • die Wegschnecke • la babosa • la lumaca

snail • l'escargot • die Schnecke • el caracol • la chiocciola

worm • le ver • der Wurm • el gusano • il verme

starfish • l'étoile de mer • der Seestern • la estrella de mar • la stella di mare

mussel • la moule • die Muschel • el mejillón • la cozza

crab • le crabe • der Krebs • el cangrejo • il granchio

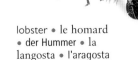

lobster • le homard • der Hummer • la langosta • l'aragosta

octopus • la pieuvre • der Seepolyp • el pulpo • la piovra

squid • le calmar • der Tintenfisch • el calamar • il calamaro

jellyfish • la méduse • die Qualle • la medusa • la medusa

plants • les plantes • die Pflanzen • las plantas • le piante

tree • l'arbre • der Baum • el árbol • l'albero

branch
la branche
der Ast
la rama
il ramo

leaf
la feuille
das Blatt
la hoja
la foglia

twig
la brindille
der Zweig
la ramita
il ramoscello

willow • le saule • die Weide • el sauce • il salice

bark
l'écorce
die Rinde
la corteza
la corteccia

root
la racine
die Wurzel
la raíz
la radice

trunk
le tronc
der Stamm
el tronco
il tronco

oak • le chêne • die Eiche • el roble • la quercia

poplar • le peuplier • die Pappel • el álamo • il pioppo

eucalyptus • l'eucalyptus • der Eukalyptus • el eucalipto • l'eucalipto

larch • le mélèze • die Lärche • el alerce • il larice

beech • le hêtre • die Buche • la haya • il faggio

birch • le bouleau • die Birke • el abedul • la betulla

pine • le pin • die Kiefer • el pino • il pino

cedar • le cèdre • die Zeder • el cedro • il cedro

maple • l'érable • der Ahorn • el arce • l'acero

elm • l'orme • die Ulme • el olmo • l'olmo

lime • le tilleul • die Linde • el tilo • il tiglio

holly • le houx • die Stechpalme • el acebo • l'agrifoglio

berry
la baie
die Beere
la baya
la bacca

palm • le palmier • die Palme • la palmera • la palma

flowering plant • la plante à fleurs • die blühende Pflanze • la planta de flor • la pianta da fiori

flower
la fleur
die Blüte
la flor
il fiore

stamen
l'étamine
das Staubgefäß
el estambre
lo stame

petal
le pétale
das Blütenblatt
el pétalo
il petalo

calyx
le calice
der Kelch
el cáliz
il calice

stalk
la tige
der Stängel
el tallo
lo stelo

bud
le bouton
die Knospe
el capullo
il bocciolo

stem
la tige
der Stiel
el tallo
il gambo

buttercup • la renoncule
• **der Hahnenfuß**
• el ranúnculo
• il ranuncolo

daisy • la pâquerette
• **das Gänseblümchen**
• la margarita
• la pratolina

thistle • le chardon
• **die Distel** • el cardo
• il cardo

dandelion • le pissenlit
• **der Löwenzahn**
• el diente de león
• il dente di leone

heather • la bruyère
• **das Heidekraut** • el
brezo • l'erica

poppy • le coquelicot
• **der Klatschmohn** • la
amapola • il papavero

foxglove • la digitale
• **der Fingerhut**
• la dedalera
• la digitale

honeysuckle • le
chèvrefeuille • **das
Geißblatt** • la madreselva
• il caprifoglio

sunflower
• le tournesol
• **die Sonnenblume**
• el girasol • il girasole

clover • le trèfle
• **der Klee** • el trébol
• il trifoglio

bluebells • les jacinthes des
bois • **die Sternhyazinthen**
• los jacintos silvestres
• i giacinti di bosco

primrose • la
primevère • **die
Schlüsselblume** • la
prímula • la primula

lupins • les lupins
• **die Lupinen** • las
altramuces • i lupini

nettle • l'ortie
• **die Brennnessel** • la
ortiga • l'ortica

town • la ville • die Stadt • la ciudad • la città

street
la rue
die Straße
la calle
la strada

kerb
le bord du trottoir
die Bordkante
el bordillo
il ciglio

street corner
le coin de la rue
die Straßenecke
la esquina
l'angolo della strada

shop
le magasin
der Laden
la tienda
il negozio

intersection
le carrefour
die Kreuzung
el cruce
il crocevia

one-way system
la voie à sens
unique • die
Einbahnstraße
• la calle de
sentido único
• il senso unico

pavement
le trottoir
der Bürgersteig
la acera
il marciapiede

office block
• l'immeuble de
bureaux • das
Bürogebäude
• el edificio de
oficinas • il
complesso di
uffici

apartment block
• l'immeuble
• der Wohnblock
• el bloque de
pisos • il
caseggiato

alley
la ruelle
die Gasse
el callejón
il vicolo

car park
le parking
der Parkplatz
el aparcamiento
il parcheggio

street sign
le panneau de signalisation
das Straßenschild
la señal de tráfico
la targa stradale

bollard
la borne
der Poller
la baliza
la colonnina

street light
le lampadaire
die Straßenlaterne
la farola
il lampione

buildings • les bâtiments • die Gebäude • los edificios • gli edifici

town hall • la mairie • das Rathaus • el ayuntamiento • il municipio

library • la bibliothèque • die Bibliothek • la biblioteca • la biblioteca

cinema • le cinéma • das Kino • el cine • il cinema

theatre • le théâtre • das Theater • el teatro • il teatro

university • l'université • die Universität • la universidad • l'università

skyscraper • le gratte-ciel • der Wolkenkratzer • el rascacielos • il grattacielo

school • l'école • die Schule • el colegio • la scuola

areas • les environs • die Wohngegend • las zonas • le zone

industrial estate • la zone industrielle • das Industriegebiet • la zona industrial • la zona industriale

city • la ville • die Stadt • la ciudad • la città

suburb • la banlieue • der Vorort • la periferia • la periferia

village • le village • das Dorf • el pueblo • il villaggio

pedestrian zone la zone piétonnière die Fußgängerzone la zona peatonal la zona pedonale	side street la rue transversale die Seitenstraße la bocacalle la via laterale	manhole la bouche d'égout der Kanalschacht la boca de alcantarilla il tombino	gutter le caniveau der Rinnstein la alcantarilla la cunetta	church l'église die Kirche la iglesia la chiesa
avenue l'avenue die Allee la avenida il viale	square la place der Platz la plaza la piazza	bus stop l'arrêt de bus die Bushaltestelle la parada de autobús la fermata dell'autobus	factory l'usine die Fabrik la fábrica la fabbrica	drain l'égout der Abwasserkanal el sumidero il canale di scolo

architecture • l'architecture • die Architektur • la arquitectura • l'archittettura

buildings and structures • les bâtiments et structures • die Gebäude und Strukturen • los edificios y las estructuras • edifici e strutture

skyscraper • le gratte-ciel • der Wolkenkratzer • el rascacielos • il grattacielo

turret
la tourelle
der Mauerturm
el torreón
la torre

moat
la douve
der Burggraben
el foso
il fossato

castle • le château • die Burg • el castillo • il castello

church • l'église • die Kirche • la iglesia • la chiesa

dome
le dôme
die Kuppel
la cúpula
la cupola

mosque • la mosquée • die Moschee • la mezquita • la moschea

temple • le temple • der Tempel • el templo • il tempio

synagogue • la synagogue • die Synagoge • la sinagoga • la sinagoga

dam • le barrage • der Staudamm • la presa • la diga

bridge • le pont • die Brücke • el puente • il ponte

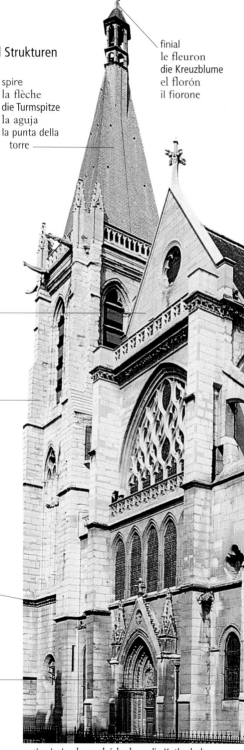

finial
le fleuron
die Kreuzblume
el florón
il fiorone

spire
la flèche
die Turmspitze
la aguja
la punta della
    torre

gable
le pignon
der Giebel
el frontón
il frontone

tower
la tour
der Turm
la torre
la torretta

vault
la voûte
das Gewölbe
la bóveda
la volta

cornice
la corniche
das Gesims
la cornisa
il cornicione

pillar
la colonne
die Säule
la columna
la colonna

cathedral • la cathédrale • die Kathedrale • la catedral • la cattedrale

styles • les styles • die Baustile • los estilos • gli stili

gothic • gothique • **gotisch** • gótico • gotico

architrave
l'architrave
der Architrav
el arquitrabe
l'architrave

Renaissance • Renaissance • **Renaissance-** • Renacimiento • Rinascimento

baroque • baroque • **barock** • barroco • barocco

rococo • rococo • **Rokoko-** • rococó • rococò

arch
l'arc
der Bogen
el arco
l'arco

frieze
la frise
der Fries
el friso
il fregio

choir
le chœur
der Chor
el coro
il coro

pediment
le fronton
das Giebeldreieck
el frontón
il frontone

buttress
le contrefort
der Strebepfeiler
el contrafuerte
il contrafforte

neoclassical • néoclassique • **neoklassizistisch** • neoclásico • neoclassico

art nouveau • art nouveau • **der Jugendstil** • el estilo modernista • lo stile liberty

art deco • art déco • **Art déco-** • art decó • art déco

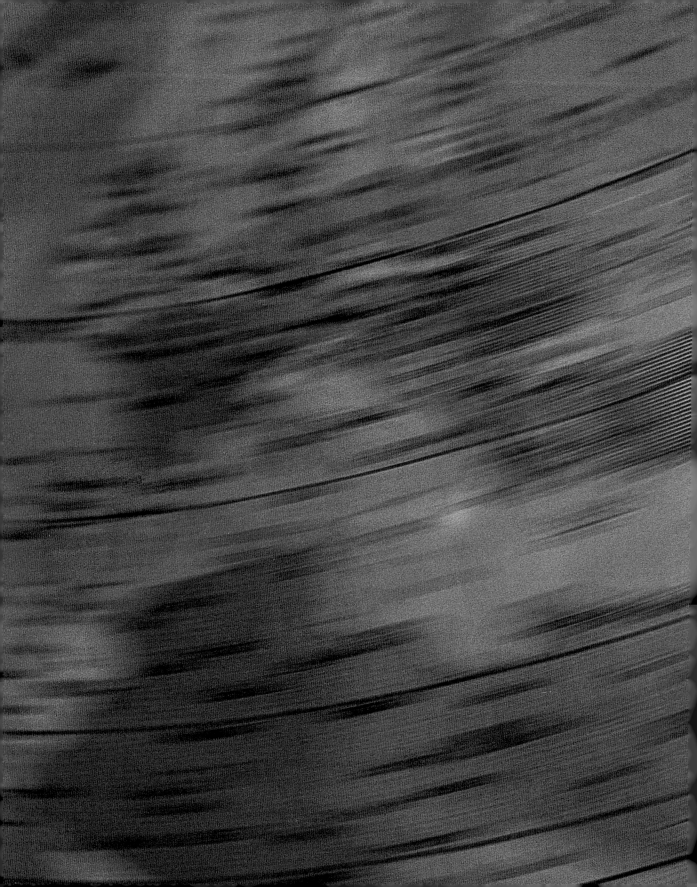

reference
l'information
die Information
los datos
i dati

time • l'heure • die Uhrzeit • el tiempo • l'ora

minute hand
la grande aiguille
der Minutenzeiger
el minutero
la lancetta dei minuti

hour hand
la petite aiguille
der Stundenzeiger
la aguja de la hora
la lancetta delle ore

clock • l'horloge • die Uhr • el reloj • l'orologio

second	now	a quarter of an hour
la seconde	maintenant	un quart d'heure
die Sekunde	jetzt	eine Viertelstunde
el segundo	ahora	un cuarto de hora
il secondo	adesso	un quarto d'ora
minute	later	twenty minutes
la minute	plus tard	vingt minutes
die Minute	später	zwanzig Minuten
el minuto	más tarde	veinte minutos
il minuto	più tardi	venti minuti
hour	half an hour	forty minutes
l'heure	une demi-heure	quarante minutes
die Stunde	eine halbe Stunde	vierzig Minuten
la hora	media hora	cuarenta minutos
l'ora	una mezz'ora	quaranta minuti

What time is it? — It's three o'clock.
Quelle heure est-il? — Il est trois heures.
Wie spät ist es? — Es ist drei Uhr.
¿Qué hora es? — Son las tres en punto.
Che ore sono? — Sono le tre.

five past one • une heure cinq • fünf nach eins • la una y cinco • l'una e cinque

ten past one • une heure dix • zehn nach eins • la una y diez • l'una e dieci

quarter past one • une heure et quart • Viertel nach eins • la una y cuarto • l'una e un quarto

twenty past one • une heure vingt • zwanzig nach eins • la una y veinte • l'una e venti

second hand • la trotteuse • der Sekundenzeiger • el segundero • la lancetta dei secondi

twenty five past one • une heure vingt-cinq • fünf vor halb zwei • la una y veinticinco • l'una e venticinque

one thirty • une heure trente • ein Uhr dreißig • la una y media • l'una e trenta

twenty five to two • deux heures moins vingt-cinq • fünf nach halb zwei • las dos menos veinticinco • le due meno venticinque

twenty to two • deux heures moins vingt • zwanzig vor zwei • las dos menos veinte • le due meno venti

quarter to two • deux heures moins le quart • Viertel vor zwei • las dos menos cuarto • le due meno un quarto

ten to two • deux heures moins dix • zehn vor zwei • las dos menos diez • le due meno dieci

five to two • deux heures moins cinq • fünf vor zwei • las dos menos cinco • le due meno cinque

two o'clock • deux heures • zwei Uhr • las dos en punto • le due

night and day • la nuit et le jour • die Nacht und der Tag • la noche y el día • la notte e il giorno

midnight • le minuit • die Mitternacht • la medianoche • la mezzanotte

sunrise • le lever du soleil • der Sonnenaufgang • el amanecer • il sorgere del sole

dawn • l'aube • die Morgendämmerung • el alba • l'alba

morning • le matin • der Morgen • la mañana • il mattino

sunset • le coucher du soleil • der Sonnenuntergang • la puesta de sol • il tramonto

midday • le midi • der Mittag • el mediodía • il mezzogiorno

dusk • le crépuscule • die Abenddämmerung • el anochecer • l'imbrunire

evening • le soir • der Abend • la noche • la sera

afternoon • l'après-midi • der Nachmittag • la tarde • il pomeriggio

early	You're early.	Please be on time.	What time does it finish?
tôt	Tu es en avance.	Sois à l'heure, s'il te plaît.	Ça finit à quelle heure?
früh	Du bist früh.	Sei bitte pünktlich.	Wann ist es zu Ende?
temprano	Llegas temprano.	Por favor, sé puntual.	¿A qué hora termina?
presto	Sei in anticipo.	Per favore, vieni in orario.	A che ora finisce?
on time	You're late.	I'll see you later.	How long will it last?
à l'heure	Tu es en retard.	À tout à l'heure.	Ça dure combien de temps?
pünktlich	Du hast dich verspätet.	Bis später.	Wie lange dauert es?
puntual	Llegas tarde.	Hasta luego.	¿Cuánto dura?
in orario	Sei in ritardo.	A più tardi.	Quanto durerà?
late	I'll be there soon.	What time does it start?	It's getting late.
tard	J'y arriverai bientôt.	Ça commence à quelle heure?	Il se fait tard.
spät	Ich werde bald dort sein.	Wann fängt es an?	Es ist schon spät.
tarde	Llegaré dentro de poco.	¿A qué hora comienza?	Se está haciendo tarde.
tardi	Arrivo subito.	A che ora inizia?	Si sta facendo tardi.

calendar • le calendrier • der Kalender • el calendario • il calendario

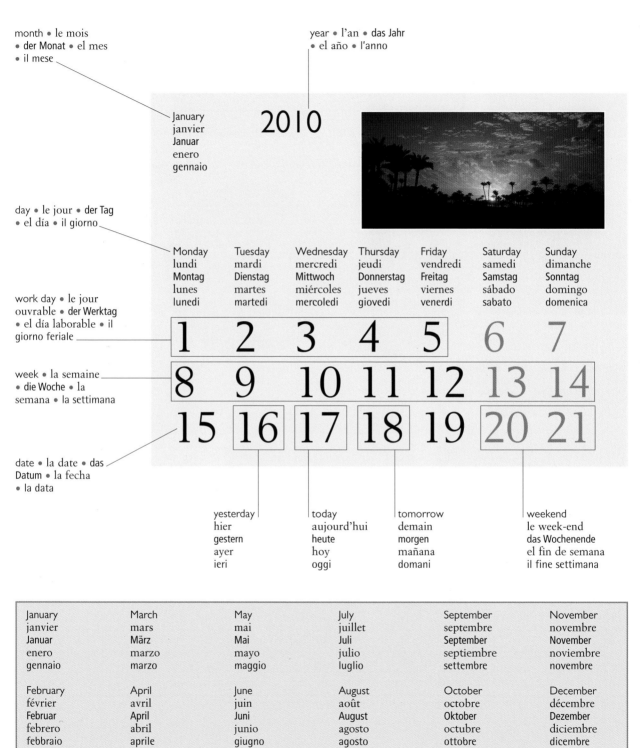

month • le mois
• der Monat • el mes
• il mese

year • l'an • das Jahr
• el año • l'anno

January
janvier
Januar
enero
gennaio

2010

day • le jour • der Tag
• el día • il giorno

Monday	Tuesday	Wednesday	Thursday	Friday	Saturday	Sunday
lundi	mardi	mercredi	jeudi	vendredi	samedi	dimanche
Montag	Dienstag	Mittwoch	Donnerstag	Freitag	Samstag	Sonntag
lunes	martes	miércoles	jueves	viernes	sábado	domingo
lunedi	martedi	mercoledi	giovedi	venerdi	sabato	domenica

work day • le jour
ouvrable • der Werktag
• el día laborable • il
giorno feriale

1	2	3	4	5	6	7

week • la semaine
• die Woche • la
semana • la settimana

8	9	10	11	12	13	14
15	16	17	18	19	20	21

date • la date • das
Datum • la fecha
• la data

yesterday
hier
gestern
ayer
ieri

today
aujourd'hui
heute
hoy
oggi

tomorrow
demain
morgen
mañana
domani

weekend
le week-end
das Wochenende
el fin de semana
il fine settimana

January	March	May	July	September	November
janvier	mars	mai	juillet	septembre	novembre
Januar	März	Mai	Juli	September	November
enero	marzo	mayo	julio	septiembre	noviembre
gennaio	marzo	maggio	luglio	settembre	novembre
February	April	June	August	October	December
février	avril	juin	août	octobre	décembre
Februar	April	Juni	August	Oktober	Dezember
febrero	abril	junio	agosto	octubre	diciembre
febbraio	aprile	giugno	agosto	ottobre	dicembre

years • les ans • die Jahre • los años • gli anni

1900 nineteen hundred • mille neuf cents • neunzehnhundert • mil novecientos • millenovecento

1901 nineteen hundred and one • mille neuf cent un • neunzehnhunderteins • mil novecientos uno • millenovecentouno

1910 nineteen ten • mille neuf cent dix • neunzehnhundertzehn • mil novecientos diez • millenovecentodieci

2000 two thousand • deux mille • zweitausend • dos mil • duemila

2001 two thousand and one • deux mille un • zweitausendeins • dos mil uno • duemilauno

seasons • les saisons • die Jahreszeiten • las estaciones • le stagioni

spring • le printemps • der Frühling • la primavera • la primavera

summer • l'été • der Sommer • el verano • l'estate

autumn • l'automne • der Herbst • el otoño • l'autunno

winter • l'hiver • der Winter • el invierno • l'inverno

century • le siècle • das Jahrhundert • el siglo • il secolo

decade • la décennie • das Jahrzehnt • la década • la decennio

millennium • le millénaire • das Jahrtausend • el milenio • il millennio

fortnight • quinze jours • vierzehn Tage • quince días • quindici giorni

this week • cette semaine • diese Woche • esta semana • questa settimana

last week • la semaine dernière • letzte Woche • la semana pasada • la settimana scorsa

next week • la semaine prochaine • nächste Woche • la semana que viene • la settimana prossima

the day before yesterday • avant-hier • vorgestern • antes de ayer • l'altroieri

the day after tomorrow • après-demain • übermorgen • pasado mañana • il dopodomani

weekly • hebdomadaire • wöchentlich • semanal • settimanale

monthly • mensuel • monatlich • mensual • mensile

annual • annuel • jährlich • anual • annuale

What's the date today?
Quelle est la date aujourd'hui?
Welches Datum haben wir heute?
¿Qué día es hoy?
Oggi che giorno è?

It's February seventh, two thousand and two.
C'est le sept février deux mille deux.
Heute ist der siebte Februar zweitausendzwei.
Es el siete de febrero del dos mil dos.
È il sette febbraio, duemiladue.

numbers • les nombres • die Zahlen • los números • i numeri

0	zero • zéro • null • cero • zero	20	twenty • vingt • zwanzig • veinte • venti
1	one • un • eins • uno • uno	21	twenty-one • vingt et un • einundzwanzig • veintiuno • ventuno
2	two • deux • zwei • dos • due	22	twenty-two • vingt-deux • zweiundzwanzig • veintidós • ventidue
3	three • trois • drei • tres • tre	30	thirty • trente • dreißig • treinta • trenta
4	four • quatre • vier • cuatro • quattro	40	forty • quarante • vierzig • cuarenta • quaranta
5	five • cinq • fünf • cinco • cinque	50	fifty • cinquante • fünfzig • cincuenta • cinquanta
6	six • six • sechs • seis • sei	60	sixty • soixante • sechzig • sesenta • sessanta
7	seven • sept • sieben • siete • sette	70	seventy • soixante-dix • siebzig • setenta • settanta
8	eight • huit • acht • ocho • otto	80	eighty • quatre-vingt • achtzig • ochenta • ottanta
9	nine • neuf • neun • nueve • nove	90	ninety • quatre-vingt-dix • neunzig • noventa • novanta
10	ten • dix • zehn • diez • dieci	100	one hundred • cent • hundert • cien • cento
11	eleven • onze • elf • once • undici	110	one hundred and ten • cent dix • hundertzehn • ciento diez • centodieci
12	twelve • douze • zwölf • doce • dodici	200	two hundred • deux cents • zweihundert • doscientos • duecento
13	thirteen • treize • dreizehn • trece • tredici	300	three hundred • trois cents • dreihundert • trescientos • trecento
14	fourteen • quatorze • vierzehn • catorce • quattordici	400	four hundred • quatre cents • vierhundert • cuatrocientos • quattrocento
15	fifteen • quinze • fünfzehn • quince • quindici	500	five hundred • cinq cents • fünfhundert • quinientos • cinquecento
16	sixteen • seize • sechzehn • dieciséis • sedici	600	six hundred • six cents • sechshundert • seiscientos • seicento
17	seventeen • dix-sept • siebzehn • diecisiete • diciassette	700	seven hundred • sept cents • siebenhundert • setecientos • settecento
18	eighteen • dix-huit • achtzehn • dieciocho • diciotto	800	eight hundred • huit cents • achthundert • ochocientos • ottocento
19	nineteen • dix-neuf • neunzehn • diecinueve • diciannove	900	nine hundred • neuf cents • neunhundert • novecientos • novecento

english • français • deutsch • español • italiano

1000	one thousand • mille • **tausend** • mil • mille
10,000	ten thousand • dix mille • **zehntausend** • diez mil • diecimila
20,000	twenty thousand • vingt mille • **zwanzigtausend** • veinte mil • ventimila
50,000	fifty thousand • cinquante mille • **fünfzigtausend** • cincuenta mil • cinquantamila
55,500	fifty-five thousand five hundred • cinqante-cinq mille cinq cents • **fünfundfünfzigtausend-fünfhundert** • cincuenta y cinco mil quinientos • cinquantacinquemilacinquecento
100,000	one hundred thousand • cent mille • **hunderttausend** • cien mil • centomila
1,000,000	one million • un million • **eine Million** • un millón • un milione
1,000,000,000	one billion • un milliard • **eine Milliarde** • mil millones • un miliardo

first • premier • erster • primero • primo

second • deuxième • zweiter • segundo • secondo

third • troisième • dritter • tercero • terzo

fourth • quatrième • **vierter** • cuarto • quarto

fifth • cinquième • **fünfter** • quinto • quinto

sixth • sixième • **sechster** • sexto • sesto

seventh • septième • **siebter** • séptimo • settimo

eighth • huitième • **achter** • octavo • ottavo

ninth • neuvième • **neunter** • noveno • nono

tenth • dixième • **zehnter** • décimo • decimo

eleventh • onzième • **elfter** • undécimo • undicesimo

twelfth • douzième • **zwölfter** • duodécimo • dodicesimo

thirteenth • treizième • **dreizehnter** • decimotercero • tredicesimo

fourteenth • quatorzième • **vierzehnter** • decimocuarto • quattordicesimo

fifteenth • quinzième • **fünfzehnter** • decimoquinto • quindicesimo

sixteenth • seizième • **sechzehnter** • decimosexto • sedicesimo

seventeenth • dix-septième • **siebzehnter** • decimoséptimo • diciassettesimo

eighteenth • dix-huitième • **achtzehnter** • décimo octavo • diciottesimo

nineteenth • dix-neuvième • **neunzehnter** • décimo noveno • diciannovesimo

twentieth • vingtième • **zwanzigster** • vigésimo • ventesimo

twenty-first • vingt et unième • **einundzwanzigster** • vigésimo primero • ventunesimo

twenty-second • vingt-deuxième • **zweiundzwanzigster** • vigésimo segundo • ventiduesimo

twenty-third • vingt-troisième • **dreiundzwanzigster** • vigésimo tercero • ventitreesimo

thirtieth • trentième • **dreißigster** • trigésimo • trentesimo

fortieth • quarantième • **vierzigster** • cuadragésimo • quarantesimo

fiftieth • cinquantième • **fünfzigster** • quincuagésimo • cinquantesimo

sixtieth • soixantième • **sechzigster** • sexagésimo • sessantesimo

seventieth • soixante-dixième • **siebzigster** • septuagésimo • settantesimo

eightieth • quatre-vingtième • **achtzigster** • octogésimo • ottantesimo

ninetieth • quatre-vingt-dixième • **neunzigster** • nonagésimo • novantesimo

one hundredth • centième • **hundertster** • centésimo • centesimo

weights and measures • les poids et mesures • die Maße und Gewichte • los pesos y las medidas • i pesi e le misure

pan • le plateau• die
Waagschale • la bandeja
• il piatto

area • la superficie • die
Fläche • el área • la superficie

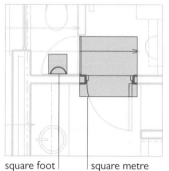

square foot
le pied carré
der Quadratfuß
el pie cuadrado
il piede quadro

square metre
le mètre carré
der Quadratmeter
el metro cuadrado
il metro quadro

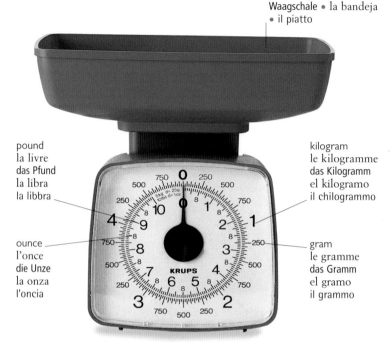

pound
la livre
das Pfund
la libra
la libbra

ounce
l'once
die Unze
la onza
l'oncia

kilogram
le kilogramme
das Kilogramm
el kilogramo
il chilogrammo

gram
le gramme
das Gramm
el gramo
il grammo

scales • la balance • die Waage • la balanza • la bilancia

distance • la distance
• die Entfernung • la
distancia • la distanza

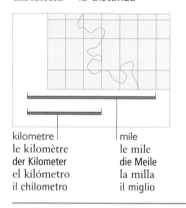

kilometre
le kilomètre
der Kilometer
el kilómetro
il chilometro

mile
le mile
die Meile
la milla
il miglio

yard	tonne	measure (v)
le yard	la tonne	mesurer
das Yard	die Tonne	messen
la yarda	la tonelada	medir
la iarda	la tonnellata	misurare
metre	milligram	weigh (v)
le mètre	le milligramme	peser
der Meter	das Milligramm	wiegen
el metro	el miligramo	pesar
il metro	il milligrammo	pesare

length • la longueur • die Länge • la longitud • la lunghezza

foot • le pied • der Fuß
• el pie • il piede

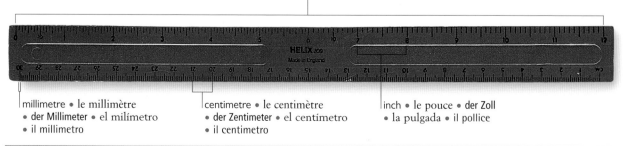

millimetre • le millimètre
• der Millimeter • el milímetro
• il millimetro

centimetre • le centimètre
• der Zentimeter • el centímetro
• il centimetro

inch • le pouce • der Zoll
• la pulgada • il pollice

capacity • la capacité • das Fassungsvermögen • la capacidad • la capacità

half-litre • le demi-litre • der halbe Liter • el medio litro • il mezzo litro

pint • la pinte • das Pint • la pinta • la pinta

volume • le volume • das Volumen • el volumen • il volume

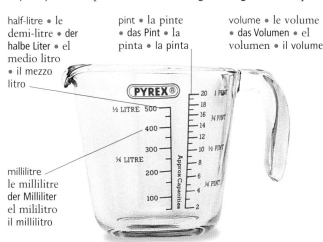

millilitre • le millilitre • der Milliliter • el mililitro • il millilitro

gallon
le gallon
die Gallone
el galón
il gallone

quart
deux pintes
das Quart
el cuarto de galón
il quarto di gallone

litre
le litre
der Liter
el litro
il litro

measuring jug • le pichet gradué • der Messbecher • la jarra graduada • il misurino

liquid measure • la mesure pour les liquides • das Flüssigkeitsmaß • la medida de capacidad • la misura di liquido

container • le récipient • der Behälter • el recipiente • il contenitore

carton • le carton • die Tüte • el tetrabrik • il cartone

packet • le paquet • das Päckchen • el paquete • il pacchetto

bottle • la bouteille • die Flasche • la botella • il bottiglia

bag • le sac • der Beutel • la bolsa • il sacchetto

tub • le pot • der Becher • la tarrina • la vaschetta

jar • le pot • das Glas • el tarro • il barattolo

can • la boîte • die Dose • la lata • la lattina

tin • la boîte • die Dose • la lata • la scatoletta

liquid dispenser • le pulvérisateur • der Sprüher • el pulverizador • il nebulizzatore

bar
le pain
das Stück
la pastilla
la saponetta

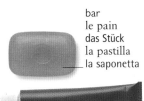

tube • le tube • die Tube • el tubo • il tubetto

roll • le rouleau • die Rolle • el rollo • il rotolo

pack • le paquet • das Päckchen • el paquete • il pacchetto

spray can • la bombe • die Sprühdose • el spray • la bomboletta spray

world map • la carte du monde • die Weltkarte • el mapamundi • il mappamondo

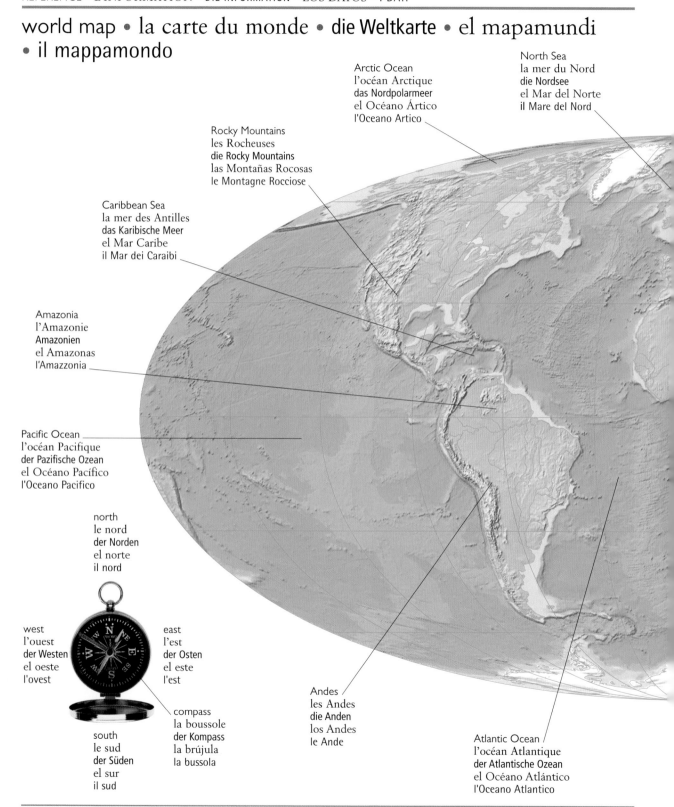

Arctic Ocean
l'océan Arctique
das Nordpolarmeer
el Océano Ártico
l'Oceano Artico

North Sea
la mer du Nord
die Nordsee
el Mar del Norte
il Mare del Nord

Rocky Mountains
les Rocheuses
die Rocky Mountains
las Montañas Rocosas
le Montagne Rocciose

Caribbean Sea
la mer des Antilles
das Karibische Meer
el Mar Caribe
il Mar dei Caraibi

Amazonia
l'Amazonie
Amazonien
el Amazonas
l'Amazzonia

Pacific Ocean
l'océan Pacifique
der Pazifische Ozean
el Océano Pacífico
l'Oceano Pacifico

north
le nord
der Norden
el norte
il nord

west
l'ouest
der Westen
el oeste
l'ovest

east
l'est
der Osten
el este
l'est

compass
la boussole
der Kompass
la brújula
la bussola

south
le sud
der Süden
el sur
il sud

Andes
les Andes
die Anden
los Andes
le Ande

Atlantic Ocean
l'océan Atlantique
der Atlantische Ozean
el Océano Atlántico
l'Oceano Atlantico

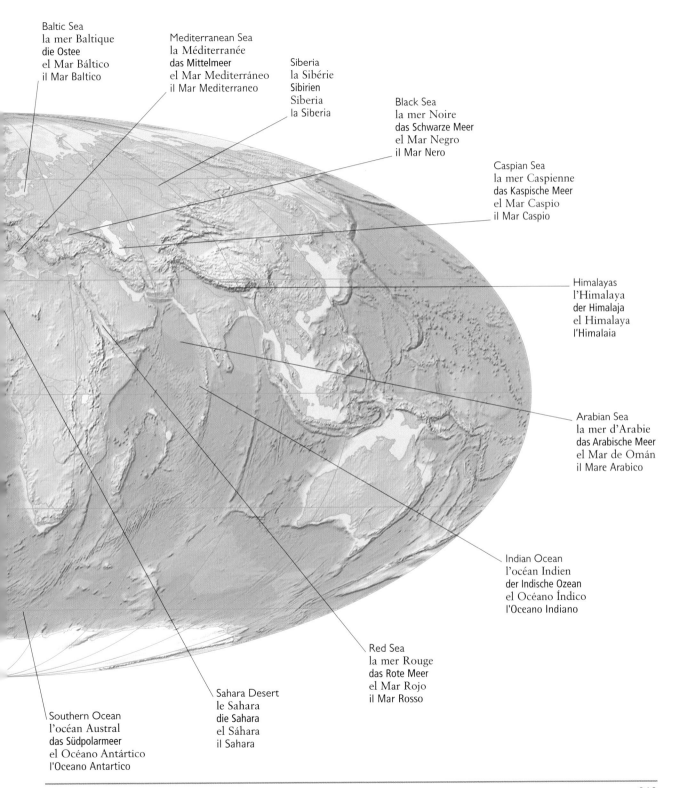

Baltic Sea
la mer Baltique
die Ostee
el Mar Báltico
il Mar Baltico

Mediterranean Sea
la Méditerranée
das Mittelmeer
el Mar Mediterráneo
il Mar Mediterraneo

Siberia
la Sibérie
Sibirien
Siberia
la Siberia

Black Sea
la mer Noire
das Schwarze Meer
el Mar Negro
il Mar Nero

Caspian Sea
la mer Caspienne
das Kaspische Meer
el Mar Caspio
il Mar Caspio

Himalayas
l'Himalaya
der Himalaja
el Himalaya
l'Himalaia

Arabian Sea
la mer d'Arabie
das Arabische Meer
el Mar de Omán
il Mare Arabico

Indian Ocean
l'océan Indien
der Indische Ozean
el Océano Índico
l'Oceano Indiano

Red Sea
la mer Rouge
das Rote Meer
el Mar Rojo
il Mar Rosso

Sahara Desert
le Sahara
die Sahara
el Sáhara
il Sahara

Southern Ocean
l'océan Austral
das Südpolarmeer
el Océano Antártico
l'Oceano Antartico

North and Central America • l'Amérique du Nord et centrale • Nord- und Mittelamerika • América del Norte y Central • l'America del Nord e Centrale

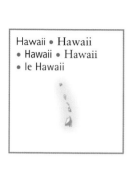

Hawaii • Hawaii • Hawaii • Hawaii • le Hawaii

1 Alaska • l'Alaska • Alaska • Alaska • l'Alaska

2 Canada • le Canada • Kanada • Canadá • il Canada

3 Greenland • le Groenland • Grönland • Groenlandia • la Groenlandia

4 United States of America • les États-Unis d'Amérique • die Vereinigten Staaten von Amerika • Estados Unidos de América • gli Stati Uniti d'America

5 Mexico • le Mexique • Mexiko • México • il Messico

6 Guatemala • le Guatemala • Guatemala • Guatemala • il Guatemala

7 Belize • le Bélize • Belize • Belice • il Belize

8 El Salvador • Le Salvador • El Salvador • El Salvador • l'El Salvador

9 Honduras • le Honduras • Honduras • Honduras • l'Honduras

10 Nicaragua • le Nicaragua • Nicaragua • Nicaragua • il Nicaragua

11 Costa Rica • le Costa Rica • Costa Rica • Costa Rica • il Costa Rica

12 Panama • le Panama • Panama • Panamá • il Panama

13 Cuba • Cuba • Kuba • Cuba • Cuba

14 Bahamas • les Bahamas • die Bahamas • Bahamas • le Bahamas

15 Jamaica • la Jamaïque • Jamaika • Jamaica • la Giamaica

16 Haiti • Haïti • Haiti • Haití • Haiti

17 Dominican Republic • la République dominicaine • die Dominikanische Republik • República Dominicana • la Repubblica Dominicana

18 Puerto Rico • la Porto Rico • Puerto Rico • Puerto Rico • Puerto Rico

19 Barbados • la Barbade • Barbados • Barbados • Barbados

20 Trinidad and Tobago • la Trinité-et-Tobago • Trinidad und Tobago • Trinidad y Tobago • Trinidad e Tobago

21 St. Kitts and Nevis • Saint-Kitts-et-Nevis • Saint Kitts und Nevis • Saint Kitts y Nevis • Saint Kitts-Nevis

22 Antigua and Barbuda • Antigua-et-Barbuda • Antigua und Barbuda • Antigua y Barbuda • Antigua e Barbuda

23 Dominica • la Dominique • Dominica • Dominica • Dominica

24 St Lucia • Sainte-Lucie • Saint Lucia • Santa Lucía • Saint Lucia

25 St Vincent and The Grenadines • Saint-Vincent-et-les-Grenadines • Saint Vincent und die Grenadinen • San Vicente y las Granadinas • Saint Vincent e Grenadine

26 Grenada • la Grenade • Grenada • Granada • Grenada

South America • l'Amérique du Sud • Südamerika • América del Sur • l'America del Sud

1 Venezuela • le Venezuela • Venezuela • Venezuela • il Venezuela

2 Colombia • la Colombie • Kolumbien • Colombia • la Colombia

3 Ecuador • l'Équateur • Ecuador • Ecuador • l'Ecuador

4 Peru • le Pérou • Peru • Perú • il Perù

5 Galapagos Islands • les îles Galapagos • die Galapagos-Inseln • las Islas Galápagos • le Isola Galapagos

6 Guyana • la Guyane • Guyana • Guyana • la Guyana

7 Suriname • le Surinam • Suriname • Suriname • il Suriname

8 French Guiana • la Guyane française • Französisch-Guyana • la Guayana Francesa • la Guyana Francese

9 Brazil • le Brésil • Brasilien • Brasil • il Brasile

10 Bolivia • la Bolivie • Bolivien • Bolivia • la Bolivia

11 Chile • le Chili • Chile • Chile • il Cile

12 Argentina • l'Argentine • Argentinien • Argentina • l'Argentina

13 Paraguay • le Paraguay • Paraguay • Paraguay • il Paraguay

14 Uruguay • l'Uruguay • Uruguay • Uruguay • l'Uruguay

15 Falkland Islands • les îles Malouines • die Falkland-Inseln • las Malvinas • le isole Falkland

continent	province	zone
le continent	la province	la zone
der Kontinent	die Provinz	die Zone
el continente	la provincia	la zona
il continente	la provincia	la zona
country	territory	district
le pays	le territoire	le district
das Land	das Territorium	der Bezirk
el país	el territorio	el distrito
il paese	il territorio	il distretto
nation	principality	region
la nation	la principauté	la région
die Nation	das Fürstentum	die Region
la nación	el principado	la región
la nazione	il principato	la regione
state	colony	capital
l'État	la colonie	la capitale
der Staat	die Kolonie	die Hauptstadt
el estado	la colonia	la capital
lo stato	la colonia	la capitale

Europe • l'Europe • Europa • Europa • l'Europa

1 Ireland • l'Irlande • Irland • Irlanda • l'Irlanda

2 United Kingdom • le Royaume-Uni • Großbritannien • Reino Unido • il Regno Unito

3 Portugal • le Portugal • Portugal • Portugal • il Portogallo

4 Spain • l'Espagne • Spanien • España • la Spagna

5 Balearic Islands • les Baléares • die Balearen • las Islas Baleares • le Isole Baleari

6 Andorra • l'Andorre • Andorra • Andorra • Andorra

7 France • la France • Frankreich • Francia • la Francia

8 Belgium • la Belgique • Belgien • Bélgica • il Belgio

9 Netherlands • les Pays-Bas • die Niederlande • los Países Bajos • i Paesi Bassi

10 Luxembourg • le Luxembourg • Luxemburg • Luxemburgo • il Lussemburgo

11 Germany • l'Allemagne • Deutschland • Alemania • la Germania

12 Denmark • le Danemark • Dänemark • Dinamarca • la Danimarca

13 Norway • la Norvège • Norwegen • Noruega • la Norvegia

14 Sweden • la Suède • Schweden • Suecia • la Svezia

15 Finland • la Finlande • Finnland • Finlandia • la Finlandia

16 Estonia • l'Estonie • Estland • Estonia • l'Estonia

17 Latvia • la Lettonie • Lettland • Letonia • la Lettonia

18 Lithuania • la Lituanie • Litauen • Lituania • la Lituania

19 Kaliningrad • Kaliningrad • Kaliningrad • Kaliningrado • Kaliningrad

20 Poland • la Pologne • Polen • Polonia • la Polonia

21 Czech Republic • la République tchèque • die Tschechische Republik • República Checa • la Repubblica Ceca

22 Austria • l'Autriche • Österreich • Austria • l'Austria

23 Liechtenstein • le Liechtenstein • Liechtenstein • Liechtenstein • il Liechtenstein

24 Switzerland • la Suisse • die Schweiz • Suiza • la Svizzera

25 Italy • l'Italie • Italien • Italia • l'Italia

26 Monaco • Monaco • Monaco • Mónaco • Monaco

27 Corsica • la Corse • Korsika • Córcega • la Corsica

28 Sardinia • la Sardaigne • Sardinien • Cerdeña • la Sardegna

29 San Marino • le Saint-Marin • San Marino • San Marino • San Marino

30 Vatican City • la Cité du Vatican • Vatikanstadt • la Ciudad del Vaticano • la Città del Vaticano

31 Sicily • la Sicile • Sizilien • Sicilia • la Sicilia

32 Malta • Malte • Malta • Malta • Malta

33 Slovenia • la Slovénie • Slowenien • Eslovenia • la Slovenia

34 Croatia • la Croatie • Kroatien • Croacia • la Croazia

35 Hungary • la Hongrie • Ungarn • Hungría • l'Ungheria

36 Slovakia • la Slovaquie • die Slowakei • Eslovaquia • la Slovacchia

37 Ukraine • l'Ukraine • die Ukraine • Ucrania • l'Ucraina

38 Belarus • la Bélarus • Weißrussland • Bielorrusia • la Bielorussia

39 Moldova • la Moldavie • Moldawien • Moldavia • la Moldavia

40 Romania • la Roumanie • Rumänien • Rumanía • la Romania

41 Serbia and Montenegro • Serbie-et-Monténégro • Serbien und Montenegro • Serbia y Montenegro • Serbia e Montenegro

42 Bosnia and Herzogovina • la Bosnie-Herzégovine • Bosnien und Herzegowina • Bosnia y Herzegovina • la Bosnia ed Erzegovina

43 Albania • l'Albanie • Albanien • Albania • l'Albania

44 Macedonia • la Macédonie • Mazedonien • Macedonia • la Macedonia

45 Bulgaria • la Bulgarie • Bulgarien • Bulgaria • la Bulgaria

46 Greece • la Grèce • Griechenland • Grecia • la Grecia

47 Turkey • la Turquie • die Türkei • Turquía • la Turchia

48 Cyprus • Chypre • Zypern • Chipre • Cipro

Africa • l'Afrique • Afrika • África • l'Africa

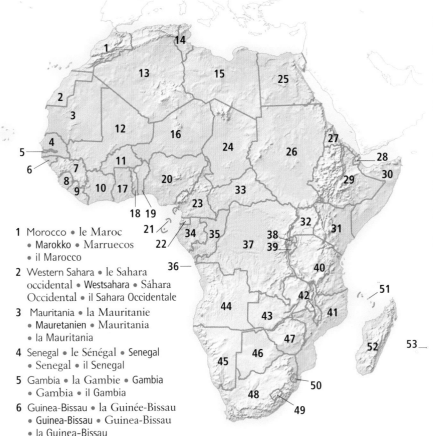

30 Somalia • la Somalie • Somalia • Somalia • la Somalia

31 Kenya • le Kenya • Kenia • Kenia • il Kenia

32 Uganda • l'Ouganda • Uganda • Uganda • l'Uganda

33 Central African Republic • la République centrafricaine • die Zentralafrikanische Republik • República Centroafricana • la Repubblica Centrafricana

34 Gabon • le Gabon • Gabun • Gabón • il Gabon

35 Congo • le Congo • Kongo • Congo • il Congo

36 Cabinda • Cabinda • Kabinda • Cabinda • Cabinda

37 Democratic Republic of the Congo • la République démocratique du Congo • die Demokratische Republik Kongo • República Democrática del Congo • la Repubblica Democratica del Congo

38 Rwanda • le Rwanda • Ruanda • Ruanda • il Ruanda

39 Burundi • le Burundi • Burundi • Burundi • il Burundi

40 Tanzania • la Tanzanie • Tansania • Tanzania • la Tanzania

41 Mozambique • le Mozambique • Mosambik • Mozambique • il Mozambico

42 Malawi • le Malawi • Malawi • Malaui • il Malawi

43 Zambia • la Zambie • Sambia • Zambia • lo Zambia

44 Angola • l'Angola • Angola • Angola • l'Angola

45 Namibia • la Namibie • Namibia • Namibia • la Namibia

46 Botswana • le Botswana • Botsuana • Botsuana • il Botswana

47 Zimbabwe • le Zimbabwe • Simbabwe • Zimbabue • lo Zimbabwe

48 South Africa • l'Afrique du Sud • Südafrika • Sudáfrica • il Sud Africa

49 Lesotho • le Lesotho • Lesotho • Lesoto • il Lesotho

50 Swaziland • le Swaziland • Swasiland • Suazilandia • lo Swaziland

51 Comoros • les Comores • Komoren • Comoras • le Comore

52 Madagascar • Madagascar • Madagaskar • Madagascar • il Madagascar

53 Mauritius • l'île Maurice • Mauritius • Mauricio • la Mauritania

1 Morocco • le Maroc • Marokko • Marruecos • il Marocco

2 Western Sahara • le Sahara occidental • Westsahara • Sáhara Occidental • il Sahara Occidentale

3 Mauritania • la Mauritanie • Mauretanien • Mauritania • la Mauritania

4 Senegal • le Sénégal • Senegal • Senegal • il Senegal

5 Gambia • la Gambie • Gambia • Gambia • il Gambia

6 Guinea-Bissau • la Guinée-Bissau • Guinea-Bissau • Guinea-Bissau • la Guinea-Bissau

7 Guinea • la Guinée • Guinea • Guinea • la Guinea

8 Sierra Leone • la Sierra Leone • Sierra Leone • Sierra Leona • Sierra Leone

9 Liberia • le Libéria • Liberia • Liberia • la Liberia

10 Ivory Coast • la Côte d'Ivoire • Elfenbeinküste • Costa de Marfil • la Costa d'Avorio

11 Burkina Faso • le Burkina • Burkina Faso • Burquina Faso • il Burkina Faso

12 Mali • le Mali • Mali • Mali • il Mali

13 Algeria • l'Algérie • Algerien • Argelia • l'Algeria

14 Tunisia • la Tunisie • Tunesien • Túnez • la Tunisia

15 Libya • la Libye • Libyen • Libia • la Libia

16 Niger • le Niger • Niger • Níger • il Niger

17 Ghana • le Ghana • Ghana • Ghana • il Ghana

18 Togo • le Togo • Togo • Togo • il Togo

19 Benin • le Bénin • Benin • Benín • il Benin

20 Nigeria • le Nigéria • Nigeria • Nigeria • la Nigeria

21 São Tomé and Principe • Sao Tomé-et-Principe • São Tomé und Príncipe • Santo Tomé y Príncipe • São Tomé e Príncipe

22 Equatorial Guinea • la Guinée équatoriale • Äquatorialguinea • Guinea Ecuatorial • la Guinea Equatoriale

23 Cameroon • le Cameroun • Kamerun • Camerún • il Camerun

24 Chad • le Tchad • Tschad • Chad • il Ciad

25 Egypt • l'Égypte • Ägypten • Egipto • l'Egitto

26 Sudan • le Soudan • der Sudan • Sudán • il Sudan

27 Eritrea • l'Érythrée • Eritrea • Eritrea • l'Eritrea

28 Djibouti • Djibouti • Dschibuti • Yibuti • Gibuti

29 Ethiopia • l'Éthiopie • Äthiopien • Etiopía • l'Etiopia

Asia • l'Asie • Asien • Asia • l'Asia

1 Russian Federation • la Fédération de Russie • die Russische Föderation • Federación Rusa • la Federazione Russa

2 Georgia • la Géorgie • Georgien • Georgia • la Georgia

3 Armenia • l'Arménie • Armenien • Armenia • l'Armenia

4 Azerbaijan • l'Azerbaïdjan • Aserbaidschan • Azerbaiyán • l'Azerbaigian

5 Iran • l'Iran • der Iran • Irán • l'Iran

6 Iraq • l'Irak • der Irak • Iraq • l'Iraq

7 Syria • la Syrie • Syrien • Siria • la Siria

8 Lebanon • le Liban • der Libanon • Líbano • il Libano

9 Israel • Israël • Israel • Israel • l'Israele

10 Jordan • la Jordanie • Jordanien • Jordania • la Giordania

11 Saudi Arabia • l'Arabie Saoudite • Saudi-Arabien • Arabia Saudita • l'Arabia Saudita

12 Kuwait • le Koweït • Kuwait • Kuwait • il Kuwait

13 Qatar • le Qatar • Katar • Qatar • il Qatar

14 United Arab Emirates • les Émirats arabes unis • Vereinigte Arabische Emirate • Emiratos Árabes Unidos • gli Emirati Arabi Uniti

15 Oman • l'Oman • Oman • Omán • l'Oman

16 Yemen • le Yémen • der Jemen • Yemen • lo Yemen

17 Kazakhstan • le Kasakhastan • Kasachstan • Kazajstán • il Kazakistan

18 Uzbekistan • l'Ouzbékistan • Usbekistan • Uzbekistán • l'Uzbekistan

19 Turkmenistan • le Turkmenistan • Turkmenistan • Turkmenistán • il Turkmenistan

20 Afghanistan • l'Afghanistan • Afghanistan • Afganistán • l'Afghanistan

21 Tajikistan • le Tadjikistan • Tadschikistan • Tayikistán • il Tagikistan

22 Kyrgyzstan • le Kirghizistan • Kirgisistan • Kirguistán • il Kirghizistan

23 Pakistan • le Pakistan • Pakistan • Pakistán • il Pakistan

24 India • l'Inde • Indien • India • l'India

25 Maldives • les Maldives • die Malediven • Maldivas • le Maldive

26 Sri Lanka • Sri Lanka • Sri Lanka • Sri Lanka • lo Sri Lanka

27 China • la Chine • China • China • la Cina

28 Mongolia • la Mongolie • die Mongolei • Mongolia • la Mongolia

29 North Korea • la Corée du Nord • Nordkorea • Corea del Norte • la Corea del Nord

30 South Korea • la Corée du Sud • Südkorea • Corea del Sur • la Corea del Sud

31 Japan • le Japon • Japan • Japón • il Giappone

32 Nepal • le Népal • Nepal • Nepal • il Nepal

33 Bhutan • le Bhoutan • Bhutan • Bhutan • il Bhutan

34 Bangladesh • le Bangladesh • Bangladesch • Bangladesh • il Bangladesh

35 Burma (Myanmar) • la Birmanie (le Myanmar) • Birma (Myanmar) • Birmania (Myanmar) • la Birmania (il Myanmar)

36 Thailand • la Thaïlande • Thailand • Tailandia • la Tailandia

37 Laos • le Laos • Laos • Laos • il Laos

38 Viet Nam • le Vietnam • Vietnam • Vietnam • il Vietnam

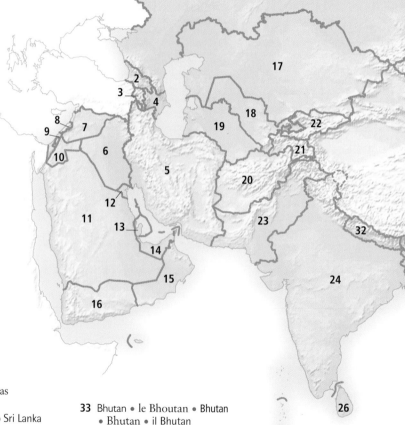

Australasia • l'Australasie • Australien und Ozeanien • Australasia • l'Oceania

1 Australia • l'Australie
  • Australien • Australia
  • l'Australia
2 Tasmania • la Tasmanie • Tasmanien
  • Tasmania • la Tasmania
3 New Zealand • la Nouvelle-Zélande
  • Neuseeland • Nueva Zelanda • la Nuova Zelanda

39 Cambodia • le Cambodge • Kambodscha • Camboya
  • la Cambogia
40 Malaysia • la Malaisie • Malaysia • Malasia • la Malaysia
41 Singapore • Singapour • Singapur • Singapur • Singapore
42 Indonesia • l'Indonésie • Indonesien • Indonesia • l'Indonesia
43 Brunei • le Brunei • Brunei • Brunei • Brunei
44 Philippines • les Philippines • die Philippinen • Filipinas • le Filippine
45 Taiwan • Taiwan • Taiwan • Taiwán • Taiwan
46 East Timor • le Timor oriental • Ost-Timor • Timor Oriental
  • Timor Est
47 Papua New Guinea • la Papouasie-Nouvelle-Guinée • Papua-
  Neuguinea • Papua Nueva Guinea • la Papua Nuova Guinea
48 Solomon Islands • les îles Saloman • die Salomonen
  • Islas Salomón • le Isole Salomone
49 Vanuatu • Vanuatu • Vanuatu • Vanuatu • Vanuatu
50 Fiji • Fidji • Fidschi • Fiyi • Figi

particles and antonyms • particules et antonymes • Partikeln und Antonyme • partículas y antónimos • particelle e antonimi

to	from	through	around
à	de	à travers	autour de
zu, nach	von, aus	durch	um
a, hacia	de, desde	a través de	alrededor de
a	da	attraverso	attorno
over	under	on top of	beside
au-dessus de	sous	sur	à côté de
über	unter	auf	neben
encima de	debajo de	encima de	al lado de
sopra	sotto	in cima	accanto
in front of	behind	between	opposite
devant	derrière	entre	en face de
vor	hinter	zwischen	gegenüber
delante de	detrás de	entre	en frente de
davanti	dietro	tra	di fronte
onto	into	near	far
sur	dans	près de	loin de
auf	in	nahe	weit
sobre	dentro de	cerca de	lejos
sopra	dentro	vicino a	lontano
in	out	with	without
dans	dehors	avec	sans
in	aus	mit	ohne
en	fuera	con	sin
dentro	fuori	con	senza
above	below	before	after
au-dessus de	au-dessous de	avant	après
über	unter	vor	nach
sobre	abajo	antes	después
sopra	sotto	prima	dopo
inside	outside	by	until
à l'intérieur de	à l'extérieur de	avant	jusqu'à
innerhalb	außerhalb	bis	bis
dentro de	fuera	antes de	hasta
all'interno	all'esterno	entro	fino
up	down	for	towards
en haut	en bas	pour	vers
hinauf	hinunter	für	zu
arriba	abajo	por	hacia
su	giù	per	verso
at	beyond	along	across
à	au-delà de	le long de	à travers
an, bei	jenseits	entlang	über
en	más allá de	a lo largo de	al otro lado de
a	oltre	lungo	attraverso

large	small	hot	cold
grand	petit	chaud	froid
groß	klein	heiß	kalt
grande	pequeño	caliente	frío
grande	piccolo	caldo	freddo

wide	narrow	open	closed
large	étroit	ouvert	fermé
breit	schmal	offen	geschlossen
ancho	estrecho	abierto	cerrado
largo	stretto	aperto	chiuso

tall	short	full	empty
grand	court	plein	vide
groß	kurz	voll	leer
alto	bajo	lleno	vacío
alto	basso	pieno	vuoto

high	low	new	old
haut	bas	neuf	vieux
hoch	niedrig	neu	alt
alto	bajo	nuevo	viejo
alto	basso	nuovo	vecchio

thick	thin	light	dark
épais	mince	clair	foncé
dick	dünn	hell	dunkel
grueso	delgado	claro	oscuro
spesso	sottile	chiaro	scuro

light	heavy	easy	difficult
léger	lourd	facile	difficile
leicht	schwer	leicht	schwer
ligero	pesado	fácil	difícil
leggero	pesante	facile	difficile

hard	soft	free	occupied
dur	mou	libre	occupé
hart	weich	frei	besetzt
duro	blando	libre	ocupado
duro	morbido	libero	occupato

wet	dry	beginning	end
humide	sec	le début	la fin
nass	trocken	der Anfang	das Ende
húmedo	seco	el principio	el final
bagnato	asciutto	l'inizio	la fine

good	bad	strong	weak
bon	mauvais	fort	faible
gut	schlecht	stark	schwach
bueno	malo	fuerte	débil
buono	cattivo	forte	debole

fast	slow	fat	thin
rapide	lent	gros	mince
schnell	langsam	dick	dünn
rápido	lento	gordo	delgado
veloce	lento	grasso	magro

useful phrases • phrases utiles • praktische Redewendungen
• frases útiles • frasi utili

essential phrases
- phrases essentielles
- **wichtige Redewendungen**
- frases esenciales
- frasi essenziali

Yes
Oui
Ja
Sí
Si

No
Non
Nein
No
No

Maybe
Peut-être
Vielleicht
Quizá
Forse

Please
S'il vous plaît
Bitte
Por favor
Per favore

Thank you
Merci
Danke
Gracias
Grazie

You're welcome
De rien
Gern geschehen
De nada
Prego

Excuse me
Pardon
Entschuldigung
Perdone
Permesso

I'm sorry
Je suis désolé
Es tut mir Leid
Lo siento
Mi dispiace

Don't
Ne... pas
Nicht
No
No

OK
D'accord
Okay
Vale
D'accordo

That's fine
Très bien
In Ordnung
Muy bien
Va bene

That's correct
C'est juste
Das ist richtig
Está bien
È giusto

That's wrong
C'est faux
Das ist falsch
Está mal
È sbagliato

greetings • salutations
- **Begrüßungen**
- saludos • saluti

Hello
Bonjour
Guten Tag
Hola
Buongiorno

Goodbye
Au revoir
Auf Wiedersehen
Adiós
Arrivederci

Good morning
Bonjour
Guten Morgen
Buenos días
Buongiorno

Good afternoon
Bonjour
Guten Tag
Buenas tardes
Buon pomeriggio

Good evening
Bonsoir
Guten Abend
Buenas tardes
Buona sera

Good night
Bonne nuit
Gute Nacht
Buenas noches
Buona notte

How are you?
Comment allez-vous?
Wie geht es Ihnen?
¿Cómo está?
Come sta?

My name is…
Je m'appelle…
Ich heiße…
Me llamo…
Mi chiamo...

What is your name?
Vous vous appelez comment?
Wie heißen Sie?
¿Cómo se llama?
Come si chiama?

Whis is his/her name?
Il/Elle s'appelle comment?
Wie heißt er/sie?
¿Cómo se llama?
Come si chiama lui/lei?

May I introduce…
Je vous présente…
Darf ich… vorstellen
Le presento a…
Le posso presentare…

This is…
C'est…
Das ist…
Éste es…
Le presento…

Pleased to meet you
Enchanté
Angenehm
Encantado de conocerle
Piacere di conoscerla

See you later
À tout à l'heure
Bis später
Hasta luego
A più tardi

signs • panneaux
- **Schilder** • letreros
- insegne

Tourist information
Office de tourisme
Touristen-Information
Información
Ufficio informazioni turistiche

Entrance
Entrée
Eingang
Entrada
Entrata

Exit
Sortie
Ausgang
Salida
Uscita

Emergency exit
Sortie de secours
Notausgang
Salida de emergencia
Uscita di emergenza

Push
Poussez
Drücken
Empujar
Spingere

Danger
Danger
Lebensgefahr
Peligro
Pericolo

No smoking
Défense de fumer
Rauchen verboten
Prohibido fumar
Vietato fumare

Out of order
En panne
Außer Betrieb
Fuera de servicio
Guasto

Opening times
Heures d'ouverture
Öffnungszeiten
Horario de apertura
Orario di apertura

Free admission
Entrée gratuite
Eintritt frei
Entrada libre
Ingresso libero

Knock before entering
Frappez avant d'entrer
Bitte anklopfen
Llamar antes de entrar
Bussare prima di entrare

Keep off the grass
Défense de marcher sur la
    pelouse
Betreten des Rasens verboten
Prohibido pisar el césped
Non calpestare l'aiuole

help • assistance • Hilfe
• ayuda • aiuto

Can you help me?
Pouvez-vous m'aider?
Können Sie mir helfen?
¿Me puede ayudar?
Mi può aiutare?

I don't understand
Je ne comprends pas
Ich verstehe nicht
No entiendo
Non capisco

I don't know
Je ne sais pas
Ich weiß nicht
No lo sé
Non lo so

Do you speak English,
    French…?
Vous parlez anglais,
    français…?
Sprechen Sie Englisch,
    Französisch…?
¿Habla inglés, francés…?
Parla inglese, francese…?

I speak English, Spanish…
Je parle anglais, espagnol…
Ich spreche Englisch, Spanisch…
Hablo inglés, español…
Parlo inglese, spagnolo…

Please speak more slowly
Parlez moins vite, s'il vous
    plaît
Sprechen Sie bitte langsamer
Hable más despacio, por
    favor
Parli più lentamente

Please write it down for me
Écrivez-le pour moi, s'il
    vous plaît
Schreiben Sie es bitte für mich auf
¿Me lo puede escribir?
Me lo scriva, per favore

I have lost…
J'ai perdu…
Ich habe… verloren
He perdido…
Ho perso…

directions • directions
• Richtungsangaben
• direcciones
• indicazioni

I am lost
Je me suis perdu
Ich habe mich verlaufen
Me he perdido
Mi sono perso/a

Where is the…?
Où est le/la…?
Wo ist der/die/das…?
¿Dónde está el/la…?
Dov'è il/la…?

Where is the nearest…?
Où est le/la…le/la plus proche?
Wo ist der/die/das nächste…?
¿Dónde está el/la… más
    cercano/a?
Dov'è il/la … più vicino/a?

Where are the toilets?
Où sont les toilettes?
Wo sind die Toiletten?
¿Dónde están los servicios?
Dov'è il bagno?

How do I get to…?
Pour aller à…?
Wie komme ich nach…?
¿Cómo voy a…?
Come si arriva a…?

To the right
À droite
Nach rechts
A la derecha
A destra

To the left
À gauche
Nach links
A la izquierda
A sinistra

Straight ahead
Tout droit
Geradeaus
Todo recto
Sempre dritto

How far is…?
C'est loin…?
Wie weit ist…?
¿A qué distancia está…?
Quant'è lontano…?

accommodation
• logement • Unterkunft
• alojamiento
• alloggio

I have a reservation
J'ai réservé une chambre
Ich habe ein Zimmer reserviert
Tengo una reserva
Ho una prenotazione

What time is breakfast?
Le petit déjeuner est à quelle
    heure?
Wann gibt es Frühstück?
¿A qué hora es el desayuno?
A che ora è la colazione?

Where is the dining room?
Où est la salle à manger?
Wo ist der Speisesaal?
¿Dónde está el comedor?
Dov'è la sala da pranzo?

eating and drinking
• nourriture et boissons
• Essen und Trinken
• comida y bebida
• cibo e bevande

Cheers!
À la vôtre!
Zum Wohl!
¡Salud!
Salute!

It's delicious/awful
C'est délicieux/terrible
Es ist köstlich/scheußlich
Está buenísimo/malísimo
È buonissimo/disgustoso

I don't drink/smoke
Je ne bois/fume pas
Ich trinke/rauche nicht
Yo no bebo/fumo
Non bevo/fumo

I don't eat meat
Je ne mange pas de la viande
Ich esse kein Fleisch
Yo no como carne
Non mangio la carne

No more for me, thank you
Je n'en veux plus, merci
Nichts mehr, danke
Ya no más, gracias
Per me basta, grazie

May I have some more?
Encore un peu, s'il vous plaît.
Könnte ich noch etwas mehr
    haben?
¿Puedo repetir?
Posso prenderne ancora?

May we have the bill?
L'addition, s'il vous plaît.
Wir möchten bitte zahlen.
¿Me trae la cuenta?
Il conto, per favore.

Can I have a receipt?
Je voudrais un reçu.
Ich hätte gerne eine Quittung.
¿Me da un recibo?
Mi dà una ricevuta?

No-smoking area
Partie non-fumeurs
Nichtraucherbereich
Zona de no fumadores
Area riservata ai non fumatori

English index • index anglais • englisches Register • índice inglés • indice inglese

english

english

english

duty-free shop 213
duvet 71
DVD disk 269
DVD player 268
dyed 39
dynamo 207

E

eagle 292
ear 14
early
earring 36
Earth 280, 282
earthenware dish 69
earthing 60
earthquake 283
easel 174, 274
east 312
East Timor 319
Easter 27
easy 321
easy cook 130
eat v 64
eat-in 154
eating 75
eau de toilette 41
eaves 58
éclair 140
eclipse 280
economics 169
economy class 211
Ecuador 315
eczema 44
Edam 142
edge 246
editor 191
eel 294
egg 20
egg cup 65, 137
egg white 137
eggs 137
Egypt 317
eight 308
eight hundred 308
eighteen 308
eighteenth 309
eighth 309
eightieth 309
eighty 308
ejaculatory duct 21
El Salvador 314
elbow 13
electric blanket 71
electric drill 78
electric guitar 258
electric razor 73
electric shock 46
electric train 208
electrical goods 105, 107
electrician 188
electricity 60
electricity meter 60
elephant 291
eleven 308
eleventh 309
elm 296
email 98, 177
email account 177
email address 177
embarrassed 25
embossed paper 83
embroidery 277
embryo 52
emerald 288
emergency 46
emergency exit 210

emergency lever 209
emergency phone 195
emergency room 48
emergency services 94
emigrate v 26
emotions 25
employee 24
employer 24
empty 321
emulsion 83
enamel 50
encore 255
encyclopedia 163
end 321
end zone 220
endive 123
endline 226
endocrine 19
endocrinology 49
engaged/busy 99
engaged couple 24
engine 202, 204, 208, 210
engine room 214
engineering 169
English breakfast 157
english mustard 135
engraving 275
enlarge v 172
enlargement 271
enquiries 168
ENT 49
entrance 59
entrance fee 260
envelope 98, 173
environment 280
epidural 52
epiglottis 19
epilepsy 44
episiotomy 52
equals 165
equation 165
equator 283
equipment 233, 238
equipment 165
Equitorial Guinea 317
equity 97
Eritrea 317
erupt v 283
escalator 104
espresso 148
essay 163
essential oils 55
estate 199
estate agent 189
estate agent's 115
Estonia 316
estuary 285
Ethiopia 317
eucalyptus 296
Europe 316
evening 305
evening dress 34
evening menu 152
events 243, 247
evergreen 86
evidence 181
examination 163
excess baggage 212
exchange rate 97
excited 25
excuse me 322
executive 174
exercise bike 250
exercises 251
exfoliate v 41
exhaust pipe 203, 204

exhibit v 261
exhibition 261
exit 210
exit ramp 194
exosphere 286
expectant 52
experiment 166
expiry date 109
exposure 271
extend v 251
extension 58
extension lead 78
exterior 198
extra time 223
extraction 50
extractor 66
eye 14, 51, 244, 276
eye shadow 40
eye test 51
eyebrow 14, 51
eyebrow brush 40
eyebrow pencil 40
eyecup 269
eyelash 14, 51
eyelet 37
eyelid 51
eyeliner 40
eyepiece 167

F

fabric 277
fabric conditioner 76
face 14
face cream 73
face mask 225
face pack 41
face powder 40
face-off circle 224
facial 41
factory 299
faint v 25, 44
fair 41
fairground 262
fairway 232
falcon 292
Falkland Islands 315
fall 237
fall in love v 26
Fallopian tube 20
family 22
famous ruin 261
fan 60, 202
fan belt 203
fans 258
far 320
fare 197, 209
farm 182, 183, 184
farmer 182, 189
farmhouse 182
farmland 182
farmyard 182
fashion 277
fast 321
fast food 154
fast forward 269
fastening 37
fat 119, 321
fat free 137
father 22
father-in-law 23
fault 230
fax 98, 172
fax machine 172
feather 293
feature film 269
February 306

feed v 183
feijoa 128
female 12, 20
feminine hygene 108
femur 17
fence 85, 182, 243
fencing 249
feng shui 55
fennel 122, 133
fennel seeds 133
fenugreek 132
fern 86
ferry 215, 216
ferry terminal 216
fertilization 20
fertilize v 91
fertilizer 91
festivals 27
fever 44
fiancé 24
fiancée 24
fibre 127
fibula 17
field 182, 222, 228, 234
field v 225, 229
field hockey 224
fifteen 308
fifteenth 309
fifth 309
fiftieth 309
fifty 308
fifty five thousand, five
    hundred 309
fifty thousand 309
fig 129
fighter plane 211
figure skating 247
Fiji 319
filament 60
file 81, 172, 177
filing cabinet 172
fill v 82
filler 83
fillet 119, 121
filleted 121
filling 50, 140, 155
film 260, 271
film chamber 270
film set 179
film spool 271
filo pastry 140
filter 270
filter coffee 148
filter paper 167
fin 210
finance 97
financial advisor 97
fingerprint 94
finial 300
finishing line 234
Finland 316
fire 95
fire alarm 95
fire brigade 95
fire engine 95
fire escape 95
fire extinguisher 95
fire fighters 95
fire station 95
firelighter 266
fireman 189
fireplace 63
firm 124
first 309
first aid 47
first aid box 47

first floor 104
first night 254
fish 107, 120, 294
fish and chips 155
fish farm 183
fish slice 68
fisherman 189
fishhook 244
fishing 244, 245
fishing boat 217
fishing permit 245
fishing port 217
fishing rod 244
fishmonger 188
fishmonger's 114, 120
fist 15, 237
fitness 250
five 308
five hundred 308
flag 221, 232
flageolet beans 131
flakes 132
flamingo 292
flan 142
flan dish 69
flare 240
flash 270
flash gun 270
flask 166
flat 59, 256
flatbread 139
flat race 243
flat wood bit 80
flavoured oil 134
flax 184
fleece 74
flesh 124, 127, 129
flex v 251
flight attendant 210
flight number 213
flint 288
flipchart 174
flip-flop 37
flipper 239, 290
float 238, 244
float ball 61
flock 183
flood 287
floor 58, 62, 71
floor exercises 235
floor plan 261
florentine 141
floret 122
florist 110, 188
flours 138
flower 297
flowerbed 85, 90
flowering plant 297
flowering shrub 87
flowers 110
flu 44
flute 139, 257
fly 244, 295
fly v 211
fly fishing 245
flyover 194
flysheet 266
foal 185
focus v 271
focusing knob 167
foetus 52
fog 287
foil 249
folder 177
foliage 110

hanging basket 84
hanging file 173
happy 25
harbour 217
harbour master 217
hard 129, 321
hard cheese 136
hard drive 176
hard hat 186
hard shoulder 194
hardboard 79
hardware 176
hardware shop 114
hardwood 79
haricot beans 131
harness race 243
harp 256
harvest v 91, 183
hat 36
hatchback 199
have a baby v 26
Hawaii 314
hay 184
hayfever 44
hazard 195
hazard lights 201
hazelnut 129
hazelnut oil 134
head 12, 19, 81, 230
head v 222
head injury 46
head office 175
head teacher 163
headache 44
headboard 70
headlight 198, 205
headphones 268
headrest 200
headsail 240
health 44
health centre 168
health food shop 115
heart 18, 119, 122, 273
heart attack 44
heater 60
heater controls 201
heather 297
heating element 61
heavy 321
heavy metal 259
hedge 85, 90, 182
hedgehog 290
heel 13, 15, 37
height 165
height bar 45
helicopter 211
hello 322
helmet 95, 204, 206, 220, 224, 228
hem 34
hematite 289
hen's egg 137
herb 55, 86
herb garden 84
herbaceous border 85
herbal remedies 108
herbal tea 149
herbalism 55
herbicide 183
herbs 133, 134
herbs and spices 132
herd 183
hexagon 164
hi-fi system 268
high 321
high chair 75

high dive 239
high heel shoe 37
high jump 235
high speed train 208
highlights 39
hiking 263
hill 284
Himalayas 313
hip 12
hippopotamus 291
historic building 261
history 162
history of art 169
hit v 224
hob 67
hockey 224
hockey stick 224
hoe 88
hold 215, 237
holdall 37
hole 232
hole in one 233
hole punch 173
holiday 212
holiday brochure 212
holly 296
home 58
home delivery 154
home entertainment 268
home furnishings 105
home plate 228
homeopathy 55
homework 163
homogenised 137
Honduras 314
honeycomb 135
honeymoon 26
honeysuckle 297
hood 31, 75
hoof 242, 291
hook 187, 276
hoop 226, 277
horizontal bar 235
hormone 20
horn 201, 204, 257, 291
horror film 255
horse 185, 235, 242
horse race 243
horse riding 242, 263
horseradish 125
horseshoe 242
hose 95
hose reel 89
hosepipe 89
hospital 48
host 64
hostess 64
hot 124, 286, 321
hot chocolate 144, 156
hot dog 155
hot drinks 144
hot tap 72
hot-air balloon 211
hotel 100, 264
hot-water bottle 70
hour 304
hour hand 304
house 58
household products 107
hovercraft 215
hub 206
hubcap 202
hull 214, 240
human resources 175
humerus 17
humid 286

hummingbird 292
hump 291
hundred 308
hundred and ten 308
hundred thousand 308
hundredth 309
Hungary 316
hungry 64
hurdles 235
hurricane 287
husband 22
husk 130
hydrant 95
hydrofoil 215
hydrotherapy 55
hypnotherapy 55
hypoallergenic 41
hypotenuse 164

I

ice 120, 287
ice and lemon 151
ice bucket 150
ice climbing 247
ice cream 149
ice cube 151
ice hockey 224
ice hockey player 224
ice hockey rink 224
ice maker 67
ice-cream 137
iced coffee 148
iced tea 149
ice-skate 224
ice-skating 247
icicle 287
icing 141
icon 177
identity badge 189
identity tag 53
idle running 203
igneous 288
ignition 200
iguana 293
illness 44
immigration 212
impotent 20
in 320
in brine 143
in front of 320
in oil 143
in sauce 159
in syrup 159
inbox 177
inch 310
incisor 50
incubator 53
index finger 15
India 318
Indian Ocean 312
indicator 198, 204
indigo 274
Indonesia 319
induce labour v 53
industrial estate 299
infection 44
infertile 20
infield 228
inflatable dinghy 215
information 261
information screen 213
in-goal area 221
inhaler 44, 109
injection 48
injury 46
ink 275

ink pad 173
inlet 61
inner core 282
inner tube 207
inning 228
innocent 181
inoculation 45
insect repellent 108, 267
inside 320
inside lane 194
insomnia 71
inspector 94
install v 177
instant camera 270
instep 15
instructions 109
instruments 256, 258
insulating tape 81
insulation 61
insulin 109
insurance 203
intensive care unit 48
inter-city train 209
intercom 59
intercostal 16
intercourse 20
interest rate 96
interior 200
internal systems 60
international flight 212
internet 177
intersection 298
interval 254
interviewer 179
into 320
in-tray 172
invertebrates 295
investigation 94
investment 97
ionosphere 286
Iran 318
Iraq 318
Ireland 316
iris 51, 110
iron 76, 109, 233, 289
iron v 76
ironing board 76
island 282
Israel 318
Italy 316
itinerary 260
IUD 21
Ivory Coast 317

J

jack 203, 273
jacket 32, 34
jade 288
jam 134, 156
Jamaica 314
January 306
Japan 318
jar 134, 311
javelin 234
jaw 14, 17
jazz 259
jeans 31
jelly bean 113
jellyfish 295
Jerusalem artichoke 125
jet 288
jet skiing 241
jetty 217
jeweller 188
jeweller's 114
jewellery 36

jewellery box 36
jewellery making 275
jigsaw 78
jigsaw puzzle 273
jodhpurs 242
jog on the spot 251
jogging 251, 263
joint 17, 119
joker 273
Jordan 318
journal 168
journalist 190
judge 180
judo 236
jug 65
juices and milkshakes 149
juicy 127
July 306
jump 237, 243
jump v 227
jump ball 226
junction 194
June 306
Jupiter 280
jury 180
jury box 180

K

kale 123
kangaroo 291
karate 236
Karliningrad 316
kayak 241
Kazakhstan 318
kebab 155, 158
keel 214
keep net 244
kendo 236
Kenya 317
kernel 122, 129, 130
ketchup 135
kettle 66
kettledrum 257
key 59, 80, 176, 207
keyboard 172, 176, 258
keypad 97, 99
kick 237, 239
kick v 221, 223
kickboxing 236
kickstand 207
kid 185
kidney 18, 119
kilogram 310
kilometre 310
king 272, 273
king prawn 121
kiosk 113
kippers 157
kitchen 66, 152
kitchen knife 68
kitchenware 68, 105
kitten 290
kiwifruit 128
knead v 138
knee 12
knee pad 205
knee support 227
kneecap 17
knee-length 34
knickers 35
knife 65, 80
knife sharpener 68, 118
knight 272
knitting 277
knitting needle 277
knock out 237

english

knuckle 15
koala 291
kohlrabi 123
koi carp 294
kumquat 126
kung fu 236
Kuwait 318
Kyrgyzstan 318

L

label 172
labels 89
labia 20
laboratory 166
lace 35, 37
lace bobbin 277
lace making 277
lace-up 37
lacrosse 249
lactose 137
ladder 95, 186
ladle 68
ladybird 295
lake 285
lamb 118, 185
lamp 62, 207, 217
land 282
land v 211
landing 59
landing gear 210
landing net 244
landlord 58
landscape 271, 284
landscape v 91
lane 234, 238
languages 162
Laos 318
lapel 32
laptop 175
larch 296
large 321
large intestine 18
larynx 19
last week 307
lat 16
late 305
later 304
latitude 283
Latvia 316
laugh v 25
launch 281
launch pad 281
launderette 115
laundry 76
laundry basket 76
laundry service 101
lava 283
law 169, 180
lawn 85, 90
lawn rake 88
lawnmower 88, 90
lawyer 180, 190
lawyer's office 180
laxative 109
lay the table v 64
lead singer 258
leaded 199
leaf 122, 296
leaflets 96
league 223
lean meat 118
learn v 163
leather shoe 37
leather shoes 32
leathers 205
Lebanon 318

lecture theatre 169
lecturer 169
leek 125
left 260
left field 228
left-hand drive 201
leg 12, 119
leg pad 225
leg press 251
legal advice 180
legal department 175
leggings 31
leisure 258, 254, 264
lemon 126
lemon curd 134
lemon grass 133
lemon sole 120
lemonade 144
length 165, 310
lens 270
lens (eye) 51
lens (glasses) 51
lens cap 270
lens case 51
Lesotho 317
lesson 163
let! 231
letter 98
letterbox 58, 99
letterhead 173
lettuce 123
lever 61, 150
lever arch file 173
Liberia 317
librarian 168, 190
library 168, 299
library card 168
Libya 317
licence plate 198
licquorice 113
lid 61, 66
Liechtenstein 316
life events 26
life jacket 240
life raft 240
lifeboat 214
lifebuoy 240
lifeguard 239, 265
lifeguard tower 265
lift 59, 100, 104
ligament 17
light 178, 321
light a fire v 266
light aircraft 211
light bulb 60
lighter 112
lighthouse 217
lighting 105
lightmeter 270
lightning 287
lights 94
lights switch 201
lily 110
lime 126, 296
limestone 288
limousine 199
line 244
line judge 220
line of play 233
linen 105, 277
linen basket 76
lines 165
linesman 223, 230
lingerie 35, 105
lining 32
lining paper 83

link 36
lintel 186
lion 291
lip 14
lip brush 40
lip gloss 40
lip liner 40
lipstick 40
liqueur 145
liquid 77
liquid dispenser 311
liquid measure 311
literature 162, 169
Lithuania 316
litre 311
little finger 15
little toe 15
live 60, 178
live rail 209
liver 18, 118
livestock 183, 185
living room 62
lizard 293
load v 76
loaf 139
loan 96, 168
loans desk 168
lob 230
lobby 100, 255
lobster 121, 295
lock 59, 207
lockers 239
log on v 177
loganberry 127
logo 31
loin 121
lollipop 113
long 32
long jump 235
long sight 51
long wave 179
long-grain 130
long-handled shears 88
longitude 283
loofah 73
loom 277
loose leaf tea 144
lorry 194
lorry driver 190
lose v 273
loser 273
lotion 109
lottery tickets 112
love 230
low 321
luge 247
luggage 100, 198, 213
luggage department 104
luggage hold 196
luggage rack 209
lumbar vertebrae 17
lunar module 281
lunch 64
lunch menu 152
lung 18
lunge 251
lupins 297
lure 244
Luxembourg 316
lychee 128
lymphatic 19
lyrics 259

M

macadamia 129
mace 132

Macedonia 316
machine gun 189
machinery 187
mackerel 120
macramé 277
Madagascar 317
magazine 112
magazines 107
magma 283
magnesium 109
magnet 167
maid service 101
mailbag 98, 190
main course 153
mains supply 60
mainsail 240
make a will v 26
make friends v 26
make the bed v 71
make-up 40
making bread 138
malachite 288
Malawi 317
Malaysia 318
Maldives 318
male 12, 21
Mali 317
mallet 78, 275
malt vinegar 135
Malta 316
malted drink 144
mammals 290
man 23
manager 24, 174
managing director 175
manchego 142
mane 242, 291
mango 128
mangosteen 128
manhole 299
manicure 41
mantelpiece 63
mantle 282
manual 200
map 195, 261
maple 296
maple syrup 134
maracas 257
marathon 234
marble 288
March 306
margarine 137
marina 217
marinated 143, 159
marine fishing 245
marjoram 133
mark v 227
market 115
marketing department 175
marmalade 134, 156
marrow 124
Mars 280
marshmallow 113
martial arts 237
martini 151
marzipan 141
mascara 40
mashed 159
masher 68
mask 189, 228, 236, 239, 249
masking tape 83
masonry bit 80
massage 54
mast 240
masters 169
mat 54, 83, 235, 271

match 230
matches 112
material 276
materials 79, 187
maternity 49
maternity ward 48
maths 162, 164
mattress 70, 74
Mauritania 317
Mauritius 317
May 306
maybe 322
mayonnaise 135
MDF 79
meadow 285
meal 64
measles 44
measure 150, 151
measure v 310
measurements 165
measuring jug 69, 311
measuring spoon 109
meat 119
meat and poultry 106
meat tenderizer 68
meatballs 158
meathook 118
mechanic 188, 203
mechanical digger 187
mechanics 202
medals 235
media 178
medical examination 45
medication 109
medicine 109, 169
medicine cabinet 72
meditation 54
Mediterranean Sea 313
medium wave 179
meeting 174
meeting room 174
melody 259
melon 127
memory 176
men's clothing 32
men's wear 105
menstruation 20
menu 148, 153, 154
menubar 177
mercury 289
Mercury 280
meringue 140
mesosphere 286
messages 100
metacarpal 17
metal 79
metal bit 80
metals 289
metamorphic 288
metatarsal 17
meteor 280
metre 310
Mexico 314
mica 289
microlight 211
microphone 179, 258
microscope 167
microwave oven 66
midday 305
middle finger 15
middle lane 194
midnight
midwife 53
migraine 44
mile 310
milk 136, 156

english

milk v 183
milk carton 136
milk chocolate 113
milkshake 137
millennium 307
millet 130
milligram 310
millilitre 311
millimetre 310
mince 119
mineral 144
minerals 289
mini bar 101
mini disk recorder 268
minibus 197
mini-dress 34
mint 113, 133
mint tea 149
minus 165
minute 304
minute hand 304
minutes 174
mirror 40, 63, 71, 167
miscarriage 52
Miss 23
missile 211
mist 287
mitre block 81
mitt 228
mittens 30
mix v 67, 138
mixed salad 158
mixing bowl 66, 69
mixing desk 179
moat 300
mobile 74
mobile phone 99
model 169, 190
model making 275
modelling tool 275
modem 176
moisturizer 41
molar 50
Moldova 316
mole 14
Monaco 316
Monday 306
money 97
Mongolia 318
monitor 172, 176
monitor 53
monkey 291
monkfish 120
monopoly 272
monorail 208
monsoon 287
month 306
monthly 307
monument 261
Moon 280
moonstone 288
moor v 217
mooring 217
mop 77
morning 305
Morocco 317
mortar 68, 167, 187
mortgage 96
moses basket 74
mosque 300
mosquito 295
mosquito net 267
moth 295
mother 22
mother-in-law 23
motor 88

motor racing 249
motorbike 204
motorbike racing 249
motorcross 249
motorway 194
moulding 63
mountain 284
mountain bike 206
mountain range 282
mouse 176, 290
mousse 141
mouth 14
mouth guard 237
mouthwash 72
move 273
mow v 90
Mozambique 317
mozzarella 142
MP3 player 268
Mr 23
Mrs 23
mudguard 205
muffin 140
muffin tray 69
mug 65
mulch v 91
multiply v 165
multivitamin tablets 109
mumps 44
mung beans 131
muscles 16
museum 261
mushroom 125
music 162
music school 169
musical 255
musical score 255
musical styles 259
musician 191
mussel 121, 295
mustard 155
mustard seed 131
Myanmar 318

N

naan bread 139
nail 15, 80
nail clippers 41
nail file 41
nail scissors 41
nail varnish 41
nail varnish remover 41
Namibia 317
nape 13
napkin 65, 152
napkin ring 65
nappy 75
nappy rash cream 74
narrow 321
nation 315
national park 261
natural 256
natural fibre 31
naturopathy 55
nausea 44
navel 12
navigate v 240
near 320
nebula 280
neck 12, 258
neck brace 46
necklace 36
neckline 34
nectarine 126
needle 109, 276
needle plate 276

needle-nose pliers 80
needlepoint 277
negative 271
negative electrode 167
negligée 35
neighbour 24
neoclassical 301
Nepal 318
nephew 23
Neptune 280
nerve 19, 50
nervous 19, 25
net 217, 222, 226, 227, 231
net v 245
net curtain 63
Netherlands 316
nettle 297
network 176
neurology 49
neutral 60
neutral zone 224
new 321
new moon 280
new potato 124
New Year 27
New Zealand 319
newborn baby 53
news 178
newsagent 112
newspaper 112
newsreader 179, 191
next week 306
nib 163
Nicaragua 314
nickel 289
niece 23
Niger 317
Nigeria 317
night 305
nightdress 35
nightie 31
nightwear 31
nine 308
nine hundred 308
nineteen 308
nineteen hundred 307
nineteen hundred and one 307
nineteen ten 307
nineteenth 309
ninetieth 309
ninety 308
ninth 309
nipple 12
no 322
no entry 195
no right turn 195
no stopping 195
non-smoking section 152
non-stick 69
noodles 158
normal 39
north 312
North and Central America
  314
North Korea 318
North pole 283
North Sea 312
northern hemisphere 283
Norway 316
nose 14, 210
nose clip 238
noseband 242
nosebleed 44
nosewheel 210
nostril 14
notation 256

note 97, 256
note pad 173
notebook 163, 172
notes 175, 191
notice board 173
nougat 113
November 306
now 304
nozzle 89
number 226
numbers 308
numerator 165
nurse 45, 48, 52, 189
nursery 74
nursing 53
nursing bra 53
nut 80
nutmeg 132
nuts 151
nuts and dried fruit 129
nylon 277

O

oak 296
oar 241
oats 130
objective lens 167
oboe 257
obsidian 288
obstetrician 52
occupations 188, 190
occupied 321
ocean 282
ocean liner 215
octagon 164
October 306
octopus 121, 295
odometer 201
oesophagus 19
off licence 115
offal 118
offers 106
office 24, 172, 174
office block 298
office equipment 172
office supplies 173
off-piste 247
off-side 223
oil 142, 199
oil paints 274
oil tank 204
oil tanker 215
oils 134
oily 41
ointment 47, 109
okra 122
old 321
olive oil 134
olives 151
Oman 318
omelette 158
on time 305
on top of 320
oncology 49
one 308
one billion 309
one million 309
one thousand 309
one-way 194
one-way system 298
onion 124
on-line 177
onto 320
onyx 289
opal 288
open 260, 321

open sandwich 155
open-top 260
opera 255
operating theatre 48
operation 48
operator 99
ophthalmology 49
opponent 236
opposite 320
optic 150
optic nerve 51
optician 51, 189
orange 126, 274
orange juice 148
orangeade 144
orbit 280
orchestra 254, 256
orchestra pit 254
orchid 111
order v 153
oregano 133
organic 91, 118, 122
organic waste 61
origami 275
ornamental 87
orthopedia 49
osteopathy 54
ostrich 292
otter 290
ounce 310
out 225, 228, 320
out of bounds 226
out of focus 271
outboard motor 215
outbuilding 182
outdoor activities 262
outer core 282
outfield 229
outlet 61
outpatient 48
outside 320
outside lane 194
out-tray 172
oval 164
ovary 20
oven 66
oven glove 69
ovenproof 69
over 320
over par 233
overalls 82
overdraft 96
overexposed 271
overflow pipe 61
overhead locker 210
overhead projector 163
overtake v 195
overture 256
ovulation 20, 52
owl 292
oyster 121
ozone layer 286

P

Pacific Ocean 312
pack 311
pack of cards 273
packet 311
packet of cigarettes 112
pad 224
paddle 241
paddling pool 263
paddock 242
pads 53, 220
paediatrics 49
painkiller 109

english

english

english

english

French index • index français • französisches Register • índice francés • indice francese

français

français

français

français

français

français

français

français

français

français

français

français

français

German index • index allemand • deutsches Register • índice alemán • indice tedesco

deutsch

deutsch

deutsch

deutsch

deutsch

deutsch

Küchenschrank m 66
Kugel f 149, 164
Kugelstoßen n 234
Kuh f 185
Kühler m 202
Kühlmittelbehälter m 202
Kühlschrank m 67
Kuhmilch f 136
Küken n 185
Kulisse f 254
Kultivator m 182
Kümmel m 131
Kumquat f 126
Kunde m 96, 104, 106, 152, 175
Kundendienst m 104
Kundendienstabteilung f 175
Kundin f 38
Kung-Fu m 236
Kunst f 162
Kunstgalerie f 261
Kunstgeschichte f 169
Kunsthandlung f 115
Kunsthandwerk n 274, 276
Kunsthochschule f 169
Künstlerin f 274
Kupfer n 289
Kuppel f 300
Kupplung f 200, 204
Kürbiskern m 131
Kurierdienst m 99
Kurkuma f 132
kurz 32, 321
kurz gebraten 159
Kurzhaarschnitt m 39
Kurzsichtigkeit f 51
Kurzwaren f 105
Kurzwelle f 179
Kuscheltier n 75
Kuskus m 130
Küste f 285
Küstenwache f 217
Kuwait 318

L

Labor n 166
Laborwaage f 166
lächeln 25
lachen 25
Lachs m 120
Lack m 79, 83
Lacrosse n 249
Lacrosseschläger m 249
Laden m 298
Lagerfeuer n 266
Laib m 139
Laken n 74
Lakritze f 113
Laktose f 137
Lamm n 118, 185
Lampe f 62
Land n 282, 315
landen 211
Landkarte f 195
Landschaft f 284
Landungsbrücke f 214
Landungssteg m 217
Landwirt m 183, 189
landwirtschaftlichen Betriebe m 183
lang 32
Länge f 165, 310
Längengrad m 283
Langkorn- 130
Langlauf m 247
Langlaufmaschine f 250
langsam 321

Längsschnitt m 282
Langwelle f 179
Laos 318
Laptop m 175, 176
Lärche f 296
Lastwagen m 194
Lastwagenfahrer m 190
Laterne f 217
Latte f 235
Lätzchen n 30
Latzhose f 30
Laubbaum m 86
Laubrechen m 88
Lauch m 125
Lauf m 228
Laufband n 250
Läufer m 272
Laufstall m 75
Lautsprecher m 176, 209, 258
Lautsprecherbox f 268
Lautstärke f 179, 269
Lava f 283
Lawine f 247
Leadsänger m 258
Lebensmittel n 106
Lebensmittelabteilung f 105
Lebensmittelgeschäft n 114
Leber f 18, 118
Lederanzug m 205
Lederschuh m 37
Lederschuhe m 32
leer 321
Leerlauf 203
Leerung f 98
legen 38
leger 34
Leggings f 31
Leguan m 293
Lehm m 85
Lehrer m 54
Lehrerin f 162, 191
leicht 321
Leichtathlet m 234
Leichtathletik f 234
Leichtflugzeug n 211
Leinen n 277
Leinwand f 255, 274
Leiste f 12
leitende Angestellte m 174
Leiter m 95, 186
Leitkegel m 187
Leitplanke f 195
Leitung f 60
Lende f 121
Lendenbereich m 13
Lendensteak n 119
Lendenwirbel m 17
Lenkrad n 201
Lenkstange f 207
lernen 163
Lernen n 162
lesen 162
Leseausweis m 168
Leselampe f 210
Lesesaal m 168
Lesotho 317
Lettland 316
letzte Woche 307
Leuchtrakete f 240
Leuchtstreifen m 205
Leuchtturm m 217
Leukoplast n 47
Levkoje f 110
Lexikon n 163
Libanon 318
Libelle f 295

Liberia 317
Libyen 317
Licht n 94
Lichtmaschine f 203
Lichtschalter m 201
Lid n 51
Lidschatten m 40
Liebesfilm m 255
Liechtenstein 316
Lied n 259
Lieferung ins Haus f 154
Liegestuhl m 265
Liegestütz m 251
Liga f 223
Likör m 145
Lilie f 110
Limonade f 144
Limone f 126
Limousine f 199
Linde f 296
Lineal n 163, 165
Linien f 165
Liniennummer f 196
Linienrichter m 220, 223, 230
Liniensystem n 256
linke Feld n 228
links 260
Linkssteuerung f 201
Linse f 51, 270
Lipgloss n 40
Lippe f 14
Lippenkonturenstift m 40
Lippenpinsel m 40
Lippenstift m 40
Litauen 316
Liter m 311
Literatur f 162
Literaturliste f 168
Literaturwissenschaft f 169
Litschi f 128
live 178
Lob n 230
Loch n 232
Locher m 173
Lockenstab m 38
Lockenwickler m 38
Löffel m 65
Löffelbiskuits n 141
Loganbeere f 127
Loge f 254
Logo n 31
Lohnliste f 175
Lokomotive f 208
Lorbeerblatt n 133
Löschfahrzeug n 95
loslassen 245
löslich 109
Lösungsmittel 83
löten 79
Lotion f 109
Lötkolben m 81
Lottoscheine n 112
Lötzinn n 79, 80
Löwe m 291
Löwenzahn m 123, 297
Luffaschwamm m 73
Luftdüse f 210
Luftfilter m 202, 204
Luftkissenboot n 215
Luftmanschette f 45
Luftmatratze f 267
Luftpostbrief m 98
Luftpumpe f 207
Luftröhre f 18
Lunge f 18
Lungenautomat m 239

Lupinen f 297
Lutscher m 113
Luxemburg 316
Luzerne f 184
lymphatische System n 19

M

Macadamianuss f 129
Madagaskar 317
Mädchen n 23
Magen m 18
Magenschmerzen m 44
magere Fleisch n 118
Magermilch f 136
Magister m 169
Magma n 283
Magnesium n 109
Magnet m 167
Mähdrescher m 182
mähen 90
Mahlzeit f 64
Mähne f 242, 291
Mai m 306
Mais m 122, 130, 184
Maisbrot n 139
Maiskeimöl n 135
Majonäse f 135
Majoran m 133
Make-up n 40
Makramee n 277
Makrele f 120
Mal n 229
mal 165
Malachit m 288
Malawi 317
Malaysia 318
Malediven 318
Malerei f 274
Malerin f 191
Mali 317
Malspieler m 228
Malta 316
Malzessig m 135
Malzgetränk n 144
Manager m 174
Manchego m 142
Mandarine f 126
Mandel f 129
Mandeln f 151
Mandelöl n 134
Mango f 128
Mangold m 123
Mangostane f 128
Maniküre f 41
Maniok m 124
Mann m 12, 23
männlich 21
Mannschaft f 220
Mansarde f 58
Mansardenfenster n 58
Manschette f 32
Manschettenknopf m 36
Mantel m 32, 282
Maracas f 257
Marathon m 234
Margarine f 137
Margerite f 110, 297
Marienkäfer m 295
Marina f 217
mariniert 143, 159
Marketingabteilung f 175
Markise f 148
Markt m 115
Marmor m 288
Marokko 317
Mars m 280

Marshmallow n 113
Martini m 151
März m 306
Marzipan m 141
Maschinen f 187
Maschinengewehr n 189
Maschinenraum m 214
Masern f 44
Maske f 236, 249
Maß n 150, 151
Massage f 54
Maße n 165
maßgeschneidert 35
Mast m 240
Mastdarm m 21
Match n 230
Material n 187
Materialien n 79
Mathematik f 162, 164
Matratze f 70, 74
matt 83, 271
Matte f 54, 235
Mauer f 58, 186, 222
Mauerturm m 300
Mauerwerkbohrer m 80
Maurer m 188
Mauretanien 317
Mauritius 317
Maus f 176, 290
Mautstelle f 194
Mazedonien 316
MDF-Platte f 79
Mechanik f 202
Mechaniker m 188, 203
Medaillen f 235
Medien f 178
Medikament n 109
Meditation f 54
Medizin f 169
Meer n 264, 282
Meeresfrüchte f 121
Meerrettich m 125
Mehl n 138
Mehl mit Backpulver n 139
Mehl ohne Backpulver n 139
mehrjährig 86
Mehrkornbrot n 139
Meile f 310
Meißel m 81, 275
Meisterschaft f 230
melken 183
Melodie f 259
Melone f 127
Mensa f 168
Menschen m 12, 16, 39
Menstruation f 20
Menübalken m 177
Merkur m 280
Mesosphäre f 286
Messbecher m 69, 150, 311
messen 310
Messer n 65, 66
Messerschärfer m 68, 118
Messleiste f 45
Messlöffel m 109
Metall n 79
Metallbohrer m 80
Metalle n 289
Metallsäge f 81
metamorph 288
Meteor m 280
Meter m 310
Metermaß n 80
Metzger m 118, 188
Metzgerei f 114
Mexiko 314

deutsch

deutsch

deutsch

deutsch

Spanish index • index espagnol • spanisches Register • índice español • indice spagnolo

español

español

español

español

español

español

español

español

español

español

español

español

español

english • français • deutsch • español • italiano

Italian index • index italien • italienisches Register • índice italiano • indice italiano

italiano

italiano

italiano

italiano

italiano

italiano

italiano

italiano

italiano

italiano

italiano

italiano

italiano

italiano

italiano

acknowledgments • remerciements • Dank • agradecimientos • ringraziamenti

DORLING KINDERSLEY would like to thank Tracey Miles and Christine Lacey for design assistance, Georgina Garner for editorial and administrative help, Sonia Gavira, Polly Boyd, and Cathy Meeus for editorial help, and Claire Bowers for compiling the DK picture credits.

The publisher would like to thank the following for their kind permission to reproduce their photographs:
Abbreviations key:
t=top, b=bottom, r=right, l=left, c=centre

Abode: 62; **Action Plus:** 224bc; **alamy.com:** 154t; A.T. Willett 287bcl; Michael Foyle 184bl; Stock Connection 287bcr; **Allsport/Getty Images:** 238cl; **Alvey and Towers:** 209 acr, 215bcl, 215bcr, 241cr; **Peter Anderson:** 188cbr, 271br. **Anthony Blake Photo Library:** Charlie Stebbings 114cl; John Sims 114tcl; **Andyalte:** 98tl; **apple mac computers:** 268tcr; **Arcaid:** John Edward Linden 301bl; Martine Hamilton Knight, Architects: Chapman Taylor Partners, 213cl; Richard Bryant 301br; **Argos:** 41tcl, 66cbl, 66bl, 66br, 66bcl, 69cl, 70bcl, 71t, 77tl, 269tc, 270tl; **Axiom:** Eitan Simanor 105bcr; Ian Cumming 104; Vicki Couchman 148cr; **Beken Of Cowes Ltd:** 215cbc; **Bosch:** 76tcr, 76tc, 76tcl; **Camera Press:** 27c, 38tr, 256t, 257cr; Barry J. Holmes 148tr; Jane Hanger 159cr; Mary Germanou 259bc; **Corbis:** 78b; Anna Clopet 247tr; Bettmann 181tl, 181tr; Bo Zauders 156t; Bob Rowan 152bl; Bob Winsett 247cbl; Brian Bailey 247br; Carl and Ann Purcell 162l; Chris Rainer 247ctl; ChromoSohm Inc. 179tr; Craig Aurness 215bl; David H.Wells 249cbr; Dennis Marsico 274bl; Dimitri Lundt 236bc; Duomo 211tl; Gail Mooney 277ctcr; George Lepp 248c; Gunter Marx 248cr; Jack Fields 210b; Jack Hollingsworth 231bl; Jacqui Hurst 277cbr; James L. Amos 247bl, 191ctr, 220bcr; Jan Butchofsky 277cbc; Johnathan Blair 243cr; Jon Feingersh 153tr; Jose F. Poblete 191br; Jose Luis Pelaez.Inc 153tc, 175tl; Karl Weatherly 220bl, 247tcr; Kelly Mooney Photography 259tl; Kevin Fleming 249bc; Kevin R. Morris 105tr, 243tl, 243tc; Kim Sayer 249tcr; Lynn Goldsmith 258t; Macduff Everton 231bcl; Mark Gibson 249bl; Mark L. Stephenson 249tcl; Michael Pole 115tr; Michael S. Yamashita 247ctcl; Mike King 247cbl; Neil Rabinowitz 214br; Owen Franken 112t; Pablo Corral 115bc; Paul A.

Sounders 169br, 249ctcl; Paul J. Sutton 224c, 224br; Peter Turnley 105tcr; Phil Schermeister 227b, 248tr; R. W Jones 309; R.W. Jones 175tr; Richard Hutchings 168b; Rick Doyle 241ctr; Robert Holmes 97br, 277ctc; Roger Ressmeyer 169tr; Russ Schleipman 229; Steve Raymer 168cr; The Purcell Team 211ctr; Tim Wright 178; Vince Streano 194t; Wally McNamee 220br, 220bcl, 224bl; Yann Arhus-Bertrand 249tl; **Dixons:** 270cl, 270cr, 270bl, 270bcl, 270bcr, 270ccr; **Education Photos:** John Walmsley 26tl; **Empics Ltd:** Adam Day 236br; Andy Heading 243c; Steve White 249cbc; **Getty Images:** 48bcl, 100t, 114bcr, 154bl, 287tr; 94tr; **Dennis Gilbert:** 106tc; **Hulsta:** 70t; **Ideal Standard Ltd:** 72r; **The Image Bank/Getty Images:** 58; **Impact Photos:** Eliza Armstrong 115cr; John Arthur 190tl; Philip Achache 246t; **The Interior Archive:** Henry Wilson, Alfie's Market 114bl; Luke White, Architect: David Mikhail, 59tl; Simon Upton, Architect: Phillippe Starck, St Martins Lane Hotel 100bcr, 100br; **Jason Hawkes Aerial Photography:** 216t; **Dan Johnson:** 26cbl, 35r; **Kos Pictures Source:** 215cbl, 240tc, 240tr; David Williams 216b; **Lebrecht Collection:** Kate Mount 169bc; **MP Visual.com:** Mark Swallow 202t; **NASA:** 280cr, 280ccl, 281tl; **P&O Princess Cruises:** 214bl; **P A Photos:** 181br; **The Photographers' Library:** 186bl, 186bc, 186t; **Plain and Simple Kitchens:** 66t; **Powerstock Photolibrary:** 169tl, 256t, 287tc; **Rail Images:** 208c, 208 cbl, 209br; **Red Consultancy:** Odeon cinemas 257br; **Redferns:** 259br; Nigel Crane 259c; **Rex Features:** 106br, 259tc, 259tr, 259bl, 280b; Charles Ommaney 114tcr; J.F.F Whitehead 243cl; Patrick Barth 101tl; Patrick Frilet 189cbl; Scott Wiseman 287bl; **Royalty Free Images:** Getty Images/Eyewire 154bl; **Science & Society Picture Library:** Science Museum 202b; **Skyscan:** 168t, 182c, 298; Quick UK Ltd 212; **Sony:** 268bc; **Robert Streeter:** 154br; **Neil Sutherland:** 82tr, 83tl, 90t, 118, 188ctr, 196tl, 196tr, 299cl, 299bl; **The Travel Library:** Stuart Black 264t; **Travelex:** 97cl; **Vauxhall:** Technik 198t, 199tl, 199tr, 199cl, 199cr, 199ctcl, 199ctcr, 199tcl, 199tcr, 200; **View Pictures:** Dennis Gilbert, Architects: ACDP Consulting, 106t; Dennis Gilbert, Chris Wilkinson Architects, 209tr; Peter Cook, Architects: Nicholas Crimshaw and partners, 208t; **Betty Walton:** 185br;

Colin Walton: 2, 4, 7, 9, 10, 28, 42, 56, 92, 95c, 99tl, 99tcl, 102, 116, 120t, 138t, 146, 150t, 160, 170, 191ctcl, 192, 218, 252, 260br, 260l, 261tr, 261c, 261cr, 271cbl, 271cbr, 271ctl, 278, 287br, 302, 401.

DK PICTURE LIBRARY:
Akhil Bahkshi; Patrick Baldwin; Geoff Brightling; British Museum; John Bulmer; Andrew Butler; Joe Cornish; Brian Cosgrove; Andy Crawford and Kit Hougton; Philip Dowell; Alistair Duncan; Gables; Bob Gathany; Norman Hollands; Kew Gardens; Peter James Kindersley; Vladimir Kozlik; Sam Lloyd; London Northern Bus Company Ltd; Lucky Luke Licensing; Tracy Morgan; David Murray and Jules Selmes; Musée Vivant du Cheval, France; Museum of Broadcast Communications; Museum of Natural History; NASA; National History Museum; Norfolk Rural Life Museum; Stephen Oliver; RNLI; Royal Ballet School; Guy Ryecart; Science Museum; Neil Setchfield; Ross Simms and the Winchcombe Folk Police Museum; Singapore Symphony Orchestra; Smart Museum of Art; Tony Souter; Erik Svensson and Jeppe Wikstrom; Sam Tree of Keygrove Marketing Ltd; Barrie Watts; Alan Williams; Jerry Young.

Additional Photography by Colin Walton.

Colin Walton would like to thank:
A&A News, Uckfield; Abbey Music, Tunbridge Wells; Arena Mens Clothing, Tunbridge Wells; Burrells of Tunbridge Wells; Gary at Di Marco's; Jeremy's Home Store, Tunbridge Wells; Noakes of Tunbridge Wells; Ottakar's, Tunbridge Wells; Selby's of Uckfield; Sevenoaks Sound and Vision; Westfield, Royal Victoria Place, Tunbridge Wells.

Front jacket image © Volkswagen

All other images are Dorling Kindersley copyright. For further information see www.dkimages.com